Crossing Borders:
Constitutional Development
and Internationalisation

Essays in Honour of
Joachim Jens Hesse

Crossing Borders: Constitutional Development and Internationalisation

Essays in Honour of
Joachim Jens Hesse

Edited by

Florian Grotz and Theo A. J. Toonen

De Gruyter Recht · Berlin

∞ Gedruckt auf säurefreiem Papier, das die US-ANSI-Norm über Haltbarkeit erfüllt.

ISBN 978-3-89949-479-2

Bibliografische Information der Deutschen Nationalbibliothek

Die Deutsche Nationalbibliothek verzeichnet diese Publikation in der Deutschen Nationalbibliografie; detaillierte bibliografische Daten sind im Internet über <http://dnb.d-nb.de> abrufbar.

Printed in Germany

Datenkonvertierung/Satz: Werksatz Schmidt & Schulz, Gräfenhainichen
Druck und Bindung: Hubert & Co., Göttingen
Einbandgestaltung: Christopher Schneider, Berlin

Contents

Introduction

Crossing Borders: Constitutional Development and Internationalisation

by Florian Grotz and Theo A. J. Toonen

I. "Crossing Borders" as Leitmotiv: The Work of *Joachim Jens Hesse*

This book is dedicated to *Joachim Jens Hesse,* a scholar who over the last three decades has produced many publications on public sector developments both in historical and cross-national perspective. While this may apply to other social scientists as well, his work definitely stands out because it has had an enormous impact on various environments – academic and non-academic alike. Doing justice to *Hesse*'s multi-faceted writings is thus no easy task, if possible at all. For the purpose of this *Festschrift* we decided to concentrate on an aspect that in our view is probably most specific to his approach: the almost continuous attempt to broaden the analytical and empirical perspectives on public sector developments. We therefore suggest that the metaphor of "crossing borders" be taken as leitmotiv for *Joachim Jens Hesse*'s academic work. This is true for at least the following three dimensions that will be outlined briefly below:

- fostering dialogue and cooperation between public sector related disciplines;
- analysing public sector developments in an international and intercultural perspective; and
- bridging the "gap" between academia and practical politics.

First, *Joachim Jens Hesse* has always highlighted the potential benefits of interdisciplinary dialogue and cooperation. Repeatedly referring to the integrated concept of *Staatswissenschaften* rooted in the German academic tradition of the 19th century,[1] he is firmly convinced that a combination of normative thinking, which is primarily found in public law, and functional categories emphasised in economics and social sciences, is the best way to analyse public sector developments. This permanent claim of "indispensable multidisciplinary" has not been mere window-dressing. Rather, *Hesse*'s own writings have been oriented towards interdisciplinary criteria, for example the well-known and widely-used monograph on the German governmental system.[2] Furthermore, he launched several "forums"

---

1 *Ellwein, T./Hesse, J. J.* (eds.): Staatswissenschaften: Vergessene Disziplin oder neue Herausforderung?, Baden-Baden, 1990.

2 *Hesse, J. J./Ellwein, T.*: Das Regierungssystem der Bundesrepublik Deutschland. 2 vol., 9th ed., Berlin, 2004.

for continuous interchange between lawyers, economists, social scientists and historians, such as *Staatswissenschaften und Staatspraxis*, the *Zeitschrift für Staats- und Europawissenschaften/Journal for Comparative Government and European Policy (ZSE)*, the *Jahrbuch für Staats- und Verwaltungswissenschaft* and the *European Yearbook of Comparative Government and Public Administration*.[3] In this way, he has rendered outstanding services in tightening cooperative relationships between the different *Staatswissenschaften* in Germany and Europe.

The second "crossing-border" dimension in *Joachim Jens Hesse*'s work seems to be closely connected with the aforementioned aspect: If public sector developments are to be analysed in a problem-adequate manner, international and intercultural comparison is of crucial significance. At this point, we could elaborate on the methodological advancements of social sciences over the last decades and then review *Hesse*'s work from this angle. For the present purpose, however, it suffices to say that he has not only published several comparative studies on key aspects of public sector development in Western countries,[4] but also, step by step, widened the empirical scope of his analyses. After the fall of the Berlin Wall, he was among the first Western scholars to study the processes of administrative transformation in Central and Eastern Europe.[5] Since the mid-1990s, when the impact of European integration on national legal and political systems considerably increased in the aftermath of the Maastricht Treaty, *Hesse* has also included the EU in his analyses.[6] More recently, his research interests have again broadened

---

3   Staatswissenschaften und Staatspraxis, Baden-Baden, 1990–1998; Zeitschrift für Staats- und Europawissenschaften (ZSE), Berlin, 2003 ff.; *Ellwein, T./Hesse, J.J./Mayntz, R./Scharpf, F.W.* (eds.): Jahrbuch zur Staats- und Verwaltungswissenschaft, Baden-Baden, 1987–1991; *Ellwein, T./Grimm, D./Hesse, J.J./Schuppert, G.F.* (eds.): Jahrbuch zur Staats- und Verwaltungswissenschaft, Baden-Baden, 1992–1997; *Hesse, J.J./Toonen, T.A.J.* (eds.): The European Yearbook of Comparative Government and Public Administration, Boulder, CO/Baden-Baden, 1995–1997.

4   Cf. for example, *Hesse, J.J./Benz, A.*: Die Modernisierung der Staatsorganisation, Baden-Baden, 1990; *Hesse, J.J.* (ed.): Local Government and Urban Affairs in International Perspective, Baden-Baden, 1991; *id./Johnson, N.* (eds.): Constitutional Policy and Change in Europe, Oxford, 1995; *id./Wright, V.* (eds.): Federalizing Europe? The Costs, Benefits, and Preconditions of Federal Political Systems, Oxford, 1996; *Hesse, J.J./Schuppert, G.F./Harms, K.* (eds.): Verfassungsrecht und Verfassungspolitik in Umbruchsituationen, Baden-Baden, 1999.

5   *Hesse, J.J.* (ed.): Administrative Transformation in Central and Eastern Europe, Oxford, 1993; *id.*: Rebuilding the State. Public Sector Reform in Central and Eastern Europe, in: Lane, J.-E. (ed.): Public Sector Reform, London, 1997, 114–146.

6   *Hesse, J.J./Grimm, D./Jochimsen, R./Scharpf, F.W.*: Zur Neuordnung der Europäischen Union, Baden-Baden, 1997; *Bruha, T./Hesse, J.J./Nowak, C.* (eds.): Welche Verfassung für Europa?, Baden-Baden, 2001; *Hesse, J.J./Grotz, F.*: Europa professionalisieren. Kompetenzordnung und institutionelle Reform im Rahmen der Europäischen Union, Berlin, 2005; *Hesse, J.J.*: Vom Werden Europas – Der Europäische Verfassungsvertrag: Konventsarbeit, politische Konsensbildung, materielles Ergebnis, Berlin, 2007; *Hesse, J.J./*

to encompass large-scale comparisons in an interregional perspective, with a special focus on East Asia.[7]

The third aspect to be addressed here is *Hesse*'s belief that *Staatswissenschaften* in general and social sciences in particular ought to conduct fundamental research but at the same time should not forget about their applied dimension. In other words, the relevant disciplines should contribute to bridging the gap between academic environments and practical politics. In our view, *Hesse* himself has definitely succeeded in meeting this ambitious demand. During the last 30 years, he has extensively worked as a consultant for national and subnational ministries, local government associations, national and transnational interest groups as well as for international organisations.[8] Furthermore, he was invited to be an expert member of various political advisory bodies and reform commissions.[9] Last but not least, he was founding director of several policy-oriented research institutions, such as the *Rhein-Ruhr-Institut für Sozialforschung und Politikberatung*, the *Centre for European Studies* at Nuffield College, Oxford University, the *European Centre for Comparative Government and Public Policy* and the *International Institute for Comparative Government and European Policy (ISE)*.[10]

Toonen, T.A.J. (eds.): The Impact of the/a "European Constitution" on the National Legal and Political Systems, Baden-Baden, forthcoming.

7 Hesse, J.J./Hood, C./Peters, B.G. (eds.): Paradoxes in Public Sector Reform, Berlin, 2003; *Hesse, J.J./Lane, J.-E./Nishikawa, Y.* (eds.): The Public Sector in Transition. The European Union and East Asia Compared, Baden-Baden, 2007.

8 Among the vast number of reports and expert opinions, cf. as a selection of the most recent ones: *Hesse, J.J.*: Überprüfung der kommunalen Verwaltungsstrukturen im Saarland. Gutachten im Auftrag des saarländischen Ministeriums für Inneres und Sport, Berlin, 2004; *id.*: Niedersachsen: Staatliche Repräsentanz in den Regionen. Funktion, Aufgaben und Organisation von „Regierungsbüros". Gutachten im Auftrag des Gesprächskreises Weser-Ems, Berlin, 2004; *id.*: Reorganisation der Hauptstadtverwaltung. Funktional- und Verwaltungsstrukturreform in Berlin. Gutachten für die FDP-Fraktion im Abgeordnetenhaus von Berlin, Berlin, 2005; *id.*: Regierungs- und Verwaltungsreformen im internationalen Vergleich: der Fall Australien. Untersuchung im Auftrag des Bundesministeriums des Innern, Berlin, 2006; *id.*: Regierungs- und Verwaltungsreformen im internationalen Vergleich: der Fall Neuseeland. Untersuchung im Auftrag des Bundesministeriums des Innern, Berlin, 2006; *id.*: Evaluation der Aufgabenträgerschaft nach dem SGB II. Jahresbericht 2006. Untersuchung im Auftrag des Deutschen Landkreistages, Berlin, 2007; *id./Götz, A./Schubert, S.*: Reform der Hoheitsverwaltung. Das Beispiel der Finanzverwaltung in Baden-Württemberg, Baden-Baden, 2007; *Hesse, J.J.*: Verwaltungsstruktur- und Funktionalreform in Schleswig-Holstein. Untersuchung im Auftrag der Landesregierung Schleswig-Holstein, Berlin, 2007.

9 To name only a very recent example, he serves as expert on the current *Bund-Länder*-Commission for Reforming the Federal Fiscal Relations. See *Hesse, J.J.*: Stellungnahme im Rahmen der Sachverständigen-Anhörung der Kommission von Bundestag und Bundesrat zur Modernisierung der Bund-Länder-Finanzbeziehungen. Verwaltungsthemen. K-Drs. 78, 08.11.2007.

10 The *Rhein-Ruhr-Institut für Sozialforschung und Politikberatung* was founded at the University of Duisburg in 1980 (cf. http://www.uni-duisburg.de/Institute/RISP/), the European Centre for Comparative Government and Public Policy was established by the three Berlin Universities in 1996, whereas the ISE began its work in 2001 (cf. http://www.internationales-institut.de).

After this quite selective overview, it should be clear that we cannot aspire to highlight all relevant facets of *Hesse*'s academic and practical work. In his honour, we rather sought to address a subject that meets the above criteria in an exemplary way: the relationship between constitutional development and internationalisation. To analyse key issues of this topic in a "cross-border" perspective, we invited a number of eminent lawyers, economists and political scientists from Europe, the United States and East Asia who worked together with *Joachim Jens Hesse* in different contexts to contribute to a concise *Festschrift*.

The following section elaborates in more detail on how the topic of constitutional development fits the leitmotiv of "crossing borders" in the threefold sense explained above. It is followed by an outline of the sections and individual contributions in this volume.

II. Constitutional Development in a Cross-Border Perspective: Theoretical and Analytical Challenges

Constitutional policy and change strike us as almost ideal topics to exemplify that "cross-border" perspectives are both needed and fruitful in analysing key issues of public sector development. First of all, the concept of constitution can be defined in very different ways.[11] "Constitution" in a formal sense is normally restricted to fundamental law texts in a country. But it can also be understood in a more functional sense, referring to the "general rules of the socio-political game" which are usually found both within and beyond constitutional frameworks. Furthermore, the main purpose of constitutions may also be interpreted in two basically distinct ways: Either constitutions are regarded as instruments to stimulate or facilitate specific policies, or they are considered to have their own objective, expressing general attitudes, opinions and views of a society.

It goes without saying that individual *Staatswissenschaften*, in accordance with their meta-theoretical and methodological preconditions, tended to highlight only one side of the abovementioned distinctions. The formal meaning of the concept predominated in constitutional analyses from a public law perspective,[12]

---

11 Cf. *Brennan, G./Hamlin, A.*: Constitutions as Expressive Documents, in: Weingast, B.R./Wittman, D.A. (eds.): The Oxford Handbook of Political Economy, Oxford, 2006, 329–341.

12 See for example *Mohnhaupt, H./Grimm, D.*: Verfassung, in: Brunner, O./Conze, W./Koselleck, R. (eds.): Geschichtliche Grundbegriffe, Vol. 6, Stuttgart, 1990, 831–899; *Böckenförde, E.-W.*: Staat, Verfassung, Demokratie, 2nd ed., Frankfurt/M., 1992; *Gosewinkel, D./Masing, J.* (eds.): Die Verfassungen in Europa 1789–1949, München, 2006.

whereas approaches in the constitutional political economy tradition were usually based on a functional and instrumental understanding of the concept.[13] In political science, the use of "constitution" has never been as uniform as in other disciplines. Nevertheless, a considerable part of mainstream literature focused on the formal as well as instrumental aspects of the term.[14] However, recent developments within the said disciplines point to a careful broadening of classical definitions and thus to rudimental processes of convergence. In European law, for example, a fundamental debate has emerged about the application of the concept of constitution beyond the nation-state, where a formal understanding in the traditional sense is certainly not appropriate.[15] In parallel, there are increasing demands to include social and political – i.e. functional – preconditions into legal analyses of national and European constitutional law.[16] Furthermore, current political science literature includes analytical approaches that stress the symbolic rather than instrumental dimension of constitutions.[17] Yet, constitutional political economy is also taking growing account of the "expressive" aspects of constitutions.[18] In a nutshell, ongoing debates and analytical advancements in constitutional research might profit enormously from "cross-border" exchange between the respective disciplines.

Secondly, constitutions seem to be almost predestined to be explored from a comparative perspective. In this context, two empirical trends require special attention. On the one hand, many nation-states have recently made substantial reforms in their constitutional frameworks. Relevant cases include "old" democracies, such as Belgium, Finland and Switzerland, "young" democracies, such as the Central and Eastern European countries, as well as non-democracies like the People's Republic of China. While each of these processes has clear idiosyncratic features, there may be similar normative and functional patterns underlying these

---

13   *Buchanan, J.*: Constitutional Economics, Oxford, 1991; *Ackerman, B.*: Constitutional Economics – Constitutional Politics, in: Constitutional Political Economy, 10/4 (1999), 403–412; *Vanberg, V.*: The Constitution of Markets, London, 2001.

14   *Lane, J.-E.*: Constitutions and Political Theory, Manchester/New York, 1996; *Lutz, D.S.*: Principles of Constitutional Design, Cambridge, 2006; *Oberreuter, H.*: Verfassung, in: Helms, L./Jun, U. (eds.): Politische Theorie und Regierungslehre, Frankfurt/New York, 2004, 45–73.

15   *Kirchhof, P.*: Europa auf dem Weg zu einer Verfassung?, in: Zeitschrift für Staats- und Europawissenschaften (ZSE), 1/3 (2003), 358–382; *Robbers, G.*: Eine neue Verfassung für die Europäische Union, in: Zeitschrift für Staats- und Europawissenschaften (ZSE), 1/3 (2003), 383–399; *Haltern, U.*: Europäische Verfassung, in: Nohlen, D./Grotz, F. (eds.): Kleines Lexikon der Politik, 4th ed., München, 2007, 125–127.

16   *Haltern, U.*: Europarecht und das Politische, Tübingen, 2005.

17   *Vorländer, H.* (ed.): Integration durch Verfassung, Baden-Baden, 2000; *Vorländer, H.* (ed.): Die Deutungsmacht der Verfassungsgerichtsbarkeit, Wiesbaden, 2006.

18   *Brennan, G./Hamlin, A.*, op. cit.

reform policies. Against this background it is not surprising that the analysis of constitutional reforms has become quite a "fashionable" field of research within comparative political science, after the discipline's mainstream had more or less ignored this issue for a long time.[19]

On the other hand, and in stark contrast to the classical view of constitutionalism, constitutional developments are no longer confined to "closed" nation-states. The emergence and evolution of international organisations where parts of the national sovereignty have been "pooled", raise questions about the possibilities and limits of constitution-giving at supranational level. The elaboration and rejection of the EU Constitution is only the most prominent case in point.[20] An even more problematic issue in this context is how and to what extent ongoing regionalisation and internationalisation processes impact on national constitutional frameworks.[21] In all the abovementioned cases we are not faced with simple causalities, but rather complex and indirect patterns of exogenous and endogenous influence. As a consequence, comparisons between nations and cultures seem to be the only way to systematically learn more about the "silent" transformation of the constitutional state in an era of internationalisation.

The third aspect of why constitutional development seems to be pre-eminently suited for illustrating the usefulness of "cross-border" perspectives is its inherent applied dimension. Since the ancient world, constitution making and constitutional reforms have been classical issues about which academics at least maintained to have specific expertise based on their research. Although by far not all current literature on constitutions and constitutionalism claims to have immediate practical value,[22] it should not be forgotten that cognitive interests in constitutional analysis are always connected to the fundamental significance which constitutions have as a "framework and programme"[23] for the public sector at

---

19 See for example *Lutz, D.S.*: Towards a Theory of Constitutional Amendment, in: American Political Science Review, 88/2 (1994), 355–370; *Schultze, R.-O./Sturm, R.* (eds.): The Politics of Constitutional Reform in North America, Opladen, 2000; *Lorenz, A.*: How to Measure Constitutional Rigidity, in: Journal of Theoretical Politics, 17/3 (2005), 339–361; *Colomer, J.P.*: Comparative Constitutions, in: Rhodes, R.A.W./Binder, S.A./Rockman, B.A. (eds.): The Oxford Handbook of Political Institutions, Oxford, 2006, 217–238. Among the "classical" studies on comparative constitutionalism cf. *Friedrich, C.J.*: Der Verfassungsstaat der Neuzeit, Berlin, 1953; *Loewenstein, K.*: Verfassungslehre, 2nd ed., Tübingen, 1969.

20 *Hesse, J.J.*: Vom Werden Europas, op. cit.; *id./Toonen, T.A.J.*: European Constitution, op. cit.

21 For a more theoretical view see *Dobner, P.*: Konstitutionalismus als Politikform. Zu den Effekten staatlicher Transformation auf die Verfassung als Institution, Baden-Baden, 2002; for a comparative study of the impact of European integration on national institutional systems, cf. *Grotz, F.*: Europäisierung und nationale Staatsorganisation, Baden-Baden, 2007.

22 One of the most prominent examples of the latter position in political science is *Sartori, G.*: Comparative Constitutional Engineering, 2nd ed., Basingstoke, 1996.

23 *Hesse, J.J./Ellwein, T.*: Regierungssystem, op. cit., 118 ff.

large. Therefore, the various *Staatswissenschaften* constantly have to consider how their research may contribute to adapting a given constitutional framework to changing national and international environments in normatively and functionally adequate ways.

III. Outline of the Volume

The contributions in this volume highlight these and other cross-border aspects of constitutional development by applying different analytical approaches to a variety of contexts. The first section deals with the historical and intellectual foundations of comparative constitutionalism. The two respective essays highlight the key role that "internationalised" concepts and comparative interpretations of national history can play for constitutional development. Although the authors analyse very different cases in specific periods, they both refer to individual academics and their work, thus underlining the – more or less indirect, but practically significant – impact which scholarly debates can have on constitutional politics in the middle and long term.

Dieter Langewiesche shows that the common view of a historical *Sonderweg*, which has characterised the discussions about political self-understanding in Germany, goes back to the *Kaiserreich* in the late 19th century. Since the institutional order of the German Empire mainly aimed at hindering the development of parliamentary democracy, it already had numerous critics, among them the leftist-liberal politician and lawyer *Hugo Preuß*. By comparing Germany with England, France and North America, he searched in national history for a reason why the country was so different from other Western states and societies. Although he produced insights that are astounding even today, *Preuß'* political influence remained limited until the end of the *Reich*. *Langewiesche's* study thus presents a relatively unfamiliar side of *Hugo Preuß*, who later became known as a "founding father" of the Weimar Constitution.

In a quite similar way, *Yoichi Nishikawa* explores the works of *Ludwig Rieß* (1861–1928), the first European historian who taught at the Imperial University of Tokyo and introduced modern historical studies there. Strongly influenced by *Leopold von Ranke's* concept of world history, *Rieß* saw the "universal meaning" of Japan's rise as regional power in its historically acquired ability to build up a nation-state in the "spirit of Western societies". It is interesting to note that this analytical concept was Eurocentric as well as outmoded in Germany by that time. However, in the context of the *Meiji* restoration, which led to a fundamental transformation of the Japanese state and society, *Rieß'* work had an enormous impact on national historiography and, eventually, on constitutional development, as for the first time Japan's history could be interpreted in an international perspective.

The first section thus focuses on examples of the "intellectual roots" of comparative constitutionalism in the late 19th century and why such cases remain worthwhile studying. The next three articles concentrate on current constitutional developments in Western democracies. As case studies on Germany and the United States show, key issues of present constitutional politics are triggered by substantial changes in the international environment.

Since the functional distinction between domestic and foreign security has become blurred because of transnational terrorism, *Peter Badura* re-examines the constitutional mandate of the Federal Armed Forces in Germany. Contrary to the widespread belief that military missions have to be strictly limited to defending the country against external enemies, he convincingly argues that the *Grundgesetz* does not rule out such operations on the state's own territory. They should, however, be confined to constitutionally enumerated cases, in which domestic security can neither be guaranteed by police danger prevention nor by deploying military abilities. In critically reviewing relevant reform initiatives, *Badura*'s essay also contributes to the current political debate on adjusting the role and function of security forces to "cross-border" threats.

Whereas in Germany, explicit amendments to the *Grundgesetz* are being discussed in order to maintain legal certainty, *Bert A. Rockman* and *Eric Waltenburg* observe a silent yet substantial constitutional change in the balance of constitutional powers in the United States. Although the American constitution provides for a system of checks and balances in which congress is the expected source of state authority, the federal executive government has been increasingly asserting itself over the years. Especially in times of crisis and war, American presidents were able to expand their prerogatives, though never without limitations. In the context of the war against terrorism in the aftermath of 9/11, the *Bush-Cheney* administration has taken its presidential authority far beyond the liberal foundations of the constitution. *Rockman* and *Waltenburg* analyse the behaviour of presidents and other institutional actors in a diachronic perspective. In doing so, they not only highlight the political preconditions for enhancing executive powers, but also make a case for a necessary constitutional debate on "rebalancing" the system in the spirit of the founding fathers.

Guy Carcassonne comments on the constitutional politics in France and shows that the institutional setting of the Fifth Republic is far less idiosyncratic than most of its advocates and opponents assume. However, the semi-presidential system has re-triggered almost cyclical debates on constitutional change after *Nicolas Sarkozy* was elected to the presidency in May 2007. Currently, the main institutional reform issues include the relationship between the president and the prime minister, the strengthening of parliamentary powers as well as the advancement of the *Conseil constitutionnel* to a fully-fledged constitutional court. In contrast to the other contributions in this section, *Carcassonne* focuses on domestic reasons for constitutional change that obviously remain decisive in the French context. At the same time, he stresses the key significance of agency for the functioning of the governmental system – independently of any change in the formal "rules of the game".

Another classical topic in the normative as well as analytical literature on comparative constitutionalism is discussed in the third section: the significance of constitutional frameworks in the context of economic and political transformation. Especially the transitions from authoritarian rule that took place in various world regions since the late 1980s have given rise to intensified legal and social research on constitutional choices favouring or hindering the institutionalisation and consolidation of new democracies.[24] The case studies highlight how dependent such constitutional choices are on context and point to the need for further comparative analyses of their effects.

According to *László Csaba*, systemic change in Central and Eastern Europe has given social scientists an extraordinary opportunity to apply their theoretical insights to a whole region under quasi-laboratory conditions. However, this opportunity has not really been seized so far, at least not where it concerns constitutional political economy. Therefore, *Csaba* presents an outline for studying the influence of constitutional development on economic change in Hungary and other new EU Member States. His analysis concludes that constitutionalism has not been a formative idea in the Hungarian transformation process, in contrast to what is argued in the neo-liberal academic literature and in the related policy discourse. Furthermore, the domestic impact of Europeanisation, i.e. the adoption of the *acquis communautaire* as "supranational constitutional framework" during the pre-accession period, has been far more limited than most Western observers first assumed.

Likewise, *Yong-duck Jung* and *Cheongsin Kim* stress the weight of historical preconditions in the Republic of Korea in establishing a "constitutional state" in

---

24   Cf. *Lijphart, A.*: Constitutional Choices for New Democracies, in: Journal of Democracy, 3/1 (1991), 72–84; *Sartori, G.*, op. cit.; *Zielonka, J.* (ed.): Democratic Consolidation in Eastern Europe. 2 Vol., Oxford, 2001.

the Western sense. Their analysis reveals that the institutionalisation of parliamentary democracy proved to be extremely difficult. The reason was that the modernisation of the Korean state and society since the late 19th century was pursued "from above", i.e. by political and bureaucratic elites rather than by common people. Given this hierarchical tradition and the cyclical sequence of regime changes since the foundation of the First Republic in 1948, the National Assembly has not been able to take root as an effective body for controlling the state executive, although its increasing reinvigoration has contributed to weakening the authoritarian legacy.

Richard Balme and *Yang Lihua* present a very remarkable case in the context of this volume: the People's Republic of China (PRC), where dynamic policy evolution and substantial socioeconomic change have not been followed by a democratisation process similar to those that many communist regimes have undergone since the early 1990s. Nevertheless, recent policy reforms of the Chinese government were accompanied by a series of constitutional amendments which might be interpreted as part of the overall modernisation process in the PRC. However, the empirical analysis of the relationship between constitutional reforms and political development suggests a more differentiated conclusion. On the one hand, constitutional politics in the PRC did not depart from the traditional communist approach, but served as a means to legitimise specific policies initiated by the Chinese Communist Party. On the other hand, the accommodation of the constitution to rule-of-law standards has triggered a self-dynamic process that brings important changes in political culture and may provoke significant tensions within the governmental system in the mid and long term.

After the historical and regional case studies in the first three sections, the fourth section focuses specifically on a core function that each "living constitution"[25] should fulfil: providing government and administration with a precise and effective framework to work with. Under the heading "state structures and constitutional reform", four comparative analyses address this issue from different angles. As *Arthur Benz* shows, constitutional arrangements have to be constantly adapted to changes in their domestic and international environments in order to maintain state effectiveness. This is especially true for federal polities where the balance of power and the relations between constituent units and their institutions are highly dynamic. At the same time, constitutional reforms in federal contexts are more likely to fail than in unitary ones, because the constellation of central and decentral actors involved in federal policy making may be generally

---

25 *Sternberger, D.*: Lebende Verfassung. Studien über Koalition und Opposition, Meisenheim, 1956.

characterised as a "joint-decision trap".[26] By comparing recent developments in Germany and Canada, *Benz* provides evidence on how federal states can escape this constitutional dilemma. Accordingly, a reform process that is open to social interest groups may form the basis for an evolutionary change of the federal constitution, both in terms of substance and legitimacy.

In a quite complementary manner, *Theo A. J. Toonen* and *Trui Steen* study the operation of constitutional structures in unitary countries. By using the concept of cooperative state, which has so far largely been applied to federal cases only, they point to the complex interrelationships between different layers of governance in traditionally unitary states such as England, Sweden, Denmark, France and the Netherlands. Their analysis shows that it is worthwhile to study historical constitutional "originals" to gain a perspective on contemporary institutional characteristics and current developments. Many constitutional and institutional design issues and developments currently discussed under the heading of internationalisation of national constitutional structures have been hotly debated before in the context of the "nationalisation" of local and regional affairs. The comparative analysis suggests that the debate on the institutional meaning of local government autonomy should be revived as – cooperative – multi-level governance within the EU might be of constitutional proportions as well. In designing relevant strategies for institutional reform, a context-sensitive understanding of local government autonomy and problem-solving capacity is required in order to secure an important position for local and regional layers in the emerging European order.

The rules of the game which keep the "*arbeitende Staat*" functioning cannot be confined to constitutional documents only.[27] This general insight is also stressed by *John Halligan*, who deals with administrative reforms in Westminster democracies. Over the last 25 years, Australia, Canada, New Zealand and the United Kingdom have restructured their public administration systems according to the – seemingly uniform – paradigm of New Public Management (NPM). Therefore, this sample of countries provides an extraordinary opportunity to study the long-term impact of extensive public sector reforms. Although the four cases are acknowledged as a coherent group based on common administrative traditions, *Halligan*'s analysis highlights how different the outcomes of NPM reforms have been.

---

26 *Scharpf, F. W.*: The Joint-Decision-Trap. Lessons from German Federalism and European Integration, in: Public Administration, 66/3 (1988), 239–278.

27 *Hesse, J. J./Benz, A.*: Staatliche Institutionspolitik im internationalen Vergleich, in: Ellwein, T./Hesse, J. J./Mayntz, R./Scharpf, F. W. (eds.): Jahrbuch zur Staats- und Verwaltungswissenschaft, 2 (1988), 69–111, here 70.

While some features have demonstrated durability and continue to be significant, others that were once considered to be "key reforms" have been demoted in significance or are subject to debate again. Nevertheless, it is also apparent that all four countries have had a pragmatic preference for better integrated and more balanced administrative systems. Therefore, the political executives' need for effective governance – whether for delivering public services or for providing international security – will continue to drive public sector change in Westminster democracies.

At the end of this section, *Tony Verheijen* points to a central feature of state effectiveness that, with some notable exceptions, has hardly been regulated by national constitutional law: a politically impartial, merit-based and professional civil service system. This classical model of personnel management is still considered as a key benchmark and is uniformly applied by international organisations. Still, many states in diverse regional contexts remain stubbornly outside this value system, or even seem to withdraw from it. Comparing the continued stalemate in most of the African continent with recent sobering experiences in Central and Eastern Europe, *Verheijen* provides an insight into why the *Weber*ian model does not make inroads outside the OECD world. His analysis shows evident limits to "cross-borderisation" where it concerns normative values beyond the formal-legal level that prove to be fundamental to running the constitutional state. The question is whether these values can be constituted and secured in a different manner, so that they might stick in ongoing transformation processes.

While the preceding contributions focus on the development of national constitutions in cross-border perspective, the fifth and last section explicitly deals with normative and functional problems of constitutionalism beyond the nation-state. In this context, the European Union is currently the only international organisation whose legal framework may be termed "quasi-constitutional". It is also the only political system beyond the nation-state that has experienced a lasting constitutional crisis after the Treaty on a Constitution for Europe was rejected in referenda in France and the Netherlands more than two years ago.[28] On 18 October 2007, the Lisbon European Council finally approved a reform of the European Treaties, which is again subject to ratification in all 27 Member States. Although many provisions of the draft Constitutional Treaty have been included in the new Reform Treaty, *Gerhard Robbers* argues that the "constitutional crisis" will continue to have enormous consequences for the systematic interpretation of Eu-

---

28 Cf. the Special Issue of the Zeitschrift für Staats- und Europawissenschaften (ZSE), 3/4 (2005), titled "The European Union in Crisis – Where to Go From Here?".

ropean law. On the one hand, the people in France and the Netherlands have politically decided that the EU should not have a constitution in the traditional sense. On the other hand, the constitutions of the Member States became "divisional constitutions" a long time ago, as Community law precedes national law. Therefore, if the European Union does not have a constitution and national constitutions only cover specific fields, large sections of law will not have any constitutional basis at all. A potential way out suggested by *Robbers* would consist in "Europeanising" the concept of constitution that refers to an evolving order rather than to a fundament of state. However, this solution will only work if the political rejection of the European Constitution is ignored.

The European Union remains the most advanced but by no means the only regional organisation. As *Jan-Erik Lane* shows, in recent years similar regimes have been mushrooming all over the world because they allow flexible responses to the challenges of globalisation. At the same time, uncertainty is a universal feature of such organisations, as participating governments tend to postpone or renege on ambitious plans for far-reaching regionalisation, not knowing the implications. But once a regional organisation engages in a common market project, constitutional decision making is called for, as the consequences of economic integration spill over into other fields of state regulation. Against this background, *Lane* elaborates on a typology of regional organisations based on their degrees of political and economic integration, and classifies existing cases according to their "constitutionalising potential".

While *Lane*'s contribution focuses on functional preconditions for supranational constitution-making, *Michiel Scheltema* discusses normative implications of the internationalisation process. He convincingly argues that as constitutional principles historically developed within the framework of sovereign nation-states, national constitutional law continues to be of crucial significance, but should at the same time "open up" to the international level. He moreover shows that the constitutional conditions for and qualities of international legal decision making are still underdeveloped and very much open to debate. However, international legal regimes for effective enforcement and compliance will remain dependent on the quality of national legal structures and actors for a considerable time to come. Therefore, a transnational legal order is required which will face the crucial challenge of establishing formal procedures through which adherence to constitutional principles in cross-border cooperation can be judged in reliable ways. While national courts will undoubtedly play a key role in this context, they will not be able to exclusively stick to their domestic legal system, but will also have to refer to common constitutional principles to be developed across borders.

In the concluding chapter, the editors try to briefly reflect on the analytical and empirical insights provided by these contributions. They point out the potential to "build bridges" between the different approaches and various contexts as well as to gain some perspective on future directions and points of attention for the academic and applied research agenda. This is methodologically inspired, to say the least, by *Joachim Jens Hesse*, who at many, often very productive, conferences and workshops presented his "ten reflections" on the given topic as a stimulus and point of departure for future activities and "cross-border" cooperation among policy-minded academics and academically-oriented practitioners. Thus, time and again he succeeded in bringing together seemingly incomparable contributions at the end of fascinating discussions – discussions which crossed the borders between disciplines, national cultures as well as academia and politics, laying the groundwork for inspiring, impressive and fruitful intellectual productivity.

I. Historical and Intellectual Foundations
  of Comparative Constitutionalism

Moderner Staat in Deutschland – eine Defizitgeschichte.
Hugo Preuß' radikale Kritik eines deutschen Sonderwegs in die Moderne

von Dieter Langewiesche

I. Die Geschichtskatastrophe um der Zukunft willen gegenwärtig halten – zur Gegenwartsaufgabe von Geschichtsbildern

Es gehört zum „vergangenheitspolitischen Grundgesetz" (*Norbert Frei*) der Bundesrepublik Deutschland, den deutschen Weg in die Moderne als einen historischen Sonderweg zu verstehen, der die Parlamentarisierung und Demokratisierung der politischen Ordnung im 1871 gegründeten ersten deutschen Nationalstaat wirksam begrenzte und eine Distanz zu den westlichen Demokratien erzeugte, die im Ersten Weltkrieg einen vorläufigen Höhepunkt erreichte und schließlich in die nationalsozialistische Barbarei führte.[1] Im Bild des Sonderwegs kann die deutsche Katastrophengeschichte als die dunkle Seite eines Lernprozesses auf dem „langen Weg nach Westen" (*Heinrich August Winkler*) gedeutet werden.[2] Die Vergangenheit wird gegenwärtig gehalten und zugleich für überwunden erklärt, die Gegenwart leuchtet vor ihrer dunklen Vergangenheit.

Das erleichtert es, die eigene Geschichte ohne Scheu vor nationalen Empfindlichkeiten zu analysieren, während der Geschichtsstolz anderer Nationen Europas es erschweren kann, die eigene Beteiligung an der Katastrophengeschichte der ersten Hälfte des 20. Jahrhunderts zu erhellen. In der Bundesrepublik Deutschland hingegen dient die Vergangenheitskritik der Zukunftsvergewisserung, indem zwischen Geschichte und Gegenwart eine scharfe Trennlinie gezogen wird. Ihr Festigkeit und Dauer zu geben, hilft eine Erinnerungspolitik, in deren Zentrum die Geschichtskatastrophe steht. Deshalb haben bislang alle deutschen

---

1   Der Text geht auf einen für den Druck stark erweiterten Vortrag vom 8. Juni 2007 an der Humboldt-Universität zu Berlin zurück. Anlass war die Vorstellung des ersten Bandes der „Gesammelten Schriften" von *Hugo Preuß* durch die Hugo-Preuß-Gesellschaft.

2   *Frei, N.*: Vergangenheitspolitik. Die Anfänge der Bundesrepublik und die NS-Vergangenheit, München, 1996, 405; *Winkler, H. A.*: Der lange Weg nach Westen. Bd. 1: Deutsche Geschichte vom Ende des Alten Reiches bis zum Untergang der Weimarer Republik. Bd. 2: Deutsche Geschichte vom „Dritten Reich" bis zur Wiedervereinigung, München, 2000.

Bundespräsidenten in ihren Geschichtsreden an die Nation der nationalsozialisti-
schen Diktatur und ihren Verbrechen einen prominenten Platz eingeräumt.[3]

Die Sonderwegsdeutung schrieb nach 1945 die deutsche Geschichte radikal
um.[4] Was zuvor als wert galt, bewahrt und verteidigt zu werden, wurde nun als
antiwestlicher Irrweg verurteilt. *Thomas Mann*s Urteilswandel bezeugt, dass dieser
Bruch im deutschen Geschichtsbild auch individuell vollzogen werden konnte.
Der erste deutsche Nationalstaat, den er 1917 in seinen „Betrachtungen eines
Unpolitischen" noch verteidigt hatte, erschien ihm nach den Erfahrungen mit
dem Nationalsozialismus als der Beginn eines unheilvollen Weges: „Durch Kriege
entstanden, konnte das unheilige Deutsche Reich preußischer Nation immer nur
ein Kriegsreich sein. Als solches hat es, ein Pfahl im Fleische der Welt, gelebt, und
als solches geht es zugrunde."[5]

Die westdeutsche Geschichtswissenschaft trug dazu bei, dass sich nach dem
Zweiten Weltkrieg die Sonderwegsdeutung zum wissenschaftlich gehärteten ge-
schichtspolitischen Fundament der Bundesrepublik entwickelte. Entworfen hat
sie dieses Geschichtsbild jedoch nicht, und die Kritik, die an ihm aus ihren Reihen
geäußert wurde, hat seine öffentliche Geltung nicht beeinträchtigt. Geschichtsbilder sind nicht auf die Hilfe der Wissenschaft angewiesen, sie entstehen aus den
gesellschaftlichen Erfahrungen heraus, und nur wenn die Gesellschaft sie an-
nimmt, gewinnen sie Geltung.[6]

Das Geschichtsbild „deutscher Sonderweg" ist von den politischen Erfahrungen der sozialdemokratischen Opposition ausgegangen, die das deutsche Kaiserreich von 1871 als einen Nationalstaat erlebt hat, dessen institutionelle Ordnung
darauf zielte, den Weg in eine parlamentarische Demokratie zu blockieren. Was
ihre Gegner als das Ergebnis deutscher Nationalgeschichte priesen, galt ihnen als
ein Fortschrittshemmnis, das sich vergeblich der politischen Zukunft zu ver-
sperren suche, indem es an einem historisch überholten staatlichen Ordnungs-

---

3 Das habe ich näher ausgeführt in: Vergangenheitsbilder als Gegenwartskritik und Zukunftsprognose:
die Reden der deutschen Bundespräsidenten; und: Der „deutsche Sonderweg". Defizitgeschichte als ge-
schichtspolitische Zukunftskonstruktion nach dem Ersten und Zweiten Weltkrieg; beides in: *Langewiesche, D.*: Zeitwende. Geschichtsdenken heute, Göttingen, 2008 (i. E.).

4 Zum Umschreiben der Geschichte als dem innovativsten Typus der Geschichtsschreibung, neben Auf-
schreiben und Fortschreiben, siehe grundlegend *Koselleck, R.*: Erfahrungswandel und Methoden-
wechsel. Eine historisch-anthropologische Skizze (1988), in: *ders.*: Zeitschichten. Studien zur Historik,
Frankfurt/M., 2000, 27–77.

5 *Mann, T.*: Essays. Bd. 2. Politische Reden und Schriften. Hg. v. H. Kurzke, Frankfurt/M., 1986, 294 f.

6 Dazu ausführlicher *Langewiesche, D.*: Die Geschichtsschreibung und ihr Publikum. Zum Verhältnis von
Geschichtswissenschaft und Geschichtsmarkt; *ders.*: Verfassungsmythen und ihr Ende. Die Präambeln
des Grundgesetzes der alten und neuen Bundesrepublik Deutschland und des Verfassungsentwurfs der
Europäischen Union; beides in: *ders.*: Zeitwende, a. a. O.

modell festhalte. So untermauerten sie ihre Gegenwartskritik durch Geschichts-opposition. Doch kaum einer dieser frühen radikalen Kritiker des Verfassungs-gehäuses, das der erste deutsche Nationalstaat erhalten hatte, argumentierte so konsequent historisch wie der linksliberale Politiker und Jurist *Hugo Preuß.*

Hugo Preuß war einer der ersten deutschen Sonderwegshistoriker, und in seiner Kritik an der deutschen Geschichte einer der radikalsten. Seine Funda-mentalkritik, die auf dem Vergleich mit der englischen, französischen und nord-amerikanischen Geschichte beruhte, machte ihn im Kaiserreich zu einem Außen-seiter, dem an der Universität eine Karriere verwehrt blieb – die Berliner Handels-hochschule bot ihm, wie anderen oppositionellen Gelehrten, eine berufliche Zu-flucht – und dessen politische Wirkung auch innerhalb des Liberalismus begrenzt war. Erst als im Untergang des Kaiserreichs für die Opposition der Griff zu den Schalthebeln der staatlichen Macht möglich wurde, schlug die Stunde des *Hugo Preuß.*[7] Allerdings nur kurz. Er war maßgeblich daran beteiligt, die Verfassung der Weimarer Republik von 1919 und die preußische Landesverfassung von 1920 zu erarbeiten, dann endete sein politischer Einfluss auf die deutsche Politik. 1925 starb er.[8]

---

7   Die Fachliteratur zu *Hugo Preuß* ist nicht umfangreich. Vgl. unter den jüngeren Studien *Lehnert, D./ Müller, C.* (Hg.): Vom Untertanenverband zur Bürgergenossenschaft. Symposion zum 75. Todestag von Hugo Preuß am 9.10.2000, Baden-Baden, 2003; *Lehnert, D.:* Verfassungsdemokratie als Bürgergenossen-schaft. Politisches Denken, öffentliches Recht und Geschichtsdeutungen bei Hugo Preuß, Baden-Baden, 1998; *ders.:* Hugo Preuß als moderner Klassiker einer kritischen Theorie der „verfaßten" Politik. Vom Souveränitätsproblem zum demokratischen Pluralismus, in: Politische Vierteljahresschrift, 33/1 (1992), 33–54; *Schönberger, C.:* Das Parlament im Anstaltsstaat. Zur Theorie parlamentarischer Repräsentation in der Staatsrechtslehre des Kaiserreichs (1871–1918), Frankfurt/M., 1997; *Mauersberg, J.:* Ideen und Konzeption Hugo Preuß' für die Verfassung der deutschen Republik 1919 und ihre Durchsetzung im Verfassungswerk von Weimar, Frankfurt/M., 1991. Ein Schriftenverzeichnis enthält die Website der Hugo-Preuß-Gesellschaft: http://www2.rz.hu-berlin.de/Hugo-Preuss-Gesellschaft/index.htm#Person.

8   Sein früher Tod (geboren 1860) ersparte ihm das Schicksal seiner Ehefrau *Else* und ihrer Söhne Dr. *Ernst Gustav* und *Hans Helmuth Preuß,* die auf Grund ihrer jüdischen Herkunft aus dem nationalsozialisti-schen Deutschland emigrieren mussten. Das Ehepaar *Preuß* hatte vier Söhne, von denen bis auf den jüngsten, 1901 geborenen *Hans Helmuth* alle als Soldaten am I. Weltkrieg teilnahmen. *Gerhard Preuß* war 1921 infolge seiner Kriegsverwundung gestorben, Dr. *Kurt Preuß* hatte sich 1935 in Berlin das Leben genommen. Angaben zur Familienbiographie finden sich auf der Website der Hugo-Preuß-Gesellschaft, a.a.O.

II. Deutschlands „*innerpolitisches Anderssein* gegenüber der westlichen Staatsstruktur"

In dieser Studie geht es nicht um den Verfassungsschöpfer *Hugo Preuß*. Dieser späte Gipfel in seinem Leben als Politiker ist auch nicht der Leitstern, auf sie ausgerichtet ist. Gefragt wird nach dem politischen Menschen in der Zeit des monarchischen Nationalstaates.[9] Er umfasst den weitaus größten Teil seiner Lebenszeit, an ihm litt er, seine Verfassungsordnung verwarf er als gänzlich ungenügend. Es geht um den Liberalen *Hugo Preuß*, für den der erste deutsche Nationalstaat, wie er 1871 geschaffen wurde, zwar ein historisch notwendiges Werk war, aber ein durch und durch unvollendetes – ein Geschöpf deutscher Geschichte, deren Fehlentwicklungen zu beheben er unermüdlich forderte. Sein Zukunftsprogramm hieß: Verwestlichung Preußens, um Deutschlands politische Ordnung grundlegend reformieren zu können.

Deutschland als „unvollendeter Nationalstaat", der in fast allem hinter den Entwicklungen in England und Frankreich zurückgeblieben sei – dieses Wort, das aus den Diskussionen um den deutschen Sonderweg vertraut ist, findet sich bei *Hugo Preuß* bereits 1915,[10] als er im Ersten Weltkrieg ein weiteres Mal die deutsche Geschichte kritisch Revue passieren ließ, um zu erkennen, warum Deutschland anders sei als andere Staaten und Gesellschaften, warum „die Antipathie des Auslands gegen uns" so umfassend ist. „Selbstprüfung" sei angesagt, nicht die Pose des Unverstandenen.[11]

Keine leichte Aufgabe in einem Krieg, den beiden Seiten als einen Krieg zwischen gegensätzlichen Staatsauffassungen begriffen.[12] *Preuß* wagte sie. Er wollte für sich und für die Deutschen ergründen: Worin besteht „unser *innerpolitisches Anderssein* gegenüber der westlichen Staatsstruktur"[13]? Seine Antwort fiel schnörkellos direkt aus – ein Gegenpol zu den vielen Selbstverteidigungsschriften, mit denen Wissenschaftler in die Kriegsdiskussion einzugreifen suchten: Das

---

9 Die Quellengrundlage stellt Band 1 der „Gesammelten Schriften" bereit: *Preuß, H.*: Politik und Gesellschaft im Kaiserreich. Hg. u. eingeleitet v. L. Albertin in Zusammenarbeit mit C. Müller, Tübingen, 2007. Sofern nicht anders angegeben, stammen alle zitierten *Preuß*-Schriften aus diesem Band.

10 *Preuß, H.*: Das deutsche Volk und die Politik (1915), 383–530, hier 510. In der späteren Diskussion wurde grundlegend für diese Geschichtsdeutung *Plessner, H.*: Die verspätete Nation. Über die politische Verführbarkeit bürgerlichen Geistes, Stuttgart, 1959 (1935). Zur deutschen Sicht auf England vgl. *Bauerkämper, A./Eisenberg, C.* (Hg.): Britain as a Model of Modern Society? German Views, Augsburg, 2006.

11 *Preuß, H.*: Das deutsche Volk, a.a.O., 400.

12 Vgl. dazu vor allem *Llanque, M.*: Demokratisches Denken im Krieg. Die deutsche Debatte im Ersten Weltkrieg, Berlin, 2000.

13 *Preuß, H.*: Das deutsche Volk, a.a.O., 550.

deutsche *Anderssein* im Vergleich zum Westen gründe auf dem „Gegensatz von Obrigkeitsstaat und Volksstaat"[14].

Vor dem Krieg hatte er mildere Worte gewählt, wenn er etwa 1886 England als das „Mutterland moderner Staatsgestaltung"[15] preist, doch im Kern ging es um dasselbe. Im Krieg wurde seine Sprache entschiedener, weil er Deutschland in einer Entscheidungssituation sah, die es zu nutzen gelte. Nicht in der „Technik des ‚Burgfriedens'", so beschwor er seine Leser, kündige sich die „neue Zeit" an, von der nun alle sprachen. Was immer sie bringen werde – das Eine sicher, „daß sie *nicht* im Zeichen des Burgfriedens stehen wird". Denn „ohne den politischen Kampf der Parteien kein politisches Leben".[16]

Diese Leitlinie zieht sich durch sein politisches Leben wie auch durch sein staatstheoretisches Denken, und sie grundiert ebenso sein Geschichtsbild: Politik ist Kampf im Gehäuse der Institutionen, durch sie geregelt. Der moderne Staat muss dieses Gehäuse bereitstellen und fortentwickeln. Dies nicht in dem erforderlichen Maße getan zu haben, beschreibt *Hugo Preuß* immer und immer wieder als den Hauptfehler des ersten deutschen Nationalstaates, ein Erbfehler aus der deutschen Geschichte, die er als eine durchgehende politische Defizitgeschichte wahrnimmt. In seinen Geschichtsbetrachtungen und in den verfassungspolitischen Folgerungen, die er daraus zog, entwarf dieser entschiedene Liberale das Bild eines unheilvollen deutschen Sonderweges in die Moderne.

Worin sah *Hugo Preuß* die Ursachen für die historischen Fehlentwicklungen, die er diagnostizierte? Welche politischen Konsequenzen leitete er daraus für die Politik im deutschen Kaiserreich ab? Wie fügte sich sein Programm der „Verwestlichung" des ostelbischen Preußen als Voraussetzung für „ein neues Preußen" in einem neuen Deutschland in den damaligen Liberalismus?[17] Betrachtet werden soll auch, welche Probleme, vor denen sich der Liberalismus im Kaiserreich gestellt sah, *Hugo Preuß* nicht ansprach, obwohl sie die Menschen seiner Zeit umtrieb.

---

14 Ebd.
15 *Ders.*: Finis Britanniae! (1886), 105–109, hier 106.
16 *Ders.*: Das deutsche Volk, a. a. O., 499.
17 *Ders.*: West-Östliches Preußen (1899), 293–314, hier 299.

III. Preußen verändern, um Deutschland nach britischem Vorbild zu parlamentarisieren

Die Kriegsschrift von 1915 „Das deutsche Volk und die Politik" endet mit dem Appell zur „rückhaltlosen Selbstüberwindung des Obrigkeitssystems". Es hafte, so mahnte *Preuß* seine Zeitgenossen, „nicht an Personen, sondern an System und politischer Struktur".[18] Beides sah er in Deutschland durch eine misslungene Geschichte zur Reformunfähigkeit erstarrt.

Die Geschichte der Neuzeit läuft auf den modernen Staat zu. Um dies vor Augen zu führen, werden die Schriften, mit denen *Hugo Preuß* in die Tagespolitik eingreifen will, zu historischen Lehrstücken. Modern ist ein Staat, wenn die Regierung aus der Entscheidung des Parlamentes hervorgeht und das Parlament von einer Gesellschaft gewählt wird, in der Parteien ungehindert um politische Macht konkurrieren können. Das „parlamentarische Regime" definierte *Preuß* als „die gleichberechtigte freie Konkurrenz der parlamentarischen Parteien um die politische Macht".[19]

Politik ist Kampf um Macht auf Zeit, die Gesellschaft muss diesen Kampf wollen, und die Institutionen des Staates müssen auf ihn ausgerichtet sein. Die „politisch fähigste Nation der modernen Welt", so nannte er England,[20] habe dies „in tausendjähriger Entwicklung"[21] gelernt und fortentwickelt zum modernen Staat. Ihn verstand *Preuß* als Volksstaat, weil er auf die politische „Teilnahme des Volkes" angewiesen ist in Gestalt von „Selbstverwaltung und Parlamentarismus". Den britischen Parlamentarismus pries er, auf die Forschungen *Rudolf von Gneist*s verweisend, als den „glänzenden Kuppelbau, der den soliden Unterbau des *Selfgovernment*, der örtlichen Selbstverwaltung, krönend abschließt"[22]. Deshalb weise der deutsche „Liberalismus unermüdlich auf England hin als das Land, von dem wir in politischer Hinsicht unendlich viel lernen können". In jüngster Zeit *Gladstone*s „Demokratisierung des Parlamentarismus", die er als dessen „Vollendung" würdigte und scharf gegen die deutsche Ablehnung von „Parteienkampf" im Parlamentarismus abhob.[23]

---

18 *Ders.*: Das deutsche Volk, a.a.O., 530.
19 *Ders.*: West-Östliches Preußen, a.a.O., 302.
20 *Ders.*: Eine Biographie des englischen Parlaments (1886), 98–105, 101.
21 *Ders.*: Finis Britanniae, a.a.O., 106. Auch das folgende Zitat.
22 *Ders.*: Biographie des englischen Parlaments, a.a.O., 100. Vgl. *Grassmann, S.*: Hugo Preuss und die deutsche Selbstverwaltung, Lübeck/Hamburg, 1965.
23 *Ders.*: Finis Britanniae, a.a.O., 105. Die Kritik am Parteienstaat wurde in Deutschland aber früh begleitet durch die Entstehung moderner Parteien (1848/49) und die hohe Bedeutung der Parlamente für die Politik in den Einzelstaaten und dann im Deutschen Reich. Das sah *Preuß* nicht. Vgl. als Überblick

In „unserem Verfassungsleben ist alles provisorisch", klagte er,[24] im Reich wie in Preußen hänge alles an Personen, nicht an Verfassungsinstitutionen, sie sind „höchst unfertig"[25], der Parlamentarismus stecke in Deutschland und ebenso in Österreich „noch arg in den Kinderschuhen"[26]. Und die Selbstverwaltung als „die notwendige Fundamentierung der parlamentarischen Verfassung"[27] – eine preußische „Leidensgeschichte"[28], und damit auch eine deutsche. Denn ohne Preußen kein deutscher Nationalstaat, ohne die Demokratisierung und Parlamentarisierung Preußens keine Demokratisierung und Parlamentarisierung des Deutschen Reiches. An Preußen krankt Deutschland. Deshalb muss Preußen reformiert, sein Verhältnis zum Reich neu gestaltet werden.[29] Den Glauben an Preußens deutscher Mission, der zum Grundbestand des deutschen Geschichtsbildes gehörte,[30] seit das preußische Militär die Reichsgründung ermöglicht hatte, teilte *Hugo Preuß*, wandte ihn aber radikal gegen das Preußen der Gegenwart und auch der Geschichte. Auf die Einseitigkeit seiner preußisch-deutschen Leidensgeschichte, die seinen Gegenwartsanalysen zugrunde liegt, werde ich noch eingehen.

Deutschland fähig machen zum Parlamentarismus und damit zum modernen Staat hieß für *Hugo Preuß* zuvörderst: Deutschland *entjunkern*. Den Junkern „das Rückgrat zu brechen", galt ihm als die wichtigste Aufgabe des „modernen Staates" und der „bürgerlichen Liberalismus".[31] Seinen politischen Widerwillen gegen die Junker färbt auch seine Sprache. Nur hier wechselt er in biologistische Bilder: das Junkertum als „schlimmster Schädling" und „soziale Schmarotzerpflanze".[32] Dieser „Anachronismus" sei als „Rudiment unwiederbringlich vergangener Zu-

---

Langewiesche, D.: Parlamentarismus – Parteienstaat. Ordnungspolitische Konzeptionen in historischer Perspektive, in: Hertfelder, T./Rödder, A. (Hg.): Modell Deutschland. Erfolgsgeschichte oder Illusion?, Göttingen, 2007, 61–77; *ders.*: Die Anfänge der deutschen Parteien. Partei, Fraktion und Verein in der Revolution von 1848/49, in: Geschichte und Gesellschaft, 4/3 (1978), 324–361.

24 *Preuß, H.*: Liberale und autokratische Revolutionäre (1887), 122–128, hier 126.
25 *Ders.*: Was uns fehlt. Politische Anregungen (1888), 129–146, hier 131.
26 *Ders.*: Nationalitäts- und Staatsgedanke (1887), 110–117, hier 112.
27 *Ders.*: Was uns fehlt, a.a.O., 138.
28 Ebd., 139.
29 Siehe insbesondere *Preuß, H.*: West-Östliches Preußen, a.a.O.; *ders.*: Die Junkerfrage (1897), 201–274.
30 Vgl. vor allem *Hardtwig, W.*: Geschichtsreligion – Wissenschaft als Arbeit – Objektivität. Der Historismus in neuer Sicht, in: Historische Zeitschrift, 252/1 (1991), 1–32; *ders.*: Von Preußens Aufgabe in Deutschland zu Deutschlands Aufgabe in der Welt. Liberalismus und borussianisches Geschichtsbild zwischen Revolution und Imperialismus (1980), in: ders.: Geschichtskultur und Wissenschaft, München, 1990, 103–160.
31 *Preuß, H.*: Die Junkerfrage, a.a.O., 202f.
32 Ebd., 202, 274.

stände" zwar unfähig, „sich in einen modernen politischen Adel zu verwandeln".[33] Doch die „Duodezpartikularisten, denen die Uckermark und die Prignitz eigene Welten sind" und „schon von preußischer Staatseinheit nichts wissen wollen", hätten es außerordentlich erfolgreich vermocht, den Nationalstaat, den sie nie gewollt hatten, in ihre „Knechtschaft" zu legen.[34] Deshalb gebe es, so *Hugo Preuß* kurz vor der Jahrhundertwende, für das liberale Bürgertum keine wichtigere Aufgabe als die „endliche und endgültige Lösung der Junkerfrage"[35].

Zerstörung des Junkertums hieß für *Hugo Preuß*: die Voraussetzung schaffen, das preußische Königtum in eine „moderne Monarchie"[36] verwandeln zu können, fähig zur Parlamentarisierung wie in England. Weil das „Reich und Preußen verbunden sind auf Gedeih und Verderb"[37], müsse jede Reichsreform in Preußen ansetzen. „Pseudo-Konstitutionalismus oben, Polizei- und Junkerherrschaft darunter", so charakterisierte er 1897 die Verhältnisse in Preußen.[38] Deshalb fordert er die Liberalen auf, ihre Zersplitterung zu überwinden in dem „Kampfrufe: *Bürgertum wider Junkertum!*"[39]. Nur so lasse sich die „Verwestlichung Preußens" erzwingen, eine „Art von Revolution für Preußen" durch die „Niederwerfung des östlichen Feudalismus".[40]

Aus diesen Worten, 1899 veröffentlicht, spricht die politische Verzweiflung eines Liberalen, der nur zehn Jahre zuvor einen konkreten Plan zur Reorganisation des Verfassungsgehäuses entworfen hatte. *Bismarck* war entlassen worden, die übermächtige Gestalt, die jeden Schritt in Richtung Parlamentarisierung des Reiches blockierte,[41] nun endlich könne das Reich und Preußen in eine Ver-

---

33 Zitate ebd., 203, 217.

34 Ebd., 239, 273.

35 Ebd., 274. Mit diesen Worten schloss seine Abrechnung mit den Junkern. Analysen auf dem heutigen Forschungsstand: *Clark, C.*: Iron Kingdom: The Rise and Downfall of Prussia, 1600–1947, London, 2006 (deutsch 2007); *Aldenhoff-Hübinger, R.*: Agrarpolitik und Protektionismus. Deutschland und Frankreich im Vergleich 1879–1914, Göttingen, 2002; *Reif, H. (Hg.)*: Adel und Bürgertum in Deutschland I. Entwicklungslinien und Wendepunkte im 19. Jahrhundert, Berlin, 2000; *Anderson, M. L.*: Practicing Democracy. Elections and Political Culture in Imperial Germany, Princeton, NJ, 2000, Kap. 6–7; *Augustine, D. L.*: Patricians and Pervenues. Wealth and High Society in Wilhelmine Germany, Oxford, 1994; *Heß, K.*: Junker und bürgerliche Großgrundbesitzer im Kaiserreich, Stuttgart, 1990. Zu *Max Weber*s Studien zu Ostelbien siehe die Bände 1.3 und 1.4 der Gesamtausgabe (Tübingen 1984, 1993).

36 *Preuß, H.*: Die Junkerfrage, a.a.O., 273.

37 Ebd.

38 Ebd., 267.

39 *Preuß, H.*: Vor den Landtagswahlen (1892), 277–287, hier 282.

40 *Ders.*: West-Östliches Preußen, a.a.O., 314.

41 Über Reichskanzler *Bismarck* als „den kommandierenden General im politischen Organismus", der „stets in der Uniform des Generals einhergeht", Gehorsam verlange und die „Macht der Institutionen"

fassungsstruktur gefügt werden, die den Weg in die parlamentarische Monarchie freigibt und zugleich institutionalisiert. Der deutsche Reichskanzler muss, so *Preuß* in seinem Organisationsplan, per Gesetz zugleich preußischer Staatskanzler sein: Premier der Reichsregierung mit einer wachsenden Zahl von Fachministerien und zugleich Premier der preußischen Staatsregierung, ebenfalls mit Fachministern als Ressortchefs.

So wollte *Hugo Preuß* zwei Strukturdefekte des jungen Nationalstaates beheben: Reich und Preußen werden verfassungsrechtlich harmonisiert, und sie zielen auch politisch in dieselbe Richtung, denn sie haben stets denselben Kopf.

Dieser Kopf ist „ein *politischer* Mann", denn er ist „für die großen, leitenden Grundsätze der Politik verantwortlich, und zwar er allein". Nicht der Monarch. „Der deutsche Reichs- und preußische Staatskanzler wäre als verantwortlicher Minister das genaue Gegenbild zum deutschen Kaiser und Könige von Preußen als unverantwortlichem Monarchen."[42]

Wie die meisten Liberalen damals, vor allem die Linksliberalen, hoffte *Hugo Preuß*, nach *Bismarck* zu erreichen, was ihnen mit ihm und auch gegen ihn verwehrt geblieben war: ein Reichsministerium, das dem Parlament gegenüber politisch verantwortlich ist und so den Weg öffnet zum parlamentarischen Regierungssystem.[43]

Ob sein Plan diesen Weg hätte ebnen können, ist durchaus fraglich. Er wollte Preußen und das Reich in den politischen Gleichschritt zwingen, indem beider Regierungspolitik von demselben Mann bestimmt werden sollte, Reichskanzler und Staatskanzler in einer Person, ausgewiesen durch ein politisches Programm, verantwortlich dem Parlament. Doch hätte diese Verantwortlichkeit einen Schritt in Richtung Parlamentarismus bedeutet? Allenfalls dann, wenn das preußische Parlament und das Reichsparlament politisch in die gleiche Richtung gezielt hätten, also nicht nur eine Personalunion an der Spitze beider Regierungen, sondern eine Meinungs- oder Programmunion zwischen den beiden Parlamenten. Eine unwahrscheinliche Konstellation, zumindest solange in Preußen nach dem Dreiklassen-Wahlrecht, „dem elendsten aller Wahlsysteme"[44], gewählt wurde. Indem *Hugo Preuß* das Reich und Preußen in der Gestalt des Regierungschefs vereinen wollte, erdachte sein Organisationsplan ungewollt eine neue Hürde

---

verblassen lasse, siehe: *Preuß, H.*: Was uns fehlt, a.a.O., 144. Vgl. *Gall, L.*: Bismarck. Der weiße Revolutionär, Berlin, 1980.

42 *Preuß, H.*: Die Organisation der Reichsregierung und die Parteien (1890), 155–176, hier 172, 174.

43 Zur Entwicklung der liberalen Parteien im Kaiserreich als Überblick *Langewiesche, D.*: Liberalismus in Deutschland, Frankfurt/M., 1988.

44 *Preuß, H.*: Vor den Landtagswahlen, a.a.O., 285.

gegen eine durchgreifende Parlamentarisierung: *ein* Kanzler verantwortlich gegenüber *zwei* Parlamenten.

Diese Konstruktion, die darauf zielte, mit einem begrenzten rechtlichen
Eingriff eine große politische Wirkung zu erzielen, lässt erkennen, warum *Hugo
Preuß* in seinen Ideen, wie Preußen fähig zur Integration in den deutschen Ge-
samtstaat gemacht werden könnte, zunehmend radikaler wurde. Nicht mehr
behutsame Reform hieß sein Programm im späten Kaiserreich, sondern „Verwestlichung Preußens", indem die Machtpositionen der Junker zerstört werden.
Nach dem Krieg ging er noch weiter: Zerlegung Preußens in mehrere Staaten
mittlerer Größe sah sein erster Entwurf einer neuen Reichsverfassung vor, den er
im Auftrage des Rates der Volksbeauftragten erarbeitet hatte und im Januar 1919
veröffentlicht wurde.[45]

In seinem Organisationsplan von 1899 erwartete er Widerstände nur von den
Gliedstaaten angesichts der enormen Machtsteigerung, welche die institutionelle
Zusammenführung von Preußen und Reich an der Spitze ihrer Regierungen bedeutet hätte. Es wäre ein Akt der Entföderalisierung geworden, dem gegenüber
Hugo Preuß von denen, die auf der Verliererseite stünden, „loyalen Partikularismus" verlangte: ein Ja zur Unitarisierung durch die preußisch-reichische Macht-
konzentration in Gestalt der Kanzlerunion. Die „nationale Monarchie" sah er
ebenfalls gestärkt. Sie müsse „nach Lage der Dinge", so *Preuß* hoffnungsfroh,
„konstitutionell und liberal sein". Deshalb könne sich der Liberalismus auf diese
Reorganisation Deutschlands einlassen. „*Hic Rhodus, hic salta!*"[46]

Das alles waren Fehleinschätzungen. Die deutsche Politik geriet nach *Bismarck*
zwar in Bewegung, doch *Hugo Preuß* erkannte darin schon bald nur noch eine
Fortsetzung der „Leidensgeschichte" des deutschen Liberalismus.[47] Die „Verwestlichung Preußens" stagniert, urteilt er, als das Jahrhundert zu Ende ging. All
das, was er als Hemmschuhe wahrnahm, fasst er in das Verdammungswort
„östlicher Feudalismus". Gegen ihn rief er das liberale Bürgertum zum politischen
Entscheidungskampf.[48]

Viele Anhänger fand er mit diesem Programm nicht; auch nicht unter den
Linksliberalen. Versagte der Liberalismus erneut, und mit ihm das Bürgertum? So
sah es *Hugo Preuß* in vielen Schriften aus dem späten Kaiserreich. Dass seine

---

45 Vgl. dazu *Anschütz, G.*: Die Verfassung des Deutschen Reiches vom 11. August 1919. Ein Kommentar für
    Wissenschaft und Praxis, Dritte Bearbeitung, 13. Auflage, Berlin, 1930, 16 f.; *Grassmann, S.*, a. a. O., 98 f.
46 *Preuß, H.*: Organisation der Reichsregierung, a. a. O., 175 f.
47 *Ders.*: Vor den Landtagswahlen, a. a. O., 278.
48 *Ders.*: West-Östliches Preußen, a. a. O., 314.

Fixierung auf Preußen den Blick auf das andere Deutschland verstellte und damit andere Geschichtsbilder und Zukunftsvorstellungen ausblendete, blieb ihm verschlossen.

IV. Preußens Verantwortung für die deutsche Defizitgeschichte – Entwicklungsblockade gegen den demokratischen Nationalstaat

Preuß' Blick auf das Deutsche Reich und auf die deutsche Geschichte, die er immer wieder aufrief, um seine Gegenwartsdiagnose zu begründen, war einzig auf Preußen gerichtet, überzeugt, an Preußen habe sich die deutsche Vergangenheit entschieden und werde sich auch die Zukunft entscheiden. Den nichtpreußischen Teilen der deutschen Nation widmete er wenig Aufmerksamkeit. Das musste die Wirkung seiner scharfzüngigen Analysen und seiner politischen Forderungen auch innerhalb des linksliberalen Milieus begrenzen.

Durchdrungen vom „deutschen Beruf Preußens"[49] sah er in der preußischen Geschichte begründet, was erreicht worden ist, und was nicht. Letzteres vor allem. Da er seine deutsche Geschichte als eine durchgehende Defizitgeschichte erzählte, mit dem Ergebnis des „innerpolitischen Andersseln" als der Westen, musste Preußen den Hauptteil dieser mächtigen Geschichtslast tragen, unter die *Hugo Preuß* das Deutschland seiner Gegenwart weiterhin gebeugt wusste. Seine Preußenmanie erzeugte keinen preußischen Triumphalismus; im Gegenteil, weil er Preußen, und nur an Preußen, das Geschick der deutschen Nation knüpfte, bürdete er ihm die ganze Verantwortungslast des Scheiterns auf dem Weg zu einem modernen entwicklungsfähigen Nationalstaat auf.

Die anderen galten ihm als zu unwichtig, um in die Pflicht genommen zu werden. Um einige Beispiele zu nennen: Die „Feudalisierung des höheren Bürgertums" unterlegte er allein mit Zahlen aus den „östlichen Provinzen Preußens"[50], die „Neue Ära" Ende der 1850er Jahre und ihr Ende erschienen bei ihm als ausschließlich preußische Phänomene, die Reformzeit zu Beginn des 19. Jahrhunderts ebenfalls, seine tiefe Sorge um die Selbstverwaltung auf dem Lande – eine der Voraussetzungen, an die er einen funktionsfähigen Parlamentarismus gebunden sah – begründete er mit dem erfolgreichen Widerstand der Junker in Ostelbien, und die vier Namen, deren „Klänge allgemein historische Bedeutung" „in unserer ganzen neueren Geschichte" zukomme, führen ebenfalls nach Preußen als Wir-

---

49 Ebd., 300; *ders.*: Die Junkerfrage, a. a. O:, 201; *ders.*: Das deutsche Volk und die Politik (1915), 473.
50 *Ders.*: Die Junkerfrage, a. a. O., 266.

kungsort: der *große Kurfürst* und *Friedrich der Große, Stein* und *Bismarck*. Alle großen Staatsmänner, mehr als vier erkannte er in der Geschichte und Gegenwart Deutschlands nicht, sind Preußen; „das ganze übrige deutsche Volk in seiner kleinstaatlichen Zersplitterung ist also ausgeschaltet. Nicht zufällig, sondern notwendig. Im Weimarischen Ländchen konnten Goethe und Schiller, Herder und Wieland den Boden ihrer Entwicklungen finden; aber kein großer Staatsmann." Ihn konnte die „Nichtigkeit deutscher Landeshoheiten" nicht erschaffen.[51]

Dem föderativ-staatenbündischen Grundzug deutscher Geschichte brachte *Hugo Preuß* kein Verständnis entgegen, er sprach ihm sogar ab, überhaupt Staaten hervorgebracht zu haben, abgesehen von Preußen und Österreich. Auch hier radikalisierte sich im Laufe der Jahre sein Urteil. Es war eine Radikalität, in der sich sein Leiden an Deutschland bekundete, an der deutschen Unfähigkeit zum modernen parlamentarischen Staat. 1915 schließlich sprach er von der „trostlosen Enge dieses in Wahrheit staatlosen Daseins" in der „deutschen Kleinstaaterei der Vergangenheit". „Das deutsche Volk besaß keinen Staat; so mußte es sich denn mit diesem seltsamen Gewimmel von Staatssurrogaten abfinden."[52]

Worin die „Jahrhunderte deutscher Staatlosigkeit"[53] begründet waren, lässt *Preuß* offen: Fehlte dem deutschen Volk zu seiner politischen Entfaltung der Staat? Oder entstand kein Staat, weil das deutsche Volk „unpolitisch" war? Unpolitisch wie *Martin Luther,* erläuterte er im Vergleich mit *Oliver Cromwell*. Während der Engländer die „Triebkraft gläubiger Inbrunst in politische Energie" umsetzte, endete der Deutsche, „der zum größten Volksführer der deutschen Geschichte berufen war, [...] als kursächsischer Hofprediger und Konsistorialrat!"[54]

Im „staatenlosen Reiche", einem „Chaos von Hunderten landesfürstlichen Dynastien", die Preußen nicht zu vereinigen vermochte als anderswo die „absolute Monarchie" ihr Einigungswerk vollbrachte[55], wähnte *Hugo Preuß*

> „die historische Wurzel des *Andersseins* unserer politischen Struktur gegenüber anderen Staatsvölkern. Im Anfang war hier keinerlei politisches Gemeinwesen; sondern im Anfang war der Zufall einer landesfürstlichen Dynastie. An sie setzten sich die beiden einzigen Organe staatlichen Handelns im staatlosen Deutschland an: stehendes Heer und berufsamtliche Obrigkeit. Beide fanden ihre Einheit in sich und mit einander einzig und allein in der Person des Fürsten als Kriegsherrn und Dienstherrn, keineswegs in der Idee eines Staates oder Volkes, eines irgendwie gestalteten politischen Gemeinwesens."[56]

---

51 Ebd., 418 f.
52 Ebd., 419, 443.
53 Ebd., 440.
54 Ebd., 442.
55 Ebd., 555.
56 Ebd., 444.

Das war starke Geschichtskost für Menschen aus Bayern oder Württemberg, Sachsen oder Weimar, für Bürger alter Reichsstädte und Hansestädte wie Hamburg oder Bremen. Die Eigenheit und die fortwirkende historische Prägekraft des Alten Reichs vermochte er nicht abwägend einzuschätzen – ein Merkmal der Sonderwegshistorie bis heute.[57] Wie durchdringend die föderativen Traditionen gewirkt haben, also das, was *Hugo Preuß* in seinen Geschichtsbetrachtungen mangelnde Staatlichkeit nennt und zum Wurzelgrund deutscher Defizitgeschichte erklärt, wie anhaltend diese Föderativtraditionen damals, als er darüber nachdachte, die politische Gegenwart prägten, lässt sich schlechterdings nicht übersehen. Von der staatlichen Organisation des deutschen Nationalstaates bis zur kirchlichen, Militär und Schule, Interessenverbände und Parteien, Sprache und politische Kultur, im Bürgertum ebenso wie am Hofe, sogar im politischen Selbstverständnis der deutschen Monarchen – überall eine große Spannweite an charakteristischen Unterschieden zwischen den historisch-politischen Räumen, aus denen sich das nationalstaatlich geeinte Deutschland zusammensetzte, überall Merkzeichen, wie durchdringend die deutsche Gesellschaft historisch-föderativ imprägniert war.[58] *Hugo Preuß* vermochte die Reichsgeschichte und ihre föderative Gegenwart ausschließlich als Versagen Preußens zu deuten, seinen historischen Beruf nicht erfüllt zu haben, „Zwingherr zur Deutschheit" zu sein.[59]

Ob der junge, durch militärische Erfolge ermöglichte deutsche Nationalstaat so schnell von den Eliten und in der gesamten Gesellschaft angenommen worden wäre, wenn es die föderative Abfederung der nationalstaatlichen Unitarisierung nicht gegeben hätte, ist durchaus fraglich. *Hugo Preuß* blickte ausschließlich auf die partikularistischen Hemmnisse im Ausbau des Nationalstaates zur parlamentarischen Monarchie, nicht auf die föderativen Hilfen zur keineswegs selbstverständlichen raschen Akzeptanz dieses Nationalstaates. Italien, das als Kontrast hätte dienen können,[60] lag außerhalb seines Geschichtsfeldes.

---

57 Vgl. *Langewiesche, D.*: Das Alte Reich nach seinem Ende. Die Reichsidee in der deutschen Politik des 19. und frühen 20. Jahrhunderts. Versuch einer nationalgeschichtlichen Neubewertung in welthistorischer Perspektive, in: Schindling, A./Taddey, G. (Hg.): 1806 – Souveränität für Baden und Württemberg. Beginn der Modernisierung?, Stuttgart, 2007, 27–51; *ders.*: Der europäische Kleinstaat im 19. Jahrhundert und die frühneuzeitliche Tradition des zusammengesetzten Staates, in: ders. (Hg.): Kleinstaaten in Europa, Schaan, 2007, 95–117.

58 Vgl. dazu *Langewiesche, D./Schmidt, G. (Hg.):* Föderative Nation. Deutschlandkonzepte von der Reformation bis zum Ersten Weltkrieg, München, 2000; *Langewiesche, D.*: Nation, Nationalismus, Nationalstaat in Deutschland und Europa, München, 2000.

59 *Preuß, H.*: Das deutsche Volk und die Politik, a. a. O., 482.

60 Vgl. *Janz, O.*: Nazionalismo e coscienza nazionale nella prima guerra mondiale. Italia e Germania a confronto, in: ders./Schiera, P./Siegrist, H. (Hg.): Centralismo e federalismo tra otto e novecento. Italia e Germania a confronto, Bologna, 1997, 219–250.

Preuß rückte ins Zentrum seiner Kaiserreichkritik, dass die föderative Struktur mit dem Bundesrat als Hauptorgan zu einer Parlamentarisierungsblockade wurde. Das trifft zu. Deshalb kritisierten auch Demokraten wie *Theodor Heuss* oder *Veit Valentin* den Föderalismus und setzten auf nationale Zentralisierung, um Demokratisierung und Parlamentarisierung voranzubringen.[61] Als Haupthemmnis, das dem entgegenstand, verurteilte *Hugo Preuß* die Gegenwart des alten Preußen. Der in der Wolle gefärbte Preuße, der an Preußen leidet, erkannte scharf, was es bedeutet hat, dass dieser Staat dank seines Militärs und *Bismarck*s an die Spitze Deutschlands trat, obwohl – so seine schöne Charakterisierung – „innerlich unvorbereitet, mit einer Verfassung, die [...] halb noch Rohbau und halb schon Ruine war"[62]. Wie kann man diesen Staat, „der die Zukunft ganz Deutschlands in sich trug", befähigen, die „moderne Staatsform auch mit modernem Staatsleben" zu erfüllen?

Seiner Antwort – durch die „Entjunkerung Preußens" es vom „Moder des östlichen Feudalismus" befreien und damit ganz Deutschland zu modernisieren[63] – stimmten durchaus viele Nicht-Preußen zu. Selbst dort, wo der selbstbewusste Bürger *Hugo Preuß* es nicht vermutete: im Hochadel, allerdings im süddeutschen, den er nicht zur Kenntnis nahm. Als 1898 der damalige Reichskanzler Fürst *Chlodwig zu Hohenlohe-Schillingsfürst* auf einer kaiserlichen Hofjagd wieder einmal „Ulanenmusik und die übliche lärmende Unterhaltung des preußischen Militärs" ertragen musste, notierte er in seinem Tagebuch:

> „Wenn ich so zwischen den preußischen Excellenzen sitze, wird mir der Gegensatz zwischen Nord- und Süddeutschland so recht klar. Der süddeutsche Liberalismus kommt gegen die Junker nicht auf. Sie sind zu zahlreich, zu mächtig und haben das Königtum und die Armee auf ihrer Seite. Alles, was ich in diesen 4 Jahren [als Reichskanzler] erlebt habe, erklärt sich aus diesem Gegensatz. Die Deutschen haben recht, wenn sie meine Anwesenheit in Berlin für eine Garantie der Einheit ansehen. Wie ich schon von 1866–70 für die Vereinigung von Nord und Süd gewirkt habe, so muß ich hier dahin streben Preußen beim Reich zu erhalten; denn alle diese Herren pfeifen auf das Reich und würden es lieber heute als morgen aufgeben."[64]

---

61 Zu *Valentin*s Geschichtsbild siehe *Langewiesche, D.*: Föderalismus und Unitarisierung – Grundmuster deutscher Geschichte im 19. und 20. Jahrhundert, in: Handbuch der baden-württembergischen Geschichte. 4. Bd., Stuttgart, 2003, 1–21; zu *Heuss'* Föderalismuskritik *ders.*: Liberalismus und Demokratie im Staatsdenken von Theodor Heuss, Stuttgart, 2005. Vgl. generell *Ritter, G. A.*: Föderalismus und Parlamentarismus in Deutschland in Geschichte und Gegenwart, München, 2005.

62 *Preuß, H.*: West-Östliches Preußen, a. a. O., 307; auch das folgende Zitat.

63 Ebd., 307 f.

64 Tagebucheintrag vom 15.12.1898, zit. nach *Zachau, O.*: Die Kanzlerschaft des Fürsten Hohenlohe 1894–1900. Politik unter dem „Stempel der Beruhigung" im Zeitalter der Nervosität, Hamburg, 2007, 374 f.

Das hätte *Hugo Preuß* ebenso schreiben können, aber nur mit Blick auf die preußischen Exzellenzen, nicht über den süddeutschen Liberalismus, zu dem sich der hochadlige Grandseigneur im Kanzleramt rechnete. Diese Form eines Liberalismus blieb *Preuß* fremd. Er dachte in den Bahnen preußischer Geschichte. Süddeutsche Föderalisten, auch unter den Liberalen, waren ihm keine politischen Bündnispartner. Er suchte Alliierte im Kampf um Preußen als Voraussetzung für ein starkes parlamentarisiertes Reich, das die Unitarisierung des Nationalstaates vorantreiben würde. Preußen aus seinem antiwestlichen Geschichtsweg befreien – so hieß *Preuß*' historisch begründetes politisches Gegenwartsprogramm, das die Zukunft Deutschlands als parlamentarische Demokratie in einem starken Nationalstaat sichern sollte.

V. „Neuer Liberalismus" und Imperialismus

Weil sein politisches Denken den Bahnen preußischer Geschichte verhaftet blieb, fand *Hugo Preuß* auch in einem anderen Bereich damaliger Politik keinen Zugang zu dem Neuen, das er beobachtete und ablehnte: das Ausgreifen des Nationalstaates über seine Grenzen. Als politischer Mensch wuchs *Hugo Preuß* in der Zeit des Hochimperialismus auf. Die Folgen, außenpolitisch wie im Innern, tauchen in seinen Schriften kaum auf. Er fand sympathisch deutliche Worte gegen den Chauvinismus seiner Zeit, den er als „krankhafte Hypertrophie der Vaterlandsliebe" beschrieb. Gerade in Deutschland berausche man sich an dem „ungewohnten Tranke nationaler Größe und Herrlichkeit [...] bis zur Sinnlosigkeit".[65] *Preuß* dachte aber nicht darüber nach, so fremd war ihm diese Form des imperialistischen Nationalismus, was es für die politischen Handlungsmöglichkeiten der Liberalen bedeutete, wenn die Idee der Nation, als deren Sprecher der Liberalismus politisch einflussreich geworden ist, sich nun als ein Expansionsprogramm nach außen wandte. Und dies nicht nur vorangetrieben von illiberalen Kreisen, sondern mit großer Resonanz auch im liberalen Bürgertum.

Der „neue Liberalismus", wie man die Aufbruchsbewegung unter den Liberalen Europas um 1900 genannt hat,[66] zog seine Impulse gerade aus der Emphase, mit der er Weltpolitik und innere Reform zu verbinden hoffte. Davon ließ sich

---

65 *Preuß, H.*: Deutschland und sein Reichskanzler gegenüber dem Geist unserer Zeit (1885), 69–94, hier 83.

66 Vgl. *Freeden, M.*: The New Liberalism. An Ideology of Social Reform, Oxford, 1982; *Langewiesche, D.* (Hg.): Liberalismus im 19. Jahrhundert. Deutschland im europäischen Vergleich, Göttingen, 1988; *Berry, J. M.*: The New Liberalism. The Rising Power of Citizen Groups, Washington, DC, 1999.

Hugo Preuß nicht anstecken. Er wandte sich ab. Erst in seinen Weltkriegsschriften finden sich Überlegungen, dass die Dominanz des alten Preußen im neuen Deutschland nicht nur den Erhalt des Obrigkeitsstaates erzwungen habe, sondern mit ihm auch dessen „kontinentale Beschränkung".

> „Muß und will das Reich aus dieser Beschränkung heraus, so muß es auch die obrigkeitliche Struktur abstreifen wollen, weil es für seine weltpolitische Entfaltung der materiellen und ideellen Kräften nicht entbehren kann, die in der einheitlichen Individualität eines Staatsvolkes, in der Identität von Staat und Volk wurzeln."[67]

Weltpolitik als innenpolitischer Reformhebel, diese Hoffnung vieler Liberaler – *Max Weber* teilte sie –, nahm *Hugo Preuß* erst im Weltkrieg auf, und selbst in dieser Ausnahmesituation beeindruckend moderat. Auch im Kriege lehnte er *Otto Hintze*s geopolitische Begründung der deutschen Staatsstruktur entschieden ab. Hintze hatte 1913 unter Berufung auf den britischen Historiker *John Seeley* geschrieben, dass „das Maß von Freiheit in den Staaten normalerweise umgekehrt proportional sein muß dem militärisch-politischen Druck, der auf seinen Grenzen lastet"[68]. Er leitete daraus historisch zwei unterschiedliche Staatstypen in Europa ab: einen kontinentalen, um Militär und Bürokratie formiert – am reinsten ausgeprägt in Frankreich und Preußen –, und den englischen, in dem unbedrohte Grenzen und eine ferne Flotte eine frühe Selbstverwaltung der Gesellschaft erlaubt haben. Die „peripherischen Staaten" wie Schweden, Polen und Ungarn ordnete er dem englischen Typus zu.[69]

Hugo Preuß stellte dieser Geschichtsdeutung, welche den deutschen Weg machtpolitisch als einen spezifisch kontinentaleuropäischen rechtfertigte und seiner Besonderheit entkleidete, seine ebenfalls geschichtlich argumentierende Überzeugung entgegen, dass nur die Nation im demokratisch geordneten Nationalstaat zur höchsten Kraftentfaltung im Krieg befähigt sei. Deutschland zum demokratisch-parlamentarischen Nationalstaat zu reformieren, galt ihm deshalb *auch* als ein Gebot der Machtpolitik. *Preuß* entwickelte daraus aber kein imperialistisches Expansionsprogramm.

---

67 *Preuß, H.*: Das deutsche Volk, a. a. O., 513 f.
68 *Hintze, O.*: Machtpolitik und Regierungsverfassung (1913), in: ders.: Staat und Verfassung. Gesammelte Abhandlungen zur allgemeinen Verfassungsgeschichte. Bd. 1, hg. v. G. Oestreich, 3. Aufl., Göttingen, 1970, 424–456, hier 433. Zu *Seeley* siehe *Wormell, D.*: Sir John Seeley and the Uses of History, New York, 1980. *Preuß*' Kritik an Hintze findet sich in *Preuß, H.*: Obrigkeitsstaat und großdeutscher Gedanke (1916), 547–582, hier 551.
69 *Hintze, O.*, a. a. O., 432. Zum heutigen Stand vergleichender Konstitutionalismusforschung, die anders argumentiert, aber ebenfalls die deutsche Entwicklung im 19. Jahrhundert entdramatisiert, siehe *Kirsch, M.*: Monarch und Parlament im 19. Jahrhundert. Der monarchische Konstitutionalismus als europäischer Verfassungstyp – Frankreich im Vergleich, Göttingen, 1999.

Weltpolitik war für ihn vor 1914 auch kein Thema, wenn er England, das Mutterland des Parlamentarismus, als Vorbild für den modernen deutschen Staat pries, um den er unermüdlich warb. Parlamentarisiert und entjunkert, so entwarf er nach englischem Muster das moderne Deutschland der Zukunft, ein Staat in festen Grenzen, ausgreifend in die Welt, aber wirtschaftlich, nicht militärisch, nicht kolonial. *Preuß* hatte ein insulares England vor Augen als Vorbild für Deutschland, nicht das britische Empire seiner Zeit. Diesen auf Europa verengten Blick teilt er, der Sonderwegshistoriker im Kaiserreich, mit seinen Nachfolgern in diesem Geschichtsbild, wenn sie Großbritannien und Frankreich als Repräsentanten westlicher Demokratie vorstellen und dabei deren Kolonialismus und Imperialismus ausblenden.[70]

Wahrnehmungsgrenzen im politischen Denken von *Hugo Preuß* anzusprechen, heißt nicht, seine harten Defizitanalysen und politischen Urteile gering zu achten. Sein Leiden an der preußisch-deutschen Geschichte und am deutschen Liberalismus schärften seinen Blick für Probleme. Zu ihnen gehörte, wie sich der moderne Staat und der bürgerliche Liberalismus zu Minderheiten verhielten.

VI. Staat – Gesellschaft – Religion

Die innere Reichsgründung, nachdem die äußere durch den Krieg gegen Frankreich ermöglicht worden war, führte im ersten Jahrzehnt des Kaiserreichs zum raschen Ausbau einer nationalen Rechts- und Wirtschaftsordnung. Es war einer der bedeutendsten Reformschübe in der jüngeren deutschen Geschichte, der viele, die einen anderen Nationalstaat erhofft hatten, mit dem Deutschen Reich versöhnten. *Hugo Preuß* zählte nicht zu ihnen. Was man „bei uns die ‚liberale Epoche‘" nenne, sei doch nichts anderes als „die unversehrte Herübernahme der preußischen Obrigkeitsregierung in das neue Reich."[71]

Preuß blickte auf die andere Seite der inneren Reichsgründung – auf den Kampf gegen die vermeintlichen Reichsfeinde: Katholiken, Sozialisten, Juden. Hier fand er unmissverständlich klare Worte, auch gegenüber den liberalen Gesinnungsfreunden, die ihm nicht eindeutig genug Position bezogen. *Preuß* vertraute auf die Kraft des modernen Staates, in seinem Gehäuse den geregelten

---

70 Dazu ausführlich *Langewiesche, D.*: Das Alte Reich, a. a. O.
71 *Preuß, H.*: Das deutsche Volk, a. a. O., 497. Dass dieser Reformschub vom Deutschen Bund vorbereitet wurde, hat die damalige Öffentlichkeit nicht gesehen. Den Beitrag des Deutschen Bundes zur deutschen Nationsbildung würdigt nun *Müller, J.*: Deutscher Bund und deutsche Nation 1848–1866, Göttingen, 2005.

Austrag gesellschaftlicher Konflikte zu ermöglichen, ohne selber in die Kämpfe der Gesellschaft einzugreifen.

Das Verhältnis von Staat und Kirche und die soziale Ordnung der Gesellschaft nannte *Preuß* „zwei große, weltbewegende Fragen", bei denen die Regierung und ihre Helfer, zu denen ein beträchtlicher Teil der Liberalen gehörte, „in wahrhaft monumentaler Weise Schiffbruch" erlitten, indem sie den „sogenannten Kulturkampf" führten und das „Anwachsen der Sozialdemokratie" nicht verhindern konnten.[72] *Bismarck* habe die Prinzipien der Außenpolitik auf das Innere des Staates übertragen, und viele folgten ihm darin, indem sie „die Beziehungen der politischen Parteien wie Beziehungen feindlicher Nationen" behandelten.[73] Das deutsche „Volk erkennt sich nicht als ein mündig gewordenes Volk", es „erkennt sich nicht als Träger des eigenen Rechts", es „erkennt sein Reich nicht als einen lebendigen Organismus". Auch hier empfahl er „England zum Muster" zu nehmen.[74]

Dem Katholizismus blieb *Hugo Preuß* fremd, er galt ihm als modernitätswidrig. Diese Haltung teilte er mit den meisten Liberalen seiner Zeit. Dem „modernen Geist" sei „jegliche Art von religiöser Orthodoxie ewig unvereinbar"[75], und das Zentrum missdeutete er als die Partei, welche die „Ansprüche katholischer Orthodoxie an den Staat"[76] repräsentiere. Liberalismus und Katholizismus verstanden sich nicht. Das bezeugte auch *Hugo Preuß*, zugleich jedoch verurteilte er jeden Versuch des Staates, in kirchliche Bereiche einzugreifen, und umgekehrt. Deshalb sprach er sich entschieden dagegen aus, die Position religiöser Minderheiten durch Paritätsregelungen oder Toleranz-Zusagen zu stärken. Das seien Instrumente des vormodernen Obrigkeitsstaates, jederzeit widerrufbar und stets gefährdet, denn in der Toleranz lauere die „latente Intoleranz", in der Parität die „latente Imparität"[77]. Ein Staat, der religiös oder kirchlich Partei ergreife, falle zurück in die Rolle einer despotischen, bestenfalls wohlmeinenden Obrigkeit.

---

72 *Preuß, H.*: Was uns fehlt, a.a.O., 145.

73 Ebd., 143.

74 Ebd., 145.

75 *Ders.*: Deutschland und sein Reichskanzler, a.a.O:, 79. Siehe auch seinen Artikel: Novae epistolae obscurorum virorum (1903), 338–354.

76 *Ders.*: Konfessionelle Kandidaturen (1898), 288–293, hier 290. Ein präziser Überblick über die damaligen Parteien findet sich bei *Ullmann, H.-P.*: Das Deutsche Kaiserreich 1871–1918, Frankfurt/M., 1995. Zur Bedeutung des Kulturkampfes für die deutschen Liberalen vorzüglich *Gross, M.B.*: The War against Catholicism. Liberalism and the Anti-Catholic Imagination in Nineteenth-Century Germany, Ann Arbor, MI, 2004.

77 *Preuß, H.*: Das deutsche Volk, a.a.O., 527.

Trennung der Sphären Religion und Staat, staatsbürgerliche Gleichheit ohne jeden Vorbehalt – diese Prinzipien, an denen er die Modernität des Staates maß, sah er vom deutschen Liberalismus der Gegenwart nur ungenügend gewahrt. Er erläutert dies 1898 in einem Artikel, in den seine persönlichen Erfahrungen als Staatsbürger jüdischer Herkunft einflossen.[78] Die „antisemitische Infektion" sei „endemisch" geworden, habe auch „Gegner des offiziellen Antisemitismus befallen", selbst die Liberalen, denn auch sie hätten die durch „Verfassung und Reichsgesetz verbürgte religiöse Gleichberechtigung stillschweigend [...] beseitigt". Ein schwerer Vorwurf, den *Preuß* überzeugend belegte: Den „jüdischen Bürgern im Reich und in Preußen, soweit sie nicht unter sozialdemokratischem Schutze stehen, [ist] das passive Wahlrecht für die Parlamente tatsächlich entzogen." Nur die Sozialdemokratie wage es noch, jüdische Kandidaten aufzustellen, die liberalen Parteien nicht mehr. Das prangerte er an als „Anfälligkeit des Liberalismus gegenüber der antisemitischen Infektion", ein Verstoß gegen „einen Kardinalpunkt jedes Liberalismus". Der Liberalismus handelt „gegenwärtig in dieser Frage nicht seinem Prinzip gemäß", und er erkenne nicht einmal die „tödliche Gefahr", die darin für ihn selber liege. Aus dieser bitteren Diagnose leitete er als einzig wirksame Therapie ab: „politische Regeneration des liberalen Bürgertums" durch „Stärkung der liberalen Idee".

Aber was hieß damals „liberale Idee"? Sie musste erneuert werden, nicht zuletzt gegenüber einer Sozialgruppe, deren beruflichen und politischen Organisationen den Minderheitenstatus überwunden hatten: die Arbeiterschaft. *Hugo Preuß* gehörte im Liberalismus des Kaiserreichs zu den engagiertesten Befürwortern einer Öffnung gegenüber der Sozialdemokratie. Nicht gegenüber ihrem Ziel, die sozialistische Gesellschaft, die er mit aller Entschiedenheit ablehnte. Er setzte auf die Kraft des parlamentarischen Systems, jede Partei, die sich auf die Spielregeln dieses Systems einlässt, so zu formen, dass sie auf Utopien verzichtet, die in diesem System keine Mehrheiten finden.

Deshalb beobachtete *Hugo Preuß* sehr genau die innerparteilichen Auseinandersetzungen der Sozialdemokraten. Früher als die meisten Liberalen setzte er auf die Möglichkeit einer Zusammenarbeit mit der Sozialdemokratie, überzeugt, der „Parlamentarismus wirkt auf die Utopien der sozialdemokratischen Lehren wie das Scheidewasser auf Truggold"[79].

78 Das geschah selten, wie *Lothar Albertin* in seiner ausführlichen Einleitung zum Band 1 der „Gesammelten Schriften" betont (1–65, hier 23). Alle folgenden Zitate aus: *Preuß, H.*: Konfessionelle Kandidaturen, a.a.O. Vergleichend zum damaligen Antisemitismus *von der Dunk, H.*: Antisemitismus zur Zeit der Reichsgründung. Unterschiede und Gemeinsamkeiten: ein Inventar, in: Alter, P./Bärsch, C.-E./Berghoff, P. (Hg.): Die Konstruktion der Nation gegen die Juden, München, 1999, 65–91.

79 *Preuß, H.*: Sozialdemokratie und Parlamentarismus, a.a.O., 176f. Zum damaligen Verhältnis von

Als Hauptindiz für diese Überzeugung wertete er, dass auch in der Sozialdemokratie unter den Bedingungen des allgemeinen Männerwahlrechts Füh-
rungspersönlichkeiten nach oben kamen, die im Parlament ihren politischen
Wirkungsort fanden. Er nannte *August Bebel* und *Wilhelm Liebknecht, Paul Singer,
Georg von Vollmar* und *Eduard Bernstein,* und immer wieder verwies er auf *Ferdi-
nand Lassalle,* den er als einen „selbstbewußten Geistesaristokraten" würdigte.[80]

Eine neue Aristokratie ermöglichen, das traute *Hugo Preuß* dem Parlamentarismus zu, und er erwartete es von ihm. „Die natürliche Aristokratie unserer
Tage ist keine Geburts-, keine Amts-, auch keine reine Geldaristokratie, sondern
ein höchst kompliziertes *mixtum compositum* aus vielerlei Elementen."[81] Entstehen können sie nur in allgemeinen und gleichen Wahlen – auch dies eine
Forderung, die damals nur eine Minderheit unter der Liberalen teilte –, denn das
demokratische Wahlrecht teste nicht den Wähler, sondern den Gewählten. Zum
Beruf des Abgeordneten qualifiziere man sich, in dem man sich „im freien
Kampfe zum Führer einer gewissen Anzahl von Bürgern zu machen versteht".

VII. Deutschlands historisch begründete Unfähigkeit zum modernen Staat – Ausgangspunkt für die Systemreform von 1919

„Politischer Kampf", gebunden an die Regeln des Rechtsstaates, ausgetragen in
seinem Institutionengehäuse, darin sah *Hugo Preuß* das Lebenselixier des modernen Staates. Seit dem Weltkrieg pflegte er ihn *Volkstaat* zu nennen. In diesem
Kampf sei der politische Sieg „der einzig gültige Adelsbrief"[82].

Was er im Kaiserreich als „natürliche Aristokratie" bezeichnete, um sie gegen
die ererbte abzusetzen, würde man heute politische Elite nennen. Sie herauszu-
bilden bestimmte er als eine der Hauptaufgaben von Parteien und Parlamenten –
Stätten der Führungsauslese, Arenen des politischen Kampfes, in denen der Staat

---

Sozialdemokratie und Liberalismus siehe *Tober, H. J.*: Deutscher Liberalismus und Sozialpolitik in der
Ära des Wilhelminismus. Anschauungen der liberalen Parteien im parlamentarischen Entscheidungs-
prozeß und in der öffentlichen Diskussion, Husum, 1999; *Kieseritzky, W. v.*: Liberalismus und Sozialstaat.
Liberale Politik in Deutschland zwischen Machtstaat und Arbeiterbewegung (1878–1893), Köln, 2002.

80 *Preuß, H.*: Sozialdemokratie und Parlamentarismus, a.a.O., 178, 180; *ders.*: Sozialismus und Konstitutionalismus (1903), 322–337. In der Schrift von 1903 kritisierte er den Theorieverfall im Liberalismus, der
wirtschaftstheoretisch nichts Neues zu bieten habe – im Gegensatz zur Sozialdemokratie: Politische
Literaturglossen (1909), 361–366. Diese Studien zeigen, dass *Preuß* sich zunehmend der Sozialdemokratie öffnete und den Liberalismus kritisierte.

81 *Ders.*: Sozialdemokratie und Parlamentarismus, a.a.O., 185; auch das folgende Zitat.

82 Ebd., 184.

mit seinen Institutionen nichts zu suchen habe. Sich hier nicht einzumischen, das sei das Kennzeichnen des modernen Staates.

Ihn zu entwickeln habe Deutschland nichts beigetragen, nicht in der Vergangenheit, nicht in der Gegenwart. Das ist das bittere Fazit, das *Preuß* immer wieder seinen Lesern vorlegte. Die „drei Wurzelstöcke der modernen Staatsform"[83] verortete er in England, Frankreich[84] und Nordamerika. Jedes Volk habe sie mit „eigenartigem Lebensinhalt" gefüllt, doch der Kern sei stets der gleiche: der „Gegensatz zur Obrigkeitsregierung". In England und Nordamerika habe sie sich nicht entfalten können, in Frankreich und den meisten Staaten sei sie seit der Revolution verdrängt worden. Nur in „Preußen-Deutschland", Österreich und Russland überdauere sie immer noch.[85]

Diesen „Kern der modernen Staatsform" nach Deutschland zu verpflanzen, wie auch immer modifiziert, um es endlich nachholend zu verwestlichen, verlangte er von den Liberalen. Daß dies im ersten deutschen Nationalstaat nicht gelang, daran hegte er keinen Zweifel. Das war für den liberalen *homo politicus* eine Selbstdiagnose, die vom Scheitern der Liberalismus sprach, vor allem aber war es eine Systemdiagnose. Sie suchte er 1919 in eine Verfassung umzusetzen, mit der er den Deutschen die institutionelle Möglichkeit schaffen wollte, das zu überwinden, was er „unser *innerpolitisches Anderssein* gegenüber der westlichen Staatsstruktur" nannte.[86]

---

83 *Ders.*: Das deutsche Volk, a. a. O., 423.

84 Dass er die englische Demokratie höher schätzte als die französische, zeigt sein Artikel „Die Jubelfeier der französischen Revolution" (1888) (146–155). Die „Ideen von 1789" pries er aber im schroffen Widerspruch zu den Verfechtern eines deutschen Weges als „Gemeingut der modernen politischen Welt" (ebd., 155). 1789 galt ihm als ein „Wendepunkt", der „unermeßlichen Fortschritt in der Geschichte Europas" (149) bedeute. Zur Gegenposition siehe *Faulenbach, B.*: Ideologie des deutschen Weges. Die deutsche Geschichte in der Historiographie zwischen Kaiserreich und Nationalsozialismus, München, 1980.

85 *Preuß, H.*: Das deutsche Volk, a. a. O., 424. Österreich beurteilte er milder, es sei mehr in Bewegung geraten als in Preußen-Deutschland.

86 In seinen Schriften zur Verteidigung der Reichsverfassung von 1919 griff er auf seine früheren Defizitanalysen zurück. Siehe insbesondere *Preuß, H.*: Deutschlands republikanische Reichsverfassung, Berlin, 1923; *ders.*: Der deutsche Nationalstaat, Frankfurt/M., 1924; *ders.*: Um die Reichsverfassung von Weimar, Berlin, 1924.

„Genius des Okzidents": zur Bedeutung der deutschen Geschichtswissenschaft für das moderne Staatsdenken in Japan

von Yoichi Nishikawa

I. Einleitung

In der vergleichenden Verfassungsgeschichtsforschung nimmt die *Meiji*-Restauration in Japan (1868) eine besondere Stellung ein.[1] Die Verbreitung der ersten „Globalisierungswelle" nach Ostasien unter dem Druck der westlichen Großmächte zwang die Länder in der Region, mehr oder weniger tiefgreifende Reformen vorzunehmen. Im Vordergrund standen eine Stärkung der militärischen Macht sowie eine Erhöhung der wirtschaftlichen Leistungsfähigkeit. Die Erreichung dieser Ziele war jedoch nicht ohne eine tief greifende Umgestaltung der gesellschaftlichen und rechtlichen Verfassung möglich. Im Falle Japans machte zudem die Revision der ungleichen Verträge eine weitgehende Anpassung der Rechtsordnung an das europäische Rechtssystem erforderlich. Letzteres erwies sich als eine außerordentlich schwierige Aufgabe für ein Land, das nicht nur bis kurz davor von der westlichen Welt abgeschottet war, sondern auch das eigentliche Ziel der Restauration darin sah, die unmittelbaren Herrschaft des „ewig kontinuierlichen Kaiserlichen Geschlechtes"[2] wiederherzustellen.

Die umfangreiche Kodifikationstätigkeit während der *Meiji*-Zeit, die unter der Mitwirkung europäischer und vor allem deutscher Juristen vorgenommen wurde, ist allgemein bekannt und auch weitgehend erforscht.[3] Allerdings musste eine derart fundamentale Umstrukturierung der positiven Rechtsordnung auch von einem grundlegend veränderten Verständnis von Recht und Staat begleitet werden. Diese Veränderung wiederum war ein überaus komplizierter historischer Prozess, der sich auf unterschiedlichen Ebenen, nicht immer gleichgerichtet und

---

1   Ich danke Herrn PD Dr. *Thomas Henne* (Frankfurt/a.M., z. Zt. Tokio) dafür, dass er das Manuskript nicht nur sprachlich korrigiert, sondern auch viele wertvolle Hinweise gegeben hat.

2   Art. 1 der Verfassung des Großjapanischen Reiches (1889).

3   Vgl. etwa *Siemes, J.*: Hermann Roesler and the Making of the Meiji State, Tokio, 1968; *Schenck, P.-C.*: Der deutsche Anteil an der Gestaltung des modernen japanischen Rechts- und Verfassungswesens. Deutsche Rechtsberater im Japan der Meiji-Zeit, Stuttgart, 1997; *Ando, J.*: Die Entstehung der Meiji-Verfassung. Zur Rolle des deutschen Konstitutionalismus im modernen japanischen Staatswesen, München, 2000.

in Wechselwirkung mit traditionellen Strukturen vollzog. Der vorliegende Beitrag befasst sich mit einem Teilaspekt dieses Gesamtprozesses: der Entwicklung des Staatsdenkens unter dem Einfluss der deutschen Geschichtswissenschaft.

Bekanntlich war *Ludwig Rieß* (1861–1928) der erste europäische Fachhistoriker, der in Japan lehrte und dort die moderne europäische Geschichtswissenschaft einführte. Der Ruhm dieses deutsch-jüdischen Gelehrten steht jedoch im merklichen Kontrast zu der Tatsache, dass es kaum fundierte Studien zu seiner Forschung und Lehre gibt. Eine eingehende Monographie über seine Lehrtätigkeit an der Kaiserlichen Universität Tokio von 1887–1902 liegt nicht vor.[4] Seine wissenschaftliche Tätigkeit nach seiner Rückkehr an die Friedrich-Wilhelms-Universität zu Berlin, zunächst für mehr als 20 Jahre als Privatdozent, dann erst ab 1925 als nichtbeamteter außerordentlicher Professor, ist kaum erforscht, obwohl er nicht wenige Schriften hinterließ.

Freilich gehörte *Rieß* nicht zu den Großen des 19. Jahrhunderts,[5] des Jahrhunderts der Geschichte. Aber das rechtfertigt es beileibe nicht, Forschung zu ihm zu unterlassen: Die Einführung einer neuen Haltung gegenüber der Geschichte in einem sich schnell wandelnden Land kann doch nicht unbedeutend sein. Was haben Lehre und Forschung dieses fast vergessenen Historikers für die alte und zugleich junge Nation in Ostasien bedeutet? Welchen Einfluss hat der Aufenthalt in Ostasien auf den jungen Historiker ausgeübt? Diese Fragen sind umso wichtiger, als sich in den Jahren, in denen er sich in Japan aufhielt, umwälzende Reformen des politischen und gesellschaftlichen Systems vollzogen: die

---

4   Auch in der japanischen Literatur gibt es, abgesehen von allgemeinen oder kursorischen Erwähnungen über die Historiographiegeschichte, keine eingehenden Studien hierzu. Die Arbeiten des Verfassers des vorliegenden Beitrags sind praktisch die ersten Versuche, auf Grund einer systematischen Untersuchung der einschlägigen Quellen das Werk des Historikers wissenschaftsgeschichtlich zu würdigen. Vgl. *Nishikawa, Y.*: Berurin Kokuritsu Toshokan shozō Rūtovihi Rīsu Shokan ni tsuite [Über die Briefe von Ludwig Rieß in der Staatsbibliothek zu Berlin], in: Kokka-Gakkai-Zasshi, 115 (2002), 179–223; *ders.*: Tōkyō to Berurin ni okeru Rūtovihi Rīsu [Ludwig Rieß in Tokio und Berlin], in: Tōkyō Daigaku Shriyōhensanjo [Historiographisches Institut der Universität Tokio] (Hg.): Rekishigaku to Shiryō-kenkyū [Geschichtswissenschaft und Quellenforschung], Tokio, 2003, 202–233. Siehe darüber hinaus *Hayashi, K.*: Ludwig Rieß, einer der Väter der Geschichtswissenschaft in Japan, in: Bonner Zeitschrift für Japanologie, 3 (1981), 31–45; *Taranczewski, D.*: Einige Aspekte der Rezeption deutscher Geschichtswissenschaft in Japan, in: Kreiner, J./Mathias, R. (Hg.): Deutschland-Japan in der Zwischenkriegszeit, Bonn, 1990. 385–401, hier 390 f.; *Martin, B.*: Deutsche Geschichtswissenschaft als Instrument nationaler Selbstfindung in Japan, in: Hübinger, G./Osterhammel, J. (Hg.): Universalgeschichte und Nationalgeschichten, Freiburg i. Br., 1994, 209–229; *Mehl, M.*: History and the State in Nineteenth-Century Japan, New York, 1998, 97–102. Im Folgenden wird grundsätzlich auf die Anführung der japanischsprachigen Sekundärliteratur verzichtet.

5   Sein Name erscheint auch nicht in dem gewichtigen Sammelband von *Hansen, R./Ribbe, W.* (Hg.): Geschichtswissenschaft in Berlin im 19. und 20. Jahrhundert, Berlin/New York, 1992.

Verkündung der Verfassung, die Eröffnung des Parlaments, der Japanisch-Chinesische Krieg, die zähen Verhandlungen über die Vertragsrevision und der Abschluss des japanisch-englischen Bündnisses, was zu einem atemberaubenden Wandel der nationalen und internationalen Lage Japans und damit auch Ostasiens führte.

II. Studium an der Universität Berlin

Weil er nicht lange nach seiner Promotion im Juli 1884 die Lehre in Tokio aufnahm (1887), lässt sich vermuten, dass seine Lehrtätigkeit, auf jeden Fall in der Anfangsphase, noch wesentlich durch sein Studium in Berlin geprägt war.

Rieß studierte im Historischen Seminar der Universität Berlin vom Wintersemester 1880 bis zum Sommersemester 1884. Er belegte die Lehrveranstaltungen unter anderem der Historiker *Harry Bresslau, Hans Delbrück, Gustav Droysen, Rudolf von Gneist* und *Julius von Weizsäcker,* aber auch Vorlesungen aus weiteren geisteswissenschaftlichen Bereichen wie die von *Wilhelm Scherer* sowie *Eduard Zeller.*[6] Ab dem zweiten Semester nahm er am Seminar von *Delbrück* teil, bei dem er promovierte. Interessanterweise vermied er vollkommen die Lehrveranstaltungen von *Heinrich Treitschke,* einem der damals meistgehörten Berliner Professoren.[7] Seine Dissertation „Geschichte des Wahlrechts zum englischen Parlament im Mittelalter"[8] wurde erweitert und erschien 1885 beim Verlag Duncker & Humblot.[9] *Rieß'* Name ist außerhalb des Kreises von Spezialisten der japanischen Geschichte fast ausschließlich durch dieses Werk bekannt.[10]

---

6   Anmeldungsbuch der Universität Berlin, Riess Ludwig, Archiv der Humboldt Universität zu Berlin: Acta der Königlichen Friedrich-Wilhelms-Universität zu Berlin betreffend Abgangszeugnisse vom 1. bis 31. Dezember 1884, No. 1 bis 61, Vol. 736.

7   *Hertz-Eichenrode, D.:* Die „Neuere Geschichte" an der Berliner Universität. Historiker und Geschichtsschreibung im 19./20. Jahrhundert, in: Hansen, R./Ribbe, W. (Hg.), a.a.O., 261–322, hier 273. Bekanntlich hatte *Treitschke* im November 1879 den sog. „Berliner Antisemitismusstreit" entfacht.

8   Inaugural-Dissertation zur Erlangung der Doktorwürde eingereicht von der Philosophischen Fakultät der Universität Berlin genehmigt und am Dienstag den 11. November 1884 öffentlich verteidigt von Ludwig Riess aus Deutsch-Krone, 1884.

9   *Rieß, L.:* Geschichte des Wahlrechts zum englischen Parlament. Erste Abteilung: Im Mittelalter, Leipzig, 1885. In den folgenden Zitaten wird die originale Schreibweise beibehalten.

10 Die Monographie wurde 1940 ins Englische übersetzt. *Rieß, L.:* The History of the English Electoral Law in the Middle Ages, translated with additional notes by K. L. Wood-Legh, Cambridge, 1940. Auch bis in die Gegenwart wird das Werk erwähnt. So bezeichnet *C. E. McClelland* (The German Historians and England: A Study in Nineteenth-Century Views, Cambridge, 1971, 196) *Rieß,* der die liberale Auffassung von *Gneist* kritisierte, als „a sign of the German's decreasing need of constitutional dogmas drawn from English examples".

Während sich die Dissertationen der Schüler von *Delbrück* fast ohne Ausnahme militär- und kriegsgeschichtlichen Themen widmen,[11] hat *Rieß* sich mit
einem Problem aus der mittelalterlichen Verfassungsgeschichte Englands befasst.
Das heißt aber nicht, dass die Dissertation ohne Zusammenhang mit dem wissenschaftlichen Interesse des Lehrmeisters entstand.

Die Gestaltung der konstitutionellen Verfassung Deutschlands war ein wichtiges politisches Anliegen *Delbrück*s. Er hielt zwar die politischen Parteien für
notwendig, aber war strikt gegen eine Verstärkung der Parteienherrschaft. Von
diesem Standpunkt aus verteidigte er die historisch gewachsene konstitutionelle
Monarchie Preußens mit ihrer starken Regierung.[12] Daher war es für ihn von gro-
ßem Belang, die historische Entwicklung des deutschen Konstitutionalismus mit
der von den Liberalen als ein Vorbild angesehenen englischen zu vergleichen.

Dass die Dissertation von *Rieß* tatsächlich in diesem Zusammenhang stand,
belegt eine Rezension zu den Werken von *Gneist* und *Rieß*, die *Delbrück* selbst in
den Preußischen Jahrbüchern veröffentlichte. *Delbrück* kritisiert *Gneist* dahin-
gehend, dass dieser die Parallele zwischen der deutschen und der englischen Entwicklung zu sehr betone.[13] Er hebt daher die Bedeutung einer genauen historischen Untersuchung des englischen Parlamentarismus hervor und sieht im Werk
von *Rieß* eine Arbeit, die diese Aufgabe vollkommen erfüllt. Aus den benannten
Tatsachen können wir den Schluss ziehen, dass *Rieß'* Dissertation nicht nur auf-
grund einer Anregung von *Delbrück* entstand, sondern auch durch das Interesse
an der gegenwärtigen politischen Situation mitbestimmt war und sich nicht auf
eine eng begrenzte mediävistische Problemstellung beschränkte.[14]

Das wissenschaftliche Interesse von *Rieß* während seines Studiums zeigt ferner
der Beitrag „Grundprobleme der römischen Geschichte", den er 1886 in den von

---

11 Vgl. Bundesarchiv Koblenz, Nachlass Hans Delbrück. Nr. 18, „Verzeichnis der auf meine Anregung unter-
    nommenen oder aus meinem Seminar hervorgegangenen Dissertationen oder sonstigen historischen
    Forschungen".

12 *Thimme, A.*: Hans Delbrück als Kritiker der wilhelminischen Epoche, Düsseldorf, 1955, 22–31. Vgl. auch
    Delbrück, H.: Programm, in: Politische Wochenschrift, No. 1, 18. März (1882), 1–2, hier 1.

13 Vgl. *Delbrück, H.*: Rezensionen zu *Gneist, R. v.*: Das Englische Verwaltungsrecht der Gegenwart in
    Vergleichung mit den deutschen Verwaltungssystemen, 3. Aufl., 2. Bd., Berlin, 1884, sowie *Rieß, L.*:
    Geschichte des Wahlrechts zum englischen Parlament im Mittelalter, Leipzig, 1885, in: Preußische Jahr-
    bücher, 55 (1885), 104–109, besonders 105: „Die Unterscheidung von Parlamentarismus und Constitutio-
    nalismus wird von Gneist kaum gestreift, und wo er es thut, da läßt er den parlamentarischen Charakter
    der englischen Verfassung nicht genügend hervortreten. Das *deutsche* System des Constitutionalismus
    unterscheidet sich aber nicht nur von jenem, sondern, was Gneist niemals ausgesprochen hat, es
    unterscheidet sich zu seinem Vortheil von ihm. Unser System ist ein dem englischen unendlich
    überlegenes."

14 Dass der von Duncker & Humblot veröffentlichte Band als „Erste Abteilung: Im Mittelalter" bezeichnet
    wurde, lässt vermuten, dass *Rieß* die Forschung bis zur modernen Zeit fortzusetzen beabsichtigte.

Delbrück herausgegebenen Preußischen Jahrbüchern veröffentlichte. In diesem Rezensionsaufsatz der beiden Meisterwerke der römischen Geschichte, nämlich der „Römischen Geschichte" von *Theodor Mommsen* und des zweiten Bandes der „Weltgeschichte" von *Leopold von Ranke,* versucht *Rieß* die grundlegende Haltung der zwei großen Historiker zu vergleichen. Er stellt die beiden folgendermaßen gegenüber:

> „Der fundamentale Gegensatz in der Auffassung unserer beiden Autoren documentirt sich also darin, daß der eine [= *Mommsen,* Y. N.] den Beginn einer spontanen, den Stammesverhältnissen genau entsprechenden nationalen Consolidirung darzuthun sucht, während der andere [= *Ranke,* Y. N.] schon in den Anfängen Roms die Durchbrechung der die italischen Populationen beherrschenden Stammesverbindungen und Stammesgegensätze wahrnimmt. Dem einen ist das Volksthum, dem anderen die politische Formation das eigentliche Element der fortschreitenden Entwickelung."[15]

Während *Mommsen* alles, auch die politische Entwicklung, auf den Volkscharakter zurückführe, sehe *Ranke* in der Persönlichkeit das Element, das über das Nationale hinausgeht. Auch die Nation sei bei *Ranke* keine gegebene Einheit, sondern gebildet worden „aus einer Zusammenfassung Einzelner unter der Einwirkung mannigfaltigster Antriebe, durch die Entscheidung zahlloser Ereignisse"[16]. Der Volkscharakter der Römer sei bei *Ranke* „ein historisches, der unbegrenzten Veränderung fähiges Element der Entwickelung, das variable Produkt variabler Faktoren"[17]. *Rieß* verbirgt nicht seine Sympathie für *Rankes* Geschichtsauffassung. Er kritisiert *Mommsen,* dass durch die in der Nation oder dem Volkscharakter verwurzelte Zivilisation oder Kultur der individuelle Entwicklungsgang der Römischen Republik nicht zu verstehen sei. Im Gegensatz zu *Mommsen* suche *Ranke* das

> „Wesen der Welteroberer [...] in ganz abstracten Momenten, in der Spannkraft der eigenthümlichen Gedanken und Bestrebungen, mit denen sie [= die Römer, Y. N.] ihre Gemeinsamkeit durchdrangen und ihm zu den anderen die Erde erfüllenden Mächten seine Stellung gaben. Die in der römischen Geschichte zur Entwickelung kommenden geistigen, Leben hervorbringenden, schöpferischen Kräfte, moralischen Energien gilt es ihm zu erfassen."[18]

Auch *Rieß* will also nicht in der vorgegebenen nationalen Gemeinsamkeit, sondern in der Summe der moralischen Entscheidungen der Persönlichkeiten die historische Grundlage der Weltgeltung Roms sehen.

---

15 *Rieß, L.:* Grundprobleme der römischen Geschichte, in: Preußische Jahrbücher, 56 (1886), 543–588, hier 549.
16 Ebd., 554.
17 Ebd., 555.
18 Ebd., 567 f.

Die oben erläuterten Werke von *Rieß* zeigen bereits die grundlegenden und zugleich bleibenden Charakterzüge seiner Arbeiten. Nämlich das Interesse an der vergleichenden Geschichte (besonders dem Vergleich mit der englischen Geschichte)[19] einerseits und andererseits die Neigung, die geschichtliche Entwicklung weniger von dem Standpunkt der nationalen Besonderheit, sondern mehr von einem, etwa an *Ranke* und *Wilhelm von Humboldt* orientierten, universalen Blickwinkel aus zu betrachten.[20]

Vor seiner Abreise nach Japan kann man *Rieß'* Schriften kein besonderes Interesse für Japan oder Ostasien entnehmen. Vermutlich war es *Delbrück*, der, weil er über eine enge Beziehung zum Auswärtigen Amt und zum preußischen Königshof verfügte, auf Anfrage des japanischen Gesandten *Rieß* in Berlin empfahl.[21] Interessanterweise finden sich im Umkreis *Delbrück*s auch sonst nicht wenige junge Akademiker, die als Lehrer in Japan tätig waren.[22] *Delbrück* erläuterte etwas später im Zusammenhang mit der Notwendigkeit einer deutschen Kolonialpolitik, dass die Deutschen versuchen müssten, „große außereuropäische Gebiete [zu] schaffen, in denen die deutsche Nationalität, die deutsche Sprache

19 Die englische Geschichte blieb bis zum Ende seines Lebens ein wichtiges Arbeitsfeld. Seine letzten Arbeiten zwischen 1926 und 1928 hatten sämtlich England zum Thema.

20 Über das Verhältnis zwischen dem nationalen und universalen Gesichtspunkt bei *Ranke* vgl. *Schulin, E.*: Universalgeschichte und Nationalgeschichte bei Leopold von Ranke, in: Mommsen, W. J. (Hg.): Leopold von Ranke und die moderne Geschichtswissenschaft, Stuttgart, 1988, 37–72; *ders.*: Universal History and National History: Mainly in the Lectures of Leopold von Ranke, in: Iggers, G. (Hg.): Leopold von Ranke and the Shaping of the Historical Disciplines, Syracuse, NY, 1990, 70–81.

21 Da das Interesse der japanischen Führungsschicht am deutschen Staatssystem und den deutschen Wissenschaften im Zusammenhang mit der geplanten Einführung einer konstitutionellen Regierung deutlich gewachsen war, wurden in diesem Jahr gleichzeitig drei junge Geisteswissenschaftler von der *Faculty of Letters* der Universität Tokio eingestellt. Neben *Rieß* kamen der Philosoph *Ludwig Busse* (1862–1907, später Professor an den Universitäten Rostock, Königsburg, Münster und Halle) und der Pädagoge *Emil Hausknecht* (1853–1927). Zu letzterem vgl. *Möller, J.*: Damit „in keinem Haus ein Unwissender zu finden sei". Zum Wirken von Emil Hausknecht und der Herbart-Rezeption in Japan, München, 1995.

22 Sein Bruder *Ernst* und sein Neffe *Felix* kamen nach Japan als Assessoren mit der Aufgabe, die deutschen Kodifikationen ins Englische zu übersetzen. GStPK Berlin, Geheimes Zivilkabinett, Auswärtiges – Außereuropa – Asien, Nr. 13370: Preußische Beamte im japanischen Staatsdienst (1884–1900), Bl. 11, Justizministerium, Berlin, den 15. Dezember 1886. Sie lehrten auch an der neu gegründeten Oberstufe der „Schule des Vereins für deutsche Wissenschaften" [Doitsugaku Kyōkai Gakkō]. Von seinen Schülern haben nicht nur *Rieß*, sondern auch *August Menge* (Dozent an der Ersten Höheren Schule in Tokio) und *Otto Becker* (Dozent an der Sechsten Höheren Schule in Okayama, später Professor an den Universitäten Halle und Kiel) in Japan gelehrt. Auch der Philosoph *Busse* (s. o.) hatte bereits vor seinem Japan-Aufenthalt Kontakte mit *Delbrück*. *Busse* publizierte nämlich einen Rezensionsaufsatz über koloniale Fragen in den Preußischen Jahrbüchern (*Busse, L.*: Die Begründung der deutschen Machtstellung in Ostafrika, in: Preußische Jahrbücher, 58 (1886), 253–282) und schickte aus Tokio ausführliche Briefe an den Berliner Historiker. Vgl. Briefe von Ludwig Busse an Hans Delbrück, SBBPK, Nachlass Hans Delbrück 76, 6 Br., 3 Br. Lten (42 Bl.) 1887–1896.

und das deutsche Geistesleben die Möglichkeit weiterer Entfaltung haben", und schlug vor, zu diesem Zweck die Akademiker einzusetzen. „Mit unseren überzähligen Assessoren, Doktoren der Philosophie, Technikern und Kaufleuten könnten wir ein Indien regieren, so gut wie die Engländer."[23] *Delbrück* hat offensichtlich großen Wert darauf gelegt, aus außenpolitischen Gründen junge deutsche Akademiker auch nach Ostasien zu schicken, damit sie dort zur Verbreitung der deutschen Kultur beitrugen.

III. Das Konzept der Universalgeschichte

Die oben dargelegte Vermutung über den Hintergrund der Empfehlung *Delbrück*s gewinnt noch an Plausibilität, wenn man die Briefe von *Rieß* aus Tokio an seinen Lehrer analysiert. Sein Japanaufenthalt fiel in die Zeit der Entwicklung Deutschlands zu einer Kolonialmacht einerseits und des raschen Aufstiegs Japans zu einem selbstständigen modernen Staat in Ostasien andererseits. Aus den Briefen von *Rieß* an *Delbrück* lässt sich ersehen, dass der junge Dozent die politische Entwicklung in Japan und Ostasien mit regem Interesse verfolgte und seine eigene Analyse dem Lehrmeister eingehend mitteilte. Ausführliche Berichte über das Alltagsleben oder die Lehrtätigkeit in Japan sind dagegen nur am Anfang des Aufenthaltes zu finden. Aber auch in dem ersten Brief aus Japan, der ausnahmsweise eingehend über seine Lehrtätigkeit berichtet, bekundet er sein starkes Interesse an den internationalen Beziehungen. Er beklagt sich nämlich, dass der Geschichtsunterricht an den japanischen Schulen anhand der elementaren amerikanischen Lehrbücher[24] durchgeführt werde und schreibt: „Eigentlich hätte ich die Pflicht, den Japanern eine einheitliche Darlegung der sich entwickelnden Völkerverbindung zu verfassen, die als Textbuch verwertet werden kann."[25] Auch für den schulischen Geschichtsunterricht war er anscheinend der Meinung, dass die Entwicklung der internationalen Beziehungen in den Mittelpunkt gestellt werden müsste.

---

23 *Delbrück, H.*: Das Programm der Preußischen Jahrbücher, in: ders.: Erinnerungen, Aufsätze und Reden, Berlin, 1902 (zuerst in: Preußische Jahrbücher, 75 (1899)), 478–497, hier 488.

24 Die folgenden beiden Lehrbücher waren besonders weit verbreitet: *Swinton, W.*: Outlines of the World's History: Ancient, Mediaeval, and Modern: With Special Relation to the History of Civilization and the Progress of Mankind, Tokio, 1883; *Parley, P.*: Peter Parley's Universal History on the Basis of Geography, Tokio, 1886.

25 Rieß an Delbrück, 24. Juni 1887. Briefe von Ludwig Riess an Hans Delbrück, SBBPK, Nachlass Hans Delbrück 133, 23 Br., 1 Anl: (64 Bl.) 1884–1922. Im Folgenden werden die Briefe von Rieß an Delbrück nach dem Datum zitiert.

Auch über verschiedene außenpolitische Fragen, die damals die öffentliche Meinung in Japan beschäftigten, hat er *Delbrück* ausführlich seine Beobachtungen mitgeteilt. In einem Brief vom 28. Juni 1889 diskutiert er die wichtigste außenpolitische Frage während der ersten Jahrzehnte der *Meiji*-Zeit in Japan, nämlich die Verhandlungen über die Vertragsrevision.[26] Er schreibt im nüchternen Ton über das Scheitern des Versuchs der japanischen Regierung, die ungünstigen Vertragsklauseln zu revidieren: „Doch wird die naive Zuversicht, dass mit einem kindlich offenen Sich anschmiegen an das europäische Wesen keinerlei Gefahren verbunden und auf gradem Wege die Gleichstellung Japans zu erreichen sei, niemals wiederkehren."[27] Nicht nur an dieser Stelle lässt sich ablesen, dass es für *Rieß* eine selbstverständliche Tatsache war, dass die großen westlichen Länder die bestimmende Macht in der internationalen Politik innehaben. Im Zusammenhang mit den wachsenden Spannungen zwischen Japan und China im Gefolge der Bauernaufstände in Korea (1894)[28] schreibt er:

> „Hoffentlich helfen die europäischen Mächte durch annehmbare Vorschläge den zunächst Betheiligten aus der Verlegenheit. Dazu wäre eine Ansammlung von Kriegsschiffen in den ostasiatischen Gewässern sehr dienlich, um namentlich China zur Nachgiebigkeit zu zwingen. Das wäre gar keine unberechtigte Einmischung, sondern internationale Pflicht der Kulturwelt. Daß dies ein wichtiger Faktor in der ganzen europäischen Geschichte seit dem Emporkommen der Römer ist, und daß er in der übrigen Welt nicht existierte, gehört in denjenigen Theil der historischen Methodologie, der bei uns herkömmlicher Weise nicht gelesen wird."[29]

Die Beteiligung Deutschlands zusammen mit Russland und Frankreich an der Intervention zur Änderung des ursprünglichen Friedensvertrags mit China (des Shimonoseki-Vertrags 1895) zuungunsten Japans[30] beurteilte er zwar als schädlich für das Ansehen der Deutschen in Japan, rechtfertigte es aber dennoch: „Als eine Mahnung an die Thatsache, daß in der alten Welt noch immer die Einwilligung der großen Mächte suprema lex ist, war der Schritt wohl angemessen."[31]

Trotzdem scheint *Rieß* – wie übrigens viele andere Beobachter – nach dem Japanisch-Chinesischen Krieg seine Einschätzung der historischen Rolle Japans verändert zu haben. Er teilt in einem Brief vom 7. Mai 1896 die Erneuerung seines

---

26 Zur Frage der Vertragsrevision siehe *Iriye, A.*: Japan's Drive to Great-Power Status, in: Jansen, M. B. (Hg.): The Nineteenth Century (The Cambridge History of Japan Vol. 5), Cambridge u. a., 1989, 721–782, hier 736–739.

27 Rieß an Delbrück, 28. Juni 1889.

28 Zu dieser unmittelbaren Ursache des Japanisch-Chinesischen Kriegs vgl. *Iriye, A.*, a. a. O., 763.

29 Rieß an Delbrück, 16. Juni 1894.

30 Vgl. *Iriye, A.*, a. a. O., 768.

31 Rieß an Delbrück, 14. Dezember 1895.

Vertrags mit und begründet seinen Entschluss folgendermaßen: „Mit beigetragen zu meinem Entschlusse hat auch das Interesse an dem Umschwung, der sich hier vor unseren Augen vollzieht."[32] Die teilweise gelungene Vertragsrevision, die Gründung der Verwaltung im neu erworbenen Taiwan, die Verstärkung des Heeres und der Marine, die Entwicklung der Privatunternehmen – der Aufbruch Japans als eines selbständigen Akteurs auf der Weltbühne und einer neuen Kolonialmacht hat den Historiker tief beeindruckt.[33] In einem späteren Brief analysiert er eingehend den Verlauf des sog. Boxeraufstands, in dem Japan zusammen mit den westlichen Ländern als eine neue imperialistische Macht auftrat.[34]

Es ist nicht schwer zu sehen, dass die häufigen brieflichen Erwähnungen der internationalen Lage in Ostasien nicht nur dem Wunsch entsprangen, seinen Lehrer in Deutschland mit Informationen über ostasiatische Verhältnisse zu versorgen. Auch für *Rieß* selbst war die Entwicklung der politischen Beziehungen zwischen den Nationalstaaten der wichtigste Gegenstand der historischen Forschung. In der Vorlesung „*Universal History*", die ihn während seiner Professur in Japan vermutlich am stärksten beschäftigte, stützte er sich auf das Konzept der „Weltgeschichte" von *Ranke*. Am Anfang der Vorlesung stellte er das methodische Fundament des unvollendeten Lebenswerks des Altmeisters vor:

> „He [= Ranke, Y. N.] distinguished the subject of his (unfortunately unfinished) Weltgeschichte from that of any national history so that the former only consists of those ties and relations that always existed between different nations. From the whole mass of events, which concerned only the condition of one nation, he separates those through which one has influenced the other so that many of them now form one living community. In the totality of such events he hoped to comprehend the growth of one great community of nations, as it now exists. [...] we gain the important principle, that only phenomena that at the time or later affected all or nearly all members of the community or that have left traits still perceivable in the present state of that community, find a fitting place in our short survey."[35]

32 Rieß an Delbrück, 7. Mai 1896.

33 Im selben Schreiben (ebd.) stellt er einen interessanten Vergleich zwischen den Stimmungen Japans und Deutschlands an: „[...] so daß man das belebende Gefühl hat, es geht vorwärts mit diesem Lande meines zeitweiligen Aufenthaltes, und Jederman wirft sich hoffnungsvoll ins Zeug. Bis etwa 1884 hatten wir diesen frischen Lebenstrieb bei uns auch noch. Seitdem sind wir in steigendem Maße griesgrämig geworden. Ob wohl ein künftiger Historiker herausbekommt; weshalb eigentlich? Ich glaube, weil seit dieser Zeit das Gefühl emporkam, daß Preußen im Kulturkampf unterlegen ist, sodaß der Liberalismus seine optimistische Grundstimmung, ohne die er sich nicht bethätigen kann, definitiv eingebüßt hat."

34 Rieß an Delbrück, 19. Oktober 1900. Dieser Brief wurde während seines Urlaubs in Deutschland verfasst.

35 Weil *Rieß* wiederholt seine Vorlesungsmanuskripte drucken ließ, sind für einige Vorlesungen mehrere Auflagen überliefert. Auch für die Vorlesung „Universalgeschichte" gibt es mehrere Versionen unter dem Titel „*Course of Lectures on Universal History*" oder „*A Short Survey of Universal History*". Inhaltlich

Nach *Rieß* tragen die zwischenstaatlichen Konkurrenzen und Gegensätze, die die Wurzeln der internationalen Beziehungen darstellen, zur Entwicklung der Zivilisation bei. Er schreibt:

> „*Wherever a nation has been content to lead an isolated life, we find that its abilities were developed principally in the same direction which from the beginning was taken, that traditional manners, customs and institutions, although highly valuable and worthy to be carefully preserved, still formed after some centuries a trammel for future progress, that the ideas and thoughts were restricted within narrow limits. To participate in the fluctuating Universal Life, where many nations and states influence each other, may bring with it some dangers for the independence and purity of the national development, but will surely also multiply the forces and faculties, awake new energies, free and enlarge the horizon, of any nationality. A country is all the more civilized, the more it exposes itself to the whirlwind of Universal Life or with other words the more eagerly its inhabitants participate in the general competition for subjugating the forces of nature, for producing the truest ideas, for regulating state and society in the best way possible.*"[36]

Aus diesen Worten, die für seine damaligen Zuhörer in Japan sehr hohe Aktualität gehabt haben müssen, wird auch der Blickwinkel klar ersichtlich, der etwa auch der oben zitierten Anerkennung der Machtposition europäischer Staaten in Ostasien zugrunde liegt. Die von Europa ausgehende und in Ostasien eindringende Konkurrenz zwischen den europäischen Großmächten (und jetzt auch Japan) sei nicht nur eine unumkehrbare geschichtliche Entwicklung, sondern, wie einst *Ranke* die Entstehung des neuzeitlichen Staatensystems beurteilte,[37] ein Vorgang, der die allgemeine Freiheit erhalten und nach der *Ranke*anischen Diktion zur Erweckung der schöpferischen Energien der Nationen sowie zur moralischen Verbesserung führen könne.

Auch in seinen wissenschaftlichen Publikationen während des Japanaufenthaltes ist derselbe Blickwinkel erkennbar. In dieser Zeit veröffentlichte er kaum wissenschaftliche Arbeiten über europäische Geschichte.[38] Stattdessen lag sein

---

jedoch unterscheiden sich die einzelnen Auflagen wenig. Die folgenden Zitate basieren auf *Rieß, L.*: Notes of a Course of Lectures on Universal History, 2nd ed., Vol. 1, Tokio, 1897, 6.

36 *Rieß, L.*: Universal History, a. a. O., 16 f.

37 *Ranke, L. v.*: Die großen Mächte, in: ders.: Abhandlungen und Versuche, Leipzig, 1872, 3–40; *ders.*: Politisches Gespräch, Berlin, 1924, 37 f.; vgl. *Muhlack, U.*: Das europäische Staatensystem in der deutschen Geschichtsschreibung des 19. Jahrhunderts, in: ders.: Staatensystem und Geschichtsschreibung. Ausgewählte Aufsätze zu Humanismus und Historismus, Absolutismus und Aufklärung, Berlin, 2006, 313–353, hier 321 f.

38 Ausnahme war *Rieß, L.*: Zum Ursprung des englischen Unterhauses, in: Historische Zeitschrift, 60 (1888), 1–33. Dieser Aufsatz war eine Ergänzung zu seiner Dissertation. Außerdem veröffentlichte er zwei Aufsätze zu biblischen Fragen in den Preußischen Jahrbüchern: *Rieß, L.*: Waren die Kinder Israels jemals in Aegypten?, in: Preußische Jahrbücher, 74 (1893), 430–448; *ders.*: Die Rekonstruktion des Debora-Liedes, in: Preußische Jahrbücher, 91 (1898), 295–304.

Forschungsschwerpunkt in der japanischen und ostasiatischen Geschichte vor allem aus der Perspektive der internationalen Beziehungen. Diese Veröffentlichungen entstanden in den meisten Fällen im Zusammenhang mit seiner Lehrtätigkeit an der Kaiserlichen Universität. Der Aufsatz „Der Aufstand von Shimabara" (1890) zum Beispiel ist das Ergebnis einer Übung und stellt eine historische Rekonstruktion des stark christlich gefärbten Aufstandes im Südwesten Japans gegen das Schogunat 1637–1638 dar.[39] *Rieß* untersuchte darin nicht nur die von den Europäern verfassten Quellen kritisch, sondern auch die japanischen Überlieferungen, die er von den Studenten übersetzen ließ, und rekonstruierte den historischen Verlauf des Aufstandes und seiner Niederwerfung. Aufbau, Methode und Stil des Aufsatzes entsprechen genau den kriegsgeschichtlichen Arbeiten, die aus der *Delbrück*-Schule hervorgingen. Inhaltlich befasst er sich jedoch mit einem wichtigen Ereignis in dem Verhältnis des *Tokugawa*-Schogunats zum Christentum in Japan, das einen Anstoß zur Abschottung des Landes gegenüber dem Westen geliefert hat.[40] Auch seine anderen in Japan verfassten Aufsätze haben Themen aus der Geschichte der Beziehungen Japans zu den westlichen Ländern in der frühen Neuzeit zum Gegenstand.[41]

Dass *Rieß* sowohl in der Forschung als auch in der Lehre die internationalen Beziehungen Japans, besonders dessen Begegnungen mit der europäischen Welt in der frühen Neuzeit, bevorzugte, war zwar teilweise bedingt durch die Schwierigkeit, sich die für die Erforschung der „eigentlichen" europäischen Geschichte notwendigen Literatur und Quellen zu beschaffen.[42] Zugleich aber muss man betonen, dass die Beziehungen zwischen Japan und den Europäern in der Frühen Neuzeit, d. h. der erste Kontakt Japans mit der europäischen Staatenwelt, eine

---

39 *Rieß, L.*: Der Aufstand von Shimabara, in: Mittheilungen der Deutschen Gesellschaft für Natur- und Völkerkunde Ostasiens in Tokio, 5/45 (1890), 191–214.

40 Zu diesem Aufstand vgl. *Bolitho, H.*: The *han*, in: Hall, J. W. (Hg.): Early Modern Japan (The Cambridge History of Japan Vol. 4), Cambridge u. a., 1991, 183–234, hier 204 f.

41 *Rieß, L.*: Die Goldausfuhr aus Japan im 16., 17. und 18. Jahrhundert, in: Zeitschrift für Social- und Wirtschaftsgeschichte, 6 (1898), 144–169; *ders.*: Die Ursachen der Vertreibung der Portugiesen aus Japan (1614–1639), in: Mittheilungen der Deutschen Gesellschaft für Natur- und Völkerkunde Ostasiens in Tokio, 7 (1898/99), 1–52; *ders.*: History of the English Factory at Hirado, in: Transactions of the Asiatic Society of Japan, 26 (1898), 1–114; *ders.*: William Adams und sein Grab in Hemimura, in: Mittheilungen der Deutschen Gesellschaft für Natur- und Völkerkunde Ostasiens in Tokio, 8 (1902), 239–253. Sogar in der ausführlichen historisch-geographischen Studie *Rieß, L.*: Geschichte der Insel Formosa, in: Mittheilungen der Deutschen Gesellschaft für Natur- und Völkerkunde Ostasiens in Tokio, 6/59 (1897), 406–447, wird sein Interesse an den japanisch-chinesischen Beziehungen sichtbar.

42 In einem Brief an *Delbrück* beklagt er sich über den desolaten Zustand der Universitätsbibliothek: „Selbst die Universitätsbibliothek ist äußerst dürftig und mit einer preußischen Gymnasiallehrer- und Schülerbibliothek kaum zu vergleichen" (Rieß an Delbrück, 24. Juli 1887).

wichtige Entwicklungsstufe innerhalb der *Rieß*'schen „Universalgeschichte" bilden. Im Herbst 1888 hielt er einen Vortrag über „Das Zeitalter der Entdeckungen" im Rahmen einer Vortragsreihe der protestantischen Kirche in Japan und veröffentlichte einen Aufsatz gleichen Titels im Jahr 1903.[43] Es handelt sich um einen Überblick zur Bedeutung und zum Charakter der Beziehungen zwischen Europa und der asiatischen Welt im 13. und im 15./16. Jahrhundert. Die Erforschung der Ost-West-Beziehungen in der frühen Neuzeit bildete als Fortsetzung dieses Ansatzes einen wesentlichen Bestandteil seiner „Universalgeschichte". In diesem Zusammenhang ist auch erwähnenswert, dass er in einem Gutachten über die Gründung des Historischen Seminars, das er beim Rektor der Kaiserlichen Universität Tokio einreichte, empfahl, die Quellen der holländischen Niederlassung in Nagasaki, die im Rijksarchief in Den Haag aufbewahrt waren, zu erforschen.[44] Auch er selbst hat während seines Urlaubs im Jahre 1893 die Archive in London und Holland besucht und viele Quellen transkribiert.[45] Die Ost-West-Beziehungen wurden nicht nur als ein „bequemes" Thema gewählt, um den japanischen Studenten die Methoden der modernen Geschichtswissenschaft beizubringen, sondern waren auch für ihn ein wichtiger Forschungsbereich.

Das Konzept und die Sinngebung der Weltgeschichte, die wir bei *Rieß* erkennen, zeigen, dass er zu den sog. „Neorankeanern"[46] gezählt werden kann. Das Postulat der unparteiischen Wissenschaftlichkeit der historischen Forschung,[47]

---

43   *Rieß, L.*: Das Zeitalter der Entdeckungen, in: Die Wahrheit: erste deutsche Zeitschrift in Japan. Allgemeiner Evangelisch-Protestantischer Missionsverein Tokio, 4 (1903), 107–114, 133–138.

44   Japanische Übersetzung in: Tōkyō Teikoku Daigaku Gojūnenshi, Jō-Satsu [Die 50-jährige Geschichte der Kaiserlichen Universität Tokio, Bd. 1], Tokio, 1932, 1299–1303. Das Original ist nicht mehr vorhanden.

45   Die Transkription ist zum größten Teil durch das Erdbeben in Tokio (1923) verloren gegangen, während einige Blätter, die *Rieß* nach Deutschland mitnahm, in seinem Nachlass im Bundesarchiv Koblenz aufbewahrt sind. Bundesarchiv Koblenz, Nachlass Ludwig Rieß, Nr. 11, „Tagebuch der Faktorei in Hirado (1637)".

46   Zu den „Neorankeaner" siehe *Dehio, L.*: Ranke und der Deutsche Imperialismus, in: Historische Zeitschrift, 170 (1950), 307–328; *Krill, H. H.*: Die Rankerenaissance: Max Lenz und Erich Marcks: ein Beitrag zum historisch-politischen Denken in Deutschland, 1880–1935, Berlin, 1962; *Fehrenbach, E.*: Rankerenaissance und Imperialismus in der wilhelminischen Zeit, in: Faulenbach, B. (Hg.): Geschichtswissenschaft in Deutschland, München, 1974, 54–65; *Jaeger, F./Rüsen, J.*: Geschichte des Historismus. Eine Einführung, München, 1992, 92–95. Für den Begriff „Neorankenaner" ist allerdings weder eine klare Grenzziehung noch eine eindeutige Zuordnung der betreffenden Historiker möglich. Sogar *Erich Marcks,* der von *Dehio* und dann von *Krill* zu den Hauptvertretern der Schule gezählt wurde, wurde kürzlich einer Neubewertung unterzogen: *Nordalm, J.*: Historismus und moderne Welt: Erich Marcks (1861–1938) in der deutschen Geschichtswissenschaft, Berlin, 2003.

47   „That historical studies of the type as they are now carried on in France, England and other countries, but most extensively in Germany, are of a *scientific* character, will be admitted by anybody who is thoroughly acquainted with them and competent to judge about this point. On this basis we venture to build the generalization, that all historical subjects and problems are capable, and in need, of scientific

die Hervorhebung der Individualität der historischen Subjekte[48] und die daraus resultierende Ablehnung der zivilisations- bzw. kulturgeschichtlichen Betrachtung[49] sind die Charakterzüge dieser Forschungsrichtung, die für die Wiederbelebung der Wissenschaftsideale *Ranke*s und die Erweiterung seiner Konzeption der Staatenverhältnisse in dem entstehenden imperialistischen Zeitalter plädierte.

Eine grobe Etikettierung hilft indes wenig, wenn man die wissenschaftsgeschichtliche Bedeutung der Tätigkeit von *Rieß* verstehen will. Im seinem Fall ist eine solche Vorgehensweise besonders unzureichend, weil seine wissenschaftliche und pädagogische Tätigkeit nicht nur im Verhältnis zum imperialistischen Streben der europäischen Großmächte, sondern auch im Hinblick auf die Entwicklung von Politik und Wissenschaft im sich rasch modernisierenden Japan untersucht werden müssen.

IV. Staat und Nation

Die deutschen Historiker, die als „Neorankeaner" bezeichnet werden, kritisierten die sog. borussische Geschichtsschreibung der vorhergehenden Generation, die sich leidenschaftlich für die nationalstaatliche Einigung Deutschlands engagiert hatte. Sie wandten sich von der politisierenden Haltung der Lehrergeneration ab und plädierten für die Rückkehr zur strengen Wissenschaftlichkeit und dem *Ranke*'schen Bild des Gleichgewichts der Mächte, jetzt aber nicht mehr beschränkt auf Europa, sondern in der ganzen Welt.

Gleichwohl hatten nicht nur die Vollendung der deutschen Nationalstaatsbildung unter *Bismarck,* sondern auch die allgemeinen wirtschaftlichen und politischen Entwicklungen seit den letzten Jahrzehnten des 19. Jahrhunderts die Rahmenbedingungen des historischen Denkens gründlich verändert; eine einfache Rückkehr zur Zeit *Ranke*s war nicht mehr realisierbar. Die „olympisch-gelassene und universal-weiträumige Betrachtungsweise"[50] *Ranke*s wurde von einem starken nationalistischen Elan überlagert. *Wolfgang J. Mommsen* schreibt sogar: „*With some justification it has been argued that the Neo-Rankeans were far more influenced by Heinrich von Treitschke than by Ranke, however much they condemned*

---

treatment: that historical treatises everywhere ought to partake, as a matter of course, of similar requirements and thereby justify their being credited as scientific productions" (*Rieß, L.*: Notes of a Course of Lectures on Methodology of History, First Part, Tokio, 1896, 1 f.).

48 *Rieß, L.*: Universal History, a. a. O., 2 f.

49 Er kritisiert wiederholt die zivilisationsgeschichtliche Geschichtsschreibung à la Buckle sowie die kulturgeschichtlichen Forschungen der *Lamprecht*-Schule.

50 *Dehio, L.*, a. a. O., 307.

the former's partisanship."[51] Vor dem Hintergrund dieser wissenschaftsgeschicht-
lichen Entwicklung stellt sich nun die Frage, wie *Rieß* „Nation" und „Staat" begriff. Diese Frage ist wichtig, nicht nur um seine historischen Arbeiten allgemein
zu charakterisieren, sondern vor allem auch um die Bedeutung seines Wirkens in
Japan und für die japanische Wissenschaft einschätzen zu können.

Rieß entwickelt selten in theoretischer Form seine Vorstellungen von Nation
oder Staat. Ausnahmsweise erläutert er jedoch am Anfang seiner Vorlesung über
„*History of Politics*" an der juristischen Fakultät seine Auffassung vom Staat. Der
Gegenstand dieser Vorlesung war weder eine systematische Analyse der politischen Institutionen noch die Darlegung der politischen Theorien in der Vergangenheit. Das Thema der Vorlesung sollte sein: „*a historical Analysis of political
life in the community of nations into which Japan has entered*"; konkreter: „*the
actual state of public affairs and social circumstances in the various epochs when
advanced political systems had been worked out and became the subject of discussions and struggle or of admiration and imitation*"[52]. Der Sinn dieser abstrakten
Formulierung ist nicht sehr klar, aber inhaltlich könnte man die Vorlesung etwa
als eine Verfassungsgeschichte unter Berücksichtigung der politischen Ideengeschichte seit der hebräischen Zeit bis zur Französischen Revolution charakterisieren.[53] Nach *Rieß* war der Staat die umfassendste und überragende Verbands-
form:

> „*Indeed there could be no historical life, if there would not be a coercive power authorised
> to keep every struggle of individuals within certain well defined limits, suppressing violence
> used by a physically strong man for selfish purposes, compelling both parties of an agree-
> ment to fulfill their promises, excluding certain methods of gaining individual advantages
> and bringing an embittered contention between individuals to a close. An overwhelming
> physical power at the disposal of the political authorities is undoubtedly the first condition
> of civilized life.*"[54]

Rieß apostrophiert hier zwar den Staat als die Voraussetzung für „historisches
Leben", sieht aber seinen Rechtfertigungsgrund in der grundlegenden Freiheit der

51 *Mommsen, W. J.*: Ranke and the Neo-Rankean School in Imperial Germany: State-oriented Historiography as a Stabilizing Force, in: Iggers. G. (Hg.), a.a.O., 124–140, hier 135 (Original auf Englisch). Auf
die Nähe der Neorakeaner zu *Treitschke* wird auch ansonsten hingewiesen: *Iggers, G.*: The Crisis of the
Rankean Paradigm in the Nineteenth Century, in: ders. (Hg.), a.a.O., 170–179, hier 175; *Muhlack, U.*,
a.a.O., 349.

52 *Rieß, L.*: A Course of Lectures on "History of Politics" delivered in the Law College of Tokyo Teikoku
Daigaku [Kaiserliche Universität Tokio] in the First and Second Term of the Academic Year 1899–1900,
Tokio, 1900, 1.

53 In dieser Zusammenstellung könnte man auch die Widerspiegelung seiner idealistischen Geschichtsauffassung sehen. Vgl. *Fehrenbach, E.*, a.a.O., 57f.

54 *Rieß, L.*: History of Politics, a.a.O., 4.

Staatsmitglieder; die Bedeutung der individuellen Freiheit wird auch sonst in dieser Vorlesung oft hervorgehoben.[55] In diesem Sinne stützt sich *Rieß'* Staatsauffassung im Grunde genommen auf eine Dichotomie von freien Individuen und Staatsgewalt als der höchsten Zwangsgewalt; von einer genossenschaftlichen oder gemeinschaftlichen Staatsauffassung ist dagegen wenig zu spüren. Zwar zeigt er sich nicht republikanisch oder besonders freiheitsliebend. Aber aus seiner Darstellung, in der neben der Entwicklung der neuzeitlichen europäischen Großstaaten zu den von den großen *„statesmen"* geleiteten „Mächten"[56] auch die aufklärerische Komponente in der modernen europäischen Verfassungs- und Ideengeschichte stark hervortritt,[57] kann man ersehen, dass er eine Staatsauffassung vertrat, die letztendlich von den aufklärerischen Ideen Europas stammt.

Auf welche Weise begriff *Rieß* dann die Nation und welche Bedeutung hat er ihr beigemessen? In seiner Vorlesung „*Methodology of History"* gibt er Definitionen der verschiedenen menschlichen Verbandsformen als grundlegende Gegenstände der geschichtlichen Erkenntnis. Die Nation (*„Nationality"*) sei die letzte Einheit in der Reihe „*natural unions"*, die bei der Familie beginnt und über Sippe (*gens*) und Stamm bis zur Nation reicht. Außer den *natural unions* stellt er die Begriffe *industrial unions, economic unions, social unions, religious units, ideal units* und *political units* auf.[58] Aber die Nation als *natural union* fasst er in einer recht differenzierten Weise auf. *Rieß* führt aus, dass in den meisten Kulturen (außer in Japan!) die großen Verbände aus gemeinsamer Herkunft bereits zerstört und durch Mischungen ergänzt seien:

> „*In reality most nations owe their origin to the fact, that under peculiar circumstances particles of one or more natural units have been combined, have secured some successes in common action, have suffered the same fate and lived together in close intercourse and intermarriage for so many generations, that a strong feeling of identity keeps now all its individuals together.*"[59]

Mit anderen Worten: Er stellt die Nation nur als eine durch die Geschichte erzeugte sekundäre Verbindung dar. Wir hören hier gewisse Anklänge an seine

---

55 Bereits im ersten Abschnitt über die althebräische Verfassungsgeschichte betont er die weltgeschichtliche Bedeutung der Verselbständigung des Nordreichs Israels und der Ideen der provinziellen Selbständigkeit und Freiheit, die in der Parole „To your tents, o Israel" enthalten gewesen seien. Vgl. ebd., 8.

56 Vor allem im französischen Absolutismus der Neuzeit (ebd., 71–79).

57 Besonders ausführlich legt er die demokratischen Entwicklungen in England und Schottland während des 17. Jahrhunderts dar. Daneben geht er auf den aufgeklärten Absolutismus in Russland und Preußen sowie die Lehren von *Locke* und *Montesquieu* ein.

58 *Rieß, L.*: Methodology of History, a.a.O., 126–143. Aber in dieser Auflage wird nur auf die *natural unions* eingegangen, und die anderen Verbandsformen werden nur als Stichworte eingeführt.

59 Ebd., 133.

frühe Würdigung der *Ranke*'schen Auffassung von der römischen Geschichte. Auch sonst findet sich in den Schriften von *Rieß* keine starke nationalistische Voreingenommenheit. Vielfach kritisiert er ausdrücklich die rassistische Geschichtsauffassung.[60] Als stark assimilierter jüdischer Intellektueller[61] teilte er auch die allgemeine nationale Gesinnung, die für deutsche Hochschullehrer dieser Zeit eine Selbstverständlichkeit war. Für ihn war etwa die Verbreitung der deutschen Kultur in Ostasien in Konkurrenz mit England von hoher Bedeutung.[62] Gleichwohl zeigt er auch in den an weite Leserkreise gerichteten Schriften während des Ersten Weltkrieges keine aggressive nationalistische Haltung, die unter vielen deutschen Historikern, auch den Vertretern der *Ranke*-Renaissance, zu beobachten war.[63] Daraus kann man folgern, dass *Rieß* im Unterschied zu den vielen „Mandarinen"[64] dieser Zeit eher eine Version der Weltgeschichte vertrat, die noch die universalistischen Charakterzüge von *Ranke* und *Wilhelm von Humboldt* widerspiegelte.

60 In seiner Vorlesung zur japanischen Geschichte, die er im Wintersemester 1904/05 an der Berliner Universität hielt, behandelte er die Vorgeschichte Japans eingehend, wobei er vor den Schriften „unsere(r) phantasievollen Rassentheoretiker, die durch die Kühnheit ihrer Behauptungen zu blenden suchen", warnte. Bundesarchiv Koblenz, Nachlass Ludwig Rieß, Nr. 14 „Japanische Geschichte im Überblick W. S. 1904/5 Aud. 53."

61 Unmittelbar vor seiner Heimkehr ließ er sich zum evangelischen Christen taufen. Er begründet diesen Entschluss mit seiner lang gehegten Sympathie zur liberalen protestantischen Religiosität. Vgl. Rieß an Delbrück, 8. Dezember 1901. Auf die Bedeutung seiner jüdischen Herkunft für sein Scheitern, ein Ordinariat in Deutschland zu erhalten, wird hier nicht eingegangen.

62 So engagierte er sich für die Gründung einer deutschsprachigen Zeitung in Japan, um das Monopol der Engländer in der fremdsprachigen Presse in Japan aufzubrechen. Vgl. Rieß an Delbrück, 14. Juli 1901. Auch in seinen ersten Briefen zeigte er ein starkes Konkurrenzbewusstsein gegenüber den englischen Professoren, die bis zur Ankunft der drei jungen Deutschen an der *Faculty of Letters* der Universität Tokio eine dominante Stellung innehatten.

63 Auch in einer während des Ersten Weltkriegs veröffentlichten Broschüre schilderte er die Entwicklung der politischen Beziehungen zu Großbritannien in einer sehr differenzierten und nüchternen Weise. *Rieß, L.*: Der Stufengang des deutsch-englischen Gegensatzes, Jena, 1917. Im Vergleich dazu vertraten bekanntlich viele Historiker eine chauvinistische Haltung, die Gegenstand heftiger Kritik durch *Max Weber* wurde. Auch die deutschen Ostasien-Spezialisten waren nicht immun gegen den pathetischen Nationalismus und die militant-antienglische Haltung. Vgl. etwa die Schriften von *Otto Franke*, einem der Begründer der deutschen Sinologie: *Franke, O.*: Deutschland und England in Ostasien (Deutsche Vorträge Hamburgischer Professoren), Hamburg, 1914; *ders.*: Die Großmächte in Ostasien von 1894–1914. Ein Beitrag zur Vorgeschichte des Krieges, Braunschweig und Hamburg, 1923, bes. VII (Vorwort).

64 *Ringer, F. K.*: The Decline of the German Mandarins: The German Academic Community 1890–1933, Cambridge, MA, 1969 (deutsche Übersetzung: Die Gelehrten. Der Niedergang der Deutschen Mandarine 1890–1933, Stuttgart, 1983).

V. Japan im Rahmen der Universalgeschichte

Welche Stellung nimmt Japan in der so verstandenen Universalgeschichte ein? Verständlicherweise findet man darüber nicht viele Bemerkungen in seinen in Japan veröffentlichten Schriften. Dagegen äußert er sich nach seiner Rückkehr nach Deutschland dazu öfters. Sein Interesse an der japanischen Entwicklung wird sehr deutlich zu Beginn seiner Vorlesung über japanische Geschichte, die er im Wintersemester 1904/05 an der Universität Berlin hielt:

> „Uns steht hier speziell die universale Bedeutung des japanischen Inselreichs vor Augen; wie der dort vereinigte Personalbestand die Kraft gewann, in einer sonst nirgends beobachteten Art Fremdes bald aufzunehmen, bald schroff von sich zu werfen, sich zu organisieren und zu bewahren mit Waffen und Wissenschaft, wie außerhalb der Kultur-gemeinschaft der abendländischen Nationen kein Volk der Erde. Dass dabei in der Entwicklung Japans die geschichtliche Tradition eine größere Rolle spielt als bei irgend-einem Volk außer den alten Israeliten sei ebenfalls schon im Voraus erwähnt."[65]

Diesen Sätzen kann man entnehmen, dass *Rieß* die „universale Bedeutung" der japanischen Geschichte besonders darin sah, dass es dem Land gelungen ist, trotz des Drucks seitens der westlichen Mächte seine Selbstständigkeit und Autonomie beizubehalten und sich rasch zu modernisieren. Der Maßstab der Bewertung blieb dabei ein Ideal, die „Kulturgemeinschaft der abendländischen Nationen". Der Begriff, auf den *Rieß* mehrmals zurückgriff, um diesen Charakterzug der modernen Entwicklung Japans zu bezeichnen, war „der Genius des Okzidents" von *Ranke*.[66] Der Ausgang jenes Ereignisses, das zum Aufstieg Japans und da-durch zur weiteren Intensivierung der Konkurrenz unter den „Mächten" in Ost-asien beitrug, wird durch diesen Begriff erläutert:

> „Wenn man nach den letzten Gründen fragt, um derentwillen das neugeordnete Japan den chinesischen Koloß so leicht hat überwältigen können, so muß man auf die innere Ueberlegenheit der Gesittung, auf die größere Aktionsfähigkeit des Volksgeistes hinweisen. In Bezug auf moderne Waffen und Kriegsgeräte hatte China einen erheb-lichen Vorsprung. […] Aber durch stramme Organisation, europäische Taktik und Strategie, Konzentration seiner Kräfte, hat das kleinere und entferntere Land erst in Korea, dann auch auf chinesischem Boden den Sieg davongetragen. Japan besitzt eben unzweifelhaft viel mehr als China von dem, was Ranke den Genius des Okzidents nennt; d. h. von dem Geiste, ‚der die Völker zu geordneten Armeen umschafft, der die

---

65 Vorlesung „Japanische Geschichte im Überblick" (vgl. Anm. 60).

66 *Ranke* benutzte diesen Begriff, um das „Übermannen" des osmanischen Reiches durch die westlich-christlichen Kräfte zu schildern. *Ranke, L. v.*: Serbien und die Türkei im neunzehnten Jahrhundert, in: Leopold von Ranke's Sämtliche Werke, Bd. 44, Leipzig, 1879, 518 f.

Straßen zieht, die Kanäle gräbt, alle Meere mit Flotten bedeckt' und auf allen Gebieten des Wissens sich mit immer frischer Arbeit betätigt."[67]

Er benutzt diesen *Ranke*'schen Begriff auch in einem interessanten Vortrag, „Lafcadio Hearn als Interpret japanischer Volksart"[68], den er am 13. Mai 1908 auf einer Versammlung der Japanisch-Deutschen Gesellschaft (*Wa-Doku-Kai*) zu Berlin hielt.[69] *Rieß* erläutert darin das Leben und die literarischen Werke dieses höchst originellen Schriftstellers und ehemaligen Kollegen in Tokio[70] und unterzieht besonders sein posthumes Buch „*Japan. An Attempt at Interpretation*" einer eingehenden Kritik. Er würdigt einerseits sehr positiv, dass *Hearn* in seinem letzten Buch versuchte, eine objektivere Beurteilung der japanischen Volksart zu geben als in seinen früheren Werken, die das Exotische, das Mythische und das Unverständliche an der japanischen Kultur einseitig hervorhoben, erhebt aber andererseits Einspruch dagegen, dass der Autor an der Fähigkeit der Japaner zweifelt, sich schnell den Gesetzen der industriellen Konkurrenz anzupassen. So schreibt *Hearn*:

> „*The capacity for industrial competition […] must depend upon the intelligent freedom of the individual; and the society which suppresses this freedom, or suffers it to be suppressed, must remain too rigid for competition with societies in which the liberties of the individual are strictly maintained. While Japan continues to think and to act by groups, even by groups of industrial companies, so long she must always continue incapable of her best. Her ancient social experience is not sufficient to avail her for the future international struggle, – rather it must sometimes impede her as so much dead weight.*"[71]

Dagegen weist *Rieß* darauf hin, dass die gesellschaftliche und politische Elite des modernen Japans wohl wüsste, welche Möglichkeiten diese Nation habe und was getan werden müsse, um diese Möglichkeiten realisieren zu können. Denn „Japan hat es bereits bewiesen, dass es dem, was man früher den Genius des Okzidents genannt hat, einen neuen Wirkungskreis im eigenen Lande und in der Nachbarschaft eröffnet hat."[72] Im Gegensatz zu *Hearn*, der vom „Alten Japan" bezaubert

---

67 *Rieß, L.*: Ein Mangel in der japanischen Kulturentwicklung, in: ders.: Allerlei aus Japan (Deutsche Bücherei Bd. 27), Bd. 1, Berlin, [o. J.], 95.

68 *Ders.*: Lafcadio Hearn als Interpret japanischer Volksart, in: Mitteilungen der Deutsch-Japanischen Gesellschaft, 1 (1908), 2–14.

69 *Rieß* war von 1907 bis 1912 Vorstandsvorsitzender dieser Gesellschaft. Vgl. *Haasch, G.* (Hg.): Die Deutsch-Japanischen Gesellschaften von 1888–1996, Berlin, 1996, 34–56.

70 *Lafcadio Hearn* (1850–1904) lehrte von 1896 bis 1903 englische Literatur an der Kaiserlichen Universität Tokio und war damit Kollege von *Rieß*. Im Zusammenhang mit der „postkolonialen" Literaturbewegung verstärkt sich jetzt wieder das Interesse an diesem interessanten anglo-griechischen Schriftsteller.

71 *Hearn, L.*: Japan. An Attempt at Interpretation, London, 1907, 496.

72 *Rieß, L.*: Lafcadio Hearn, a. a. O., 13.

war und gerade deshalb die Konkurrenzfähigkeit dieses Landes im industriellen Zeitalter bezweifelte, bestand für *Rieß* der hervorstechende Zug Japans in seiner Modernisierungskapazität im Sinne der europäischen Staaten.

In der oben zitierten Stelle aus der Berliner Vorlesung deutet er auch darauf hin, dass die historische Tradition wesentlich zu dieser grundlegenden Modernisierungskapazität beigetragen hat. In seinem Aufsatz „Der Volksgeist Japans und der Bushido" (1907) versucht er, historisch zu erklären, wie es zur raschen Festigung eines modernen Nationalstaates kommen konnte.[73] Dabei geht es um die Frage, ob die Standesethik der Krieger (*Bushidō*) oder die nationale Gesinnung (*Yamato Damashī*) die bestimmende historische Tradition im modernen Japan darstellt.[74] Nach *Rieß'* Ansicht war es wichtig, dass bereits in der *Nara*-Periode (710–794) eine schriftlich fixierte nationale Tradition entstanden war, die zwar stark von der chinesischen Kultur beeinflusst war, sich aber dennoch durch die Verschmelzung mit den einheimischen Elementen als ein Neues darstellte und dadurch die Nation „verjüngte".[75] In der so entstandenen verschriftlichten Entwicklungsgeschichte erschien das „ganze Volk […] als eine große Familie der Abkömmlinge der ersten Eroberer oder der vom Kaiser angesiedelten Fremden oder der in Dienst genommenen älteren Ansiedler". Mit dieser Entwicklungsgeschichte hätten sich der starke Ahnenkult, das Bewusstsein der Einzigartigkeit des Herrschergeschlechts, die Pflege selbständiger Kunstgattungen, vor allem der kurzen Dichtungen, verbunden; diese Elemente hätten den japanischen Volksgeist begründet, der sich „in erster Linie als Nationalstolz und als schnell entschlossenes Zusammenstehen aller Volksgenossen den Fremden gegenüber" betätigt habe.[76]

In der nachfolgenden Zeit der Herrschaft der Krieger (*Samurai*) sei zwar der *Bushidō* in den Vordergrund getreten, aber auch damals habe es nicht an Kritik vom nationalen Gesichtspunkt aus gefehlt, die sich besonders nach dem Ende der Abschließungspolitik (1854) zum glühenden Nationalismus mit dem Kaiser im Mittelpunkt entwickelte und schließlich zum Sturz des Schogunats (Kriegerherrschaft) geführt habe. Die Führer der Opposition gegen das Schogunat hätten

---

73 *Ders.*: Der Volksgeist Japans und der Bushido, in: Asien. Organ der Deutsch-Asiatischen Gesellschaft, 6, Hefte 5, 6, 7 (1907), 65–68, 86–88, 104–106.

74 Den Hintergrund dieser Fragestellung bildete der Umstand, dass seit dem Ende des 19. Jahrhunderts, besonders durch das Erscheinen des Büchleins „*Bushido*" von *Inazō Nitobe* (*Nitobe, I.*: Bushido: The Soul of Japan, Tokio, 1900), die früher in der *Meiji*-Restauration in Misskredit geratene kriegerische Ethik der *Samurai*-Schicht wieder „entdeckt" und gepriesen wurde.

75 *Rieß* legt diesen Vorgang in Analogie zur Entstehung der griechisch-römischen Kultur in der Zeit von *Augustus* dar.

76 *Rieß, L.*: Bushido, a. a. O., Heft 5, 68.

aber die Notwendigkeit nicht nur der Zentralisierung des Landes, sondern auch der Umbildung der Einrichtungen nach europäischem Muster erkannt, „um eine gleichgeachtete Stellung in der Welt für seinen [= des japanischen Volksgeistes, Y. N.] Staat zu erringen und damit vor dem eigenen Selbstgefühl zu bestehen"[77]. Die nationale Gesinnung des Volkes (*Yamato Damashī*) sei gelegentlich gegen die Regierung gerichtet worden (etwa wegen eines für Japan ungünstigen Vertragsrevisionsplans), allerdings habe sie zugleich der Verstärkung der Loyalität gegenüber dem Kaiser gedient, was die rapide Überwindung des Partikularismus der Fürstentümer (*Daimyō*) und die Vereinigung des Landes ermöglicht habe. In diesem Sinne sei das *Yamato Damashī* „viel tiefer geschichtlich begründet, viel umfassender (weil allen Volksklassen gemeinsam) und viel heilsamer für die weitere Entwickelung Japans" als der *Bushidō*.[78]

Auch die anderen Aufsätze und Vorträge von *Rieß* zeigen, dass er nicht nur über umfassende Kenntnisse der japanischen Geschichte verfügte, sondern auch imstande war, selbständig Thesen zur Besonderheit der japanischen Entwicklung sowie die Stellung Japans im Rahmen der von ihm konzipierten „Universalgeschichte" zu entwickeln.[79] In der Tat kann man schwerlich die Auffassung von *Rieß* bestreiten, dass die Bildung eines modernen Nationalstaates in Japan, trotz der weiteren Existenz diskriminierter und unterdrückter Minderheiten, in einem erstaunlich kurzen Zeitraum vonstatten ging und dies nur durch die Verbindung traditioneller Elemente mit der aktuellen internationalen Konstellation erklärbar ist. Wie wir gesehen haben, war seine Sicht durch und durch geprägt von dem Idealbild eines Gleichgewichts zwischen den konkurrierenden selbständigen Nationalstaaten, das dem neuzeitlichen Europa entnommen war. Für ihn war dies der nie bezweifelte Maßstab, an dem auch die historische Entwicklung Ostasiens gemessen werden musste.

Aus der Perspektive des „postkolonialen" 21. Jahrhunderts fällt es leicht, dieser Geschichtsauffassung einen naiven Eurozentrismus, sogar eine Rechtfertigung der imperialistischen Außenpolitik nicht nur des Westens, sondern auch Japans vorzuwerfen. Aber eine wissenschaftsgeschichtliche Würdigung darf sich nicht auf eine pauschale Verurteilung beschränken, sondern muss immer die realen Ausgangsbedingungen sowohl des deutschen Historikers als auch des Geschichts-

---

77 Ebd., Heft 7, 104.

78 Ebd., 106.

79 In seinem Nachlass im Bundesarchiv Koblenz sind Manuskipte und Materialien für die Vorträge, die er in Berlin hielt, überliefert. Besonders das Manuskript „Der Bild- und Filmvortrag. Japan, die Weltmacht im stillen Ozean" (Bundesarchiv Koblenz, Nachlass Ludwig Riess, Nr. 8) enthält scharfsinnige Beobachtungen zur Gesellschaft und zum Leben der Japaner.

denkens und der Geschichtswissenschaft Japans mitberücksichtigen. Zum Schluss
dieses Beitrages sei daher auf die historische Bedeutung der wissenschaftlichen
Tätigkeit von *Rieß* eingegangen.

Der traditionellen Geschichtsforschung Japans, die bereits eine lange Geschichte vor der Einführung der europäischen Wissenschaften hinter sich hatte,
fehlte es beileibe nicht an kritischen Methoden. Sowohl in den vom chinesischen
Imperium eingeführten Wissenschaften (*Kangaku*) als auch in den national-japa-
nischen Wissenschaften (*Kokugaku*), die vor allem in der späten *Tokugawa*-Zeit
aufblühten, existierte eine Einstellung, die tradierten Überlieferungen der philo-
logischen Untersuchung zu unterziehen und durch kritische Analyse sowohl den
textlichen Sinn als auch die geschichtlichen Fakten festzustellen.[80] Auch an der
neu gegründeten Universität Tokio wurde – neben der von *Rieß* eingeführten
europäischen Geschichtswissenschaft – solche traditionelle Geschichtsforschung
weiterhin betrieben, wobei partielle Einflüsse von der neuen westlichen Geschichtswissenschaft nicht völlig auszuschließen sind.[81]

Was jedoch in der traditionellen japanischen Geschichtsforschung nicht aus-
gebildet war, war eine Haltung, die Geschichte Japans in einem objektivierten
theoretischen Rahmen zu erfassen, der einen Vergleich mit den anderen Ländern
ermöglicht hätte. Die Vorstellung der Einzigartigkeit, der Unvergleichbarkeit des
japanischen Staates, die sich vor allem in dem Glauben an die einzigartige Kontinuität der kaiserlichen Familie seit der mythischen Gründung des Landes bis
zur Gegenwart ausdrückte, erschwerte es, die japanische Geschichte anhand mehr
oder weniger abstrakter universaler Begrifflichkeiten zu konstruieren. Nicht nur
die Gelehrten, die in unmittelbarer Kontinuität zur geistigen Welt der Zeit vor der
Meiji-Restauration standen, sondern auch die Universitätsprofessoren für japanische Geschichte, die durchaus von den europäischen Wissenschaften beeinflusst waren, beschränkten sich entweder auf die (hyper-)kritische Tatsachen-

---

80 *Krämer, H. M./Schölz, T./Conrad, S.*: Geschichtswissenschaft in Japan. Entwicklung und aktueller Diskus-
     sionsstand, in: dies. (Hg.): Geschichtswissenschaft in Japan, Göttingen, 2006, 9–30, hier 10–12; *Goch, U.*:
     Die Entstehung einer modernen Geschichtswissenschaft in Japan, in: Bochumer Jahrbuch zur Ostasien-
     forschung, 1 (1978), 238–271, hier 254–259. Die nach der *Meiji*-Restauration wieder aufgenommene Arbeit
     an der „amtlichen Geschichtsschreibung", die 1888 in die Universität eingegliedert wurde, stützte sich auf
     diese alten Traditionen. Die Forschung und Lehre der japanischen Geschichte an der Kaiserlichen
     Universität wurde zunächst hauptsächlich von den Historikern, die sich dieser Arbeit widmeten,
     getragen. Vgl. *Mehl, M.*, a.a.O.

81 *Yasutsugu Shigeno* (1827–1910), die repräsentative Figur der traditionellen Geschichtsforschung anhand
     der chinesischen philologisch-kritischen Methode und seit 1888 Professor für japanische Geschichte an
     der Kaiserlichen Universität, zeigte reges Interesse an der europäischen Geschichtswissenschaft, obwohl
     er keine europäische Sprache beherrschte.

feststellung oder erläuterten in den wichtigsten Handbüchern den einzigartigen mythischen Ursprung des Landes.[82]

Rieß dagegen verstand die japanische Geschichte durchaus als Teil der Universalgeschichte und behandelte sie entsprechend. In der oben erwähnten Vorlesung „*History of Politics*" hat er auch die politische Entwicklung Japans anhand von geschichtlichen Begriffen und Theorien, die ihre Wurzeln im Okzident haben, rekonstruiert und mit anderen Kulturen verglichen.[83] Dadurch entstand die Voraussetzung, den japanischen Staat und seine historische Entwicklung auf die gleiche Ebene mit allen anderen Ländern und Nationen zu stellen und mit ihnen zu vergleichen.

Mit Sicherheit hing es mit dieser Haltung von *Rieß* zusammen, dass viele seiner Schüler in Japan die internationalen Beziehungen Japans vor der Abschließung des Landes gegenüber der westlichen Welt (1641) als zentrales Forschungsthema gewählt haben. Besonders die Arbeiten von *Naojirō Murakami* (1868–1966) und *Shigetomo Kōda* (1873–1954) zeichnen sich durch ihr gründliches Quellenstudium und ihre kritische Methode aus. Auch *Kengo Murakawa* (1875–1946), der die Forschungen zur westlichen antiken Geschichte in Japan begründete, interessierte sich in der Frühphase seiner Forschungstätigkeit für die Aktivität der Europäer im Südostasien in der frühen Neuzeit und veröffentlichte Forschungen sowie Übersetzungen der wichtigen europäischen Quellen. Die Ost-West-Beziehungen vom 16. bis zum 18. Jahrhundert erwiesen sich somit als der fruchtbarste Forschungsbereich der jungen japanischen Geschichtswissenschaft. Es belegt das hohe Niveau der Lehrtätigkeit von *Rieß*, die in kurzer Zeit Fachhistoriker hervorbrachte, die es verstanden, unter Verwendung moderner geschichtswissenschaftlicher Methoden mit den japanischen und europäischen Quellen originelle Forschungsergebnisse zu erzielen.

Für vertiefte Forschungen zur Geschichte Europas im engeren Sinne, *Rieß*' eigentlichem Arbeitsgebiet, fehlte es dagegen entscheidend an notwendigen Bedingungen. Er scheint daher auch den Studenten der europäischen Geschichte

---

82 *Katsumi Kuroita* (1874–1946), ein einflussreicher Professor für japanische Geschichte, hat in seinem viel gelesenen Handbuch zur japanischen Geschichte den „Wesenszweck der Forschung zur japanischen Geschichte" in der „Erklärung der unvergleichbaren Staatsform (*Kokutai*) Japans, die sich in dem seit dem Anfang ununterbrochene Kontinuität des kaiserlichen Geschlechts verkörpert" gesehen (*Kuroita, K.*: Kokushi no Kenkyū [Das Studium der Japanischen Geschichte], 1. Aufl., Tokio, 1908, 313). Diese bekenntnisartige Aussage ist umso bemerkenswerter, als andere Stellen des Werkes, vor allem die Abschnitte über die Hilfswissenschaften, umfangreiche Kenntnisse des Verfassers von den europäischen Geschichtswissenschaften belegen.

83 Er vergleicht etwa die feudale Verfassung Japans im Mittelalter mit der von Westeuropa sowie derjenigen der Türkei (*Rieß, L.*: History of Politics, a.a.O., 40).

oft Themen aus der japanischen Geschichte gegeben zu haben. *Katsurō Hara* (1871–1924) etwa befasste sich zunächst mit der Geschichte der freien Stadt Sakai im Mittelalter.[84] Diese Arbeit, vor allem ihre quellenkritische Methode sowie ihr Vergleich mit den freien Reichsstädten sowie den Hansestädten, wäre undenkbar gewesen ohne die starken Einflüsse der *Rieß*'schen Lehrtätigkeit.

Das neorankeanische Geschichtsbild von *Rieß* eröffnete auf diese Weise den japanischen Historikern einen neuen globalen Horizont und eine vergleichende Perspektive, die die Geschichte Japans in die globale historische Entwicklung einzuordnen half. Mit Sicherheit war dieses Bild einseitig eurozentrisch. Aber unter den damaligen Bedingungen war es doch unerlässlich, sich einmal gründlich mit der Begrifflichkeit der europäischen Wissenschaft auseinanderzusetzen, wenn die japanische Geschichtswissenschaft ihre eigene Nationalgeschichte unter einem universalen Blickwinkel betrachten können sollte, um dadurch die Dialogfähigkeit mit der Historie anderer Länder zu erreichen.[85] Darüber hinaus war es wichtig, dass *Rieß* auch die Nation nicht als etwas Vorgegebenes, sondern als durch das Zusammenwirken verschiedener Gegebenheiten und politischer Entscheidungen Hervorgebrachtes auffasste.

Diese universalistische Geschichtsbetrachtung von *Rieß* mag zwar im Kontext des damaligen deutschen Geschichtsdenkens bereits überholt gewesen sein. Sie konnte jedoch die japanischen Historiker davor bewahren, einer Mythisierung der Nationalgeschichte zu erliegen oder ihre Unvergleichbarkeit einseitig hervorzuheben[86] und so darauf zu verzichten, sich allgemeinen wissenschaftlichen Maßstäben zu stellen.[87] Sein durch die Aufklärung bestimmtes Staatsdenken forderte,

---

84 *Hara, K.*: Ashikaga Jidai no Sakai-Kō [Der Hafen Sakai während der Ashikaga-Zeit], in: Shigaku-Zasshi, 7 (1896). *Hara* wurde später Professor für Europäische Geschichte an der neu gegründeten Kaiserlichen Universität Kioto.

85 Auch die Gründer der „postkolonialen" Bewegungen wie *Frantz Fanon* mussten sich in der Regel zunächst gründlich mit den europäischen Wissenschaften und der europäischen Literatur auseinandersetzen. Erst dadurch konnte eine sie relativierende Perspektive gewonnen werden.

86 Dass diese Gefahr keineswegs unrealistisch war, bezeugt das Wuchern der *tennō*-zentrierten Geschichtsauffassung in den 1920er und 30er Jahren, die die Ideologie der Einzigartigkeit der japanischen Staatsverfassung, die man in der „ununterbrochenen Kontinuität des Kaisergeschlechts" verkörpert sah, zum Einsatz der Nation zur militärischen Unterjochung der Nachbarländer verwendete. Zu diesem „Kōku-Shikan" [Geschichtsauffassung des Kaiserlichen Staates] genannten Geschichtsbild vgl. *Krämer, H. M./Schölz, T./ Conrad, S.*, a. a. O., 16.

87 Auch eine andere Strömung der „eurozentrischen" Geschichtsbetrachtung, die rechts- und verfassungsgeschichtliche Forschung unter dem Einfluss des Rechtspositivismus, die besonders mit dem Namen des Rechtshistorikers *Kaoru Nakata* (1877–1967) verbunden ist, war als Ausgangsbasis einer fruchtbaren komparatistischen Geschichtsforschung in Japan wichtig. Vgl. *Nishikawa, Y.*: Feudalismus und Staat – Zur Entstehung der Systematik der japanischen Rechtsgeschichte, in: Zeitschrift für Neuere Rechtsgeschichte, 25/1–2 (2003), 19–38.

dass nicht nur die positivrechtliche Ordnung des Staates, sondern auch die traditionellen Beziehungen zwischen Staat und Individuen nach dem modernen europäischen Muster uminterpretiert werden mussten.[88] In diesem Sinne bedeutete die Einführung der deutschen Geschichtswissenschaft des 19. Jahrhunderts nicht nur eine zunehmende Verwissenschaftlichung und Spezialisierung, sondern auch eine Möglichkeit der gründlichen Umwandlung der Idee des Staats und der Nation für *Meiji*-Japan.

---

[88] Daher seine kritischen Bemerkungen über die Einschränkung der Freiheit der Forschung in Japan, wenn die ideellen Fundamente des Glaubens an die Einzigartigkeit der kaiserlichen Herrschaft berührt werden: „Ich hoffe, die Zeit ist nicht mehr fern, wo man auch in Japan von dieser Beschränkung der Freiheit der Wissenschaft absehen kann. Denn ein Volksgeist, der sich solcher Leistungen fähig erwiesen hat, wie der japanischen in den letzten Jahren, bedarf keiner Gängelung mehr. Die weitere Entwicklung der Dinge kann ihm getrost ohne jede Vorsichtsmaßregel anvertraut werden, die der Freiheit des Geisteslebens widerspricht" (*Rieß, L.*: Bushido, a. a. O., Heft 7, 106).

II. Constitutional Developments
   in Western Democracies

Der Verfassungsauftrag der Streitkräfte im Grundgesetz

von Peter Badura

I. Die Bundeswehr

1. Wehrverfassung

Der Bund stellt Streitkräfte zur Verteidigung auf. Außer zur Verteidigung dürfen die Streitkräfte nur eingesetzt werden, soweit das Grundgesetz es ausdrücklich zulässt. Durch die Vorschriften der Art. 87a, 73 Abs. 1 Nr. 1 GG wird eine selbständige Bundeskompetenz der Gesetzgebung und der vollziehenden Gewalt begründet, die Aufstellung von Streitkräften zur Verteidigung als Verfassungsauftrag ausgesprochen und eine spezifische Begrenzung der den Streitkräften zukommenden Aufgabe festgelegt. Mit den durch die Novellen von 1954 und 1956 in das Grundgesetz eingefügten wehrverfassungsrechtlichen Bestimmungen[1] hat der Verfassungsgeber zugleich eine Grundentscheidung für die wirksame militärische Landesverteidigung getroffen.[2] Diese Grundentscheidung vervollständigt das Recht des Bundes, sich zur Wahrung des Friedens einem System gegenseitiger kollektiver Sicherheit einzuordnen (Art. 24 Abs. 2 GG), und verbindet sich mit dem Verbot von Handlungen, die geeignet sind und in der Absicht vorgenommen werden, das friedliche Zusammenleben der Völker zu stören (Art. 26 Abs. 1 GG). Die Notstands-Novelle von 1968[3] hat, im Zuge der vollständigen Ablösung des Besatzungsregimes, staatsrechtliche Vorkehrungen für den Verteidigungsfall getroffen (Art. 53a, 115a ff. GG) und begrenzte Regelungen des „inneren Notstands" eingeführt (Art. 87a, 91, 35 Abs. 2 und 3 GG).

Die Streitkräfte gehören zu den verfassungsmäßig bestehenden Machtmitteln des Staates. Ihre Verwendung ist nicht, sozusagen von Natur aus, auf Verteidigung gegen einen äußeren Feind beschränkt, zumal die Trennung von „innen" und „außen" im Hinblick auf gewaltsame Konflikte seit dem letzten Krieg und angesichts des organisierten internationalen Terrorismus an Realität verloren hat. Es gibt jedoch gute Gründe dafür, einen Einsatz der Streitkräfte auf dem eigenen

---

1   Gesetz zur Ergänzung des Grundgesetzes vom 26.03.1954 (BGBl. I, 130); Gesetz zur Ergänzung des Grundgesetzes vom 19.03.1956 (BGBl. I, 111).
2   BVerfGE 48, 127 ff., hier 159 ff.; BVerfGE 69, 1 ff., hier 22.
3   Siebzehntes Gesetz zur Ergänzung des Grundgesetzes vom 24.06.1968 (BGBl. I, 709).

Staatsgebiet, im „Innern", auf verfassungsrechtlich enumerierte Fälle zu beschränken, die allein im Rahmen der polizeilichen Aufgabe der Gefahrenabwehr
oder ohne den Einsatz militärischer Fähigkeiten nicht zur Gewährleistung der
inneren Sicherheit bewältigt werden können. Das Grundgesetz hat selbst die
Abwehr einer drohenden Gefahr für den Bestand oder die freiheitliche demokratische Grundordnung des Bundes oder eines Landes als Gegenstand nur des
polizeilichen Einschreitens aufgefasst (Art. 91 GG) und auch bei einer derartigen
Sachlage den Einsatz der Streitkräfte unter engen Voraussetzungen und nur zur
Unterstützung der Polizei des Landes und der Bundespolizei lediglich beim
Schutz von zivilen Objekten und bei der Bekämpfung „organisierter und mili-
tärisch bewaffneter Aufständischer" zugelassen (Art. 87a Abs. 4 GG).

Ungeachtet des eindeutigen Wortsinns des Art. 87a Abs. 2 GG soll nach einer
verbreiteten – teleologisch reduzierten – Auslegung dieser Verfassungsvorbehalt
nur den Einsatz der Streitkräfte im Bundesgebiet, d. h. zur Gewährleistung der
inneren Sicherheit, von einer ausdrücklichen Zulassung durch das Grundgesetz
abhängig machen.[4] Danach wären Auslandseinsätze der Bundeswehr, außer zur
Verteidigung (Art. 87a Abs. 1 GG) und im Rahmen eines Systems kollektiver
Sicherheit (Art. 24 Abs. 2 GG), auch sonst ohne ausdrückliche Zulassung durch
die Verfassung und nur kraft „konstitutiver Zulassung" des Deutschen Bundestages[5] verfassungsrechtlich erlaubt. Entstehungsgeschichte und Regelungszusammenhang können diese Rechtsauffassung stützen. Die an die Stelle des Art. 143
GG in der Fassung des Gesetzes vom 19. März 1956 mit dessen Verfassungsvorbehalt für die Inanspruchnahme der Streitkräfte „im Falle eines inneren Notstandes" getretene Regelung des Art. 87a Abs. 2 GG soll verhindern, dass für die
Verwendung der Streitkräfte als Mittel der vollziehenden Gewalt „ungeschriebene
[…] Zuständigkeiten aus der Natur der Sache"[6] abgeleitet werden. Maßgeblich
war demnach das Ziel, die Möglichkeiten für einen Einsatz der Bundeswehr im
Inneren durch das Gebot strikter Texttreue zu begrenzen.[7]

---

4   *Stein, T.*: Landesverteidigung und Streitkräfte im 40. Jahr des Grundgesetzes, in: Hailbronner, K./
    Ress, G./Stein, T. (Hg.): Staat und Völkerrechtsordnung. Festschrift für Karl Doehring. Berlin u. a., 1989,
    935–949, hier 941 ff.; *Randelzhofer, A.*: Art. 24 Abs. II, in: Maunz, T./Dürig, G. (Hg.): Grundgesetz, Mün-
    chen, 1992, Rn. 63; *Kokott, J.*: Art. 87a, in: Sachs, M. (Hg.): Grundgesetz. Kommentar. 4. Aufl., München,
    2007, Rn. 13.

5   Die im Hinblick auf Art. 24 Abs. 2 GG entwickelte Verfassungsauslegung ist ein allgemeiner Grundsatz:
    Für den militärischen Einsatz von Streitkräften ist dem Grundgesetz das „Prinzip eines konstitutiven
    Parlamentsvorbehalts" zu entnehmen (BVerfGE 90, 286 ff., hier 383 ff.).

6   Schriftlicher Bericht des Rechtsausschusses zu dem Entwurf einer Notstandsverfassung, BT-Drs. 5/2873,
    13.

7   BVerfGE 90, 286 ff., hier 356 f.; BVerfGE 115, 118 ff., hier 142.

Art. 87a Abs. 2 GG begrenzt den „Einsatz" der Streitkräfte außer zu Verteidigung. Einsatz der Streitkräfte in diesem Sinne ist deren funktionsgerechte Verwendung im Rahmen der militärischen Befehlsgewalt zur Ausübung der vollziehenden Gewalt, insbesondere unter Inanspruchnahme hoheitlichen Zwangs mit der Möglichkeit zur Anwendung von Waffengewalt. Der Einsatz der Streitkräfte unterscheidet sich von der als allgemeine Amtshilfe gemäß Art. 35 Abs. 1 GG in Betracht kommenden Bereitstellung ihrer technischen, wissenschaftlichen und logistischen Fähigkeiten, ihres Personals und ihrer Sachmittel zur Unterstützung anderer Behörden, ohne dass die Soldaten selbst Zwang anwenden. Derartige Unterstützungsleistungen, etwa auch zur Abwehr von Anschlägen mit nuklearen, biologischen oder chemischen Mitteln, sind dem Verfassungsvorbehalt des Art. 87a Abs. 2 GG nicht unterworfen.[8]

2. Streitkräfte „zur Verteidigung" und „zur Wahrung des Friedens"

Die primäre Aufgabe der Streitkräfte ist die Landesverteidigung, die Abwehr eines bewaffneten Angriffs, der mit militärischen Mitteln gegen das Gebiet der Bundesrepublik Deutschland gerichtet ist und einem auswärtigen Staat zugerechnet werden kann (Art. 87a Abs. 1 GG). Für diesen Fall des „äußeren Notstandes" enthält das Grundgesetz Vorkehrungen zur staatsrechtlichen Bewältigung des Spannungs- und Verteidigungsfalles (Art. 87a Abs. 3; Art. 53a, 115a ff. GG).[9] Der Bund hat die ausschließliche Gesetzgebung über die Verteidigung einschließlich des Schutzes der Zivilbevölkerung (Art. 73 Abs. 1 Nr. 1 GG). In neuerer Zeit hat die internationale Staatspraxis, nicht zuletzt im Sicherheitsrat der Vereinten Nationen, das Recht der Staaten zur Selbstverteidigung (Art. 51 UN-Charta) auch auf die Abwehr von die staatliche Existenz und Friedensordnung bedrohende bewaffnete und organisierte Angriffe nichtstaatlicher Gruppen erstreckt, sodass es naheliegt, den verfassungsrechtlichen Verteidigungsauftrag auf derartige Angriffe auszudehnen. Auf dieser Grundlage wäre die Abwehr bestimmter nicht-staatlicher

---

8 Antwort der BReg. auf eine Kleine Anfrage „Einsatz der Bundeswehr im Innern", BT-Drs. 15/3892, 2 f.; Antwort der BReg. auf eine Kleine Anfrage betr. Einsatz der Bundeswehr beim G8-Gipfel in Heiligendamm, BT-Drs. 16/5148, 5 f.; *Stein, T.*, a.a.O., 941; Antwort der BReg. auf eine kleine Anfrage „Einsatz der Bundeswehr im Inneren anlässlich des G8-Gipfels", BT-Drs. 16/6046; *Wiefelspütz, D.*: Sicherheit vor den Gefahren des internationalen Terrorismus durch den Einsatz von Streitkräften?, in: Neue Zeitschrift für Wehrrecht, 45/1 (2003), 45–65, hier 58; *Danwitz, Th. v.*: Art. 35, in: Mangoldt, H. v./Klein, F./Starck, C. (Hrsg.): Grundgesetz, 5. Aufl., München, 2005, Rn. 15.

9 *Stein, T.*, a.a.O., 940; *Depenheuer, O.*: Der verfassungsrechtliche Verteidigungsauftrag der Bundeswehr. Grundfragen des Außeneinsatzes deutscher Streitkräfte, in: Deutsches Verwaltungsblatt, 112/11 (1997), 685–688, hier 687.

Angriffe, wenn und soweit sie nicht mit polizeilichen Mitteln bekämpft werden können, Fälle eines Einsatzes der Streitkräfte zur Verteidigung im weiteren Sinne (Art. 87a Abs. 1 GG).[10] Das Prinzip des konstitutiven Parlamentsvorbehalts für den militärischen Einsatz der Streitkräfte außerhalb des Spannungs- und Verteidigungsfalles i. e. S. führt zu der Notwendigkeit jedenfalls einer generellen Regelung derartiger Einsätze der Bundeswehr. Der hier beschrittene Weg einer an der Entwicklung der äußeren Sicherheit und des Völkerrechts orientierten erweiterten Auslegung des Verteidigungsauftrags der Streitkräfte bleibt allerdings eng begrenzt und erfasst nicht etwa das gesamte Spektrum der Bedrohung durch den internationalen Terrorismus.[11]

Die im Lichte der politischen und internationalen Entwicklung nach dem II. Weltkrieg als ein Verfassungsauftrag zu verstehende Ermächtigung des Bundes, sich zur Wahrung des Friedens einem System gegenseitiger kollektiver Sicherheit einzuordnen, gibt dem Verteidigungsauftrag der Streitkräfte eine über die eigentliche Landesverteidigung hinausweisende Dimension (Art. 24 Abs. 2 GG). Der Beitritt zu einem so beschaffenen Bündnis bedeutet nicht nur die Gewährleistung der eigenen äußeren Sicherheit der Bundesrepublik, sondern auch die Mitwirkung an der Garantie einer internationalen Friedensordnung bis hin zum Schutz dritter Staaten gegen rechtswidrige Angriffe.[12] Das Urteil des Bundesverfassungsgerichts vom 12 Juli 1994[13] hat im Wege verfassungsändernder Rechtsfortbildung[14] Voraussetzungen und Grenzen des auf Art. 24 Abs. 2 GG beruhenden Verfassungsauftrags der Streitkräfte anerkannt und näher bestimmt. Die Ermäch-

---

10 *Wiefelspütz, D.*, a. a. O., 54 ff., 64; *Kokott, J.*, a. a. O., Rn. 17, 34; *Ladiges, M.*: Die Bekämpfung nicht-staatlicher Angreifer im Luftraum, Berlin, 2007, 33 ff.

11 *Tomuschat, C.*: Internationale Terrorismusbekämpfung als Herausforderung für das Völkerrecht, in: Die öffentliche Verwaltung, 59/9 (2006), 357–369.

12 *Kirchhof, P.*: Der Verteidigungsauftrag der deutschen Streitkräfte, in: Beyerlin, U. u. a. (Hg.): Recht zwischen Umbruch und Bewahrung. Festschrift für Rudolf Bernhardt, Berlin u. a., 1995, 797–824.

13 BVerfGE 90, 286 ff. Vgl. dazu *Isensee, J.*: Bundeswehr als internationale Krisenfeuerwehr und Friedenstruppe. Mitverantwortung der Deutschen in der Völkergemeinschaft, in: Wellershoff, D. (Hg.): Frieden ohne Macht? Sicherheitspolitik und Streitkräfte im Wandel, Berlin, 1991, 210–221; *Nolte, G.*: Bundeswehreinsätze in kollektiven Sicherheitssystemen: Zum Urteil des Bundesverfassungsgerichts vom 12. Juli 1994, in: Zeitschrift für ausländisches öffentliches Recht und Völkerrecht, 54/3–4 (1994), 652–685; *Dau, K./Wöhrmann, G.* (Hg.): Der Auslandseinsatz deutscher Streitkräfte, Heidelberg, 1996. Siehe weiter BVerfGE 104, 151 ff. (neues Strategisches Konzept der NATO von 1999); BVerfG, Urteil vom 03.07.2007, 2 BvE 2/07 (Beteiligung an dem erweiterten ISAF-Mandat).

14 *Roellecke, G.*: Bewaffnete Auslandseinsätze – Krieg, Außenpolitik oder Innenpolitik? Ein verfassungsänderndes Urteil, in: Der Staat, 36/3 (1995), 415–428; *Badura, P.*: Staatsrecht, 3. Aufl., München, 2003, G Rn. 83; *Starck, C.*: Auslegung und Fortbildung der Verfassung und des Verfassungsprozessgesetzes durch das Verfassungsgericht, in: Depenheuer, O. u. a. (Hg.): Staat im Wort. Festschrift für Josef Isensee, Heidelberg, 2007, 215–227, hier 218.

tigung des Art. 24 Abs. 2 GG berechtigt den Bund nicht nur zum Eintritt in ein System gegenseitiger kollektiver Sicherheit und zur Einwilligung in damit verbundene Beschränkungen seiner Hoheitsrechte. Sie bietet vielmehr auch die verfassungsrechtliche Grundlage für die Übernahme der mit der Zugehörigkeit zu einem solchen System typischerweise verbundenen Aufgaben und damit auch eine Verwendung der Bundeswehr zu Einsätzen, die im Rahmen und nach den Regeln dieses Systems stattfinden. Hat der Gesetzgeber der Einordnung in ein System gegenseitiger kollektiver Sicherheit zugestimmt (Art. 59 Abs. 2 Satz 1 GG), so ergreift diese Zustimmung auch die Eingliederung von Streitkräften in integrierte Verbänden des Systems oder eine Beteiligung von Soldaten an militärischen Aktionen des Systems unter dessen militärischem Kommando, soweit Eingliederung oder Beteiligung in Gründungsvertrag oder Satzung, die der Zustimmung unterlegen haben, bereits angelegt sind. Zu dem durch Gesetz erfolgenden Beitritt der Bundesrepublik zu dem Bündnis muss die konkrete Entscheidung des Bundestages über einen von der Bundesregierung beabsichtigten Einsatz hinzutreten.[15] Nicht der Zustimmung des Bundestages bedarf die Verwendung von Personal der Bundeswehr für Hilfsdienste und Hilfsleistungen im Ausland, sofern die Soldaten dabei nicht in bewaffnete Unternehmungen einbezogen sind. Die Fortentwicklung eines Systems gegenseitiger kollektiver Sicherheit im Sinne des Art. 24 Abs. 2 GG, die keine Vertragsänderung ist, bedarf keiner gesonderten Zustimmung des Bundestages. Der Wahrung des internationalen Friedens können auch Krisenreaktionseinsätze dienen.

3. Einsatz der Streitkräfte „außer zur Verteidigung"

Die Gefahrenabwehr im Bereich der inneren Sicherheit ist eine polizeiliche Aufgabe. Soweit das Grundgesetz einen Einsatz der Streitkräfte zulässt, ist dieser nur „zur Hilfe" oder „zur Unterstützung" der Polizeikräfte der Länder und des Bundes erlaubt, selbst im Fall einer Bekämpfung organisierter und bewaffneter Aufständischer (Art. 35 Abs. 2 Satz 2, Abs. 3 Satz 1, Art. 87a Abs. 4 GG). Das Recht der Gesetzgebung und die Ausübung der vollziehenden Gewalt im Bereich der

---

15 Siehe z. B. den Antrag der BReg. betr. Beteiligung bewaffneter deutscher Streitkräfte an der EU-geführten Operation EUFOR RD CONGO zur zeitlich befristeten Unterstützung der Friedensmission MONUC der Vereinten Nationen während des Wahlprozesses in der der Demokratischen Republik Kongo auf Grundlage der Resolution 1671 (2006) des Sicherheitsrates der Vereinten Nationen vom 25.04.2006, BT-Drs. 16/1507; beschlossen in der 37. Sitzung des Bundestages am 01.06.2006 (Pl.-Prot. 3259 C). Antrag der BReg. betr. Einsatz deutscher Streitkräfte zur Evakuierung deutscher Staatsbürger und unter konsularischer Obhut befindlicher Staatsangehöriger anderer Nationen aus Albanien (BT-Drs. 13/7233).

Gefahrenabwehr zum Schutz der öffentlichen Sicherheit und Ordnung fallen in die Kompetenz der Länder. Ein unmittelbar aus Art. 35 Abs. 2 Satz 2 und Abs. 3 Satz 1 GG ableitbares Gesetzgebungsrecht des Bundes besteht für Regelungen, die das Nähere über den Einsatz der Streitkräfte bei der – auch präventiven – Bekämpfung besonders schwerer Unglücksfälle und bei der Katastrophenhilfe nach diesen Vorschriften und über das Zusammenwirken mit den beteiligten Ländern festlegen;[16] Entsprechendes muss für die Unterstützung nach Art. 87a Abs. 3 und 4 GG gelten.

Die Streitkräfte wirken an der Erfüllung der Aufgabe der Länder durch Amtshilfe nach Maßgabe des Art. 35 GG mit. Diese Regelung ist ein Bestandteil der bundesstaatlichen Ordnung und außerdem eine Befugnis des Bundes und seiner Streitkräfte gemäß Art. 87a Abs. 2 GG.[17] Die Streitkräfte können hier nur zur Unterstützung der Länder bei der Erfüllung polizeilicher Aufgaben handeln und dabei lediglich von den Befugnissen Gebrauch machen, die ihnen das Landesrecht einräumt. Eine originäre Zuständigkeit des Bundes und seiner Streitkräfte besteht im Rahmen der Amtshilfe nicht, auch nicht im Fall des überregionalen Einsatzes der Bundeswehr. Die Klausel von der Erforderlichkeit einer „wirksamen Bekämpfung" in Art. 35 Abs. 3 GG könnte auf einen Grundsatz der effektiven Gefahrenbekämpfung und damit auch auf die Zulässigkeit des Einsatzes militärischer Mittel hindeuten.[18] Dem steht der akzessorisch begrenzte Einsatzauftrag der Streitkräfte im Verhältnis zur polizeilichen Gefahrenabwehr *de constitutione lata* entgegen, so dass Art. 87a Abs. 2 in Verbindung mit Art. 35 GG einen Einsatz der Streitkräfte mit ihren besonderen Fähigkeiten nicht rechtfertigt.[19] Ein Kampfeinsatz der Bundeswehr „mit spezifisch militärischen Waffen" ist im Rahmen des Art. 35 GG ausgeschlossen.[20]

---

16 BVerfGE 115, 118 ff., hier 140 f.

17 *Danwitz*, Th. v., a.a.O., Rn. 76, 84; *Gramm, C.*: Der wehrlose Verfassungsstaat? Urteilsanmerkung zur Entscheidung des BVerfG zum LuftSiG vom 15. Februar 2006 – 1 BvR 35705, in: Deutsches Verwaltungsblatt, 121/11 (2006), 653–661.

18 *Gramm, C.*, a.a.O., 654 f.; *Hillgruber, C.*: Der Staat des Grundgesetzes – nur „bedingt abwehrbereit"?, in: JuristenZeitung, 62/5 (2007), 209–217, hier 214.

19 *Danwitz*, Th. v., a.a.O., Rn. 71; *Starck, C.*: Anmerkung zu BVerfG, 15.2.2006 – 1 BvR 357/05, in: JuristenZeitung, 61/8 (2006), 417–419.

20 BVerfGE 115, 118 ff., hier 146 ff.; *Schenke, W.-R.*: Die Verfassungswidrigkeit des § 14 LuftSiG, in: Neue Juristische Wochenschrift, 59/11 (2006), 736–139; *Winkler, D.*: Verfassungsmäßigkeit des Luftsicherheitsgesetzes, in: Neue Zeitschrift für Verwaltungsrecht, 25/5 (2006), 536–537; *dies.*: Die Systematik der grundgesetzlichen Normierung des Bundeswehreinsatzes unter Anknüpfung an die Regelung des LuftSiG, in: Die öffentliche Verwaltung, 59/4 (2006), 149–157; *Linke, T.*: Eine unendliche Geschichte oder lässt sich das Luftsicherheitsgesetz durch eine Verfassungsänderung retten?, in: Nordrhein-Westfälische Verwaltungsblätter, 21/3 (2007), 101–105. – Zweifel daran, dass der im LuftSiG geregelte Einsatz der Streitkräfte mit Art. 87a Abs. 2 GG in Verbindung mit Art. 35 GG und auch mit Art. 2 Abs. 2 Satz 1 in Verbindung

Diese Grenze der Amtshilfe durch einen Einsatz der Bundeswehr könnte an sich durch eine Ergänzung des Art. 35 GG beseitigt werden, durch die den Streitkräften ausdrücklich eine Unterstützung der Polizeikräfte auch mit „spezifisch militärischen Waffen" zugestanden würde. Für die Abwehr von Gefahren durch Luftzwischenfälle mithilfe von Zivilflugzeugen hat das Bundesverfassungsgericht jedoch eine weitere grundrechtliche Schranke aufgerichtet, die in die Sphäre des absoluten Verbotes einer Verfassungsänderung (Art. 79 Abs. 3 GG) reicht. Die Ermächtigung der Streitkräfte, gemäß § 14 Abs. 3 des Luftsicherheitsgesetzes durch unmittelbare Einwirkung mit Waffengewalt ein Luftfahrzeug abzuschießen, das gegen das Leben von Menschen eingesetzt werden soll, ist mit dem Recht auf Leben nach Art. 2 Abs. 2 Satz 1 GG in Verbindung mit der Menschenwürdegarantie des Art. 1 Abs. 1 GG nicht vereinbar, soweit davon tatunbeteiligte Menschen an Bord des Luftfahrzeugs betroffen werden. Es wäre danach jedenfalls eine Regelung im Sinne des § 14 Abs. 3 LuftSichG, bei der der Einsatz der Streitkräfte auf ein Luftfahrzeug beschränkt wäre, das keine „tatunbeteiligten" Menschen an Bord hätte, nicht verfassungswidrig, wenn durch Verfassungsänderung eine entsprechende Befugnis des Bundes eingeführt würde.[21] Der Gesetzgeber müsste sich mit der Prognoseunsicherheit auseinandersetzen, die hier für das Vorliegen der konkreten Gefahr und für die Geeignetheit und Verhältnismäßigkeit des Einsatzes militärischer Gewalt gegeben wäre. Er kann hier offen bleiben, ob es Art. 2 Abs. 2 Satz 1 in Verbindung mit Art. 1 Abs. 1 GG schlechthin ausschließt, zur Verhinderung eines besonders schweren Unglücksfalls Waffengewalt gegen ein Passagierflugzeug anzuwenden.

mit Art. 1 Abs. 1 GG vereinbar sei, waren schon vor dem Urteil des Bundesverfassungsgerichts eindringlich vorgebracht worden. Die Notwendigkeit einer Ergänzung des Grundgesetzes war der Beweggrund für die erfolglose Initiative der CDU/CSU-Fraktion und die Bundesratsinitiative einiger Länder (siehe unten II.2., FN 29). Vgl. *Sattler, H.*: Terrorabwehr durch die Streitkräfte nicht ohne Grundgesetzänderung. Zur Vereinbarkeit des Einsatzes der Streitkräfte nach dem Luftsicherheitsgesetz, in: Neue Zeitschrift für Verwaltungsrecht, 23/11 (2004), 1286–1291; *Gramm, C.*: Die Aufgaben der Bundeswehr und ihre Grenzen in der Verfassung, in: Neue Zeitschrift für Wehrrecht, 47/4 (2005), 133–146; *Lose, J.*: Streitkräftefunktion und Katastrophenschutz, in: Die Verwaltung, 38/4 (2005), 471–491; *Pieroth, B./Hartmann, B. J.*: Der Abschuss eines Zivilflugzeugs auf Anordnung des Bundesministers für Verteidigung, in: Jura, 27/11 (2005), 729–734; *Hase, F.*: Das Luftsicherheitsgesetz: Abschuss von Flugzeugen als „Hilfe bei einem Unglücksfall"?, in: Die öffentliche Verwaltung, 59/5 (2006), 213–217. – Aufschlussreich ist die Kontroverse beim *Benda*-Kolloquium am 22. Januar 2005. Vgl. dazu *Schily, O.*: Das Notstandsrecht des Grundgesetzes und die Herausforderungen der Zeit, in: Europäische Grundrechte-Zeitschrift, 32/11–12 (2005), 290–294; *Schäuble, W.*: Neue Bedrohungen und die Antwort des Notstandsrechts, in: Europäische Grundrechte-Zeitschrift, 32/11–12 (2005), 294–296.

21 BVerfGE 115, 118 ff., hier 160 ff., 165. Kritik, allerdings ohne klare Lösung durch eine alternative Befugnisnorm: *Depenheuer, O.*: Das Bürgeropfer im Rechtsstaat. Staatsphilosophische Überlegungen zu einem staatsrechtlichen Tabu, in: ders. u. a. (Hg.): Staat im Wort. Festschrift für Josef Isensee. Heidelberg, 2007, 43–60; *Hillgruber, C.*, a. a. O., 214 ff.

II. Schutz der äußeren und inneren Sicherheit

1. „Schutzlücke"

Für die verfassungspolitische Frage, nach welchen Kriterien es zu beurteilen ist, ob das Grundgesetz eine den Einsatz der Streitkräfte im Inland oder im Ausland betreffende Schutzlücke für die Gewährleistung der inneren oder äußeren Sicherheit der Bundesrepublik Deutschland aufweist, muss als Richtschnur gelten, dass die Gefahrenabwehr durch Polizeikräfte und der militärische Einsatz der Streitkräfte unterschiedliche Staatsaufgaben sind und bleiben müssen und dass die Abwehr von Gefahren für die innere Sicherheit, die mit den Befugnissen und Mitteln der Polizeikräfte bewältigt werden können, keine originäre Aufgabe des Bundes und seiner Streitkräfte ist und sein kann. Ein Einsatz der Streitkräfte mit ihren spezifischen militärischen Fähigkeiten und Mitteln kann nur in Gefahrenlagen für die innere Sicherheit in Betracht kommen, die mit den Befugnissen und Mitteln der Polizeikräfte nicht bewältigt werden können. Wenn und soweit mit derartigen Gefahrenlagen zu rechnen ist, muss ein Einsatz der Streitkräfte zur Unterstützung der Polizeikräfte oder als originäre Aufgabe ermöglicht werden, wenn der Bestand der Einrichtungen des Bundes oder eines Landes oder die wesentlichen Bedingungen der inneren Rechts- und Friedensordnung sonst beeinträchtigt werden würden. Unter diesen Umständen müsste die Bundeswehr auch im Innern eingesetzt werden können, wenn nur *sie* über die Fähigkeiten und Mittel verfügt, die notwendig sind, um gravierende Gefahren für gemeinschaftswesentliche Verfassungsgüter oder durch Anschläge des internationalen Terrorismus abzuwehren.

> „Es wäre eine Sinnverkehrung des Grundgesetzes, wollte man dem Staat verbieten, terroristischen Bestrebungen, die erklärtermaßen die Zerstörung der freiheitlichen demokratischen Grundordnung zum Ziel haben und die planmäßige Vernichtung von Menschenleben als Mittel zur Verwirklichung dieses Vorhabens einsetzen, mit den erforderlichen rechtsstaatlichen Mitteln wirksam entgegenzutreten. Die Sicherheit des Staates als verfasster Friedens- und Ordnungsmacht und die von ihm zu gewährleistende Sicherheit seiner Bevölkerung sind Verfassungswerte, die mit anderen im gleichen Rang stehen und unverzichtbar sind, weil die Institution Staat von ihnen die eigentliche und letzte Rechtfertigung herleitet (BVerwGE 49, 202/209)."[22]

Die Erweiterung der Unterstützung der Polizeikräfte im Rahmen der Amtshilfe (Art. 35 Abs. 2 und 3 GG) durch die auch einen Einsatz mit spezifisch militärischen Waffen ermöglichte Hilfsleistung der Streitkräfte bleibt auf die – auch

---

22 BVerfGE 49, 24 ff., hier 56 f. (Kontaktsperregesetz); zust. *Hillgruber, C.*, a.a.O., 210.

präventive – Gefahrenabwehr bei einer Naturkatastrophe oder einem besonderes schweren Unglücksfall beschränkt. Immerhin würde damit eine Schutzlücke bei terroristischen Angriffen zu Lande, im Luftraum und im Küstenmeer der Bundesrepublik geschlossen werden. In anderen Fällen des inneren Notstandes zur Verhinderung oder zur Abwehr terroristischer Gefahren im Inland müsste im Regelungszusammenhang der Amtshilfe oder als neuer Tatbestand der Zulassung des Einsatzes der Streitkräfte (Art. 87a GG) eine Befugnis des Einschreitens geschaffen werden. Es liegt nahe, eine gewisse Parallele zu der Bekämpfung organisierter und militärisch bewaffneter Aufständischer (Art. 87a Abs. 4 GG) zu sehen. Auf einer anderen Ebene liegen die dem Bund zugewiesenen Materien der Abwehr von Gefahren des internationalen Terrorismus durch das Bundeskriminalpolizeiamt, den Verfassungsschutz und die Nachrichtendienste (Art. 73 Abs. 1 Nr. 9a und 10, 87 Abs. 1 Satz 2 GG), die polizeiliche und nachrichtendienstliche Aufgaben der Gefahrenabwehr und Strafverfolgung sowie die dazu erforderlichen Ermittlungen betreffen.[23] Keine Aufgaben der Streitkräfte sind die Bewältigung von nichtkriegerischen, gewalttätigen Zusammenstößen im Inland und die Bewachung von Liegenschaften und kritischer Infrastruktur außerhalb der Anwendungsfälle des Art. 87a Abs. 3 und 4 GG.[24] Außergewöhnliche Gefahrenlagen könnten einen militärischen Objektschutz im Rahmen der Amtshilfe nötig erscheinen lassen.

Folgt man der Auffassung, dass Art. 87a Abs. 2 GG den Einsatz der Streitkräfte im Ausland nicht umfasst,[25] sind bewaffnete Auslandseinsätze der Bundeswehr, die nicht zur Verteidigung und nicht zur Wahrung des Friedens im Rahmen eines Systems gegenseitiger kollektiver Sicherheit gemäß Art. 24 Abs. 2 GG (NATO, UN) dienen, nicht von einer ausdrücklichen Zulassung durch das Grundgesetz abhängig und nach Völkerrecht zu beurteilen. Nach dem Prinzip eines konstitu-

---

23 § 129a StGB; Gesetz zur Bekämpfung des internationalen Terrorismus (Terrorismusbekämpfungsgesetz) vom 09.01.2002 (BGBl. I, 361); Gesetz zur Ergänzung des Terrorismusbekämpfungsgesetzes (Terrorismusbekämpfungsergänzungsgesetz) vom 05.01.2007 (BGBl. I, 2); Rahmenbeschluss 2002/475/JI des Rates vom 13.06.2002 zur Terrorismusbekämpfung , ABlEU. Nr. L 164/3 vom 22.06.2002. Art. 73 Abs. 1 Nr. 9a GG ist aus der Föderalismusreform hervorgegangen (Gesetz zur Änderung des Grundgesetzes vom 28.08.2006, BGBl. I, 2034). Der Initiativentwurf zur dieser Grundgesetznovelle (BT-Drs. 16/813, 12) sagt zur Begründung, der Begriff des internationalen Terrorismus sei durch das internationalen und nationalen Normen zugrundeliegende Verständnis vorgeprägt, aber zugleich für künftige Entwicklungen offen. Vgl. *Möstl, M.*: Die neue dogmatische Gestalt des Polizeirechts. Thesen zur Integration eines modernen informationellen Vorfeldrechts in das klassische rechtsstaatliche Gefahrenabwehrrecht, in: Deutsches Verwaltungsblatt, 122/10 (2007), 581–589; *Tams, C. J.*: Die Zuständigkeit des Bundes für die Abwehr terroristischer Gefahren. Anmerkungen zum neuen Art. 73 Abs. 1 Nr. 9a GG, in: Die öffentliche Verwaltung, 60/9 (2007), 367–375; *Middel, S.*: Innere Sicherheit und präventive Terrorismusbekämpfung. Baden-Baden, 2007.

24 Antwort der BReg., 2004, a. a. O., 4; Antwort der BReg., 2007, a. a. O., 5.

25 *Wiefelspütz, D.*, a. a. O., 64. Siehe oben unter I.2.

tiven Parlamentsvorbehalts, den das Bundesverfassungsgericht dem Grundgesetz entnimmt, wird jedoch ein Beschluss des Bundestages für die Zulassung des Einsatzes zu verlangen sein, dessen Voraussetzungen durch ein allgemeines Gesetz festgelegt sein sollten. Verwendungen der Streitkräfte im Ausland, die nicht als bewaffneter Einsatz durchgeführt werden, etwa Katastrophenhilfe, Rettungsmaßnahmen, Staatsbesuche der Flotte etc., sind der auswärtigen Gewalt des Bundes zuzurechnen [26] und setzen eine parlamentarische Mitwirkung nicht voraus.

Die schon länger erkannte Notwendigkeit, die Aufgabe der Streitkräfte angesichts neuartiger Gefährdungen der inneren und äußeren Sicherheit zu überprüfen und erforderlichenfalls das Grundgesetz zu ändern, hat durch die Auseinandersetzung über das Luftsicherheitsgesetz und durch das Urteil des Bundesverfassungsgerichts vom 28. Februar 2007 eine verstärkte Dringlichkeit erhalten. Gesetzliche Regelungen über den militärischen Einsatz der Streitkräfte müssen in der Verfassung eine klare Grundlage darüber finden, unter welchen Voraussetzungen und mit welchen Befugnissen ein Einsatz der Bundeswehr nach Maßgabe der Art. 87a, 35 GG zulässig ist. Hinsichtlich der inneren Sicherheit kreisen die verfassungspolitischen Bestrebungen vor allem um die Frage, ob dem Bund für den die polizeiliche Aufgabe einer Abwehr von Gefahren aus der Luft oder von See her eine originäre Zuständigkeit eingeräumt werden soll, soweit eine wirksame Abwehr nur mithilfe des Einsatzes militärischer Mittel möglich wäre. Es zeichnet sich ab, dass der bewaffnete Einsatz der Streitkräfte bei einer Gefährdung der inneren Sicherheit, zu deren Bewältigung die Polizeikräfte im Rahmen ihrer polizeilichen Aufgabe, ihrer Befugnisse und mit ihren Mitteln nicht in der Lage sind, eine dritte Fallgruppe neben der Verteidigung und Friedenssicherung durch militärischen Kampfeinsatz und der Amtshilfe zur Unterstützung der Polizeikräfte im Grundgesetz vorgesehen werden könnte. Diese Fallgruppe erscheint bisher nur in Art. 87a Abs. 4 GG für zwei eng begrenzte Gefahrenlagen. Sie könnte gesetzestechnisch und sachlich richtig in einem neuen Art. 91 Abs. 3 GG Aufnahme finden, wenn nicht überhaupt der Wehrverfassung einschließlich der militärischen und nicht-militärischen Aufgabe der Bundeswehr ein eigener Abschnitt des Grundgesetzes gewidmet würde.

2. Initiativen und Vorschläge zur Änderung des Grundgesetzes

Der Entwurf eines Gesetzes zur Änderung des Grundgesetzes (Artikel 35), den die Freistaaten Bayern und Sachsen als Gesetzesantrag im Bundesrat eingebracht hatten, sollte es durch eine Neufassung des Art. 35 Abs. 2 GG ermöglichen, die

---

26 *Kirchhof, P.*, a. a. O., 808, Fn. 52.

Streitkräfte zum Schutz ziviler Objekte auf Anforderung eines Landes in Fällen von besonderer Bedeutung, wie etwa im Falle terroristischer Bedrohungen einzusetzen, wenn die Polizeikräfte des Bundes und der Länder zur Aufrechterhaltung oder Wiederherstellung der öffentlichen Sicherheit oder Ordnung nicht mehr ausreichen. Maßnahmen der Streitkräfte im Rahmen ihres Verteidigungsauftrags (Art. 87a Abs. 1), insbesondere zur Abwehr von Angriffen aus der Luft, sowie die Verpflichtung zur Amtshilfe nach Art. 35 Abs. 1 GG sollten unberührt bleiben.[27] Die Begründung des Antrags unterstreicht, dass angesichts der grundsätzlich verschiedenen Aufgaben von Polizei und Streitkräften der Einsatz der Streitkräfte zum Schutz ziviler Objekte *ultima ratio* sein müsse und dass die Zuständigkeit der Länder bei der Wahrnehmung polizeilicher Aufgaben zu wahren sei, indem der Einsatz der Streitkräfte nur auf Anforderung eines Landes im Wege der Amtshilfe vorgesehen sei. Im Übrigen wird angenommen, dass „nach überkommenem Verständnis" der gesamte Bereich der Luftabwehr, also insbesondere die Identifizierung und – im Bedrohungsfall – die Bekämpfung von Luftfahrzeugen, die sich unberechtigt oder mit feindlicher Absicht im Luftraum der Bundesrepublik Deutschland bewegen, zur Verteidigung im Sinne des Grundgesetzes gehörten und mit den militärische Mitteln der deutschen und alliierten Luftstreitkräfte wahrzunehmen sei. Der Bundesrat hat in seiner 271. Sitzung am 20. Dezember 2001 gegen die Empfehlung seines Ausschusses für Innere Angelegenheiten, und der Empfehlung seines federführenden Rechtsausschusses und seines Ausschusses für Verteidigung folgend beschlossen, den Gesetzentwurf beim Deutschen Bundestag nicht einzubringen.

Ein erweiterter Entwurf eines Gesetzes zur Änderung des Grundgesetzes (Artikel 35 und 87a) war Gegenstand eines Gesetzesantrages der Länder Bayern, Hessen, Sachsen und Thüringen beim Bundesrat.[28] Die Amtshilfe durch einen Einsatz der Streitkräfte auf Anforderung eines Landes sollte danach im Falle terroristischer Bedrohungen zur Unterstützung der Polizei beim Schutze von zivilen Objekten möglich sein, wenn die Polizei ohne diese Unterstützung die Aufgabe nicht oder nur unter erheblichen Schwierigkeiten erfüllen könnte und auch die Unterstützung durch Kräfte und Einrichtungen des Bundesgrenzschutzes nicht ausreichen würde. Klarstellend sollten die Worte „bei einer Naturkatastrophe oder bei einem besonders schweren Unglücksfall" ersetzt werden durch die Worte „bei der Verhinderung einer unmittelbar drohenden Katastrophe oder eines unmittelbar drohenden besonders schweren Unglücksfall oder bei der Bewältigung ihrer Fol-

---

27 BR-Drs. 993/01.
28 BR-Drs. 181/04.

gen" (Art. 35 Abs. 2 Satz 2 GG). Weiter sollte Art. 87a Abs. 2 GG wie folgt gefasst werden: „Außer zur Verteidigung und zur Abwehr von Gefahren aus der Luft und von See her, zu deren wirksamen Bekämpfung der Einsatz der Streitkräfte erforderlich ist, dürfen die Streitkräfte nur eingesetzt werden, soweit dieses Grundgesetz es ausdrücklich zulässt." Die vorgesehene Änderung des Art. 87a Abs. 2 GG hält zwar, wie die Begründung des Antrags ausführt, daran fest, dass die Luftabwehr zum Verteidigungsauftrag der Streitkräfte gehöre. Die Zuständigkeit der Streitkräfte müsse jedoch unabhängig davon bestehen, von wem und von wo (Ausland oder Inland) der Angriff unternommen wird, und vor allem auch unabhängig davon, ob der Angriff militärischer oder sonstiger Art sei. Bereits insoweit könnten sich Unsicherheiten über die Zulässigkeit des Einsatzes der Streitkräfte im Rahmen ihres Verteidigungsauftrages ergeben. Aber auch bei sonstigen Gefahren aus der Luft müsse ein Einsatz der Streitkräfte zweifelsfrei zulässig sein, soweit dies zur wirksamen Bekämpfung erforderlich sei. Darüber hinaus solle durch die Aufnahme von Gefahren von See her eine Rechtsgrundlage für den Einsatz von Streitkräften geschaffen werden, etwa für die Durchführung von Kontrollen auf See beim Verdacht von Waffenlieferungen oder Umweltdelikten, wenn ihr Einsatz zur wirksamen Bekämpfung solcher Gefahren erforderlich sei.

Mit dieser Bundesratsinitiative stimmt ein Gesetzentwurf überein, den die Fraktion der CDU/CSU im Bundestag eingebracht hatte.[29] Mit demselben Inhalt ist der Initiativentwurf der CDU/CSU-Fraktion erneut Anfang 2005 im Bundestag eingebracht worden.[30] An den Vorschlägen für eine Novellierung des Grundgesetzes aus den Jahren 2004 und 2005 ist bemerkenswert, dass die „Abwehr von Gefahren aus der Luft und von See her" als eine neben der Verteidigung bestehende originäre Aufgabe des Bundes und seiner Streitkräfte erscheint und auch nicht als Unterstützung der Polizeikräfte im Wege der Amtshilfe geregelt ist. In der 16. Wahlperiode des Bundestages ist es bisher nicht zu einer neuen Initiative im Bundestag gekommen.

---

29 BT-Drs. 15/2649. Der Länderantrag ist im Bundesrat nicht zu Ende beraten worden. Der textgleiche Initiativantrag wurde in der 1. Beratung des Bundestages in der 100. Sitzung am 25. März 2004 an den Innenausschuss federführend und an den Rechtsausschuss und den Verteidigungsausschuss zur Mitberatung überwiesen. Er stand im Zusammenhang mit dem Entwurf der BReg. für ein Gesetz zur Neuregelung von Luftsicherheitsaufgaben (BT-Drs. 15/2361). Der Beschlussempfehlung und dem Bericht des Innenausschusses (BT-Drs. 15/3338) folgend lehnte der Bundestag den Gesetzesentwurf zur Novellierung des GG in der 115. Sitzung am 18.06.2004 ab (Pl.-Prot. 10545 D). Für die Amtshilfe der Bundeswehr, wie sie im LuftSichG vorgesehen sei, biete Art. 35 GG eine ausreichende Rechtsgrundlage (Beschlussempfehlung und Bericht a.a.O., 28).

30 BT-Drs. 15/4658. Der Gesetzantrag wurde in der 155. Sitzung des Bundestages am 28.01.2005 an den Innenausschuss federführend und an den Rechtsausschuss und den Verteidigungsausschuss zur Mitberatung überwiesen (Pl.-Prot. 14490 D, 14504 D).

Im Januar 2007 wurde ein – dann nicht zur Kabinettsreife gelangender – Vorschlag des Bundesministeriums des Innern bekannt, der in einem neuen Absatz 4 des Art. 35 GG vorsieht, dass die Bundesregierung den Einsatz der Streitkräfte mit militärische Mitteln anordnen kann, wenn zur Abwehr eines besonders schweren Unglücksfalles polizeiliche Mittel nicht ausreichen, und der dem Art. 87a Abs. 2 GG folgende Fassung geben will: „Außer zur Verteidigung sowie zur unmittelbaren Abwehr eines sonstigen Angriffs auf die Grundlagen des Gemeinwesens dürfen die Streitkräfte nur eingesetzt werden, soweit dieses Grundgesetz es ausdrücklich zulässt." Hinsichtlich des neuen Art. 35 Abs. 4 GG ist fraglich, ob der Einsatz der Streitkräfte zur Unterstützung der Polizeikräfte, wie bei Art. 35 Abs. 3 GG, stattfindet und ob hier überhaupt noch ein Fall der Amtshilfe vorliegt. Der Vorschlag zu einer Ergänzung des Art. 87a Abs. 3 GG lehnt sich offenbar an eine eher beiläufige Ausführung des Bundesverfassungsgerichts an,[31] hat aber lebhaften Widerspruch erfahren.[32] Eine diese Klausel nutzende gesetzliche Regelung, die normenklar und praktikabel zum Einsatz der Streitkräfte ermächtigt, ist schwer vorstellbar, abgesehen davon, dass die Klausel eigentlich nur den Grundgedanken andeutet, weswegen eine staatliche Gemeinschaft überhaupt eine militärische Wehrhaftigkeit organisiert. Die Abwehr von Gefahren aus der Luft und von See her würde nicht erfasst und wird offenbar als Einsatz im Sinne des neuen Art. 35 Abs. 4 GG verstanden. In keinem Fall könnte so die vom Bundesverfassungsgericht aufgerichtete grundrechtliche Hürde (Art. 2 Abs. 2 Satz 1 in Verb. mit Art. 1 Abs. 1, 79 Abs. 3 GG) überwunden werden.

Legt man die Rechtsauffassung zugrunde, dass der Verfassungsvorbehalt des Art. 87a Abs. 2 GG für Einsätze der Bundeswehr außerhalb des deutschen Staatsgebiets nicht gilt, bedarf es für die Zulässigkeit derartige Verwendungen der Streitkräfte keiner Verfassungsänderung. Der verfassungsgerichtlich entwickelte Parlamentsvorbehalt schränkt die militärpolitische Entscheidungsgewalt der Exekutive für den Einsatz der Streitkräfte ein. Der Vorschlag eines neuen Abs. 5 des Art. 87a GG soll die Rechtslage klarstellen: „Die Streitkräfte dürfen nach den Regeln des Völkerrechts, auch zur Unterstützung der zuständigen Behörden, eingesetzt werden. Einsätze bedürfen der Zustimmung des Deutschen Bundestages; das Nähere regelt ein Bundesgesetz."[33]

---

31 BVerfGE 115, 118 ff., hier 159 (Bewahrung des rechtlich verfassten Gemeinwesens vor Angriffen, „die auf dessen Zusammenbruch und Zerstörung abzielen").

32 *Pestalozza, C.*: Inlandstötungen durch Streitkräfte – Reformvorschläge aus ministeriellem Hause, in: Neue Juristische Wochenschrift, 60/8 (2007), 492–495; *Sittard, U./Ulbrich, M.*: Neuer Anlauf zu einem Luftsicherheitsgesetz – Ein Schuss in die Luft?, in: Neue Zeitschrift für Wehrrecht, 49/2 (2007), 60–69.

33 *Wiefelspütz, D.*: Änderung des Art. 35 GG, „Quasi-Verteidigungsfall" oder Neuordnung der Wehrver-

Hinsichtlich des Einsatzes der Streitkräfte im Innern ist die wesentliche Weichenstellung, ob eine Erweiterung der Amtshilfe – ein Einsatz zur Unterstützung der Polizeikräfte – oder eine originäre Zuständigkeit des Bundes in Betracht gezogen wird. Im ersten Fall müsste Art. 35 GG ergänzt werden, wie in folgendem Vorschlag für neue Absätze 4 und 5 dieser Verfassungsnorm: „Wenn ein besonders schwerer Unglücksfall nach Abs. 2 oder Abs. 3 aus dem Luftraum oder von See her unmittelbar droht, dürfen die Streitkräfte auch militärische Mittel zur Gefahrenabwehr einsetzen, wenn die Polizei die Gefahr mit ihren Mitteln nicht abwenden kann. Näheres regelt ein Bundesgesetz."[34] Der mögliche Einsatz der Streitkräfte mit militärischen Mitteln bleibt auf Gefahren aus dem Luftraum und von See her begrenzt. Weitergehend wird durch einen anderen Vorschlag (Art. 87a Abs. 5 neu GG) der Zusammenhang mit der Amtshilfe durch eine originäre Bundeskompetenz gelöst und allein darauf abgestellt, dass mit den Befugnissen der Länder zur Gefahrenabwehr eine „Gefährdungssituation" nicht bewältigt werden kann: „Besteht innerhalb der Bundesrepublik Deutschland eine Gefährdungssituation, welche durch ein Land oder die betroffenen Länder im Rahmen der allgemeinen Gefahrenabwehr nicht bewältigt werden kann, so ist der Einsatz der Streitkräfte zur Gefahrenabwehr im Innern der Bundesrepublik Deutschland zulässig, soweit ein Gesetz nach Art. 73 Abs. 1 Nr. 1a GG dazu ermächtigt oder im Eilfall der Bundestag und der Bundesrat darüber entscheiden."[35] Dieser Vorschlag paraphrasiert im wesentlichen den Grundsatz der Verhältnismäßigkeit für die Gefahrenabwehr zur Gewährleistung der inneren Sicherheit und verlässt den Grundgedanken des Art. 87a Abs. 2 GG, den militärischen Einsatz der Streitkräfte im Innern an bestimmte, in der Verfassung ausdrücklich zugelassene Tatbestände zu binden. Richtig ist jedoch, den militärischen Einsatz der Streitkräfte zur Gewährleistung der inneren und äußeren Sicherheit, soweit er die engeren Grenzen der Amtshilfe nach Art. 35 Abs. 2 und 3 GG überschreiten muss, als eine grundsätzliche Frage der Wehrverfassung – gesetzestechnisch also in erster Linie einer Regelung im Rahmen des Art. 87a GG – anzusehen[36] und in dieser Hinsicht einer Novellierung des Grundgesetzes zur Klärung und Sicherung des Verfassungsauftrags der Streitkräfte näherzutreten.

---

fassung. Der Umgang mit dem Luftsicherheitsurteil des Bundesverfassungsgerichts, in: Zeitschrift für Gesetzgebung, 22/2 (2007), 97–134.

34 *Ders.*: Vorschlag zur Neufassung des Art. 35 GG, in: Zeitschrift für Rechtspolitik, 40/1 (2007), 17–20.

35 *Giemulla, E./van Schyndel, H.*: Kommentar zum Luftsicherheitsgesetz. Neuwied, 2006, Vorbem. zu Abschnitt 3 des LuftsichG, Rn. 33 ff. Der neue Art. 73 Abs. 1 Nr. 1a GG gibt dem Bund das Gesetzgebungsrecht für den Einsatz der Streitkräfte im Inneren nach Maßgabe des Art. 87a Abs. 5 GG.

36 *Gramm, C.*, a.a.O., 143 ff.; *Sattler, H.*, a.a.O., 1291; *Schäuble, W.*, a.a.O., 296.

The American Constitution, the State, and Executive Prerogative

by Bert A. Rockman and Eric Waltenburg

I. The Constitutional Founding

The federal constitution, which is the basic law of the United States, was developed under unusual circumstances. The current constitution, written in 1787 with ten amendments known more commonly as the Bill of Rights added to the text to achieve ratification, is not only the oldest written basic law of any current constitutional system, but is also the 2nd constitution of the United States. It replaced the Articles of Confederation which failed to provide adequate conformity of law and sufficient clarity of authority across the 13 former British colonies subsequently known as states after the colonies attained independence.

This second constitution was written hastily during a hot Philadelphia summer. The delegates had been given authority by the Continental Congress to amend the existing constitution in order to deal with the chaos that ensued in the absence of sufficient central authority. The delegates essentially staged a coup d'état and created a new constitutional order and a new set of governing institutions. Previously, power had largely been dispersed to the states and what little federal authority there was had been lodged in the Continental Congress. The setting in Philadelphia pitted a need for power against the fear of power.

The American constitution is the oldest written constitution partly because it is the most difficult to amend and partly because it is so sparse in its specification of powers and obligations leaving to future generations much of its meaning. There have been only 27 amendments to the document in the last 220 years, and ten of them (the Bill of Rights) came shortly after the main body of the document had been presented. The Bill of Rights principally deals with protections against the state and in the 10th amendment (the so-called doctrine of residual powers) the sovereignty of states vis-à-vis federal authority.

Being vaguely constructed, the US constitution is partly what it says on paper and partly what it implies from tradition and case law. For example, the aforementioned 10th amendment gives to the states all powers not otherwise expressly given to the federal government. That seems clear enough. However, the commerce clause of the constitution enables the federal government to regulate interstate commerce – a clause that provided the rationale for the equal accommodations section of the 1964 Civil Rights Act. The meaning of this reasoning is that if, let us say, you were operating a restaurant in Savannah, Georgia and the condiments on the table came from, say, Pittsburgh (where many do come from), you could be regulated by the federal government to ensure that all individuals would be served. The reach that seemed so constricted by the 10th amendment can be stretched quite extensively once a dash of creativity in interpretation is provided and a need to find legal justification for a desired action becomes compelling. Furthermore, constitutional traditions frequently derive from case law as much from what is actually written in the document itself. For example, the United States Supreme Court constructed the "doctrine of implied powers" in a famous court case known as *McCulloch v. Maryland*[1] in 1819. In this case, the Court unanimously held that the State of Maryland could not impede the operations of a branch of the Second Bank of the United States because that branch had not been chartered by the state of Maryland which required all banks operating in the state to be chartered by it. The implication of the decision clearly placed "the doctrine of implied powers" (what was being implied was federal supremacy) at odds with the "doctrine of residual powers" deriving from the 10th amendment to the constitution. There is no seemingly clear voice for all time on the role of federal vs. state powers. There has been and continues to be plenty of ambiguity. This, of course, is one reason why the judiciary, especially the appellate courts and the Supreme Court in the US are politically controversial, for there is no doubt that the more ambiguous the situation the greater the room for interpretation. And judges do a great deal of interpreting.

The US constitution is a post-modernist's dream. There is much to interpret. Similarly, that is true with respect to the powers and functions attributed to the branches of government – the so-called separation of powers system which is, in reality, a competitively shared powers system. The first three articles of the constitution specify the functions of the various branches. The first, and most explicit, has to do with the legislative function. The legislative function was explicit perhaps because under the prior constitution (i.e., the Articles of Confederation) the legislature was the one relatively developed institution and the one with which proponents of a more popular representative system felt most comfortable. The second article deals with the executive function. It is both shorter and less explicit than the 1st article, and it seems largely to imagine the president as an executor rather than as a prime mover. The third article deals with the judiciary. The constitutional stipulations more or less establish the existence of a judiciary

---

1   4 Wheaton 316 (1819).

and the terms of appointment and little else. So, how did the courts come to play such a large role in the United States and be so politically controversial? The answer lies nowhere in the constitution. It derives instead from case law that the US Supreme Court carved out as its function through the case of *Marbury v. Madison*[2] (1803). In this case, the court reserved for itself the right of judicial review and by implication the capability to hear cases involving the authority of the federal government and the discretionary powers of the executive among other things. The absence of certainty provides room for creativity and adaptability over time but also sets fewer bounds on arbitrary definitions of authority. Some jurists and legal scholars claim that it is essential to divine the original intent of the constitution's framers. The trouble is that sometimes the framers left little evidence by which to decipher their intentions. In other instances, the framers were frequently divided and the product they produced under intense pressure of time and the necessity to reach agreement was a patchwork of compromises which inevitably would receive sharper and more controversial, but not immutable, definition in the future.

While the courts are passive actors, being unable to respond until litigants come before them, the legislature (Congress) and the executive (president) are initiating actors, though the executive may not have been defined in that way by the constitution itself. Three subjects were among the mostly hotly contested in the constitutional debates by the framers and these were articulated in a set of essays justifying the new constitution prior to its ratification. These essays are known as the Federalist Papers. The first made famous in Federalist 51, mainly written by the chief architect of American governing institutions, *James Madison*, emphasised competition between institutions, each with partially overlapping yet distinctive constituencies, so as to deter a given faction from gaining control of all of the instrumentalities of government. Ambition, as *Madison* put it, would counter ambition – a perspective based on scepticism about human nature, despite the constitution's founding during the time of the Enlightenment and that epoch's more optimistic assessments about the human condition and its progress.

Federalist 10 puts forth yet another notion by which concentration of power could be avoided, and that was through the solution of federalism. *Madison* emphasised, in an unusual argument for federalism, that building authority to larger entities and sharing power between a federal government and state governments could dissipate the power of any one faction. In this document, *Madison* em-

2   1 Cranch 137 (1803).

phasises that the larger the compass of authority (the broader its territorial and jurisdictional swath) the more pluralised factions are likely to be and the less likely that any particular one will dominate. This is an intriguing argument for the protection of minority rights and for a pluralistic system. It is essentially a vertical version of the arguments set forth in Federalist 51. The scope of state and federal authority has been at the core of constitutional debates throughout history and the courts have often gone in different directions in cases that seemingly evoked similar constitutional principles.

Indeed, recounting the tale of the judiciary's near schizophrenic understanding of the federal relationship could occupy volumes. By way of example, however, a brief review of the Supreme Court's various constructions of the national government's commerce power should suffice. Accordingly, in *Gibbons v. Ogden,*[3] decided in 1824, the Supreme Court ruled that powers delegated to the national government were exclusive. Consequently, Congress's commerce power was plenary. By 1852 the Supreme Court's construction of the national commerce power was more limited. In *Cooley v. Board of Wardens*[4] the Court held that the Congress's commerce power was neither complete nor absolute. Its exercise was in fact circumscribed by the existence of the states which had their own powers with respect to commerce and that in some aspects (such as sales or production), the states' powers were controlling. In 1903, however, in *Champion v. Ames*[5] the Supreme Court cycled back to a far more expansive view of national power, holding that Congress's commerce power was as absolute as if it were vested in a unitary government. Fifteen years later, in *Hammer v. Dagenhart,*[6] the Court adhered yet again to its more cramped vision, ruling that Congress's commerce power was merely "ample" and that any constitutional grant of authority to the national government was limited per se by the 10th amendment. By 1941 the Supreme Court had reversed itself anew. In *U.S. v. Darby* the Court expressly overturned *Hammer,* declaring that Congress's commerce power was plenary and that the 10th amendment was but a truism and therefore was not intended to limit the exercise of the national government's powers. It took nearly a half century before the Supreme Court again checked Congress's exercise of its commerce power, but in *U.S. v. Lopez*[7] the Court held that although Congress's powers are broad, they are not unlimited. In the case of commerce, the Supreme Court ruled that it must not

3   9 Wheaton 1 (1824).
4   12 Howard 299 (1852).
5   188 U.S. 321 (1903).
6   247 U.S. 251 (1918).
7   514 U.S. 519 (1995).

construe this enumerated power so as to allow Congress to usurp the sovereignty of the states to police the conduct of their own citizens. The broader point is that there is no conclusive final word with respect to judicial understandings of the balance of federal and state authority.

Finally, Federalist 70 is an argument for acquiring sufficiency of authority in the form of executive power. It was authored by *Alexander Hamilton* who was a powerful proponent of an "energetic executive" and proclaimed it to be best invested in a single office. *Hamilton*'s view, coinciding with the party of his day, the Federalists, was to strengthen federal authority and to strengthen the central focus of that authority in the president.

As we have noted, article 2 of the constitution does not say a great deal about the authority of the president. But there are two critical elements that in the future would be interpreted, especially by presidents, quite generously. One of these is popularly known as the "take care" clause of article 2, section 3 which stipulates that the president is to take care that the laws be faithfully executed. The phrasing makes the president sound like a clerk. The implied power in that wording, however, gives a president who is willing to exercise his (and possibly his imagined) authority to the utmost tremendous powers of initiative and prerogative in defining what laws mean. The wording enables presidents, among other things, to define precisely what statutory laws may mean through the more precise definitions of administrative law. It also enables presidents to issue executive orders – a form of law that lacks statutory status and can be overridden by statutory law or by a successor acting unilaterally.

In modern times especially and during the omnipresent national security state of the cold war and the most recent global war on terror (GWOT), the seemingly innocuous role given to the president in article 2, section 2 as the commander-in-chief of the armed forces also has provided an opening for presidents to pursue "inherent powers" and to sometimes short circuit Congress which, on matters of war, seems often to prefer to be short-circuited. Although Congress was assigned the responsibility for declaring war, it has not done so in 66 years, though US forces have been engaged in numerous hostilities both big and small during that interval. Whilst presidents often have requested an enabling resolution to legitimate their use of military forces, they also frequently have not. It is hard to know exactly what the framers meant by the "commander-in-chief" role assigned to the president since at the time the United States had no standing army. But, for sure, the national security state and the now open-ended war against Salafist terrorists have dramatically expanded this role and presidential interpretations of it.

II. Constitutional Evolution

The American patriarch *Benjamin Franklin,* who presided at an advanced age over the Constitutional Convention in Philadelphia in the summer of 1787, reputedly was asked at the end by someone outside of the convention hall what had been produced. Equally reputedly, *Franklin* responded, "a republic if you can keep it". Whether apocryphal or not, the story suggests that institutions are deeply influenced by norms, by the intensity of cleavages in the social order, and by the willingness to compromise and find solutions. The republic was challenged internally by the searing division of slavery, the expansion of US territory, and the rent between an emerging industrial economy and an agrarian one. Like many states, it had a costly civil war because it could not solve these issues through political means, perhaps because of rather than in spite of an institutional architecture designed to force compromise. The westward manifest destiny (which also involved trampling over the aboriginal societies that stood in the way to that expansionary end) ironically forced the slavery issue because it was unlikely that any further states could come into the union as slave states, meaning that the Senate would soon become unbalanced between states where slavery was forbidden and those where it was permitted. When losers see themselves as permanent, they usually seek what *Albert Hirschman* called the "exit" option.[8] Ultimately, the eleven southern states that formed the Confederacy were reincorporated into the national state though at the cost 30 years later of a persisting American racial apartheid that remained until the 1960s.

The evolution of the American federal state, especially to meet the demands of industrialisation, economic depression, and its emergence as a major world power undoubtedly created over time a stronger federal government than likely could have been foreseen by the founders. The growth of revenue resources at the federal level spurred a more active federal role. Reactions to the Great Depression of the 1930s fostered an economic security state which also became part of the *Roosevelt* administration's efforts to create a long term coalition for an ascendant Democratic Party, based on labour, intellectuals, and the economically marginalised. The emergence of the welfare state was immediately followed by the emergence of the warfare state. And war is always a stimulant to state-building for though states make wars, wars also are state-makers.

---

8   *Hirschman, A. O.:* Exit, Voice, and Loyalty: Responses to Decline in Firms, Organizations, and States, Cambridge, MA, 1970.

It is these crisis conditions that especially create tension between the normal system of diffused and fragmented power bequeathed by the institutional arrangements of the American constitutional order and the emphasis on concentrating executive power to make things happen. Crisis is a president's friend in the American system. Fragmented authority and a system of multiple veto points often work as *Madison* intended. They frustrate power. And the frustration of power is often the normal condition despite the fact that presidents have become increasingly enamoured of unilateral exercises of authority and of concentrating executive authority in the White House. Large-scale change is more typically than not frustrated under normal conditions. Under conditions of crisis, especially national security crises, there is a tendency for the other branches of government to concede territory to the president whether by grants of authority from Congress or by congressional unwillingness or inability to effectively challenge assertions of executive authority. In sum, clashes between the normal constitutional regime and an abnormal crisis regime are especially frequent and consequential in the United States. Emphasis on a president's inherent powers is given more opportunity to come into play under crisis circumstances. The rise of the US as a leading world power certainly induces more crisis situations during which time the authority of the president comes to the fore, whether intended by the founders or simply inevitable in the evolution of constitutional practice. Perhaps, however, the sternest tests of executive authority and the federal government came during the US civil war (1861–1865). Certainly, the civil war laid the foundation for unprecedented extensions of executive power. And once this foundation was set, subsequent crises contributed to the continuing evolution of an enlarged executive. To be sure, the executive branch did not achieve this movement toward what some have referred to as the "Imperial Presidency"[9] and the pre-eminence of the federal government single-handedly. Indeed, a combination of historical moments and the performance of other political institutions (most notably the Supreme Court) came together to produce these outcomes.

III. Crises, the Court, and the Extensions of Presidential Power

Edwin Corwin declared, "the history of the presidency is a history of aggrandisement, but the story is a highly discontinuous one. That is to say, what the presidency is at any particular moment depends in important measure on who is the

---

9 See *Schlesinger, A. M.*: The Imperial Presidency, Boston, 1973.

President."[10] The ability of each occupant of the White House to determine to a large degree the outer limits of presidential authority is a function of the imprecision with which presidential power is laid out in the constitution.

As we suggested in our discussion of a president's vested interest in crises, the open-ended and personalised nature of presidential power can be seen with exceptional clarity in times of war or national emergency. These are the occasions that place a premium on the energy and dispatch associated with a powerful executive. The executive branch's claims of broad discretionary authority are given great deference at these moments. This is not to suggest, however, that presidential power even in the context of crisis is not without potential limitation. Quite the opposite: The breadth and scope of presidential power during periods of national emergency remains a question of constitutional politics more than what actually can be found in the constitution itself. The unsettled nature of the extent of the president's discretionary power is not a consequence of the issue's novelty. There is a rich vein of historical examples and court cases to explore. And it is to that task that we direct our energies in this section.

Perhaps the principal duty of the president is to defend the nation, and on this score, there is the tendency to allow the president substantial latitude. As *Thomas Jefferson*, a noted defender of individual rights, put it: "A strict observance of the written laws is doubtless one of the highest duties of a good citizen, but it is not the highest. The laws of necessity, of self-preservation, of saving our country when in danger are of higher obligation."[11] Threats to the nation's self-preservation can stem from external war or internal crisis. When it comes to waging war, the president's inherent powers are on firm footing, despite the constitutional division of war-making authority. The constitution names the president as the commander-in-chief of the armed forces. Congress is vested with the power to declare war, and it is charged with the responsibility of raising and maintaining the armed forces, including calling forth the militia (forces that were essentially under the supervision of state authorities but which could be federalised and commanded by the president) to suppress insurrection. The Supreme Court has been very reluctant to question the authority of the president's *military decisions* during a crisis or war itself. For example, in *The Prize Cases*,[12] a majority of the justices upheld *Abraham Lincoln*'s assumption of a war power (the blockade of southern ports) in the face of the secession crisis. The majority found that,

---

10 *Corwin, E.*: The President, 5th, ed., New York, 1984, 29 f.
11 Quoted in *O'Brien, D. M.*: Constitutional Law and Politics, 2 Volumes, New York, 1995, 254.
12 67 U.S. 935 (1863).

although Congress had not declared war, a state of war existed, and the president's decision to meet force with force was well within constitutional parameters.

A noted scholar of the American judiciary, *David O'Brien,* suggests that the willingness of the Supreme Court to countenance the president's exercise of broad discretionary authority in military affairs is merely a recognition of dire conditions and a need so imperative that to rule against the president would see the Court interpose its will contrary to national security and interest. As a result, "restraints on the president's power to wage war remain almost entirely in the hands of Congress".[13] Given the speed of modern transportation and troop movement as well as the extremely limited and politically non-viable (very blunt) instruments available to Congress to compel a recalcitrant president to withdraw troops engaged in an armed conflict by basically de-funding them,[14] the president's military powers as commander-in-chief are effectively unilateral.

This nearly unconstrained discretionary authority of a president to make war is not present in the case of the president's management of domestic affairs during a war or national crisis. To be sure, presidents are quick to claim inherent powers over both domestic and foreign affairs when a national crisis presents itself. Justifying their actions under the constitution's "take care" provision and their powers as commander-in-chief, presidents have treated their ambiguous article 2 authority as something of a blank check and have arrogated to themselves unauthorised powers, ignored constitutional limitations, and suspended basic rights.[15] Upon review of the historical record, though, it is worth noting that the lion's share of presidential takings of discretionary authority in the area of domestic affairs during times of crisis were done with eventual congressional approval or in response to broad congressional delegations of authority. Thus, for the most part, the president's *takings* of discretionary authority became *grants* of discretionary authority.

Certainly, no other internal crisis has threatened national self-preservation to the same extent as the civil war, and no president prior to *Abraham Lincoln* exercised greater discretionary power. Faced with the disintegration of the Union and armed resistance to national authority, *Lincoln* claimed sweeping powers under his authority as commander-in-chief and his constitutional oath obliging him to protect, preserve, and defend the constitution. Thus, along with calling for troops to suppress the rebellion, he blockaded southern ports, authorised large expansions in the size of the regular army and navy, authorised the expenditure

13 *O'Brien, D. M.,* op. cit., 253.
14 The War Powers Act (passed over the president's veto in 1973) has never been constitutionally tested.
15 *O'Brien, D. M.,* op. cit., 217.

of $ 2 million from the federal treasury and pledged the nation's credit to the sum of a quarter of a billion dollars, suspended the writ of habeas corpus, and authorised the military detention and trial of civilians. Each of these actions was taken without prior congressional approval. More significantly still, many of them were more clearly within the ambit of congressional power than executive authority; yet, *Lincoln* took the initiative in each case and acted unilaterally. To be sure, he justified each of his actions on the grounds that it was within the constitutional competence of Congress, and he expected Congress would eventually ratify each action as necessary.[16] To a large degree, this is just what Congress did. Accordingly, by the end of its 1861 session Congress had validated all but two of *Lincoln*'s extraordinary actions. Thus, the path along which takings of authority eventually become grants of authority was first blazed by *Lincoln.*

Kelly, Harbison, and *Belz* point out that as the War went on, *Lincoln* continued to take and exercise broad discretionary authority. Sometimes these takings became grants upon eventual congressional authorisation. For example, *Lincoln* suspended the writ of habeas corpus in May 1861, despite the fact that the power to take such an action is found in the constitution's organisation of congressional authority. By 1863, and following a judicial decision finding *Lincoln*'s suspension of habeas corpus unconstitutional,[17] Congress attempted to clarify the constitutional question through passage of the Habeas Corpus Act, conferring the power to suspend the writ on the president. At other times, however, *Lincoln* took discretionary authority in disregard of congressional authorisation. For example, he based his Emancipation Proclamation of 1863 freeing all slaves on his power as commander-in-chief, despite a section in the Second Confiscation Act that spoke to emancipation. Occasionally, he openly flouted it. In 1863 he announced his own Reconstruction programme to Congress. When Congress passed a programme that would have imposed greater penalties on the South, he killed it with a "pocket veto"[18], which allows a president to simply not sign legislation if Congress is no longer in session. After ten days, without congressional action to override, the veto goes into effect.

---

16 *Kelly, A. H./Harbison, W. A./Belz, H.*: The American Constitution: Its Origins and Development, New York, 1983, 301.

17 *Ex parte Merryman* (17 Fed. Cases 144 [1861]). Here, Chief Justice *Taney*, while serving in his capacity as a circuit court judge, ruled *Lincoln*'s suspension of the writ of habeas corpus unconstitutional on the grounds that the suspension was an exclusive congressional power because the habeas corpus clause is found in article 1. *Lincoln* effectively ignored *Taney*, responding to the *Merryman* decision by pointing out that the constitution does not clearly specify which branch has the power to suspend the writ and that the exigencies of the moment gave him warrant for the action.

18 *Kelly, A. H./Harbison, W. A./Belz, H.*, op. cit., 305.

Of course, wars need not be contested on American soil for presidents to assume broad inherent powers over domestic affairs during their prosecution. World War I is an excellent illustration of this. At approximately 8:30 on the evening of 2 April 1917, *Woodrow Wilson* addressed a joint session of Congress to request a declaration of war against the Central Powers. In his address, he called for several extraordinary policy choices – a bold tax programme; the compulsory draft of millions; the forced loyalty of all Americans to a cause with which many disagreed; and the "preeminence of the Executive, 'upon which the responsibility of conducting war and safeguarding the nation will most directly fall'"[19]. With respect to his final point, the pre-eminence of the executive, *Wilson* tacitly recognised one of *Lincoln*'s greatest accomplishments – namely, that he "constitutionalize[d] the doctrine of emergency prerogative"[20]. Ironically, despite making a call for arming the president with broad discretionary authority in order to effectively lead the nation "into the most terrible and disastrous of all wars"[21], *Wilson* was very careful not to assume extraordinary powers in the same unilateral manner as *Lincoln*. Rather, throughout most of the war years, *Wilson* "sought express congressional authority for nearly all of his actions"[22].

During the war, *Wilson*'s discretionary authority knew virtually no bounds. But this was due to Congress's willingness to delegate nearly its entire legislative authority to the president, not *Wilson*'s seizure of power in the fashion of *Lincoln*. Authorised by congressional statute (most notably the Lever and Overman Acts), then, *Wilson* was able to force preferential compliance with governmental contracts, seize and operate certain industries deemed essential to the war effort, regulate foreign language presses, conscript an army, establish food and fuel price controls, and fully reorganise executive agencies without congressional oversight. "Legislative delegation on this scale was unprecedented and little short of revolutionary."[23]

The sweeping delegation of legislative authority to the president in the area of domestic affairs during World War I raises a fundamental question. Why didn't the Supreme Court invalidate them? One reason is simply logistical in nature. The US Supreme Court is a reactive institution. That is, it must wait for constitutional questions to be put to it. Most of the controversial wartime measures were never taken to the Court, and of the few that were, all but one arrived in the Court well

---

19 Quoted in *Kennedy, D. M.*: Over Here: The First World War and American Society, New York, 1980, 14.
20 *Kelly, A. H./Harbison, W. A./Belz, H.*, op. cit., 306.
21 Quoted in *Kennedy, D. M.*, op. cit., 14.
22 Ibid., 125.
23 *Kelly, A. H./Harbison, W. A./Belz, H.*, op. cit., 449.

after the armistice was signed and the constitutional question was no longer of pressing concern.[24] A second reason is that it is impractical to expect the Court to rule unfavourably on a vital piece of war legislation while the war was in progress. Had the Court done so, "ways and means would have probably been discovered to ignore or to circumvent the decision"[25].

Two Court decisions, separated by about three-quarters of a century, illustrate this point quite nicely. In *Korematsu v. United States*[26] the Court evinced a strong reluctance to find a wartime order of the president or an act of Congress unconstitutional *while the war was in progress*. Within two months of the Japanese attack on Pearl Harbor, President *Roosevelt* issued an executive order establishing curfews and military zones in which military commanders could exclude individuals so as to prevent espionage and sabotage. One month later, Congress enacted legislation authorising *Roosevelt*'s executive order. As a result, tens of thousands of Japanese-Americans were relocated to "internment camps" farther inland. By 1944, a constitutional challenge concerning the forced relocations had worked its way up to the Supreme Court. Faced with fears over possible invasion, national security, and citizen loyalty, the Court ruled that the relocation was a constitutional exercise of the emergency prerogative:

> "We uphold the exclusion order as of the time it was made. [...] In doing so, we are not unmindful of the hardships imposed. [...] But hardships are a part of war, and war is an aggregation of hardships. [...] Korematsu was not excluded from the Military Area because of hostility to him or his race. He was excluded because we are at war with the Japanese Empire, because the properly constituted military authorities feared an invasion of our West Coast [...], because they decided that the military urgency of the situation demanded that all citizens of Japanese ancestry be segregated [...], and finally, because Congress [...] determined that [military leaders] should have the power to do just this."[27]

Ex parte Milligan[28] concerned *Lincoln*'s suspension of habeas corpus and his order that all persons disloyal to the Union be tried in military courts. The case arose from a trial of an Indiana citizen before a military tribunal despite the fact that Indiana was never a state in rebellion and the civil courts there were never threatened. The Supreme Court ruled unconstitutional the trial of civilians in military courts in regions where the civil judiciary was unaffected by the war. *Kelly, Harbison,* and *Belz* aver that "the Court's opinion was not a realistic ap-

---

24   Ibid., 447.
25   Ibid.
26   323 U.S. 214 (1944).
27   323 U.S. 214 at 219, 223 (1944).
28   71 U.S. 2 (1866).

proach in relation to the Civil War experience". They go on to contend that "there was ample ground for believing, as Lincoln did, that disloyalty in the North [...] might materially bolster Confederate morale and [...] prolong the war"[29]. Thus, arbitrary arrests and military trials made perfect sense given the circumstances. Notably, however, *Milligan* was decided *after the South's surrender* at Appomattox Courthouse and the crisis under which the action had been taken had passed.

The Court, however, does not always "roll-over" in the face of presidential exercises of emergency powers during times of crisis. Take the "steel seizure case", *Youngstown Sheet and Tube Co. v. Sawyer.*[30] It is the most noteworthy example of an instance where the Court was unwilling to countenance the president's claim of emergency inherent power in domestic affairs during a period when the president claimed national security was at stake. In 1952, with an undeclared war with Korea underway, the United Steelworkers struck, shutting down the nation's steel mills. President *Truman,* pursuant to no statutory authority, and in fact contrary to a "cooling-off" provision of the Taft-Hartley Act, issued an executive order calling for the Secretary of Commerce to seize and operate the mills. The steel companies immediately sought and obtained an injunction in a federal district court preventing the order from being effectuated, whereupon the Steelworkers struck again. The *Truman* administration then obtained a stay of the district court order, pending expedited review by the Supreme Court. The Court agreed to hear the case and handed down its ruling within a month. The president could have waited longer.

In a 6-3 decision the Supreme Court found against *Truman*'s assertion of inherent, emergency powers. Significantly, however, only two of the justices in the majority took the position that the president had no claim whatsoever to broad, discretionary authority during a period of national crisis. The four remaining justices ruled against *Truman*'s exercise of emergency power in this instance, because his action ran contrary to an express or implied policy of Congress. As Justice *Burton* put it in a concurring opinion:

> "The controlling fact here is that Congress [...] has prescribed for the President specific procedures, exclusive of seizure, for his use in meeting the present type of emergency. Congress has reserved for itself the right to determine where and when to authorize the seizure of property in meeting such an emergency. Under these circumstances the President's order [...] invaded the jurisdiction of Congress."[31]

---

29 *Kelly, A. H./Harbison, W. A./Belz, H.*, op. cit., 315.
30 342 U.S. 579 (1952).
31 343 U.S. 579 at 660 (1952).

Thus, the Court did not find against the existence of presidential discretionary authority per se. Indeed, the president may well have extensive implied powers, particularly when those powers are made in pursuance of congressional authorisation or Congress is quiescent on the issue. When Congress, either implicitly or explicitly, makes a choice of policy with respect to a given issue, however, the president's discretionary authority begins to be walled. And that was the case here.

In the end, what can we take from this brief discourse on the history of the president's discretionary authority during periods of crisis? First, it is clear that most extensions of presidential claims of inherent power during crises have been authorised by Congress. Not surprisingly, presidents are quick to invoke crisis as a justification for their claims and takings of power. Indeed, cloaking their extension of authority as being done in the context of a crisis may all but guarantee congressional and judicial approval. Occupying the bully pulpit and having first mover status, the president is in an excellent position to convince the public that a crisis is at hand, and, therefore, extensions of the emergency prerogative are essential for protecting and preserving the nation. Congress, susceptible to the public mood, will then be especially apt to authorise the president's taking of discretionary power. And the Court, often characterised as "the least dangerous branch", has little ability or desire to buck the policy choices of the elected institutions when they are in agreement with one another and in line with the public mood. It is a classic example of *Neustadt*'s observation that the essence of presidential power lies in the ability of the office holder to convince others that what he wants is in their interest.

This is not to suggest, however, that presidential claims of the emergency prerogative always trump the constitutional system of separation of powers and checks and balances. When the Court is faced with an instance where a president's exercise of emergency power is in conflict with a statutory provision of Congress, the Court is apt to decide against the president. Doctrinally, then it appears that the Court has effectively written *Theodore Roosevelt*'s broad construction of executive power into constitutional law:

> "I declined to adopt the view that what was imperatively necessary for the Nation could not be done by the President unless he could find some specific authorization to do it. My belief was that it was not only his right but his duty to do anything that the needs of the Nation demanded unless such action was forbidden by the Constitution or by the laws." [32]

---

32 Quoted in *O'Brien, D. M.*, op. cit., 219.

IV. Toward Presidential Supremacy?

Especially during times of crisis and threat, presidents gain the upper hand vis-à-vis the other governing institutions with whom they are supposedly in competition. The extent to which presidential prerogative is pressed is a function both of a secular trend toward executive power and of the actions of particular presidents. In addition, the claim of inherent powers is often open-ended since, by definition, that claim cannot be resolved by reference to documentary text but only by reference to practice. When presidents find it propitious to interpret their powers expansively and when conditions are congenial to such generous inter-pretations, other institutions tend, when asked, to grant such discretionary au-thority to the president. The alignment of political parties across the branches and the appointment of judges with expansive perspectives toward executive au-thority are conditions conducive to, though not fully determinative of, grants of presidential discretion. National security emergencies clearly provide presidents with a distinct advantage over the other branches – advantages they sometimes yield without great struggle. During such perceived emergencies "the second sober thought", which is presumably reflected in the checks and balances system, often has been bypassed in favour of the first intoxicating thought. Exactly two US Senators, for example, voted against the Vietnam War resolution sought by the *Johnson* administration in 1964, and subsequently cited as the source of its authority to conduct military activities in Southeast Asia. Exactly one US Senator voted against the USA Patriot Act of 2001 (an Orwellian tag) which gave federal authorities and the executive immense powers of surveillance and investigation – in reality, significant powers of intimidation – in the immediate aftermath of the Al Qaeda attacks of 11 September. The reality is that in the face of commonly perceived threat and powerful if momentary political consensus, politicians, whatever their private thoughts, are reluctant to risk their political careers to become profiles in courage. No legislator wishes to be an outlier during a national security emergency, though those few who have been on the outer rather than the inner circle often proved to be prophetic. Emergency legislation is rarely examin-ed with care or prudence. This gives presidents significant advantages in defining the terms of debate, and, indeed, frequently in avoiding debate altogether.

The events of 11 September 2001 and subsequent terrorist threats play directly into the hands of a president willing to exercise inherent powers to the fullest. Virtually any president would have come away with enhanced powers after the 11 September events. Modern presidents, and especially *George W. Bush,* not only have taken the biggest bite possible to expand the ambit of inherent powers, they also have sought legislation at moments that seem propitious for action and inadequate for reflection to provide them with capabilities granted through legislative authority.[33] National security issues are a president's trump card. Congress, under these circumstances, often lacks the fortitude to respond. And when it has the will to respond, it often lacks teeth as illustrated by the War Powers Act legislated during the end of the *Nixon* administration. The last effort on the part of Congress to invoke the War Powers Act was in 1982 when the *Reagan* administration sent US forces into Lebanon during the civil war there. *Reagan* acted as though the Act didn't exist, and there was little the congressional leadership could do. The law has scarcely been heard of since. Strategically, Congress is at a disadvantage because it is in the position of reacting to a presidential move that may not be consistent with statutory intent even if a single intent could be inferred from the passage of legislation. Presidents with a will to get away with a lot usually can and few have been so emboldened to do exactly that as has President *Bush*.

The notion of inherent powers has been taken to new extremes by the *Bush* administration because of the equally boundless war on terror. The expansion of presidential authority and the expansion of federal authority are by no means perfectly correlated, but they are generally so. In the era of shadow watching and a soft form of the garrison state, more federal powers have meant enlarged executive authority and a vigorous pursuit by the *Bush-Cheney* administration to claim vast inherent powers residing in the presidency along with expansive interpretations of presidential authority provided by statutes.[34]

An especially radical version of President *Bush*'s claims of inherent powers has come through the extraordinary use of signing statements when the president accepts into law a bill from Congress. Signing statements have been used by presidents to place their interpretation as to the meaning of statutes that they are

---

33 For example, despite the congressional attack on President *Bush*'s violation of the Foreign Intelligence Survey Act, requiring FISA court approval, to conduct surveillance on the calls of US citizens, the Congress accepted presidential terms not to require court approval for surveillance passing through routers located in the US. The effect was to make legal – albeit for a period of only six months – what previously was thought by nearly all but the *Bush* administration as an illegal exercise of presidential authority precisely because the *Bush* administration's actions had directly contravened a statute requiring prior court approval. But members of Congress wanted to go into recess and thus authorised the President to do what he – but virtually no one else – claimed he had the authority to do. See *Risen, J.*: Bush Signs Law to Widen Reach for Wiretapping: Restrictions are Eased – Rules on Eavesdropping are Altered to Match Program in Use, in: The New York Times (National Edition), 06.08.2007, A1, A14.

34 An excellent review of the *Bush-Cheney* efforts in this regard may be found in a manuscript by a noted professor of constitutional law, *Peter Shane*. See *idem:* Madison's Nightmare: How Executive Power Threatens American Democracy, Unpublished Monograph, 2007.

willing to sign into law. *Bush* has not invented this procedure. In fact, his father, *George H. W. Bush,* produced a number of signing statements designed to reserve what he and his legal counsel, *Boyden Gray,* took to be his discretionary powers if the statutes he signed were potentially to conflict with them. The American system is characterised by imprecise constitutional and often legislative documentation. This is masked by precise legal (actually political) doctrines about what legitimately may be regarded as the intent of decision makers. The doctrine of "original intent" has been in vogue for some time among right-wing constitutional interpreters, particularly notable in the arguments and writings of Associate Supreme Court Justice *Antonin Scalia.* In this context, signing statements have become a new twist in the game of what constitutes original intent in the formation of governing statutes. It puts a president on record as to his interpretation of the law. A president does have the option to veto laws but cannot do so on a piecemeal basis (the so-called line item veto) according to judicial ruling based on interpretation of the constitutional veto power.[35] President *George W. Bush* has vetoed very little legislation – his first veto did not come until late in his first term – but he has made extraordinary use of signing statements, sometimes to make claims on matters that were raised by the legislation in question. At other times, they were used to make pronouncements of presidential prerogative having virtually nothing to do with the legislation that crossed his desk. In other words, the signing statements served the purpose of issuing ex-cathedra proclamations about the discretionary powers of the president. By mid-2006, *Bush*'s signing statements numbered over 750; they have climbed to well over 1,000 since then. *Bush* has not bothered himself with vetoes; he has instead essentially produced a form of line item veto that has no official status but which preserves his administration's right to interpret the law as it sees fit – in essence uprooting the constitution by placing administrative action potentially outside of statutory authority. The scope of executive presumption here is, to say the least, extravagant. To say more than the least, it is likely subversive of American constitutional traditions and the mutual veto system of checks and balances. It is an astonishing expression of unilateral assertion. What it points out is that Congress has mainly blunt instruments to coerce a president and the use of such blunt instruments is politically injudicious and likely counter-productive.

Even the courts have been limited in forcing a president's hand when the president interprets the outcome as a consequence of a case rather than as a policy.

---

35 *Clinton v. New York City* (524 U.S. 417 (1998)).

The case of *Hamdan v. Rumsfeld*[36] decided in 2006 illustrates that even when the Supreme Court found for the plaintiff who was rounded up as a prisoner in the hunt for terrorists and terrorist sympathisers and sent to the prison in Guantanamo, its edict for the application of proper criminal justice procedures to be brought into play was circumvented by a presidential administration intent on asserting its inherent powers. That is, the administration essentially responded to the specific case but not to general policy applications since it chose to interpret the Court's decision in highly restrictive terms.[37] *Stalin* reputedly cynically and rhetorically asked in regard to the Pope's countervailing authority to his ambitions in post-war Europe: "How many divisions does the Pope have?" *Bush* could be asking the same of Congress and the judiciary even as he has worked forcefully to produce a judiciary sympathetic to his claims.

Whilst crisis and expansive definitions of "inherent power" are joined at the hip, the *Bush* administration also has made new claims based on the notion that the president is the sole proprietor of the executive branch of government rather than one of its supervisors. The Federalist Society, presumably named after *Alexander Hamilton* and the Federalists of the founding, is an association of right-wing legal scholars and jurists with a currently expansive view of executive authority, in particular the president's. It asserts that the executive branch is a unity under the direction of the president.

The Federalist Society has produced a pool of potential judicial nominees for the *Bush* administration. The last two appointments nominated by *Bush* to the Supreme Court – *John Roberts* as Chief Justice and *Samuel Alito* as Associate Justice – were both members of the Federalist Society. The perspective of the unity of the executive under the command of the president runs counter to both administrative traditions in the US and also appropriate legislative oversight of the functions of the agencies whose funds have been appropriated by the Congress and whose authority has been provided by statutory law.

The theory of a unified executive branch under unequivocal presidential control provides presidents with further prerogatives. All agencies of the federal government, in the unified executive interpretation, fall under the active control of the White House. Such a perspective is an audacious interpretation of the "take care" power. What it means in practice is that agencies' decisions produced

---

36 542 U.S. 507 (2006.)

37 The Court ruling required that *Hamdan* be tried in a court or commission with court-like proceedings. The *Bush* administration responded by meeting the letter of the decision and pressing for specific congressional authorisation to use military tribunals in cases involving enemy combatants. It certainly did not free *Hamdan* or similarly situated enemy combatants.

through the regularised means of the Administrative Procedures Act of 1947 may be overturned to accord with the priorities of the White House's occupant as those priorities are defined by the White House or its direct political agents. It also implies that "best judgments" often required by law of agencies are, when convenient, to be replaced by "correct judgments". It also means in practice that professional experience gives way to political *dictát*. The closest analogue may be the Leninist doctrine of democratic centrism. Although there has been a secular trend toward growing presidential centrism, the *George W. Bush* administration, building upon the administrations of *Ronald Reagan* and, to some extent, *George H. W. Bush,* has fervently pursued the Federalist Society vision of a unified executive under the command of the president.[38]

The constitution is unclear about the governance of the executive because the founders did not imagine a large government and the complicated issues of technical and legal discretion that agencies would possess. They could not imagine a professional corps of civil servants, especially ones with advanced technical skills who are required to offer their best judgments not merely the appropriate political line of the moment. Government was then much like a neighbourhood shop. Today, it is a mega-market. But clearly, Congress was to have a hand in the supervision of the executive branch, and, equally clearly, statutory law has often sought to define procedures of administrative discretion and to mandate on other occasions a role for professional expertise.

For presidential administrations equipped with powerful ideological certainties or needing the support of clienteles who are forceful in what they want, independence, professionalism, and expertise in the government's bureaucracy and among its career officials are annoyances. A former Surgeon General of the United States appointed by the *Bush* administration, *Richard Carmona,* whose mandated role is to provide health advice and education to the public, complained of censorship by more politically attuned *Bush* administration appointees. The cases are numerous and also go back to prior administrations. Nevertheless, the *George W. Bush* administration has set a new high (or low) in ensuring that only the White House line is adopted and in censoring officials whose role is to provide independent advice – a notable example of which was the immediate rebuttal and eventual dismissal of the Army Chief of Staff, General *Eric Shinseki,* for his response to a direct question from a congressional interrogation as to how

---

38 *Shane, P.,* op. cit. Also see *Aberbach, J. D.*: Supplying the Defect of Better Motives? The Bush II Administration and the Constitutional System, in: Campbell, C./Rockman, B. A./Rudalevige, A. (eds.): The George W. Bush Legacy, Washington, DC, 2007, 112–134.

many troops would be needed to successfully carry off an invasion of Iraq and maintain order there. *Shinseki*'s numbers failed to accord with those of the Defence department's civilian leadership, and *Shinseki* was immediately upbraided by Deputy Defence Secretary *Paul Wolfowitz.*

V. Unbalancing the Checks and Balances System

The founding of the American constitution was based on the proposition that authority is both necessary and dangerous. The founders were of differing minds as to where the balance should be struck. They constructed an ornate system of institutional checks and balances based on the supposition that the inability of any faction to command the system would result, to use contemporary language, in a *Nash* equilibrium outcome and, thus, a non-zero sum game. Norms are an important element to keeping such a system functional. But politics itself is the means by which legal-institutional constraints may be circumvented. Put another way, a government purely of laws is probably likely to be too inflexible but a government purely of politics is apt to be arbitrary, capricious, and corrupt – in a word, lawless.

The power of the presidency has grown abundantly in the 20th century. Multiple forces are at work as we have tried to emphasise. The power of the presidency, however, has grown even as its constitutional powers remain murky and ill-defined. Presidents have strategic advantages compared to other actors in the system. They can concert will more readily. They can move quickly and by being first movers, they can place other actors in reactive mode. They can define agendas and terms of debate or even muffle debate. They can stall when information is requested or choose to hold back witnesses to congressional investigation through the invented, though not implausible, claims of executive privilege – an informal American version of the British Official Secrets Act.

The founders did not foresee the role that modern political parties with strong incentives to support or oppose presidents could have as American governing practice evolved. Nor did the founders count on the political disincentives for members of Congress, fearing the adverse impact of the sound or visual bite on casually informed publics, to buck the president in the face of momentary consensus.

The will of particular presidents and their commitments to governing ideologies are vital aspects to the effort to govern unilaterally. In the case of the *Bush-Cheney* administration, the perfect storm came to pass. A serious national security threat provided opportunity for an administration committed to doing things its way. A Republican-controlled Congress, for the most part, was largely compliant and a Democratic-controlled Congress lacked the numbers to force the action – a consequence also of the non-majoritarian procedures of the US Senate. An administration obsessed with secrecy and increasing executive power has, for the most part, been in prime position to ignore what it wishes to ignore and to proclaim without legal substantiation a broad expanse of prerogatives. The courts, increasingly populated with Federalist Society perspectives, have been favourable to broad claims of discretionary executive authority.[39]

Still, a president cannot pass major legislation without congressional consent. For example, *Bush* was unable to make social security (pension) alterations, though, of course, he never actually submitted a legislative proposal. *Clinton* could not move a major health care proposal. Members of Congress also can oppose a president when they sense that compliance could turn them into political casualties, such as privatising social security. These limitations are still in place and given the complexity of Senate rules, make it even more complicated for far-reaching legislation to pass there. So, presidents will take what they can, and the *Bush* administration has illustrated how far a president can go – and get away with – governing through unilateral means.

It turns out that the constitutional founders' fears were well placed but the institutions they devised may have been insufficient to deter the threats to accommodation and liberty that have subsequently emerged. Can immense discretionary authority in the executive engendered currently by the open-ended terrorist threat be reconciled with constitutionalism and freedom? No one can be certain of the answer to that. However, history in the US and elsewhere should give those who cherish liberty pause as unchallenged executive authority threatens to become both a legal and normative reality.

---

39 Take, for example, the case of *Hein v. Freedom from Religion, Inc.* (127 S. Ct. 2553 (2007)). At issue was the ability of taxpayers to challenge the *Bush* Administration's funding of "faith-based" initiative programmes in federal courts. The Supreme Court ruled 5-4 that taxpayers had no standing to sue because the funds in question were not the result of specific congressional appropriations. Rather, they were drawn and dispersed by the president from general Treasury money. Taken to its limits, the ruling suggests that, unless limited by specific congressional appropriations, a president is free to spend money pretty much as he or she pleases.

Les institutions françaises face au réformisme sarkoziste

par Guy Carcassonne

I. La fébrilité constitutionnelle de la France

Comme toute personne sérieuse – et *Joachim Jens Hesse* l'est assurément – il a toujours porté sur le système constitutionnel français, dans nos échanges amicaux, un regard sceptique et amusé. Son scepticisme vient de la trivialité que revêtent, à ses yeux, des débats institutionnels vifs et récurrents quand notre énergie pourrait être mobilisée plus utilement au profit de réformes plus urgentes, souvent plus sérieuses. Son amusement, lui, vient des bizarreries d'un système qui n'a certes pas pour lui l'évidence rationnelle, comme si les Français, lassés du cartésianisme qu'on leur attribue à l'excès, avaient choisi, dans le domaine constitutionnel, de laisser libre cours à leur goût moins connu pour l'architecture baroque. Et c'est peut-être pour tempérer ce scepticisme, si possible sans renoncer à l'amusement, que c'est un plaisir de formuler quelques remarques en l'honneur d'un ami cher et d'un collègue très estimé.

De fait, à près de cinquante ans, qu'elle fêtera l'an prochain, la V° République continue de dérouter. Elle n'est pas la seule en Europe où le Président soit élu au suffrage universel direct. Mais il n'y a qu'ici où l'élection offre à son vainqueur la puissance d'une espèce de monarque républicain, qui cumule les attributs symboliques du chef de l'Etat et les moyens d'agir du chef de l'exécutif, à charge, pour le malheureux Premier ministre toujours placé dans une situation délicate, de s'accommoder de cette tutelle encombrante qui, même en période de cohabitation, ne disparaît jamais complètement.

A y regarder de plus près, pourtant, une autre analyse est possible, qui n'est paradoxale qu'en apparence, consistant à plaider que, tout bien considéré, la France, grâce à la V° République, a le même régime que l'Allemagne, le Royaume-Uni, le Portugal, l'Espagne et beaucoup d'autres encore, que l'ont classe généralement dans la catégorie des démocraties majoritaires.

Ramenés à l'essentiel, les caractères communs à tous ces régimes sont au nombre de trois: les gouvernés choisissent eux-mêmes leurs gouvernants, les gouvernants ont les moyens de gouverner, les gouvernants sont réellement responsables devant les gouvernés. Pour le dire en d'autres termes, plus simples, sont simultanément et clairement présents: un patron, une majorité, une durée. La France, à cet égard, ne se distingue pas vraiment de ses homologues comparables.

Bien sûr, il existe des différences, mais plus spectaculaires que substantielles. Ici, le «*patron*» est élu au suffrage universel direct. Mais n'est-ce pas, en fait, le cas ailleurs aussi, où le leader qui conduit son camp à la victoire en retire une légitimité personnelle très proche de celle d'une élection directe? Là, le chef de l'exécutif, quelle que soit sa dénomination, est responsable devant le Parlement alors que, en France, le Président, chef réel de l'exécutif, demeure politiquement irresponsable. Mais autre cette différence est-elle si importante? Combien de chefs de gouvernement ont-ils été renversés au Parlement depuis la guerre, dans les démocraties majoritaires? *James Callaghan* au Royaume-Uni en 1979, *Helmut Schmidt* en Allemagne en 1982 et c'est tout. Certes, *Margaret Thatcher* puis *Tony Blair* ont été plus ou moins poliment conduits vers la sortie, mais, d'une part, ils l'ont été par leurs partis respectifs et non par les groupes parlementaires, d'autre part et surtout, il s'est agi dans chaque cas, comme d'ailleurs dans celui d'*Helmut Schmidt*, d'une anticipation sur ce que l'on supposait être le vœu des électeurs eux-mêmes. Car, en dernière analyse, là est l'essentiel: dans ces régimes majoritaires, la responsabilité devant le Parlement n'est, le plus souvent, que théorique, tandis que, en réalité, c'est devant le suffrage universel qu'elle s'exerce, à l'occasion des élections suivantes. Or, à cet égard, le Président français ne se distingue pas vraiment des autres chefs d'exécutif européens bénéficiant du soutien d'une majorité disciplinée.

Ce qui a longtemps manqué à la France pour ressembler à ses voisines fut la durée. Elle avait déjà «*un patron*» et «*une majorité*», mais comme chaque élection nationale pouvait remettre en cause le résultat de la précédente et que présidentielles et législatives ne pouvaient être synchronisées puisque les mandats ne comptaient pas le même nombre d'années, le pouvoir n'était attribué, en fait que jusqu'à l'élection nationale suivante, laquelle intervenait dans un délai variable de un an à cinq ans: lorsque, par exemple, *Jacques Chirac* fut élu pour la première fois en 1995, il le fut pour sept ans, mais son pouvoir était limité en vérité à trois ans puisque des élections législatives devaient se dérouler en 1998[1] et pouvaient le priver de ses moyens d'agir en amenant à l'Assemblée une majorité hostile.

C'est à cela qu'a remédié l'adoption du quinquennat présidentiel, par le référendum du 24 septembre 2000. Désormais les Français élisent un Président en mai, sont ensuite appelés à confirmer – ou tempérer ou infirmer – leur choix en désignant les députés en juin, après quoi rendez-vous est pris pour cinq ans plus tard. Le patron et la majorité ont ainsi, enfin, la durée.[2] Elle est un peu plus longue

---

1   Il eut d'ailleurs l'imprudence d'accélérer cette échéance par une dissolution malencontreuse en 1997 qui le contraint ensuite à cinq ans de cohabitation.

2   Certes, cette synchronisation est fragile car elle pourrait être mise en cause par le décès ou la démission

que dans la majeure partie des autres pays comparables mais, de nouveau, cette différence n'est pas fondamentale.

Bref, à la veille de sa dernière séquence électorale, la France semblait, en profondeur, ressembler de plus en plus à ses voisines, amies et partenaires, même si des asymétries trop encombrantes empêchaient souvent d'en prendre conscience.

Mais voilà que l'élection de *Nicolas Sarkozy,* puis sa confirmation législative et le style qu'il a donné à ses premières semaines de présence à l'Elysée ont paru tout remettre en question. Présidentialisation, hyper-présidence, sont les images qui ont été le plus souvent évoquées. Le principal intéressé lui-même a fait tout son possible pour les nourrir, présent partout, dans tous les rôles, au point qu'en plus d'être chef de l'Etat on le voit Premier ministre, ministre de tout, dirigeant du Parlement et, pour faire bonne mesure, chef de l'opposition! La presse française, une nouvelle fois, s'est montrée amnésique. Que le nouveau Président ait un style bien à lui est indiscutable. Que sa volonté d'exercer le pouvoir lui-même soit franche, au point d'être presque agressive, est une évidence. Mais qu'il soit plus puissant que ses prédécesseurs, certes non.

En réalité, ce sont dix-neuf années – le second mandat de *François Mitterrand* et les deux mandats de *Jacques Chirac* – qui, placés sous le signe des rois fainéants et du chef en retrait, ont fait oublier ce qu'avait été la vie politique auparavant. De 1958 à 1988, nous avions déjà connu ce Président exerçant un pouvoir sans partage, décidant de tout, chaque fois qu'il en avait envie. *Nicolas Sarkozy* frappe les esprits en disant «*je gouverne*»? *Georges Pompidou* l'avait affirmé avant lui, exactement dans les mêmes termes, dès sa première conférence de presse en juillet 1969! *Nicolas Sarkozy* étonne en envoyant à chacun de ses ministres une «*feuille de route*» lui indiquant ce qu'il aura à faire? Dès 1974, *Valéry Giscard d'Estaing* avait inventé les «*directives gouvernementales*» qui avaient exactement le même objet! *Nicolas Sarkozy* surprend en multipliant les conseillers qu'il recrute auprès de lui? C'est avec *François Mitterrand,* en 1981, que l'Elysée a changé de dimension et que ceux qui y travaillaient ont commencé à substituer indûment aux ministres eux-mêmes! *Nicolas Sarkozy* bénéficie du soutien d'une large majorité à l'Assemblée nationale? C'est vrai, mais cette majorité n'est pas plus importante – et même plutôt moins – que celle dont bénéficièrent *Pompidou, Mitterrand* et même *Jacques Chirac.* Ainsi est-il plus juste de parler, à la rigueur, de re-présidentialisation mais non de présidentialisation.

Allons un peu plus loin encore. La France a considérablement changé au cours des dernières décennies. Sous *Pompidou,* elle était encore incroyablement centralisée; le secteur public occupait des positions majeures dans le monde économique, dont toutes les grandes banques et compagnies d'assurance; le contrôle de constitutionnalité n'en était qu'à ses balbutiements; il n'existait aucune autorité administrative indépendante pour tempérer la puissance du pouvoir politique; l'audiovisuel était un monopole d'Etat. *Valéry Giscard d'Estaing* et *François Mitterrand* avaient encore conservé une partie de ces atouts.[3]

Nicolas Sarkozy, dans ces conditions, est autant «*chef*» que l'ont été ses prédécesseurs, mais il l'est d'un Etat incomparablement moins fort, et il ne faut ni l'oublier ni le sous-estimer. Analysée froidement, la réalité est donc assez éloignée des représentations qui en sont communément faites. Pourtant, même inexactes ou caricaturales, ces représentations jouent un rôle et la conviction partagée d'assister à la naissance d'un hyper-Président a paru rendre d'autant plus indispensables la modernisation et le rééquilibrage des institutions. Après tout, peu importe que ce soit pour de mauvaises raisons qu'ils ont été décidés: cette modernisation et ce rééquilibrage sont nécessaires et bienvenus en tout état de cause. Tant mieux, donc, si l'on parvient à les réaliser et, d'abord, à y réfléchir.

C'est la mission que le nouveau Président de la République a confiée à un Comité, placé sous la présidence d'*Edouard Balladur,* ancien Premier ministre et candidat malheureux à l'élection présidentielle de 1995. A ses côtés siègent douze personnalités d'origines, de compétences et de spécialités diverses, dont, toutefois, plusieurs professeurs de droit constitutionnel au nombre desquels figure le soussigné.

La mission est vaste et aucune limite ne lui est imposée *a priori.* Seul le délai de remise du rapport – au plus tard le 31 octobre 2007 – contraint ses auteurs à aller moins loin dans le détail qu'ils pourraient le souhaiter.

Quelles que soient finalement leurs conclusions – dont on comprendra qu'il n'est pas possible de les dévoiler ici –, quel que soit le devenir de leur travail – le Président reprendra-t-il à son compte toutes leurs propositions? Le Parlement choisira-t-il de les adopter? Dans quel délai? – le simple fait que le travail soit entrepris est, en lui-même, éclairant.

Nombreux sont les pays où les règles institutionnelles ne sont pratiquement jamais mises en cause. D'autres, à l'inverse, ont comme l'Allemagne une attitude plus pragmatique, procèdent à des changements chaque fois qu'ils les estiment

---

3   Et ce dernier les avait même en partie accrus avec la grande vague de nationalisation de 1982.

nécessaires, ou simplement utiles, mais sans jamais remettre en cause les traits fondamentaux du régime.

La France ne pratique aucune de ces deux attitudes saines et en préfère une troisième, plus discutable. A peine la V° République était-elle née, en 1958, que *Maurice Duverger,* dès 1961, publia un ouvrage portant sur… la VI° République.[4] Depuis, le débat n'a jamais cessé. Longtemps, il fut animé par la gauche qui, de *Mendès France* à *Mitterrand,* n'avait jamais accepté le régime créé par le Général *de Gaulle.* Puis, au fur et à mesure que se rapprochait la perspective d'un accès au pouvoir, les socialistes se rallièrent progressivement au système, mais toujours du bout des lèvres, avec réticences, lors même, pourtant, que le premier Président de gauche usa et abusa de toutes les facilités, y compris excessives, que le système lui mettait à sa disposition. Aujourd'hui, cette remise en cause n'est plus le fait d'un camp contre l'autre, et l'on trouve de chaque côté des défenseurs de la V° autant que d'ardents – et souvent bruyants – partisans de la VI°.

Ces derniers, jusqu'à l'élection de *Nicolas Sarkozy,* se divisaient en deux factions antagoniques. La première voyait dans la République à créer un régime parlementaire, qualifié «*primo-ministériel*» qui, effaçant le chef de l'Etat, alignerait la France sur les autres démocraties majoritaires européennes. La seconde, elle, militait en faveur de l'adoption d'un régime de type présidentiel, supprimant tout ensemble le Premier ministre, la responsabilité du Gouvernement devant le Parlement et le droit de dissolution.

Depuis quelques mois, la première faction est devenue discrète. L'engouement qu'a provoqué l'élection présidentielle, à laquelle les Français ont massivement participé, puis le style que le nouveau chef de l'Etat a adopté depuis font regarder comme une erreur ou un mirage l'idée de supprimer ce scrutin ou celle, malcommode, de ramener la fonction présidentielle à un simple magistère protocolaire et moral. *Exit*, donc (mais peut-être n'est-ce que passager), la VI° République primo-ministérielle. Ne subsiste que la VI° République strictement présidentielle, au sens des catégories classiques du droit constitutionnel.

Aussi n'est-ce pas trahir un secret, car leurs positions sont publiques, que de dire que plusieurs des membres du Comité, à commencer par son président, sont sur cette ligne. S'ils sont assez lucides pour savoir que leurs travaux ne déboucheront pas sur un bouleversement de ce type – parce que le chef de l'Etat ne le veut pas et que les Français eux-mêmes n'en voudraient certainement pas non plus – ils restent persuadés que les réformes à venir ne seront qu'une étape

---

4   *Duverger, M.*: La VI° République et le régime présidentiel, Paris, 1961.

sur le chemin qui, selon eux, conduira fatalement à l'adoption par la France d'un régime de stricte séparation des pouvoirs.

A vrai dire, l'on peine à croire à cette fatalité, tout comme on rechigne à trouver une logique à l'idée selon laquelle le plus sûr moyen, pour la France, de se rapprocher de ses amis et partenaires européens consisterait à introduire un régime présidentiel unique au milieu d'autres qui ont tous en commun d'être parlementaires. Mais peu importent les pronostics. Seul compte le fait que, ici, le débat constitutionnel n'est jamais clos, parce que sont toujours présentes l'illusion que pourrait être inventé un système parfait et l'outrecuidance qui conduit à penser que la France aurait vocation à offrir au monde cet idéal.

Quoi qu'il en soit, il est vrai que le système est très déséquilibré, que le Président y dispose d'un pouvoir considérable qu'il exerce sans partage tandis que les citoyens n'ont d'autres ressources que celles qu'ils tirent, tous les cinq ans, de l'utilisation de leur bulletin de vote.

Bien des progrès sont donc possibles, qui ne seront accomplis, néanmoins, qu'à condition de ne pas se tromper de diagnostic. Pour l'illustrer, trois sujets, quoi que d'inégale importance, doivent particulièrement retenir l'attention: les rapports entre Président et Premier ministre, le rôle du Parlement, la place de la Justice constitutionnelle.

II. Les rapports entre Président de la République et le Premier ministre

Même le moins averti des Français est sensible au tour trompeur, voire mensonger, que sa Constitution a pris. Elle énonce en effet, dans son article 20, que «*Le gouvernement détermine et conduit la politique de la Nation*», alors que chacun sait qu'il n'en est rien dans la réalité, que c'est le chef de l'Etat qui détermine, et même conduit quand il en a envie, et que le gouvernement, y compris le chef de celui-ci, se borne souvent à mettre en œuvre une politique choisie et définie par un autre.

Jusqu'ici, l'on s'était assez bien accommodé de cette situation. Le texte était le plus souvent oublié et ne reprenait son sens, et seulement en partie,[5] qu'en période de cohabitation. Certes, la position du Premier ministre s'en trouvait assez inconfortable – ce qui n'est pas bien grave dans la mesure où elle n'a pas été

---

5 Même en période de cohabitation, tous les Premiers ministres concernés ont accepté que le Président continue à jouer un rôle important en matière de politique étrangère et de défense. Sans doute voulaient-ils ainsi préserver la dignité d'une fonction que tous, dès l'élection suivante, ont aspiré (en vain) à exercer eux-mêmes (*Jacques Chirac* pour 1988, *Edouard Balladur* pour 1995 et *Lionel Jospin* pour 2002).

conçue pour le confort de celui qui l'occupe – mais le système y gagnait une souplesse réelle en ceci qu'il permettait aux acteurs d'adapter leur attitude aux circonstances et à leurs souhaits. L'on avait connu des Présidents très présents ou plus en retrait, actifs sur tous les sujets ou seulement sur quelques uns, et des chefs de gouvernement disposant d'une marge de manœuvre large ou étroite. Le même couple exécutif pouvait d'ailleurs évoluer dans son fonctionnement, le même Président emprunter plusieurs registres différents durant son mandat, de sorte que c'était le rapport de forces entre les deux protagonistes, ainsi que les exigences de chaque période, qui guidaient, finalement, la réalité de leur relation. Seuls, alors, les puristes pouvaient-ils se plaindre d'un système mobile, tandis que les pragmatiques se satisfaisaient au contraire qu'il pût n'être pas immobile.[6]

L'élection de *Nicolas Sarkozy* a bouleversé ces habitudes, moins par nécessité que par volonté. Sa thèse est connue, qu'il met ostensiblement en pratique: c'est le Président de la République qui a été élu pour conduire sa politique; il doit le faire lui-même et l'assumer personnellement, sans hypocrisie, sur tous les fronts, en dictant sa volonté; le Premier ministre, alors, devient un simple exécutant, le premier de ses collaborateurs mais seulement un collaborateur, auquel il sera demandé de coordonner l'action des ministres, sans prétendre la leur commander lui-même.[7]

A partir de là, la tentation est vive qui consiste à l'écrire dans la Constitution, plutôt qu'à laisser subsister dans cette dernière une rédaction dont l'expérience a démontré et aggravé la fausseté. Le plus simple serait alors d'écrire que le Président «*détermine la politique de la Nation*» et que le Gouvernement la «*conduit*».

A cette tentation, néanmoins, il est souhaitable de résister pour une raison de principe et pour une raison de prudence. La raison de principe est que le souci d'adapter le droit au fait est souvent vain, quand il n'est pas dangereux. La pratique a toujours une longueur d'avance sur les textes, et quand ceux-ci veulent absolument coller à celle-là, ils se lancent dans une course sans fin et sans limite. En outre, le choix est intrinsèquement discutable: ce qui fait la popularité de *Nicolas Sarkozy* aujourd'hui peut très bien être ce qui fera sa défaite demain, à l'élection prochaine. Nul n'en sait rien. Donc une chose est que la Constitution rende une telle pratique possible, mais une chose très différente, et beaucoup moins acceptable, serait que la Constitution érige cette seule pratique en norme.

---

6   Il va de soi qu'il s'agit ici d'un jugement sur les règles, non sur la manière, trop souvent décevante, dont les acteurs les ont exploitées.
7   Pour faire bonne mesure, *Nicolas Sarkozy* souhaite que le chef de l'Etat puisse, à l'avenir, s'adresser aux assemblées en y prononçant lui-même des messages, ce qui lui est aujourd'hui interdit par l'article 18.

La raison de prudence est que si le quinquennat et la synchronisation des calendriers ont rendu la cohabitation improbable, ils ne l'ont pas rendue impossible. Toutes sortes de circonstances pourraient la faire ressurgir,[8] fût-ce très passagèrement. Dans cette situation, un texte constitutionnel qui aurait attribué exclusivement au chef de l'Etat, désavoué par hypothèse, le pouvoir de déterminer la politique de la Nation soit devrait à nouveau être méconnu, avec tous les débats oiseux qui en résulteraient, soit créerait une situation de blocage à peu près sans issue.

Pour ces raisons, il serait souhaitable que les retouches à la rédaction constitutionnelle soient prudentes. Qu'elles évitent la contre-vérité actuelle serait une bonne chose, mais il serait sage également qu'elle maintienne délibérément une part d'ambiguïté, qui, en évitant les précisions et rigidités inutiles, permettrait au système de continuer à fonctionner en toutes circonstances, y compris celles où, comme c'est parfaitement son droit, le suffrage universel ferait des choix présidentiels et parlementaires apparemment incohérents.[9]

III. Le rôle du Parlement

L'on touche ici au cœur des dérèglements du système français. Tous les régimes constitutionnels ont leurs mérites, mais on n'en connaît aucun qui puisse fonctionner de manière satisfaisante sans une première chambre active. La France n'en a pas.

Certes, sa Constitution la dote d'une Assemblée nationale, composée de 577 députés élus au scrutin majoritaire uninominal à deux tours et dotée de pouvoir importants. Seul problème: elle n'exerce pas les pouvoirs dont elle dispose et la majorité entretient avec le gouvernement des relations de vassalité qui confinent à l'esclavage. De là naissent tous les déséquilibres: le Président peut faire absolument tout ce qu'il veut au gouvernement qui, à son tour, peut faire absolument

---

8 Il peut s'agir de la démission ou du décès d'un Président, ou d'une dissolution ratée, comme en 1997. De surcroît, rien n'interdit aux Français, un jour, de faire un choix dissocié (auquel il faudrait alors trouver une autre dénomination que celle de cohabitation) en élisant un Président d'une couleur en mai puis une majorité parlementaire de la couleur opposée en juin.

9 Après tout, si les électeurs français voulaient, comme l'ont fait leurs voisins allemands aux dernières élections, forcer les deux grandes formations opposées à travailler quelques années ensemble, malgré leurs différences, le seul moyen dont ils disposeraient pour les y contraindre – mais il serait très efficace en ce sens – serait d'élire un Président d'un bord et une majorité parlementaire de l'autre, et les acteurs devraient bien, que cela leur plaise ou non, se plier à une telle décision.

tout ce qu'il veut au Parlement, sans limite, sans contrôle, souvent sans discussion. Ce n'est pas le texte constitutionnel qui donne au Président son incroyable puissance. Celle-ci résulte exclusivement de ce que les autres – gouvernement et Parlement – lui offrent leurs propres pouvoirs dont il peut jouir sans retenue.

Cet assujettissement aveugle de l'Assemblée nationale est le produit d'un cercle vicieux, largement né, mais pas exclusivement, de l'existence du cumul des mandats qui permet aux députés d'être, en même temps, élus locaux, voire chef d'exécutifs municipaux, départementaux ou régionaux: occupés par ces mandats locaux, les députés sont peu présents à l'Assemblée; étant peu présents, ils ne sont pas assez nombreux pour résister aux exigences du gouvernement, même les moins fondées; constatant leur impuissance, ils sont portés à préférer leur mandat local où ils ont le sentiment, justifié, d'être plus influents; privilégiant leur mandat local, ils viennent de moins en moins à l'Assemblée … et le cercle se referme sur son vice.

Les conséquences sont multiples. La première d'entre elles est que tous les gouvernements ont pris l'habitude d'entretenir avec les parlementaires des relations fondées sur l'autoritarisme: toute discussion est perçue comme une menace de rébellion. Cette culture de l'autoritarisme est à ce point répandue que l'on a pu lire dans *Le Monde*, avant l'été, un titre d'autant stupéfiant que ses auteurs n'avaient manifestement pas conscience de son énormité, qui écrivait, en gros: «*Crise dans la majorité: les députés souhaitent amender le texte du gouvernement*». Ainsi, en France, le fait que des députés entendent amender un projet de loi, même sans le remettre en cause, est perçu, par un journal réputé sérieux, comme une crise! C'est assez dire l'état d'assujettissement auquel on est parvenu.

Bien sûr, l'on sait que, à peu près partout dans les démocraties majoritaires, les députés subissent la tutelle du gouvernement et en souffrent souvent. Cela, pour autant, ne les empêche pas de continuer à jouer leur rôle et d'apporter une contribution décisive à leur fonction législative autant qu'à leur fonction de contrôle. Rien de tel en France où l'apport législatif est limité et le contrôle pratiquement inexistant.

Or, lorsqu'on se livre à des comparaisons précises et documentées,[10] il apparaît très vite que les différences ne tiennent pas à des écarts sensibles entre les pouvoirs des assemblées (ou des gouvernements), mais bien davantage à des cultures parlementaires très contrastées, plutôt consensualiste en Allemagne, majoritariste au Royaume-Uni, et clairement autoritariste en France.

---

10   V. à cet égard, la thèse très convaincante de *Mauguin-Helgeson, M.*: L'élaboration parlementaire de la loi. Etude comparative (Allemagne, France, Royaume-Uni). Paris, 2006, 514 p.

L'on a même vu, dans un passé récent, que chaque fois que l'on a doté les assemblées de capacités nouvelles, leur aliénation à l'exécutif les a aussitôt transformées en facilités nouvelles indûment offertes au gouvernement. En 1995, l'on décida que le Parlement siégerait neuf mois par an au lieu de six, dans l'idée que, disposant de plus de temps, les lois seraient mieux faites; au lieu de cela, les gouvernements se sont saisis de l'aubaine pour multiplier les projets de loi ou le nombre d'articles de chacun d'eux, moyennant quoi aucun progrès n'a été fait, au contraire, dans la recherche de la qualité législative.[11] Dans ces conditions, revaloriser le Parlement français, comme il en a bien besoin, ne suppose pas d'abord de lui donner des pouvoirs nouveaux, mais plutôt de l'amener à exercer effectivement ceux qu'il détient.

Ainsi faut-il, avant tout, inventer les moyens de ramener les élus au Parlement et, surtout, les députés à l'Assemblée nationale. A cette fin, une mesure nécessaire mais insuffisante serait évidemment d'interdire cette absurdité, typiquement française, qu'est le cumul des mandats. Etre un élu du peuple, représenter la Nation est un travail à plein temps. Il peut tolérer d'autres activités, mais non s'incliner complètement derrière elles.

Pour que la mesure soit efficace, il faut, de surcroît, et compte tenu du poids des mauvaises habitudes, amener les élus à un minimum de présence dans l'enceinte parlementaire. Ce peut être par un mécanisme d'incitation (gratifier significativement ceux qui sont présents et actifs) ou de sanction (amputer les revenus de ceux qui ne sont pas assez présents et actifs), mais ce doit être, car, ici, c'est la quantité qui fait la qualité: le même ministre qui obtient aisément ce qu'il veut de la poignée de députés présents devra expliquer, convaincre, répondre, accepter des compromis face à plusieurs centaines de parlementaires que leur nombre même amènera à refuser de marcher au simple coup de sifflet.

Alors, et alors seulement, les parlementaires découvriront qu'ils ont beaucoup plus de pouvoirs qu'ils ne croient et qu'il ne tient qu'à eux de les exercer. Alors, et alors seulement, l'on devra songer à les augmenter ou à leur en faciliter l'exercice.

Les pistes dans cette direction sont nombreuses et prometteuses. La limitation à six commissions permanentes dans chaque assemblée (article 43) est devenue inepte et ce carcan mériterait d'être desserré. Le fait que ce soit toujours le texte du gouvernement, plutôt que celui amendé par la commission, qui serve de base

---

11 Et l'on pourrait également citer l'exemple des lois de financements de la sécurité sociale, instituées en 1996. Créées pour permettre au Parlement d'exercer un contrôle annuel sur le budget social de la Nation, et devant ne compter qu'une dizaine d'articles, elles en comptent aujourd'hui des dizaines, ayant été exploitées par les gouvernements comme un moyen commode de faire adopter rapidement les dispositions législatives les plus diverses.

à la discussion en séance publique (article 42) n'a plus de sens, depuis que l'exécutif est mis à l'abri, par le fait majoritaire, d'une dénaturation grave de ses intentions. Une présence massive des députés suffira à dissuader le gouvernement d'abuser des moyens de contrainte que la Constitution lui offre (vote bloqué, article 49, alinéa 3) et qui, avec cette garantie, peuvent être conservés pour les situations extrêmes. Plus important encore, l'instauration d'un délai minimum de plusieurs semaines entre le dépôt d'un projet et son inscription à l'ordre du jour[12] permettrait de lutter contre la frénésie législative qui atteint tous les ministres. Enfin, la modernisation et le développement des moyens de contrôle autoriseraient le Parlement français à combler le honteux et coûteux retard qui est le sien, en cette matière, par rapport à ses homologues étrangers.

Evidemment, de telles réformes seraient d'autant mieux accueillies, et d'autant plus efficaces, qu'elles s'accompagneraient d'une amélioration de la représentativité de l'Assemblée nationale. Voilà des années qu'est en débat l'idée d'introduire une dose de représentation proportionnelle, afin que toutes les familles politiques tant soit peu significatives puissent avoir accès au Parlement. S'il y a un attachement assez large au mode de scrutin actuel dont on souligne l'efficacité, même ses partisans reconnaissent son injustice, d'où l'idée de conserver la première caractéristique en tempérant la seconde, pour faire en sorte qu'une fraction des sièges – d'une vingtaine à une soixantaine selon la modalité retenue – soit attribuée sur une base proportionnelle.

Bref, beaucoup de choses sont possibles, seraient utiles mais, répétons-le, demeureront vaines au mieux ou aggravantes au pire si, au préalable, l'on ne parvient pas à redonner une vie véritable à l'Assemblée nationale, en y disposant de suffisamment d'élus présents et motivés.

IV. La place de la justice constitutionnelle

Elle est le troisième grand sujet d'interrogation et, sans doute, d'évolution. Le système français est assez singulier puisque le Conseil constitutionnel, d'une part, ne contrôle la conformité des lois qu'à la Constitution, d'autre part, ne le fait qu'avant leur promulgation et, enfin, seulement s'il est saisi par soixante députés ou soixante sénateurs.

Conçu à l'origine comme un moyen de contrôle du Parlement, il a changé de nature à partir du moment, dans les années 70, où, d'un côté, le juge a pris sur lui

---

12 Sous réserve d'une dérogation possible, en cas d'urgence réelle et avec l'accord de l'opposition.

de se soucier d'une véritable protection des droits fondamentaux et où, de l'autre, l'opposition a reçu le pouvoir d'en appeler à lui. Mais la situation a encore évolué depuis, sous l'effet du droit communautaire et de la Convention européenne des droits de l'homme (CEDH). N'importe quel justiciable, en effet, peut demander et obtenir que soit écartée la loi qu'on prétend lui appliquer, si elle est contraire à n'importe quel engagement international souscrit par la France, ce qui vise en premier lieu la CEDH mais aussi tout le droit communautaire, originaire comme dérivé.

Or, dans le même temps, a été maintenu l'interdit formel au nom duquel les juridictions ordinaires ne peuvent mettre en cause la conformité d'une loi à la Constitution, privilège réservé au seul Conseil constitutionnel, dans le cadre étroit du contrôle qui est le sien.

L'on aboutit ainsi à cette situation loufoque dans laquelle les justiciables, en France, peuvent opposer à la loi le plus anodin des traités, la plus obscure des prescriptions de la moins importante des directives européennes, mais ne sont jamais autorisés à se placer sous la protection de leur propre Constitution. C'est indéfendable et, de surcroît, interdit que les citoyens s'approprient leur loi fondamentale, puisqu'elle leur apportera moins que n'importe quel texte supranational et qu'ils ne trouvent donc nul intérêt à seulement la connaître.

Il est trop tôt pour dire ce que seront les préconisations du Comité constitutionnel, mais on peut affirmer sans craindre le démenti qu'il traitera la question pour faire en sorte que les justiciables aient enfin accès à la justice constitutionnelle, cinquante ans après la naissance de celle-ci. Les spécialistes savent bien que la question est délicate, en droit comme en fait, mais ils n'ignorent pas non plus qu'ils ont une obligation de résultat pour parvenir à un système moderne, protecteur et cohérent.

V. Les joueurs et la règle du jeu

Bien d'autres sujets encore méritent examen, sur la justice – est-il normal que le chef de l'Etat préside le Conseil supérieur de la magistrature? Faut-il séparer le siège et le parquet? Faut-il créer un procureur général de la Nation? … – sur le référendum – doit-on permettre des référendums d'initiative populaire? A quelles conditions, avec quels effets? … – sur les droits des citoyens – faut-il créer une fonction similaire à celle du *Defensor del Pueblo* en Espagne? … – sur le statut de l'opposition – faut-il en créer un? Comment définir l'opposition dans un système de multipartisme? … – et les observations présentées ici n'entendent pas faire la somme de tous les débats en cours.

Elles voulaient seulement, en hommage à leur destinataire que ces sujets intéressent, faire une présentation sommaire des principaux enjeux, à la veille d'évolutions qui peuvent être importantes. Mais si innovatrices ou utiles puissent-elles être, elles ne devront jamais faire oublier un enseignement dont, je crois, tous les connaisseurs ont conscience: la meilleure règle du jeu ne dispensera jamais les joueurs d'avoir du talent …

III. Institutional Transformation and Constitutional Change

Constitutionalism, Economic Transformation and Europeanisation: the Case of Hungary

by László Csaba

One peculiarity of the social sciences is the researchers' inability to agree upon the meaning of even basic analytical concepts. This is hardly astonishing, especially in the light of constructivism and other post-modern approaches, which highlight the focal role of discourse in constituting both reality and our perceptions of actions relating to the former. For this reason and contrary to the Anglo-Saxon tradition, it matters which name we attach to individual processes or phenomena. It also matters how we structure our axioms and arguments, as this, especially in the more formal approaches, prejudges the type of outcomes we may and do expect from performing academic exercises on empirical materials or models.

I. Why Does Constitutionalism Matter for the Economy?

Against this background it may not come as a surprise that economists, even from within the same line of thought, tend to disagree on concepts and their meanings just as much as other social scientists do. In law, for instance, the more traditional approach[1] takes constitutionalism to be the broad understanding of the history and practice of constitutional arrangements *in toto*. In the post-communist environment, by contrast, an equally influential line of reasoning emerged that defines constitutionalism in terms of *limiting the state, primarily the executive.*[2]

This line of thinking underscores the relevance of checks and balances in a much broader way than is customary in political science, meaning the division of powers between the legislative, executive and judicial branches. It has its equivalent in the contemporary representatives of the Freiburg School or constitutional political economy.[3] This approach, following the political philosophy of *F. A. Hayek,*[4] lays great emphasis on the quality of the constituting components

---

1 Cf. recently *Vorländer, H.*: Europas multiple Konstitutionalismen, in: Zeitschrift für Staats- und Europawissenschaften (ZSE), 5/2 (2007), 160–180.

2 Most prominently in *Sajó, A.*: Limiting Government. An Introduction to Constitutionalism, Budapest/New York, 1999.

3 Cf. the major books by *Buchanan, J.*: Constitutional Economics, Oxford, 1991, and *Vanberg, V.*: The Constitution of Markets, London, 2001.

4 *Hayek, F. A.*: The Constitution of Liberty, Chicago, 1978.

of economic order or, to put it more simply, the *framework for the macroeconomic processes*. From this perspective, two momentums may be considered decisive:

- to save the market from its imperfections and self-destroying failures by regulatory agencies and procedures that keep the open economy and thereby the free society in operation, and
- to save mass democracy from itself, including its inherent tendency to overspend and disregard those broader concerns that do not fit into the myopia of media-led politics or maximising votes.

Given that post-communist change has been one of wholesale *social engineering* where all rules of the game, formal and informal, have been re-written, it could have been an extraordinary opportunity to test those theories. Moreover, the accession of post-communist countries to the European Union, which has been a top strategic priority for all domestic elites from the very outset, also included a fair dose of social engineering because the Maastricht Treaty and its successors have been gradually transforming the former trade bloc and customs union into a political community. Since the Amsterdam Treaty omitted the possibility of "opt-outs", new member states have become, willy-nilly, "110-percent Europeans" in their attempts to transplant existing EC/EU arrangements, irrespective of their salience. As the Commission has been entrusted to check progress in these areas in detail and on the spot, this commitment could not remain pious in intention only.

Therefore from the very outset, *transformation* has been much more than its economic backbone, commonly referred to by the English acronym SLIP, i.e. stabilisation, liberalisation, institution-building and privatisation. This process has entailed the parallel restructuring of the economic, social and political order, formal and informal institutions alike. As a large-scale social engineering experience, it has provided a potential for implementing the related insights, all the more so, because systemic change, at least in the frontrunner countries, has been taking place in the context of Europeanisation.

The latter term has a variety of meanings,[5] but for our purposes we understand Europeanisation as *interaction of domestic and EU policies and institutions,* rather than mere copying of EU institutions or the quasi-coercive use of EU policies by the new members. In so doing and in line with the research on West European experiences with integration, we stress the relevance of active feedback processes.

---

5   Cf. the broad overview in the Special Issue of the Zeitschrift für Staats- und Europawissenschaften (ZSE), 4/3 (2006).

The more we do so, the more we may think about the pivotal importance of constitutional change as the supreme and final level of formalising institution-building and political commitments alike. First, policy diffusion has been shown to have a major impact in all OECD countries, even in the old EU member states.[6] Second, a properly designed and EU-oriented constitution-building has been shown by recent econometric evidence to be a forceful commitment device, signalling both elite commitment to sound policies and accountability, thereby improving the credibility of and public support for large-scale (and oftentimes costly) market-oriented reforms.[7]

In this way we might assess constitutional progress in terms of *new political economy,* i. e. to test if, and to what degree, constitutional changes that have been taking place in a frontrunner transforming country and by now EU member state have contributed to economic improvement in one way or another. The case of Hungary might be illuminating in order to highlight the – limited, though relevant – role of history and the responsibility of those taking decisions that culminate in constitutional change. Finally, we turn to the intriguing question of *if, and how, constitutional change may contribute to fiscal consolidation.* Since this last question has been one of the oldest topics that triggered the work in the area of constitutional political economy, the test may be worth a run.[8]

II. From Form to Substance and Disregard of Economy

A characteristic specific to Hungarian "Goulash Communism" as practised under *János Kádár* from 1956 to 1989 was its pronounced respect for formalities. This served, *inter alia,* the purpose of dissociating itself from the disgraced *Rákosi* regime as well as from other communist countries, such as Romania or East Germany. Stepping into the footprints of the Soviet Constitution of 1936, which is known to have declared universal freedoms (including the right to secede from the Union), formal arrangements in Hungary have always been kept legally impeccable.

Although this kind of legalism has not immediately influenced policy outcomes, it has been important in a number of ways. First, the legal tradition based

---

6   *Pitlik, H.:* A Race to Liberalization?, in: Public Choice, 132/1–2 (2007), 159–178.

7   *Desai, R./Olofsgaard, A.:* Constitutionalism and Credibility in Reforming Economies, in: Economics of Transition, 14/3 (2006), 479–504.

8   See, among others, *Buchanan, J.,* op cit., *Vanberg, V.,* op cit., as well as *Persson, T./Tabellini, G.:* The Economic Effects of Constitutions, Cambridge/London, 2003.

on German law going back to the interwar and earlier periods was sustained. Second, following the gradual liberalisation of the post-1962 period, legal forms allowed for actual – economic and personal – freedoms to evolve. Examples of this are the Enterprise Law of 1977, allowing for major decentralising reforms in the 1980s, the liberalisation of the second economy in 1982 or the Transformation Law of 1988, allowing for the spontaneous privatisation of assets. Finally, those in power developed a sense of being constrained by legal forms and procedures.

This state of affairs differed greatly from that in other communist countries. Supported by the small freedoms of Kádárism, such as the relatively liberal travel arrangements or the respect for privacy, this paved the way to what was later termed the "negotiated revolution" in the 1989/90 period.[9] It also allowed for the National Round Table Talks during this period, which resulted in a complete regime change without adopting a new constitution.[10] For this reason, Hungary did not receive a new basic law, but rather it had to be content with the revised and improved edition of the 1949 version.

It is very telling that both the old and the new constitutional arrangements that key features of the political order such as the guarantee of property rights, personal freedoms and the multiparty system could be incorporated into what many still consider a "Stalinist" construct. On the other hand, the Hungarian political elites have obviously missed the window of opportunity to act as Founding Fathers and lay the basis of a free economy and free society for the decades to come. The "negotiated" transition has also contributed to the lack of catharsis among both common people and the political class. The switch to democracy and a market economy was conspicuously non-violent, almost "everyday-like". Therefore the petty work of political and economic transformation, including the launching of painful reforms, could not be compensated for by the euphoria about regained freedoms.

For the early period this remained a seemingly negligible circumstance since the outgoing regime had already legislated much of what was needed in terms of property ownership and privatisation. The independence of the Central Bank could be created by a mere amendment of the Law on the National Bank in 1991 and via a minor modification of the Law on Financing Public Debt in 1997 (that practically prohibited the monetisation of fiscal deficits by interdicting direct financing of government imbalances). However, as soon as the policy consensus

---

9   *Tőkés, R. L.*: Hungary's Negotiated Revolution, Cambridge/New York, 1997.
10 Cf. in more detail *Bozóki, A.* (ed.): The Roundtable Talks of 1989. The Genesis of Hungarian Democracy, Budapest/New York, 2002.

of the 1990s gave way to left- and right-wing populism without a "*Stabilitäts-kultur*" having materialised within the economics profession or in the broader public, the practice of doctoring statistics and creative accounting proliferated.[11]

It is common knowledge that several of the "old" EU member states have also been found guilty of "creative accounting", from France to Greece and, notoriously, Italy. However, references to the malpractices of others do not exempt us from the consequences of our own misdeeds. The Hungarian public has been ill-informed about the actual state of affairs and has thus not been able to make deliberate public choices. Investors have been misled too. And last but not least, the well-known crowding-out effect of public deficits has triggered a slowdown in growth, irrespective of contemporary accounting tricks.

For this reason one could have argued for introducing fiscal rules along the lines of the practice that was spreading in a number of developed and developing countries in the second half of the 1990s.[12] Introducing fiscal rules alone may or may not be conducive to more disciplined and sound public finance. Without getting into the nitty-gritty of this issue let us note that anchoring sound policies in the constitution, as in Poland, might be a rather resolute way of tying the hands of politicians and ensuring that inevitable controversies do not derail the fundamentals of economic policy. In this regard, the speaking silence of the Hungarian Constitution could perhaps be seen as omission at least, and shortcoming at worst.

Even fragmentary evidence for the democratic period may be indicative of the relevance of this issue. First, recurring attempts have been made, primarily, though, by no means exclusively, originating within the Hungarian Socialist Party and intellectuals close to it, to create a new constitution. It would have implemented two major changes:

- First, regressing to the idea to set up a bicameral system which was discussed by the National Round Table but overtaken by the political processes culminating in the free parliamentary elections of 1990. Adherents to this institutional option perceive it as a counterweight to what they consider as "partocracy" and to the majoritarian structure of the lower house.
- Second, creating a safeguard for social rights, seen by many as being threatened by marketising reforms. The latter can, in fact, lead to an ever-exploding budg-

---

11 *Csaba, L.*: Between Transition and EU Accession: Hungary at the Millennium, in: Europe-Asia Studies, 52/2 (2000), 805–828.

12 See *Kopits, G.*: Fiscal Responsibility Framework: International Experience and Implications for Hungary, National Bank of Hungary, MNB Occasional Papers 62, Budapest, 2006 (available online under www.mnb.hu).

et, since rights not covered by revenue intakes might be relegated to a formality. If enforceable via courts, these never allow the fiscal stance to be restrictive.

The political relevance of these abstract considerations has been shown through the rulings of the Constitutional Court. This body has actually taken over the role of an upper house, counterbalancing the tyranny of the 50 percent plus one vote in the legislature. This role perhaps started with the ruling against "serving historic justice" in 1991, not allowing for retroactive legislation to purge the ex-communists from public life. More importantly from the economic perspective was the ruling against restitution of property, which had been the major agenda point – if not the single issue – of the then governing Smallholders' Party. By enforcing financial compensation instead of returning confiscated property, the Court directly meddled in shaping political institutions and policy choices. Likewise, the 1993 ruling on municipalities that declared these to be fully-fledged property owners has made any centralisation of state administration impossible. It also pre-empted the attempts to leave the local municipalities without assets in the process of privatisation, and has therefore had important implications for the outcomes of this process. Last but perhaps most conspicuously, the Constitutional Court, through a series of rulings, revoked the structural reform components of the *Bokros* adjustment package of 1995, thereby setting clear limits to what the parliamentary majority of the day and the executive can deliver in terms of systemic change by a mere fiat.

While the activism of the first Constitutional Court (1990–1999) was perhaps inevitable since the nature of the Round Table Talks and the hectic pace of the events tended to overtake everybody, improvisation, ad-hoc legislation and the resultant incoherence among the various economic subsystems as well as between the economy and society could not be avoided either. The Court has assisted in spelling out the spirit of the Constitution through interpretations. And although it would be hard to deny that judges have – sometimes changing – political preferences, in the long run this gradual and continual evolution of constitutionalism has basically been a plus in creating an open economy and an open society.

However, the rulings on the *Bokros* adjustment package already underlined the paradox we are trying to address here. While by 1995 the immediate transformation of a reform socialist economy into a market economy had basically been accomplished, as reflected by Hungary's admission to the OECD (an organisation precisely checking this quality), it would have been premature to state that the new market order in all of its finesse had already been created. Therefore, one could argue both in favour of and against the adjustment package introducing structural measures going way beyond what is needed by any version of stabilisation. Adherents of the *Bokros* package have rightly emphasised the economic component, i.e. that only structural reforms allow for the sustainable adjustment of economic processes.[13] These imply changing rather than protecting the *status quo ante*, in social and economic terms alike. By contrast, opponents of the package, including the strong majority of the Constitutional Court, formulated equally weighty criteria about stability, predictability and transparency as being fundamental principles of rule of law in general and in and for the economy in particular. Arguing along those lines, the Court, in a series of rulings in 1995–1997, basically revoked most of the structural measures, such as tuition fees for universities and the payments for health services, and it curbed a number of social transfers, including pensions.

In short, given the parsimonious wording of the Hungarian Constitution on economic matters, which was due to the conditions of its inception, it has allowed not only for competing, but positively conflicting interpretations. It has not anchored any clear set of policies to be conducted, such as price stability or social rights. For this reason, as we have tried to indicate in the sketchy list of major rulings by the Court, it has not become an obstacle to systemic change, as was the surviving Soviet Constitution for Russia in its first period of stabilisation (1991–1994) when such support would have been most needed. Meanwhile, it has also not precluded the regress to policies that were oriented towards the *status quo* rather than towards developing a mature and competitive market order.

III. Europeanisation – the Overrated Promise

One commonplace to be found in the academic and polical analyses of the 1990s and early 2000s has been the belief, developed into an axiom, that Europeanisation is likely to represent a fundamental moulding factor for all countries engaging in systemic change, but particularly for new EU member states. This top-down approach tended to put the emphasis on the leverage of the Union, highlighting the various dimensions of influence the old members had on new ones.[14]

---

13 See *Kornai, J.*: Adjustment without Recession: A Case Study of Hungarian Stabilization, in: Zecchini, S. (ed.): Lessons from the Economic Transition, Dordrecht et al., 1997, 123–152; *Antal, J.*: A kiigazítás- ahogy én látom [The Adjustment Programme as Seen by an Insider], in: Közgazdasági Szemle, 44/2 (1998), 97–122.

14 This view was emphatically expressed by *Schimmelfennig, F./Engert, S./Knobel, H.*: International Socialization in Europe: European Organization, Political Conditionality and Democratic Change, New York, 2006.

Furthermore, much of the literature on the then candidate countries interpreted the EU attempts to transplant their arrangements and check institutional quality, both during *acquis*-screening and accession talk, as a quasi-colonial attempt to restrain the freedom of choice for new democracies from among the "varieties of capitalism".[15]

Against this background it might be surprising to see the resurgence of popu-list policies in the new member states in the first few years of the 21st century and their relapse into policies that were thought to have ended with the EU accession process. This applies to assertive Polish foreign policy stances as much as to Hun-garian laxity and its lagging behind in the economic arena. The latter will now be our subject for analysing the impact of constitutionalism.

Dovetailing supranational legislation with domestic traditions of EU member states has never been an easy task. The Karlsruhe ruling on the Maastricht Treaty and many other judgments indicated that old members also have their troubles in managing the interaction. For the new member states, a number of specificities have emerged.[16] Furthermore, the coordination process has become even more complex because of the political stalemate within the EU-15 that emerged by the time accession became politically feasible. Some of the most important items include the boycott of Austria in 2001, the disagreement about Afghanistan and even more about Iraq, the meagre deal in Nice, the equally minor results of the Constitutional Convention and finally the rejection of the Constitutional Treaty in 2005 and its planned replacement by a Treaty in 2008; all these events indicate that the implementation capacity of the EU, i.e. the most important feature of any institution,[17] has been severely constrained by issues that do not relate to enlarge-ment and the related distributional conflicts. As a result, the idea of the "supre-macy" of EU law has been replaced by a reference to its "primacy" over national law, rendering it a contested domain. As a consequence, the top-down controlling and guiding functions of EMU arrangements could not exert their influence either in law or in fiscal policy.

Let us address the major areas where Europeanisation could have brought about a breakthrough in the more recent past. First and foremost the entire constitutional order, primarily major components of the legal system, could and

15 *Dyson, K.* (ed.): Enlarging the Euro Area: External Empowerment and Domestic Transformation in East Central Europe, New York, 2006.

16 See *Vörös, I.*: Legal Doctrine and Legal Policy Aspects of EU Accession, in: Acta Iuridica, 44/3–4 (2003), 141–163.

17 See *North, D.*: Institutions, Institutional Change and Economic Performance, Cambridge/New York, 1990.

should have been adjusted with an eye to deepening. The *acquis communautaire* started to develop in an unprecedented manner following the Maastricht Treaty and the evolution of the three-pillar system. Also the silent, covert but continuous evolution of Community legislation, arising partly from the actions of the European Commission as policy entrepreneur and partly from policies of various pressure groups, often without explicit authorisation, resulted in the establishment and gradual implementation of a wide variety of policies at the EU level.[18] The fields that have emerged over the past 15 years include legislation relating to society, the environment, the defence arm of the EU with extraterritorial peace-keeping missions and, more recently, energy.[19]

These developments could not have taken the new members by surprise because the structured dialogue, launched at the Essen Council of 1994, already involved all ministries besides finance and foreign affairs in the consultations. While the educatory impact of this intergovernmental dialogue could hardly be overestimated, *legal harmonisation* has not lead to that level of congruity and forward-lookingness that one could optimistically have expected. In short, it has not been only about economic and other vested interest, but about broader concerns. Despite the two separate rounds of *acquis*-screening and accession negotiations in 1998–2002 and beyond, the influence of EU arrangements has remained partial, and *anticipatory adaptation* of domestic rules and policies has remained fragmentary at best.

One of the reasons for this has been the technical and substantial difficulties involved in the complex process of legal harmonisation.[20] This has to do with the very nature of the EU, which both at the constitutional and the political level (*Verfassungswirklichkeit*) continues to be much more an association of compound states[21] than a federation with central powers to enforce any legal norm. While the latter might well be derived from the basically (though by no means exclusively) intergovernmentalist structure of the EU, the evolution of policies is indicative of the presence of the contrary processes as well. However, without reference to the political stalemate and the ensuing implementation deficit referred to above (that has nothing to do with Eastern enlargement, having pre-

18 Cf. *Wallace, H./Wallace, W./Pollack, M.* (eds.): Policy-Making in the European Union, 5th ed., Oxford/ New York, 2005.

19 On the latter cf. *European Commission:* Green Paper on Market-based Instruments for Environment and Related Policy Purposes, COM (2007) 140 final of 28.03.2007.

20 See in more detail *Vörös, I.,* op. cit.

21 *Blankart, C.:* The EU: Confederation, Federation or Association of Compound States?, in: Constitutional Political Economy, 18/2 (2007), 99–106.

ceded it in the old member states during the period from 1998 to 2004), one could not convincingly interpret the foot-dragging observable in the new members.

In short, the bad example of the old members has proven much too easy to emulate. As long as the political class uses European forums as a theatre for their respective domestic electorates rather than focusing on visions and modalities of managing future challenges, it is perhaps overambitious to expect, as the present writer tended to, new members not to follow suit but to adopt the stance of the Founding Fathers and focus on issues that might be solved only through common effort. In this concept the unwillingness of the Hungarian Constitutional Court to give up its gatekeeper function and quasi-automatically condone the primacy of European law over domestic[22] is rather the expected outcome. All the more so since, in the earlier phase, the well-known lawyer, *Barna Berke* already won a precedent case in the late 1990s. In that ruling, the Court declared that, contrary to the political atmosphere of the day, the process of legal harmonisation should *not* lead to the automatic adoption of EU competition norms in the pre-accession period. While in both cases the major argument was the need to retain the internal coherence of domestic legal arrangements, which is *per se* valid, a different viewpoint emerges from the economic perspective: that of the missed opportunity to import a set of rules which already perform relatively well and with a credibility and enforceability way beyond any local arrangement, not least owing to the practice of the European Court of Justice in Luxembourg.

A second area where Europeanisation could have been expected to have immediate influence is monetary policy. Ever since Maastricht and the implementation of the EMU, monetary policy has been centralised in the hands of the European Central Bank. Because the new members were precluded from the option of opt-outs by the Amsterdam Treaty of 1997, they acceded with the commitment to join the Monetary Union. In a way the conditions applying to them are stricter than those for Britain or Denmark.

Here again, theoretical assumptions and policy considerations have been clashing. In short, economic theory is unequivocally in favour of any small open economy joining a monetary union. The more we realise the pre-eminent role of fiscal flows in setting exchange rates and interest rates in a global interaction of markets operating 24/7, the less meaningful we find the conventional terms "exchange rate policy" or "interest rate policy", implying a major deliberative

22 *Sajó, A.*: Learning Cooperative Constitutionalism the Hard Way: the Hungarian Constitutional Court Shying Away from EU Supremacy, in: Zeitschrift für Staats- und Europawissenschaften (ZSE), 2/3 (2004), 351–371.

component on the side of policy makers. The reign of the bipolar view in financial economics, considering either monetary union or free floating as the only viable and sustainable long-term alternatives, renders further discussion at this point superfluous. By implication, giving up two non-instrumental policy tools does not count as a major sacrifice for any small open economy.

It follows that it was only logical that Hungarians and foreign investors alike expected the speediest possible adoption of the euro. This would have required fiscal consolidation and the copying of the monetary arrangements of Community law. In reality, a different story emerged, and formal professional opposition to the considerations outlined above was demonstrably negligible. First, the independence of the National Bank of Hungary (NBH), though guaranteed by the 2001 edition of the law on central banking, has not been anchored in the Constitution, unlike the status of the ECB that has been enshrined in the successive EU treaties. As a consequence, the practical meaning of this independence has been open to interpretation. As long as successive governments adopted an increasingly populist line, central bank independence remained a nuisance. For this reason, a series of measures were passed, especially in the 2003–2006 period, leading to a narrow interpretation. First, with reference to the legal status of the Bank as a corporation, a supervisory board was established. Second, fiscal policies that were out of line with the inflation-targeting regime adopted by the NBH have been continued. Increasing VAT rates in 2004, decreasing them in 2005 and re-increasing them in 2006 were only the tip of the iceberg. Third, policy disagreements between fiscal and monetary authorities went public, with the pro-government press conducting a series of unfounded attacks on the political motives of the NBH. Fourth, as a consequence, in 2004 the supreme decision-making body of the Bank was expanded to include experts close to the government line. While these mishaps are being corrected in the 2007–2008 period, this is an outcome of selecting a highly esteemed commercial banker to the post of the Governor, a person who also has an extremely cordial relationship with the Premier. In other words, the rituals of the EU, including public interventions of the ECB, have not proven to be instrumental in pre-empting derailments.

It is an important technicality that, contrary to the ECB, the National Bank of Hungary has been sticking to the regime of inflation-targeting (IT), while the ECB adheres to its two-pillar strategy.[23] IT is in line with the fashion in financial economics, although clear IT regimes are being practised in countries like Britain,

---

[23] *Issing, O./Angeloni, I./Gaspar, V.*: Decision-Making in the European Central Bank, 2nd ed., Cambridge/New York, 2004.

Chile and New Zeeland, who are currently not aspiring for EMU membership. Inflation targets, constantly 3 percent per annum, have been regularly missed, and there are no chances of meeting it before 2009,[24] which is a poor performance of eight consecutive years.

As a consequence, and after a series of postponements, Hungary was forced to give up the original entry date to the euro by mid-2006. In short, EU membership has not armed the NBH to withstand fiscal policy fluctuations and thus enhance the expected credibility. Therefore, financial markets reacted to this astounding move rather condoningly, reflecting the credibility problem mentioned above.

The third area in which Europeanisation has had an impact is fiscal policy. In any monetary union, but especially in one constructed without prior political integration, fiscal policy is by definition a matter of common concern. Economic debates preceding the adoption of the euro amply demonstrated this point, leading to the famous non-bailout close in the Maastricht Treaty and it successors. This means that tolerating fiscal laxity is by no means an option since this would trigger reactions from the financial markets or translate into higher inflation in non-trespassing countries. While the efficiency of these arrangements has proven to be questionable in practice since financial markets failed to punish obvious non-compliance in old and new EU members alike in 2004–2007, this does not invalidate the objective existence of the interrelationship. This is the rationale of sustaining the various processes of policy coordination and control, including the convergence and stability programmes and their assessment by the Commission and the Council (Ecofin), the regular analyses from ECB and the involvement of the Council in debating economic matters and measures.

From this perspective, the application of the common fiscal framework, i.e. the Stability and Growth Pact, could have been seen as legitimate and practical, even following its re-interpretation in March 2005.[25] In short, two overlapping considerations may be advanced. First, conducting sound fiscal policies by avoiding the explosion of public debt is simply common-sense economics conducted not for the sake of gaining approval from any external agency but for its own virtue and uses. Second, being a candidate for the single currency immediately implies that efforts for compliance arise from the country's own efforts rather than only from external pressure.

---

24 *MNB [National Bank of Hungary]:* Inflációs jelntés-frissítés [An Update on the Report on Inflation], Budapest, August 2007 (available online under www.mnb.hu).

25 A more detailed analysis can be found in *Csaba, L.*: The New Political Economy of Emerging Europe, 2nd, revised and updated ed., Budapest, 2007, Chapters 8 and 9.

It is of course true that precisely in the period immediately before and after Hungary's entrance into the EU, large countries were regularly flouting the Stability and Growth Pact (SGB). As long as they could get away with it without even the famous "naming and shaming", governments were given the incentive to drift into populist economic policies and the precedent was created. Observing the mismatch, insightful analysts called for complementing the joint framework of SGP with national fiscal rules.[26] These have indeed been effective in a number of countries, such as Sweden, but they have remained non-existent in most new members except Poland, where a constitutional amendment in 1999 contained a provision about the automatic measures and procedures to be taken if public debt were to exceed 50 percent of GDP. However, in the case of Hungary, no such rules exist.

It might be legitimate to object that fiscal discipline is an outcome of a broad socio-economic process, in which the culture of fiscal soundness, transparency and trust among major players are formative in ensuring the outcomes.[27] In this line of reasoning, one may well get away with or without rules. For instance, in the 2000s Romania has conducted sound policies without formal rules. By contrast, elaborate procedures in Germany could not stop the country from non-compliance with Maastricht in a series of years.

From the perspective of the literature on Europeanisation, one could have expected that constitutional modifications would anchor sound public finances in the basic law of the country. This also seemed to be possible given the fact that in 2000–2002 public debt was way below the line of 51–53 percent of GDP, and deficits were also in the range of 5 percent.[28] Since growth was also around 5 percent, this could, in theory, have been the ideal time for fiscal adjustment. Reference to EU accession and the ensuing need to regularise fiscal affairs could have been a handy argument, and the "EU consensus" among various elite factions was widespread. Moreover, fiscal adjustment, if implemented under conditions of liberalising markets and social cooperation, does not necessarily imply costs in terms of production and employment. Although comparative analysis has indi-

---

26 *Buti, M./Franco, D.*: Fiscal Policy in a Monetary Union, Cheltenham/Northampton, 2005.

27 *Győrffy, D.*: Democracy and Deficits, Budapest, 2007.

28 Current reporting and final numbers often do not overlap, and the difference was significant until this practice was discontinued in August 2006. There was also a cleaning-up procedure in both election years, when misreporting of preceding years were discontinued. Although the latter may evoke the impression of a political business cycle (*Nordhaus, W.*: The Political Business Cycle, in: Review of Economic Studies, 42/1 (1975), 169–190), it is not the case. Deducing those one-time items deficits in the range of 6 percent in 2002 and 7 percent for 2006 remains, whose average is just equal to the consolidated average for the 1991–2006 period.

cated that the growth-generating/expansionary effect could not be proven, the contractionary effect can unambiguously be excluded under Hungarian conditions.[29]

However, if anything, the opposite of the normative view has happened. Between 2001 and 2007, governments were involved in populist redistribution policies. Therefore, the adoption of fiscal rules seemed anything but urgent to them. This applied to the post-election time of 2002 and 2006 and to the historic opportunity of May 2004 when accession, after 15 years of laborious efforts, finally occurred. Meanwhile, the Law on Public Finance was re-interpreted so that none of the corrective measures of its stipulations, such as the obligation to submit a supplementary budget to the legislation, ever needed to be applied. For instance in 2002, when the reported current deficit exceeded 9 percent, a re-interpretation of the Law made the formal submission of a supplementary budget obligatory only if the difference between planned and actual figures exceeded 5 percent of expenditures. Given that the majority of the day is always ready to accept a modification of fiscal targets during the year, even as late as in November, it would require an extreme exigency, such as an earthquake or a war on the territory of the country, for this to happen. Ex-post evaluation of the fiscal target and performance by the State Audit Office is normally conducted with empty rows of seats in Parliament. No politician or official has ever suffered from the consequences of the often sweeping criticism of the office, which has been public all the time. As a final consequence, general deficit ballooned to 9.6 percent by 2006 and 6.4 percent by 2007, and public debt reached 71 percent of GDP by 2007, with very gradual improvements possible in the years to come due to increasing international rates of interest.[30]

In short, a series of other policy areas could have been immediately affected. These include the rule of law and the spread of law-abiding behaviour. In reality, the latter has not happened, and the state, as exemplified by fiscal policy, has been one of the major actors in setting the bad example. Improvisations on granting or not granting concessions to foreign investors, delaying the payment of the 13th-month wage for public-sector employees and the 13th-month pension to pensioners, the two accounting for about 4.2 million persons in a country of ten million, are just the best known examples. Continuous and incoherent changes in taxes, public dues and other items of regulation, such as employment and safety

---

29 See *Benczes, I.*: Trimming the Sails. European Fiscal Reforms from a Hungarian Perspective, Budapest/ New York, 2008.
30 *MNB,* op. cit.

conditions, together with red tape, non-transparency and allegations about corruption are among the major hindrances that limit the growth of the new private sector, i. e. small and medium firms.[31] Recent attempts to conduct "patriotic economic policies" along French, Spanish and Italian lines, protecting through a special law "strategic" firms from takeover by those disliked by the government,[32] in open defiance of the basic principle of the single market, also do not bode well for the spread of law-abiding behaviour.

Likewise, recurrent tendencies of the governmental majority of the day to reinterpret any legislation in their own favour, especially those regulations that would constrain the majority's freedom to manoeuvre, are reasons for concern. Nominations for the organs overseeing public media, non-nomination of persons to positions where they could exert restraining influence, such as the post of ombudsman, judges of the Constitutional Court and even of the attorney general, are rather well publicised cases in point.

In matters of environmental policy the introduction of Community legislation has been slow, partial and delayed.[33] This sector's share of total public expenditure has been constantly decreasing since 2002 when accession negotiations were concluded. Despite a government's avowed good intention, its spending is the way to measure its actual priorities. And while private sector involvement in building waste-processing works or even supplying water has been an established practice, this only mildens lacking public sector involvement.

Finally, the influence of Europeanisation in social affairs has been limited. While the EU in general has no significant competences over social matters, discursive elements, policy evolution and rulings of the European Court of Justice have created a field for interaction. In the case of Hungary, social legislation tends to be lax and labour market regulations liberal. However, in recent years a number of new regulations emerged, such as the higher compulsory minimum wage for university leavers, limiting the opening hours of supermarket chains, or the fight against illegal employment. These changes have usually followed domestic policy considerations rather than any immediate influence of European forums, be they consultative or formal.

---

31 Cf. the extensive analysis published recently by the *Ministry of the Economy and Transport (GKM):* A kis-és középvállalatok helyzete, 2005–2006. Éves jelentés. [Annual Report on the State of Small and Medium Enterprises, 2005–2006], Budapest, August 2007.

32 See more on that in the editorial of the business weekly Figyelő, 36 (2007).

33 The Urban Waste Water Directive will be fully employable only after 20 years, i. e. 2022.

IV. Balance Sheet and Perspectives

What we have seen until now provides at least partly unexpected answers to the question raised in the title of this contribution. First, constitutionalism has not proven to be a formative idea in Hungary, despite the rather strong neo-liberal traits of the social science literature and even policy discourse in the nearly two decades of systemic change. This is a finding that may be generalised, with the usual caveats, to other new EU members as well. Second, Europeanisation, espe- cially its top-down component usually (over-)emphasised in the literature in general and on Eastern enlargement in particular, has also proven to be a largely toothless lion. The availability of EU funds – the material component – or the enthusiasm for overcoming the uncertainties of the post-1920 period and joining the great work of European construction – the ideational component – have both had insufficient impact on the conduct of actual policy-making. The latter component followed – so our third insight – its own closed, self-referential logic, rather than the norms of economics, law or political science. In matters of fiscal policy and law-abiding behaviour, it even failed to follow the basic interest of an acceding country.

Fourth, as a consequence, economic change has proven to be much less of a success story than it could have been expected. Although this finding cannot be generalised, it is not entirely surprising. Notoriously lax fiscal policies inevitably lead, as we have seen, to the crowding out of private investment. Increasing the role of the state in terms of expenditure leads to efficiency losses and limitations to the bottom-up development of the private sector and the supply side in gen- eral. Giving up the entry date to the Eurozone has opened the drift in policy- making. It has also left reform deliberations without a macroeconomic anchor and a time frame. The choice has thus been clearly counterproductive, especially seen in the broader context. Both sustainable high rates of growth and financial stability could only have benefited from an early adoption of the single currency. EU arrangements have proven to be inefficient to counteract the drift coming from domestic policies. While the final, fifth insight is by no means peculiar to new EU member states, its ramifications are perhaps weightier for those in need of a better quality regulatory frame for their global competitiveness.

On balance, the competences and the practice of the Hungarian Constitution- al Court has not followed the ideas of the new political economy cited at the outset. The Court has continued to meddle in a variety of current affairs, while it has proven unable to strengthen the basic features of the socio-economic order against the political cycle to the ideal degree. This applies especially to monetary and fiscal institutions and the enforcement of the idea of the rule of law.

Future options contain partial though potentially important improvement in the two major problem areas, fiscal and monetary policies. In fiscal policy the years of procrastination, the growing burden of debt and the despair of markets about being able to join the safe haven of the Eurozone any time soon have made the need for regularising public finance an imperative. There is a need for broader insights into the need for transparency and for rules guiding fiscal decisions in the course of the daily ups and downs of democratic politics.[34]

In September 2007, the President of the Republic convened all parties represented in Parliament in order to agree upon introducing fiscal rules, new institutions and legislative procedures meant to ensure the coherence of fiscal planning and avoid recurring public debt and overspending. In order to attain this, modifications to the Constitution are being discussed that would provide the fiscal authority and planning process with the anchor that has been missing up to now. However, the first public statements made by those participating have already raised doubts about the viability of the entire project in bringing about major and sustainable improvements in public finance. These improvements are a must if the single currency is ever to be introduced under the existing criteria.

The government's original proposal of July 2007, as published on the website of the Ministry of Finance,[35] is a mere compilation of existing alternatives, without prioritising any of the available options. Following the announcement of the Premier in April 2007, an Office of the Budget modelled on its American counterpart is being created to help create consistency in fiscal plans. However, it is well known that the fiscal performance of the USA was dismal in 2000–2007, leading to the greenback losing half its purchasing power against the single currency in the period under scrutiny. The Congressional Budget Office is not even meant to create a counterweight to the improvisations of the administration and of the legislature, the major sources of fiscal imbalances in any democracy.

While experts have advocated the introduction of stiff quantitative and procedural norms to streamline the budgeting process,[36] actual policies seem to have moved in a different direction. Not only is the new institution toothless, but also no other institution will be in a position to crosscheck the consistency of fiscal

---

34 *Cosidine, J./Duffy, D.*: Partially Sighted Persons and the Public Debt Elephant, in: Constitutional Political Economy, 17/4 (2006), 237–249.

35 See www.pm.gov.hu.

36 *Kopits, G.* (ed.): Rules-Based Fiscal Policy in Emerging Economies, New York, 2004; *Romhányi, B.*: Reforming Fiscal Rules and Institutions in Hungary, in: Public Finance Quarterly, 52/2 (2007), 341–376.

plans with medium-term targets. Setting these targets in a continuous updating of the EU convergence programmes remains basically disconnected from the annual fiscal planning and its ongoing modifications. Neither the State Audit Office nor the parliamentary committee on fiscal affairs has the right and the expertise to control *ex ante* the coherence of fiscal plans. Their opinion is by no means binding on the governmental majority.

In terms of monetary policy, the correction of previous misdeeds is in the making. At the time of writing, a joint committee of the Bank and the Ministry of Finance has even been set up to elaborate the trajectory and technicalities of introducing the euro. Quite tellingly, the Minister of Finance also stressed that the government continues not to set a fixed date for introducing the single currency.[37] This might be a problem insofar as the crux of the political economy of the euro is to gain credibility through timing and calculable actions that trigger those reforms and adjustment that are needed to qualify.

In light of the improvements reported above it is instructive to see the evident impact of Europeanisation, as Hungary does not dare to be left out of core EU policies. That is, the possibility to shape decisions is at least as significant as the reverse influence, that of the European fiscal and monetary framework on domestic arrangements. It is important to observe that flouting the SGP has not led, as many feared, to its disintegration. On the contrary, in 2006 and 2007 France, Germany and Greece adopted measures to ensure gradual compliance with the fiscal targets. By the same token, Hungary also faced the core options, i.e. being left out or adjusting to the common goals.

In the other fields listed in the previous section, the impact of Europeanisation also remains significant and favourable, especially if complemented by domestic efforts. Among these efforts, the ongoing activist stance of the Constitutional Court deserves special appreciation. Through a series of its rulings nullifying improvisational policies of the government, the Court continues to develop what many consider an unwritten constitution. In so doing, the judges follow the insights from new political economy[38] that highlight the enormous relevance of case law even under continental systems since rulings create trial-and-error processes, whereby legislation that is able to meet public preferences may and does emerge.[39]

---

37 As reported in *Világgazdaság,* 13 September 2007.
38 *Gennaidi, N./Shleifer, A.*: The Evolution of Common Law, in: Journal of Political Economy, 115/1 (2007), 43–68.
39 The authors term this as *Cardoso* law, referring to the Brazilian case in which a series of politically biased rulings have finally added up to legislation of a much better quality than before.

Also in other areas, such as competition policy, environmental policy and social policy, the slow, evolutionary change and the possibility to rely on the European Court of Justice as final arbiter allows for the continuous improvement and harmonisation of Hungarian institutions and policies. The higher the probability of overcoming the political impasse that culminated in the Dutch and French rejection of the Constitutional Treaty, the more palpable these results might be in the non-economic areas in the years to come. And the better the quality of institutions and policies, the bigger the potential gain, both for Hungary and the Community, in terms of competitiveness, growth and welfare. In this way, the objectives on which the entire process of systemic change has been focused could be realised.

The Institutionalisation of Representative Democracy in Korea, 1948–2007

by Yong-duck Jung and Cheongsin Kim

I. Introduction

The institutionalisation of representative democracy in Korea began with the establishment of the First Republic in 1948. However, this process has not proceeded smoothly during the past 60 years, as can be clearly seen in the changing key functions of the parliament (National Assembly) and in its relationship to the executive branch.

Before the establishment of the Republic, parliamentary sovereignty did not exist either as an idea or as actual practice in this country.[1] Korea's modernisation, which started in the late 19th century, was pursued by political and bureaucratic elites rather than by the common people.[2] Based on the institutional legacy which was formed during the process of modernisation from above, the Republic of Korea, from its very beginnings, was established as an administrative state.

This article analyses the changes in the key functions of the National Assembly and its politico-administrative relationship with the executive branch since the establishment of the First Republic in 1948. In doing so, it explores the characteristics of the evolution of representative democracy in a country that started off as an administrative state.[3]

II. Legislation

Legislation is supposedly one of the key functions that a legislature conducts. In general, there is a tendency to regard parliament as the core body of legislative power to ensure the authority and the binding power of laws made in democratic states. In reality, however, no country or political system grants legislative power exclusively to the legislative branch. For instance, constitutional revisions may be

---

1 *Goldsworthy, J.*: The Sovereignty of Parliament: History and Philosophy, Oxford, 1999.
2 *Jung, Y.*: Stateness in Transition: the Korean Case in Comparative Perspective, in: Zeitschrift für Staats- und Europawissenschaften (ZSE), 3/3 (2005), 410–433.
3 Parts of this contribution rely on *Kim, C./Jung, D.*: Institutionalizing the National Assembly in Korea 1948–2006, in: Korean Journal of Public Administration, 44/4 (2006), 91–129 (in Korean).

carried out by referendums, such as in Ireland, or by constitutional convention (e.g., in Belgium). In France, administrative officials often enact legal regulations based on decrees. American presidents can exercise veto power on bills passed in Congress. And the European Parliament's decision-making powers have been confined by those of the Council of Ministers from the very beginning.

Even in the case in which the legislative branch performs legislative functions, it is not always done autonomously. In most countries, the legislative branch passively conducts its legislative function by vetoing or amending bills established by the executive branch, mostly within a limited scope. Even in the American Congress, often regarded as the most independent and influential policy-maker in the world, more than 80 % of the bills to be reviewed are submitted by the president. In the case of Japan, which operates a parliamentary system of government, more than 90 % of the bills are submitted by the executive branch. Passive legislative power, an alternative for not being able to be more active, such as the right to veto or amend bills submitted by the executive branch, is executed within a very limited scope. In the United Kingdom, there are very few cases in which bills submitted by the executive branch are not passed by the government majority in the House of Commons.[4] In France, on the other hand, the number of bills proposed by the National Assembly is nearly eight times that submitted by the executive branch. However, the parliamentary bills adopted amount to only 5 % of those submitted by the executive branch. Moreover, the right to determine whether to refer the bill deliberated by the respective parliamentary committee to the Assembly is not assigned to the committee, but to the executive branch.[5]

1. Law and Administrative Order

In order to identify the relative proportion of legislative functions performed by the National Assembly and the executive branch in Korea, the following analysis refers to the relative proportions of laws and administrative orders (i. e., presidential decrees, the prime minister's decrees, or ministerial ordinances). In Korea, laws must be enacted by the National Assembly, whereas administrative orders can be established by the executive branch.

The number of laws and orders continuously increased from 1974 to 2006 (*Figure 1*). This can be interpreted as being a result of the expansion of government functions during this period. The National Assembly enacted 629 laws in

---

4   *Heywood, A.*: Politics, Basingstoke, 1997, 298.
5   *Macridis, R. C.*: Modern Political Systems, Englewood Cliffs, 1987, 98; *Rossetto, J.*: Les institutions politiques de la France, Paris, 1992, 151.

1973 and 1,145 laws in 2006. However, 1.5 times as many administrative orders were enacted in 2006 as compared to 1973: 1,762 in 1973 and 2,873 in 2006. In total, the number of laws enacted always accounted for less than 30 % of the total number of legal regulations.

Figure 1: Number of Laws and Administrative Orders Made in Korea, 1973–2006

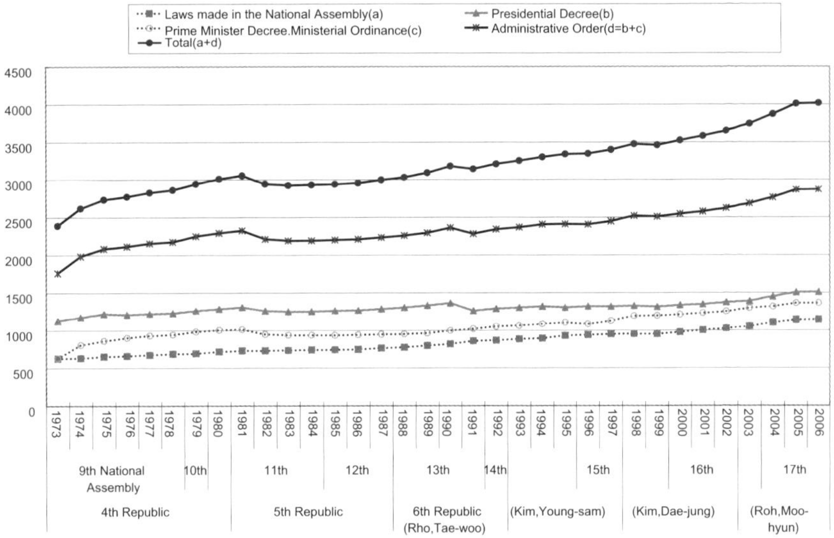

Source: Authors' compilation based on data from *Ministry of Government Legislation: The Fifty Years' History of Korean Legislation,* 1999, 2253–2256 (in Korean); *idem: The Legal Statistics,* annually (www.moleg.go.kr; in Korean).

2. Bill Submissions and Resolutions by the National Assembly

With respect to the draft laws proposed in the National Assembly, the periods when the number of bills proposed by parliamentary representatives exceeded those submitted by the executive branch have been much shorter than the opposite case (*Figure 2*). In particular, the number of bills proposed by parliamentarians was lowest under the authoritarian governments during the military junta (1961–1963), the Fourth Republic (1972–1980) and the Fifth Republic (1980–1987).

Furthermore, more bills submitted by the executive branch were passed than those proposed by members of Parliament. *Figure 2* shows that the relative proportions of bills passed among those submitted by the National Assembly and the executive branch are similar to the respective number of draft laws.

Figure 2: Bills Proposed to the Korean National Assembly, 1948–2004

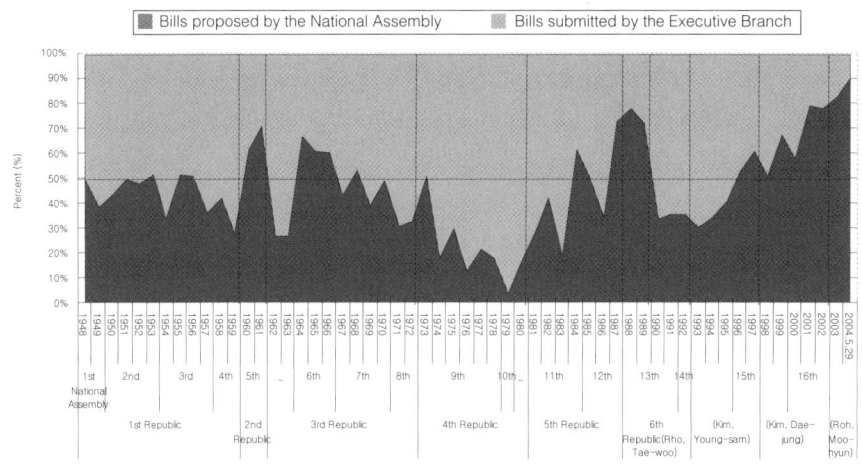

Source: Authors' compilation based on data from the Legislative Information System (likms.assembly.go.kr/bill).

The budget statement indicating the budget required for bills proposed by the National Assembly has been made faithfully since 2003, the second half-period of the 16th Korean National Assembly.[6] An analysis of only the 16th National Assembly (2000–2004) shows that the approval ratio of bills proposed by parliamentarians was 27.0 % while the approval ratio of the bills on attaching the budget statement was even lower (*Table 1*).

Table 1: Approval Ratio of the Bills Proposed by the 16th National Assembly (2000–2004)

Parliamentary period	Number of bills proposed by MPs (a)	Number of bills passed (b)	Approval ratio (b/a, in %)
16th National Assembly (2000–2004)	1,912 (total number of bills proposed)	517	27.0
	76 (total number of budget statement attached bills)	15	19.7

Source: Lim, M., op. cit., 225 (in Korean); *Legislative Information System* (likms.assembly.go.kr; in Korean).

6   *Lim, M.:* Legislative Administration, in: Korean Journal of Legislative Studies, 27 (2004), 209–234 (in Korean).

The ratio of those bills submitted by the executive branch that were amended by the National Assembly was very low during the Second Republic (1960–1961), the rule of the military junta and the Fourth and Fifth Republics (*Figure 3*). With the exception of the Second Republic, which adopted a parliamentary system of government, this was the age of authoritarian governments. Since the establishment of the Sixth Republic in 1988, the amendment approval ratio of the National Assembly has been rising.

Figure 3: Amendment-Approval Ratio of Executive Branch-Submitted Bills in the National Assembly, 1948–2004

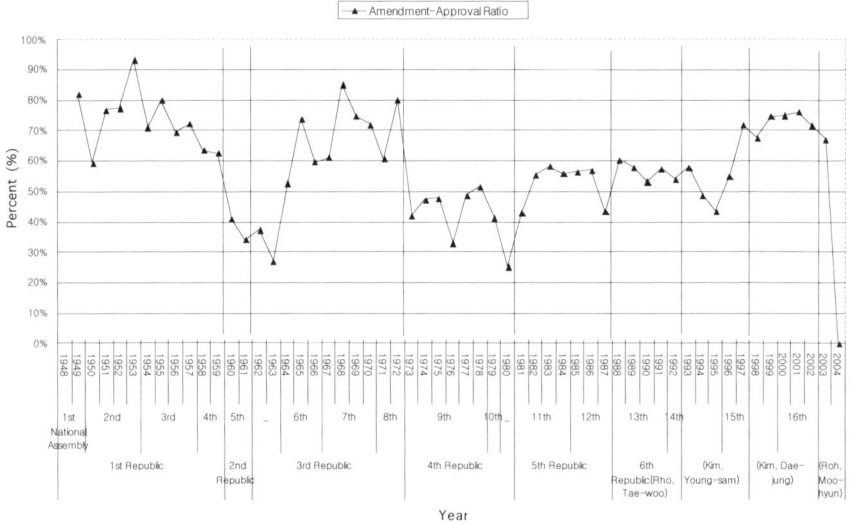

Source: Authors' compilation based on data from the Legislative Information System (likms.assembly.go.kr/bill).

3. Constitutional Referendums and Presidential Emergency Decrees

So far, there have been ten legislations related to the Korean Constitution (*Table 2*). Interestingly enough, all five decisions on this document that were made from the establishment of the First Republic in 1948 to the 4th constitutional amendment in 1960 were approved by the National Assembly, while the other five decisions made on the Constitution from 1962 to 1987 were carried out by referendum.

Actually, most constitutional amendments made in Korea were targeted mainly on changing the relative power between the National Assembly and the president. Among the ten constitutional decisions, only the three that were to establish the Constitutions of the First, Second and Sixth Republics were proposed to improve representative democracy (*Table 2*).

Table 2: Constitutional Amendments Conducted in Korea

Legislation on constitutional law	Date (period of National Assembly)	Key contents of legislation	Impact on representative democracy	Decision-making methods
Establishment of the Constitution	July 17, 1948 (Constitutional Assembly)	Established the Constitution of 1st Republic; provided the NA (unicameral) with power to select president and vice-president indirectly.	Very positive	Proposed and decided in the Constitutional Assembly
1st Amendment	July 7, 1952 (2nd NA)	Changed the presidential selection method from the NA's indirect election to the election system.	Negative	Proposed by President and NA and decided direct in NA
2nd Amendment	Nov. 29, 1954 (3rd NA)	Removed the third-term restriction for the first president; provided people with right to propose constitutional amendments directly.	Negative	Proposed and decided in NA
3rd Amendment	June 15, 1960 (4th NA)	Established the Constitution of 2nd Republic after the students' uprising of April 19; institutionalised a parliamentary government with a bicameral assembly system and local government autonomy.	Very positive	Proposed and decided in NA
4th Amendment	Nov. 29, 1960 (5th NA)	Established the special court to punish the antidemocratic activists during the First Republic.	Negative	Proposed and decided in NA
5th Amendment	Dec. 26, 1962 (the military junta)	Established the Constitution of 3rd Republic; institutionalised a presidential system and unicameral NA.	Negative	Proposed by the military junta and decided by referendum
6th Amendment	Oct. 21, 1969 (3rd Republic; 7th NA)	Removed the third-term restriction for president.	Negative	Proposed and decided in NA
7th Amendment	Dec. 27, 1972 (Emergency State Council)	Established the Constitution of the 4th Republic; changed presidential selection method from direct to indirect election system; any restrictions on presidential term; provided president with power to nominate 1/3 of NA seats.	Very negative	Proposed by President and decided by referendum under the martial law

Table 2 (continued)

Legislation on constitutional law	Date (period of National Assembly)	Key contents of legislation	Impact on representative democracy	Decision-making methods
8th Amendment	Sept. 29, 1980 (National Security Legislative Council)	Established the Constitution of 5th Republic; kept the indirect presidential election system; restricted president to only one seven-year term.	Very negative	Proposed by the National Security Legislative Council and decided by referendum
9th Amendment	Oct. 29, 1987 (5th Republic; 12th National Assembly)	Established the Constitution of 6th Republic after the citizens' uprising of June; changed presidential selection method to direct election system; restricted president to one five-year term.	Positive	Proposed by president and decided by referendum

Source: Authors' compilation based on data from the Legal Information System (nalaw.assembly.go.kr/law).

Figure 4: Presidential Emergency Decrees and Measures Instituted in Korea, 1948–2007

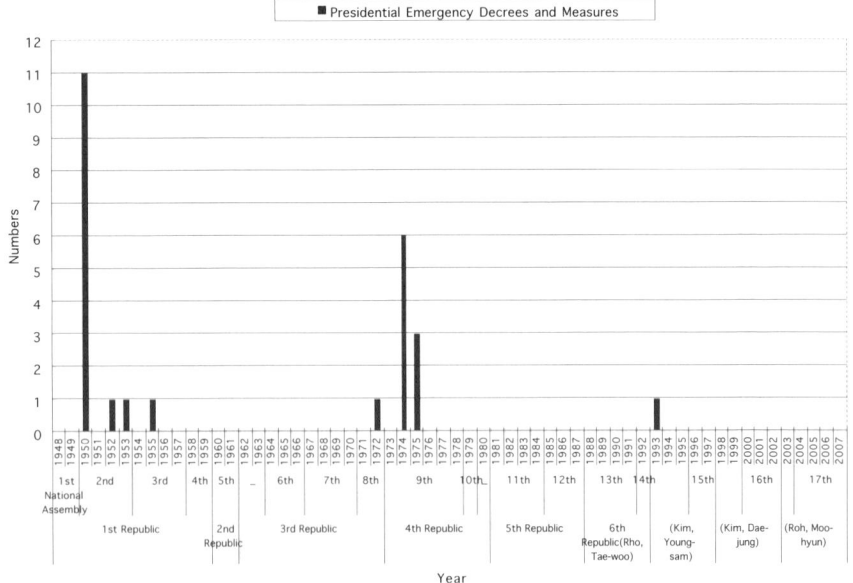

Source: Authors' compilation based on data from the *Ministry of Government Legislation* (www.klaw.go.kr); *Park, Y./Kim, Y.*: A Study on the Presidential Emergency Decree, in: Korean Legislation Research Institute Current Issues, 93/6 (1993), 1–22 (in Korean).

Another form of legislation which occurred outside of the National Assembly was the president's execution of so-called "national emergency power", such as the Emergency Presidential Decree, the Emergency Measure and the Emergency Financial Disposition.[7] Of the 25 national emergency powers exercised by past presidents, 23 were exercised during the Korean War (1950–1953) and the period of authoritarian governments during the Fourth and Fifth Republics (1972–1987; see *Figure 4*). The National Assembly did not play any significant role as a lawmaker in these processes, having no constitutional rights to declare a state of emergency.

III. Budget Approval and Administrative Review

1. Budget Approval

The legislature's budget approval is one of the key instruments for controlling the executive branch. Korea's budgetary process is quite similar to the one in the US: The executive branch prepares the presidential budget to be approved by the National Assembly one year earlier than the fiscal year, executes the approved budget during the fiscal year, and makes a report on closing accounts to the National Assembly right after the fiscal year. Though the whole process is operated on the basis of the Budget and Accounting Act, the annual budget itself is not regarded as a law in Korea as it is in the United States.

The National Assembly slightly adjusted the presidential budget within the range of ±1 % (*Figure 5*). In the fiscal year 1950 during the Korean War and the fiscal year 1973 during the Fourth Republic, the presidential budget was considerably reduced (by about −5 % and −6 %), while during the military junta in 1962 it increased immensely (by approximately +15 %). These are all exceptional cases that occurred during emergency periods. For the three years immediately after the democratic transition (1988–1990), the budget underwent another slight change within ±1 %.

After 1987, various policies were established to actively support the legislators during the processes of budget approval and administrative review. For example, the Budget and Appropriations Committee, which was organised as a temporary annual special committee and only convened at a certain period, was transformed into a standing special committee that has been convened throughout the year

---

7   *Sung, N.*: The Constitutional Law, Bubmoonsa, 2002, 701 (in Korean).

since 2000.[8] The establishment of the National Assembly Budget Office in 2003 by benchmarking the United States Congressional Budget Office is another leading example in this context.

Figure 5: Adjustment Ratio of Presidential Budget in the Korean National Assembly, 1948–2004

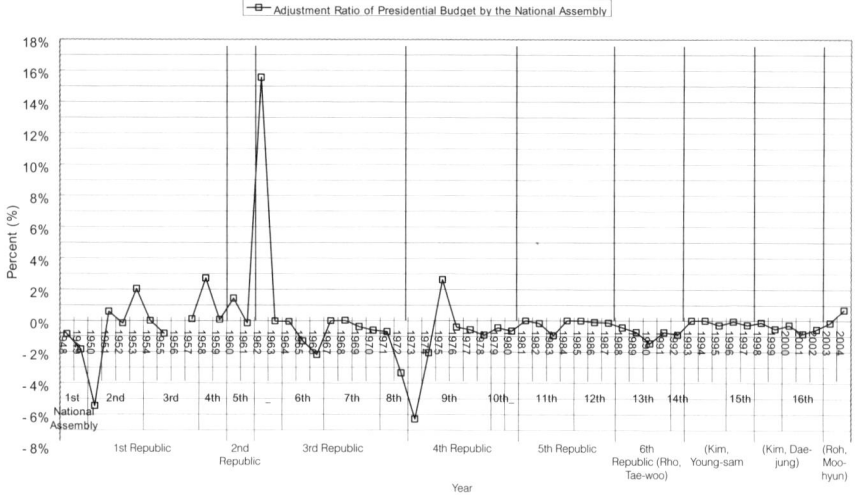

Source: Authors' compilation based on data from the *Korea Development Institute:* Forty Years' History of Korean Public Finance, 1991, 32 (in Korean); *National Assembly Secretariat:* Legislative Data, 2000, 537 (in Korean); *Ministry of Planning and Budget:* Annual Budget Report, 2004 (www.mpb.go.kr; in Korean).

2. Administrative Review

Even in Western countries where parliamentary democracy was institutionalised in an early period, the function of the representative body as legislator has gradually declined while its role of restraining the power and limiting the activities of the executive branch has gained in significance. In other words, the role of parliament as a scrutinising body has grown to ensure administrative accountability.[9] Furthermore, the legislative branch has institutionalised diverse methods to carry out its role as administrative oversight and scrutinising body. In Korea, the leading institutional framework is the National Assembly's inspection, investigation and hearing procedures.

---

8   For further information see nalaw.assembly.go.kr/law.
9   *Heywood, A.*: Key Concepts in Politics, Basingstoke, 2000.

The National Assembly's inspection of the executive branch, which is a unique review of the administration, has contributed to controlling the executive branch during the period of annual budget approval.[10] The parliamentary inspection, institutionalised during the 1st National Assembly, was regularly conducted once a year, with the exception of the 15-years' absence during the Fourth and Fifth Republics, i.e., from the 9th to the 12th National Assembly.[11]

Unlike the National Assembly's inspection of the executive branch, the National Assembly's Investigation is carried out when requested by parliament rather than being held regularly every year. The National Assembly's investigation was also institutionalised during the 1st National Assembly and was practiced annually, with the exception of the period from the Fourth Republic to the Fifth Republic.

Since 1988, immediately after the democratic transition and following the resurrection of the National Assembly's inspection and investigation, the National Assembly has institutionalised a hearing system to facilitate its administrative review. The National Assembly's hearings of those nominated as heads of the four key powerful state apparatuses, such as the director of the national intelligence service, the director of the national tax service, the Prosecutor General, and the national police commissioner, have been held in the relevant standing committee since 2003. In addition, since 2005 the scope of the National Assembly's hearings has expanded to include all cabinet members, judges of the Constitutional Court and members of the central election management committee, who are directly appointed by the president or nominated by the Supreme Court chief justice. However, unlike the prime minister, whose appointment needs parliamentary approval, the National Assembly's hearings of other positions is not required to approve or veto the appointment itself. This has led to the criticism that the National Assembly's hearing is nothing more than a formal instrument.[12] In practice, however, the hearing system has successfully been forcing the various presidents to abandon the policy of appointing their candidates ministers or other nominees for leading positions when these candidates fail to get a majority vote in the National Assembly; hence, the procedure has contributed to improving the power of the National Assembly's control of the executive branch.

---

10 *Kim, H.*: Institutions and Practices of the National Assembly Inspection 1988–1998, in: Korean Political Science Review, 33/1 (1999), 399–422 (in Korean); *Lee, K.*: National Assembly Inspection and Investigation in Korea, in: Constitutional Law Studies, 1/3 (2005), 519–535 (in Korean).

11 *Jung, Y.*: Stateness in Transition, op.cit.

12 *Lee, B.*: Functions and Dysfunction of the National Assembly Hearing in Korea, in: Korean Journal of Legislative Studies, 9/1 (2003), 193–198 (in Korean).

V. Political Recruitment

One of the National Assembly's key functions is to foster and train competent and democratic political leaders, something that is usually referred to as political recruitment. In Korea, except for President *Yun Bo-seon* and Prime Minister *Chang Myeon* in the short-lived Second Republic, no chief executives before 1990 who established their political career bases in the National Assembly. The first president, *Rhee Syngman,* was the leader of an independence movement, while the three sequential presidents from 1962 to 1993, *Park Chung-Hee, Chun Doo-Hwan* and *Roh Tae-Woo,* were former military generals. However, all three presidents who took office sequentially after 1993, President *Kim Young-sam,* President *Kim Dae-jung* and President *Roh Mu-hyun,* were leaders who began their political careers in the National Assembly.

To indirectly measure the effects of the parliamentary perspective on public policy-making within the political executive, this study analyses the proportion of career politicians (e.g., members of National Assembly and/or members of political parties) among the cabinet members (*Figure 6*). This measurement can be used for the Korean case, where a dual executive system is applied (though its legal and political framework is closer to the US presidential system than to the

Figure 6: Previous Careers of the Ministers in Korea, 1948–2006

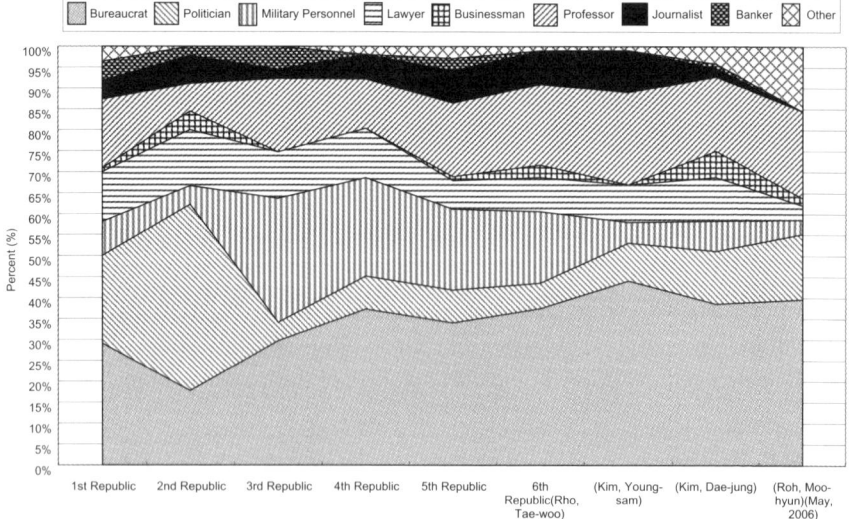

Source: Authors' compilation based on data from *Lee, S./Min, B.*: Terms and Backgrounds of Ministers in Korea, in: Korean Public Administration Journal, 11/3 (2002), 53–82, here 69 (in Korean); *Bark, D./Harm, S./Jung, K.*: Korean Ministers, Nanam, 2003, 73 (in Korean).

French-style dual executive), and where some of the incumbent members of the National Assembly used to be appointed to the cabinet.

A large number of cabinet members were recruited from members of the National Assembly or the key members of the political parties during the First (20.9 %) and Second Republics (44.4 %). However, the percentage of professional politicians was low during the Third, Fourth and Fifth Republics (4.4 %, 7.8 % and 7.8 %, respectively). Since the democratic transition in 1987, the ratio of career politicians has been gradually on the rise: i.e., the *Kim Young-sam* Administration (9.0 %), the *Kim Dae-jung* Administration (12.5 %), and the *Roh Mu-hyun* Administration (as of May 2006, 15.5 %). This data also shows that more career politicians were appointed as cabinet members under the chief executives who were previously civilians rather than under those who were previously military personnel.

VI. Politico-administrative Structure of the National Assembly

1. Divided Government

The National Assembly has been able to more effectively control the executive branch under a situation of a divided government in which the president comes from a minority party within the Assembly. From the First to the Fifth Republics, a divided government occurred only once, immediately after the students' uprising of 19 April 1960. During the period of authoritarian government (1972–1987), a distorted proportional representation system was applied to acquire more seats for the government party, which artificially helped prevent the formation of an anti-presidential majority in Parliament. However, the divided government appeared six times within a 20-year period under the Sixth Republic, which was launched after the democratic transition in 1987. Since 1996, even when a unified government was formed, the government party has never won more than 56 % of the National Assembly seats. This suggests that the National Assembly has started to control the executive branch more effectively than before.

2. Operational Principles

The effectiveness of National Assembly activities is also affected by its main operational principles: the National Assembly-oriented principle and the party-oriented principle. The point at which the introduction of a divided government becomes important is when the party-oriented principle, followed by strict party discipline based on the doctrine mandate, is applied rather than the National Assembly-oriented or "Westminster" principle. The latter is based on the so-called "Bourke principle" according to which assemblymen act as individual trustees by reflecting the preferences of their voters. In Korea, the party-oriented principle and the doctrine mandate have dominated in the National Assembly.[13]

Furthermore, the power to nominate candidates for the National Assembly was exercised by the party leaders and this was used as an effective means to enhance the loyalty of legislators to their party.[14] However, since the general election to form the 17th National Assembly, there has been a gradual spread of a nomination method in which members of local constituencies select candidates from among the primary candidates for election.

3. Committee System

As explained above, the expertise and continuity of the Budget and Appropriations Committee lies in whether or not it is convened as a temporary annual committee or as a regular standing committee. Also, if one committee handles a small number of policy agendas rather than a vast variety of issues, this contributes to improving the expertise of the legislators involved and strengthens the committee's legislative and administrative capacity for administrative review.[15]

Figure 7 is a measurement of the average number of central administrative bodies within the executive branch handled by one standing committee in the Korean National Assembly. The average number of administrative bodies overseen per standing committee was the lowest in 1950, and it was a mere 1.2 during the 2nd National Assembly (1950–1954). From the early 1960s, the ratio began to increase and reached 2.8 committees in the 11th National Assembly (1981–1985). The number of standing committees from 1961 to 1987 was fixed at 13, and the number of central government bodies greatly increased following the promotion of the government-led economic growth policy. Since the democratic transition in 1987, the number of standing committees has increased to 16 and the ratio of administrative bodies per committee has been 2.3.

13 *Park, C.*: Theory and Practice of Representation in the Legislative Branch, in: Korean Journal of Legislative Studies, 7/2 (2001), 229–237 (in Korean).
14 *Kim, Y.*: Divided Government and a New Legislative Politics in 21st Century, in: Korean Journal of Legislative Studies, 6/2 (2000), 32–53 (in Korean); *id.*: President-National Assembly Relation and Role of Political Parties, in: Korean Journal of Legislative Studies, 8/2 (2002), 6–31 (in Korean).
15 *Yim, T.*: Legislature-Executive Relations in France, in: Governmental Studies, 6/2 (2000), 103–130 (in Korean).

Figure 7: Average Number of Ministries and Agencies per Standing Committee in the National Assembly, 1948–2005

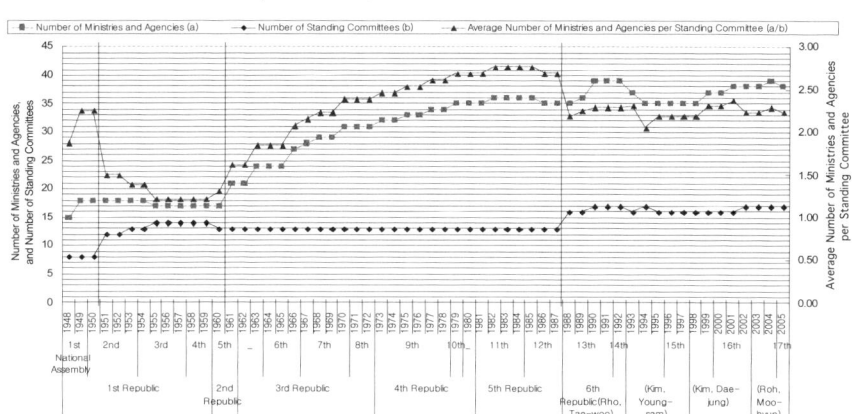

Source: Authors' compilation based on data from *Ministry of Government Administration and Home Affairs: Government Organisation Chart,* annually (in Korean); *Ministry of Government Administration and Home Affairs: A Forty Years' History of Korean Government Organisations,* 1998, 121 (in Korean); *The National Assembly* (likms.assembly.go.kr/law; in Korean).

1. Administrative Infrastructure

Support for the administrative infrastructure for legislators varies considerably among democratic countries. For example, congressmen and senators in the United States are provided with sufficient funding and human resources, whereas members of Parliament in the UK receive low monthly salaries and insufficient administrative support.[16]

Figure 8 shows the size of all administrative apparatuses of the Korean Parliament, such as the National Assembly Secretariat, the National Assembly library, the National Assembly training centre and the recently established National Assembly Budget Office, by dividing it into bureau-level and division-level organisations. The administrative organisation was temporarily expanded during the Second Republic (1960–1961), but it was completely demolished and all public officials were fired when the National Assembly was dissolved in the aftermath of the military coup in 1961. In the Third Republic, the National Assembly's administrative infrastructure gradually expanded; this expansion continued in the Sixth Republic in 1988, except for the structural adjustment period (1988–2003) following the liquidity crisis of 1997.

---

16 *Heywood, A.*: Politics, op. cit., 299.

Figure 8: Administrative Apparatus in the National Assembly in Korea, 1948–2004

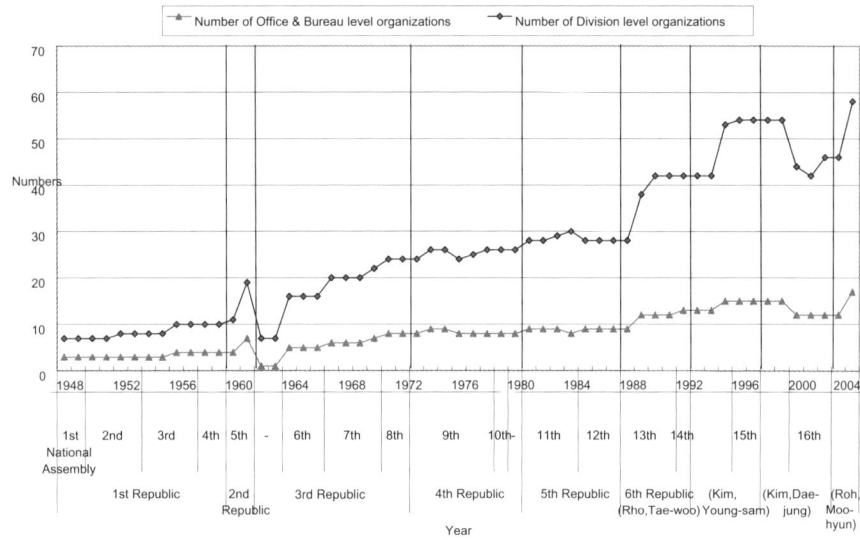

Source: Authors' compilation based on data from the National Assembly (www.assembly.go.kr/nas.na.go.kr/www. nabo.go.kr; in Korean).

The total number of administrative staff working for the National Assembly also continued to increase. However, the number of administrative staff per 100,000 citizens continued to decline from 1970 (1.5) to 1987 (1.3). Since the establishment of the Sixth Republic, the number has begun to grow again, reaching a ratio of about 1.9 in 2000. In addition to the general administrative infrastructure that jointly supports the National Assemblymen, public funds are being provided to research institutes of the political parties.

With respect to individual staff for each assemblyman, one person was assigned to each legislator for the first time in 1954; support increased to 2 in 1960, 3–5 from 1970 to 1990 and 6 since 1998.[17]

The absolute amount of the National Assembly's budget has continued to increase, but the ratio of the parliamentary budget to the total government budget has maintained a downward spiral. The decline began in the Third Republic (1963–1972) and hit bottom during the Fifth Republic (1981–1987). The ratio of National Assembly's budget for the general operational costs of the executive branch was lowest during the military junta rule (1961–1963) and the Fourth and

---

17 *The National Assembly:* The Fifth Years' History of the National Assembly, 1998, 1224 (in Korean).

Fifth Republics (1973–1987). The ratio grew slightly in the early period of the Sixth Republic but declined again following the liquidity crisis of 1997 (*Figure 9*).

Figure 9: Operational Costs of the National Assembly in Relation to the Executive Branch, 1959–2006

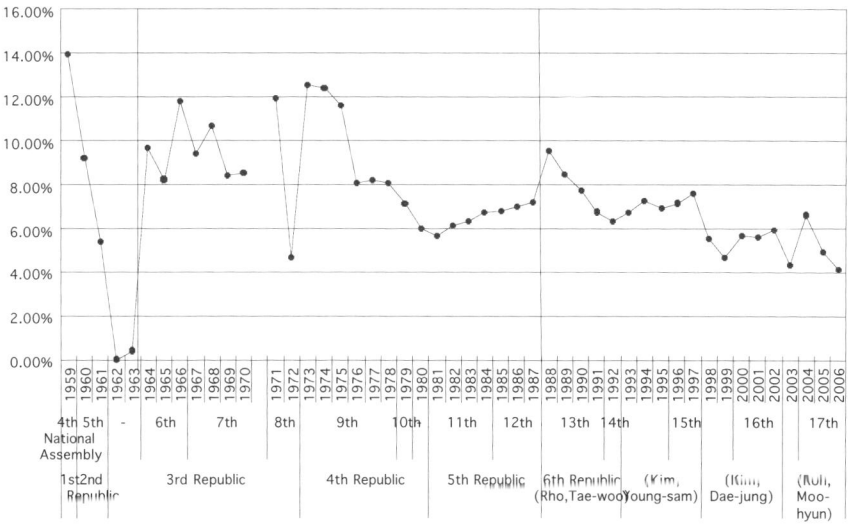

Sources: Authors' compilation based on data from Ministry of Finance and Economy (www.mofe.go.kr; in Korean); *Korea Development Institute:* The Forty Years' History of Korean Public Finance, 1991 (in Korean); *Ministry of Planning and Budget:* Budget Summary, annually (www.mpb.go.kr; in Korean).

IV. Conclusion

This article has analysed the structural developments of the Korean National Assembly during the sixty years since the establishment of the First Republic in 1948. In the First and Second Republics, the Assembly played a relatively important role. However, during the two years of the military junta (1961–1963) and the fifteen years from the Fourth Republic to the Fifth Republic (1972–1987), the National Assembly was almost completely inactive; these were also the years of its greatest vulnerability in terms of politico-administrative infrastructure. Since the establishment of the Sixth Republic (1988–2007), the National Assembly's role and its supporting politico-administrative infrastructure have continued to improve. Based on the result of the empirical analysis, the following theoretical implications may be derived.

First, representative democracy withered during the 1970s to the 1980s when Korea experienced rapid industrialisation and economic development. This clearly confirms the so-called "bureaucratic authoritarianism thesis".[18] However, representative democracy has been flourishing since the late 1980s when industrialisation had been successfully achieved. Therefore, in the longer run, Korea adds another case that backs up the "modernisation theory".[19]

Second, Korea institutionalised an Asiatic form of an administrative state with the establishment of the Republic in the late 1940s. Since the late 1980s, however, the role of the National Assembly began to gain in significance. This development is quite opposite to that of the United States, in which the administrative state was institutionalised after a century of a political or legislative state, where public policy-making was initiated mainly by representative institutions (i.e., the legislative branch).[20] Currently, there is no indication of whether a political or legislative state will be introduced in Korea in the near future.

Third, the flourishing and withering phases of parliamentary democracy may also have had specific implications for the Korean state. The reinvigoration of the National Assembly from the establishment of the Republic until the early 1970s weakened state autonomy. Since then, however, the National Assembly's atrophy of 26 years facilitated the institutionalisation of a strong state. Since the democratic transition in 1987, the institutional characteristics of this traditional strong state have again been weakened by the growing political significance of the National Assembly.

---

18 *O'Donnell, G.*: Modernization and Bureaucratic Authoritarianism, Berkeley, 1973.
19 *Huntington, S.*: Political Order in Changing Societies, New Haven, 1968.
20 *Waldo, D.*: The Administrative State, New York, 1948; *Schick, A.*: The Cybernetic State, in: TRAS-action, 7 (1970), 15–26.

The Politics of Constitutional Reform in China: Rule of Law as a Condition or as a Substitute for Democracy?

by Richard Balme and Yang Lihua

I. Introduction

This paper reviews constitutional reforms and their implications for the under-standing of political change in post-*Mao* China. Three decades after the intro-duction of the reform policy, what have been the major transformations of the Constitution of the People's Republic of China (PRC), what are their consequen-ces, and what are the contemporary dynamics of Chinese constitutionalism? The dramatic policy evolution and related economic and social changes in China strikingly contrast with the limits of political reforms, and particularly with the absence of any democratic transition similar to those followed by most com-munist countries in the last two decades. However, the Chinese government's en-gagement in its reform policy entails a number of important administrative and legal aspects as well as widely commented upon amendments to the Constitution. Understanding whether and how constitutional reform is indeed part of political modernisation in China is the purpose of this contribution. In particular, we ana-lyse substantive and procedural aspects of the PRC's constitutional reforms to ex-plore their contribution to the development of constitutionalism and the rule of law in China. By constitutionalism we mean the hierarchy of norms placing the Constitution in a position of authority above other types of rules, therefore sub-mitting to the Constitution all government decisions about their compatibility with the fundamental law. We also use the term "constitutionalisation" to desig-nate the growing reference to this idea or to the Constitution itself within the political culture and its effective use in regulating political interactions. By rule of law, we refer to the recognition, definition and effective implementation by the state of fundamental rights for citizens, including the right to formally contest and modify governmental decisions when they violate those rights.

Although the two notions of constitutionalism and rule of law are closely re-lated, they are nevertheless distinct.[1] Indeed, in common law systems the rule of

---

1 See in particular *Lane, J.-E.*: Constitutions and Political Theory, Manchester, 1996, and *Holmes, S.*: Lineages

law can be developed to a great extent on a jurisprudential basis, in some cases in the absence of a formal constitution (i.e. the "Westminster" model). In other instances, constitutions declaratively acknowledge a number of fundamental rights without any concrete implications for citizens to formally question the government's policy in the absence of rule-of-law procedures. Constitutional changes have to therefore be assessed on both dimensions. When China is considered, it is tempting to interpret the growing legalisation of public policy, including its constitutional dimension, as a substitute and possibly an alternative to more substantial political reforms, namely democratisation. We will first attempt to identify the different steps of constitutional change and the ideological evolution they represent for the political regime of the PRC. Secondly, we intend to assess whether these changes can indeed be interpreted as a constitutionalisation of Chinese politics, meaning a greater role of the constitution in the conduct of public policy and a growing submission of governmental policy to constitutional limitations. Thirdly, we will also analyse whether and, if so, when constitutional changes entail some progress in the rule of law by which citizens make use of the constitution to protect their rights against state authorities. Finally, we wish to explore whether these developments are likely to be conflicting, compatible with, or alternative to full democratisation in the PRC.

Our argumentation shows that, on the whole, constitutional changes in the PRC did not depart from a traditional communist approach and also how reforms were used to legitimise and to secure fundamental policy changes initiated by the Chinese Communist Party (CCP). Furthermore, it argues that accommodating policy change in the fundamental law triggered a genuine constitutionalisation process, one subject to severe limitations, but nevertheless signalling important changes in the political culture and imposing significant tensions on the whole political system. We start with a brief historical review of constitutional developments in China until the contemporary period before analysing the different reforms introduced since the adoption of the current constitution in 1982. We then consider in detail the process of constitutional reform and its evolution and the activism deployed by citizens and groups of legal professionals around constitutional issues. The conclusion develops the prospective implications of the trends depicted for the rule of law and democratisation in the PRC.

of the Rule of Law, in: Maravall, J.M./Przeworski, A. (eds.): Democracy and the Rule of Law, Cambridge, 2003, 29–61.

II. A Brief History of Constitutional Development in China
   since the *Qing* Dynasty

Constitutional government was properly introduced as a political concept in China in the late 19th century by reformists aiming at transforming imperial institutions to better resist foreign influences and intrusions. The word *xianfa,* which is used in Chinese for "constitution", existed in ancient China, which was endowed with vivid and burgeoning legal traditions; however the word designated the set of rules and regulations related to government more than a fundamental law in a position of hierarchy with regard to other norms. The same word, this time referring to the concept of a constitution in the Western sense, was reintroduced by Chinese intellectuals in exile in Japan during the *Meiji* era (1868–1912). Constitutionalism was then considered as the instrument needed to limit or to abolish the arbitrary power of the *Manchu* Dynasty as well as to encourage Chinese elites to promote an effective form of government in a period of trouble. It was also the legal change required for China to alter its status as a self-centred empire to a nation-state engaged in international relations.[2] Remarkably, from the contemporary perspective we will adopt here, this moment for constitutionalism coincided with the first wave of "globalisation" and with the economic, cultural and colonial expansion of industrial powers on a world-wide scale.

In this context, the *Qing* Dynasty reluctantly considered some changes, first in 1898 with the *Wuxu* Reform and then in 1908 with an imperial edict titled "General Principles of Constitutional Government" (*Qinding Xianfa Dagang*) intended to elaborate a constitution instituting a parliament, the features of which were mainly borrowed from the German Constitution of 1871 and the Japanese *Meiji* Constitution of 1889. Again in 1911 amidst the secession of a number of provinces in central and southern China, a Charter (*Shijiu Xintiao*) followed by an organic law was promulgated, but this failed to save the Emperor from having to abdicate. China then entered a long period of institutional collapse and permanent turmoil marked by rivalries among warlords, Japanese invasion, and civil war between the Guomindang (KMT) and the Communist Party. A number of constitutional projects were launched during this period, in particular at the provincial level with the development of a federalist movement. In 1921, the Hunan province adopted a constitution and was followed by others. Under the influence of Dr. *Sun Yat-Sen,*

---

2   *Xiao-Planes, X.*: Constitutions and Constitutionalism: Trying to Build a New Political Order (1908–1949), in: Balme, S./Dowdle, M. (eds.): Constitutionalism and Judicial Power in China, Basingstoke (forthcoming). A first (French) version of this article has been published in Delmas-Marty, M./Will, P.E. (eds.): La Chine et la démocratie, Paris, 2007, 259–295.

the founder of the KMT and the icon figure of Chinese republicanism, projects for a national constitution flourished and were adopted in several instances,[3] although they failed to meet the political conditions for implementation. The Constitution of the Republic of China (*Zhonghua Minguo Xianfa*) promulgated by the Guomindang government under the leadership of *Chiang Kai-shek* on 1 January 1947 still serves as the basic law of the present Taiwanese government. For a number of reasons that cannot be explained here, the collapse of the imperial regime was followed by a long period in which the edification of a constitutional state in China proved to be impossible.[4]

With the end of the civil war and the foundation of the PRC on 1 October 1949, the CCP wanted to model China's institutions under the precepts of Marxism-Leninism. The 1954 Constitution, inspired by the 1936 Constitution of the Soviet Union, guaranteed equality before the law, the separation of powers and private ownership of the means of production. Within a few years, however, this constitution fell into disuse as *Mao*'s radical economic plans and sweeping political agendas left no room for legal restrictions on state power. In 1975, following long years of political turmoil and devastation imposed by the Great Leap Forward and before the Cultural Revolution ended, the PRC adopted a second, dictatorial and ineffective, Constitution. Based on this legacy, it abolished most of the legal protections offered in the 1954 document and proclaimed the need to struggle against the capitalist elements of society. Three years later, however, the Eleventh Central Committee of the CCP concluded that official democratic centralism would necessarily require a certain measure of democracy and drafted the 1978 Constitution accordingly. Of course, the meaning of "democracy" remained grounded in the "people's democratic dictatorship" (*renmin minzhu zhuanzheng zhidu*), based on an alliance of the proletariat classes and led by the Communist Party. The 1978 Constitution was also an attempt to counteract the personality cult, the anarchy and the bloodshed of the preceding decade by superimposing a form of socialist democracy on the existing authoritarian model of government.

Departing from its predecessors, the 1982 Constitution may be viewed as an expression of *Deng Xiaoping*'s determination to lay a lasting institutional foundation for China's economic modernisation. Progressive in many respects, the current constitutional document de-emphasises class struggle, omits all direct references to the Cultural Revolution, clarifies citizens' "fundamental rights and

---

3   *Xiao-Planes* (op. cit., 2007, 294) numbers twelve constitutions or organic laws that were promulgated from 1912 to 1948.

4   *Mao, S.L.*: Recent Development of Constitutional Government in China. Paper presented at the International Conference on "The Value Base of Institutions in Times of Political Change", Taipei, July 2000.

duties" and stresses the importance of socialist law for the regulation of political behaviour.[5] Critics of the constitutional developments in today's China mainly address the subordination of the PRC Constitution to the constitution of the CCP.[6] In particular, from a comparative perspective, the absence of judicial or constitutional review imposes severe limits on Chinese characteristics of constitutionalism, suggesting that it amounts merely to party politics with a different name. However, such a position does not allow for considering the possibility of a gradual change, i.e. slowly developing the rule of law as constitutive of the state and progressively providing incentives for the government to comply with it.[7] The following section, an analysis of the constitutional amendments introduced since 1982, will examine whether or not these amendments, beyond enshrining CCP policy in the state foundations, have contributed to the development of constitutionalism in China.

III. Constitutional Changes and the Reform Policy

Since its enactment in 1982, the Constitution of the PRC has been modified by four different reforms involving a total of 31 articles. The distribution of these articles shows that 14 of them deal with economic issues to progressively acknowledge market economy,[8] eight address the political organisation of state power,[9] seven articles involve ideological issues reflecting the policy changes from the CCP,[10] while two refer to social rights and human rights issues (*Table 1*).[11]

5 *Blanchard, H.*: Constitutional Revisionism in the PRC: "Seeking Truth from Facts", in: Florida Journal of International Law, 17/2 (2005), 365–403, here 370–383.

6 The role of the CCP is acknowledged in the Preamble of the 1982 Constitution: "Under the leadership of the Communist Party of China and the guidance of Marxism-Leninism, Mao Zedong's Thought, Deng Xiaoping's Theory and the important thought of 'Three Represents', the Chinese people of all nationalities will continue to adhere to the people's democratic dictatorship and the socialist road." Art. 1 further states that "The People's Republic of China is a socialist state under the people's democratic dictatorship led by the working class and based on the alliance of workers and peasants. The socialist system is the basic system of the People's Republic of China. Disruption of the socialist system by any organisation or individual is prohibited."

7 *Cai, D. J.*: The Development of Constitutionalism in the Transition of Chinese Society, in: Columbia Journal of Asian Law, 19/1 (2005), 1–29.

8 Articles 1, 2, 5, 6, 7, 8, 9, 10, 14, 15, 16, 20, 21 and 22 of constitutional amendments.

9 Articles 11, 25, 26, 27, 28, 29, 30 and 31 of constitutional amendments deal with the division of powers between public authorities, elections, and national symbols.

10 Articles 3, 4, 12, 13, 17, 18 and 19 mainly concern the Preamble, which asserts the leading status of the CCP in the PRC's political system. These amendments are in line with the evolutions of the CCP's ideology as reflected by the CCP National Congress, which takes place every five years.

11 Articles 23 and 24 of the constitutional amendments passed in 2004 deal with issues of social and

Table 1: Distribution of Constitutional Amendments (Articles by Topic)

Amendment year/ Topic of articles	1988	1993	1999	2004	Total
Economy	2	6	3	3	14
Political Organisation	–	1	–	7	8
Ideology	–	2	3	2	7
Rights	–	–	–	2	2
Total	2	9	6	14	31

Source: Authors' compilation.

When timing is considered, it is worth noticing the gradual shift from the economy and related ideological aspects to political organisation and fundamental rights. It is more accurate to say that rights are latecomers in the constitutional reform process. In the wording of the Standing Committee of the National People's Congress (NPCSC) in its Explanation to the Drafting Amendment of the PRC Constitution, Article 23, which claims the necessity of establishing a social security system consistent with the level of economic development, is justified by the fundamental interests of the masses and as a tool to maintain the social stability needed to establish a socialist market economy.[12] The Explanation also stipulates that enacting Article 24, which proclaims the state's responsibility to protect human rights, is consistent with the CCP policy defined by its XVth and XVIth Congresses and aims at promoting international communication and cooperation with regard to human rights.[13]

In line with official ideology, Chinese media usually praise constitutional change as the hallmark of the reform policy:

> "The core of the four amendments is to establish a market economy, strengthen democracy and the rule of law and protect human rights. As the NPC now plays a more and more important role in promoting political and economic development, it attracts

---

human rights. Art. 23 indicates for the first time that "the state establishes and improves a social security system compatible with the level of economic development" (becomes paragraph 4, Art. 14 of the Constitution). Art. 24 declares, also for the first time, that "the state respects and safeguards human rights" (becomes paragraph 3, Art. 33 of the Constitution).

12 *Wang, P.Y./Quanguo Renda Chang Weihui Bangongting Mishu Erju* [Second Secretarial Office of the Standing Committee of the National People's Congress]: *Zhongguo Xianfa Wenxian Tongbian* [The Materials of the PRC Constitution], Beijing, 2004, 141.

13 Ibid.

much attention. Meanwhile, the system reform of the people's congresses at various levels has emerged as one of the cornerstones in promoting political civilisation."[14]

Academic comments are also positive, albeit in a somewhat more critical tone:

> "Our constitution has been revised at the same pace as China's reform and it has been called a 'Constitution of reform' [...] However, it is really time to reconsider the role of the Constitution and its relationship with reform. The Constitution should be not only a document acknowledging every big step in China's grand reform efforts, it should provide guidance to the overall reform programme itself."[15]

As indicated, the first constitutional reforms considered here reflected the major change in China's political economy. On 12 April 1988, the First Session of the Seventh NPC's meeting amended Article 11, formally endorsing the existence and development of the private sector as a supplement to the public economy. The reform was adopted two years after the first draft of the General Principles of the Civil Law (GPCL), which already contained various provisions on private contract relations. This was the first official recognition of the private sector in communist China. A related amendment granted permission for the transfer of land-use rights.[16]

The 1988 amendment was comprised of two articles loosening the prohibition of the private economy. The reform echoed the change in ideology of the CCP during its XIIIth Congress (*Zhongguo Gongchandong Zhongyang Weiyuanhui*) in 1987, proclaiming that China would establish an economy relying primarily on planning, but at the same time allowing market-oriented mechanisms to supplement the former.[17]

Based upon this declaration, in early 1988 the State Council (the equivalent to the Chinese government) initiated seven proposals for constitutional amendments. The seven proposed amendments included:

- adding to the Preamble, "China is in the primary stage of socialism" and "perseveres in reform and opening itself to the outside world";
- adding "the state permits other ways of distributing wealth" after the paragraph of Art. 6 which refers to the principle of "from each according to his ability" to "each according to his work";

---

14 *Li, J. G.*: All Eyes on NPC, in: Beijing Review, 47 (04. 03. 2004), 2.
15 *Xia, Y.*: Zhongguo Xianfa gaige de JIge Jiben Lilun Wenti – Cong "Gaige Xianfa Dao Xianzheng Xianfa" [The Fundamental Theoretical Issues of China's Constitutional Reform: From "A Reform Constitution" to "A Constitutional Government Constitution"], in: Zhongguo Shehui Kexue [The Social Sciences of China], February 2003, 4–17.
16 *Blanchard, H.*, op. cit., 385 f.
17 *Wang, P. Y./Quanguo Renda Chang Weihui Bangongting Mishu Erju*, op. cit., 91.

- revising Art. 10, which prohibits the lease of state-owned land;
- adding an article concerning the private economy;
- revising Art. 10, which defines the Chinese economy as primarily centrally planned but now supplemented by mechanisms of the "socialist market economy";
- stipulating the division of ownership and management for state-owned enterprises (SOEs);
- deleting the notion of Rural Peoples' Communes (*nongchun renmin gongshe*) in Art. 8 of the Constitution.[18]

Under the 1982 Constitution, the Chinese economy excluded any reference to the market, this being considered incompatible with historical socialism. As the major actor implementing reform, the State Council considered the economic regulatory system as outmoded and not suitable for upcoming economic reforms. For the Chinese executive, constitutional changes were necessary to provide the legal basis to conduct relevant reforms. Some of these amendments were decisive in legally unleashing policy changes in China, particularly the option to lease state-owned land, thus introducing the negotiability and marketability of land-use rights, which is so crucial to urban development. It is interesting to note that before the 1988 constitutional amendment, some cities had already engaged in policies leasing state-owned land under the authorisation of the China Land Administration (*Guojia Tudi Guanliju*). In 1987, the China Land Administration had authorised six cities (Shanghai, Tianjin, Shenzhen, Guangzhou, Fuzhou, Xiamen) and the island of Hainan to lease state-owned land, which had been prohibited up to then. Obviously, these administrative policies generated important controversies about their conformity with the Constitution.[19] Significantly from our perspective, the reform policy preceded constitutional change that was implemented in a second stage in order to legalise ongoing governmental practices.

However, the seven proposals from the State Council were too controversial at that time to be fully accepted within the Politburo, and only two of them were eventually endorsed by the Central Committee of the CCP.[20] One of these pro-

---

18 See *Tian, J.Y.*: Shinian Renda Shengya [Ten Years in NPC], in: Xinhua Wenzhai, September 2004.

19 In particular about compatibility with Art. 10, paragraph 4, which states that "no organisation or individual may appropriate, buy, sell or lease, or otherwise engage in the transfer of land by unlawful means". Cf. *Zhang X.R./Chen, N.*: Ershi Shiji Zhi Zhongguo Xianzheng [The 20th Century's Chinese Constitutionalism], Wuhan, 2002, 401.

20 *Tian, J.Y.*, op. cit.

posals concerns the recognition of the private economy, while the other deals with the permission to transfer the rights to use land.[21]

On 28 February 1988, the Central Committee proposed the constitutional amendment to the Standing Committee of the NPC and recommended that the latter initiate the legislative process to amend the Constitution.[22] The first session of the VIIth Meeting of the NPC passed the constitutional amendment[23] in the exact wording proposed by the Central Committee. This amendment was the first constitutional reform after the adoption of the 1982 Constitution. It was crucial in abolishing the unconstitutionality of the market economy and in defining a legal basis for the reform policy.

In its own turn, the 1993 constitutional reform followed the ideological change promoted by the CCP during its XIVth Congress of 1992. China was then declared to be in the primary stage of socialism; the nation's basic task was to concentrate its effort on socialist modernisation, this in line with the theory of building socialism with Chinese characteristics (*jianshe you zhongguo tese de shehui zhuyi*). The *aggiornamento* also indicated that the basic goal of reform was to establish a socialist market economy, confirming and allowing for further development of the private economy.[24] In line with established practices, the CCP Central Committee initiated the constitutional reform process by proposing an amendment of eight articles to the Standing Committee of the NPC. The proposal aimed mostly at further legalising the changing political economy in the Constitution.[25]

---

21 The amendment reads: "Article 1. Article 11 of the Constitution shall include a new paragraph which reads: 'The state permits the private sector of the economy to exist and develop within the limits prescribed by law. The private sector of the economy is a complement to the socialist public economy. The state protects the lawful rights and interests of the private sector of the economy and exercises guidance, supervision and control over the private sector of the economy.'
Article 2. The fourth paragraph of Article 10 of the Constitution, which provides that 'no organisation or individual may appropriate, buy, sell or lease land or otherwise engage in the transfer of land by unlawful means', shall be amended to 'no organisation or individual may appropriate, buy, sell or otherwise engage in the transfer of land by unlawful means. The right to the use of land may be transferred according to law.'"

22 *Wang, P. Y./Quanguo Renda Chang Weihui Bangongting Mishu Erju,* op. cit., 90.

23 Ibid.

24 *Pan, W. J.:* Lun Xianfa Xiugai, Xianzheng Zhixu Yu Zhongguo Renquan Fazhan Fangxiang [Constitutional Amendment, Constitutionalism and the Development of Human Rights Protection in China], in: 2004 Renquan Ruxian Yu Renquan De Fazhi Baozhang Huiyi Lunwenji [Materials of 2004 Conference of Constitutionalizing and Protecting Human Rights in China], China Academic Journal Electronic Publishing House (www.cnki.net), 2004, 300–311.

25 The final constitutional amendment adopted at the First Session of the Eighth National People's Congress and promulgated for implementation by the Announcement of the National People's Congress on 29 March 1993 reads:

Before the Central Committee conveys its proposals to the Standing Committee of the NPC, the draft is normally circulated to various authorities, social organisations and experts invited to provide comments. The Central Committee then releases explanations, particularly regarding the recommendations it has

"Article 3. The last two sentences of the seventh paragraph of the Preamble to the Constitution read: 'The basic task of the nation in the years to come is to concentrate its effort on socialist modernisation. Under the leadership of the Communist Party of China and the guidance of Marxism-Leninism and Mao Zedong's Thought, the Chinese people of all nationalities will continue to adhere to the people's democratic dictatorship and the socialist road, steadily improve socialist institutions, develop socialist democracy, improve the socialist legal system, and work hard and self-reliantly to modernise the country's industry, agriculture, national defence and science and technology step by step to turn China into a socialist country with a high level of culture and democracy'. This has been revised to read: 'China is at the primary stage of socialism. The basic task of the nation is to concentrate its effort on socialist modernisation in line with the theory of building socialism with Chinese characteristics. Under the leadership of the Communist Party of China and the guidance of Marxism-Leninism and Mao Zedong's Thought, the Chinese people of all nationalities will continue to adhere to the people's democratic dictatorship and the socialist road, persevere in reform and opening to the outside world, steadily improve socialist institutions, develop socialist democracy, improve the socialist legal system, and work hard and self-reliantly to modernise the country's industry, agriculture, national defence and science and technology step by step to turn China into a socialist country that is prosperous, powerful, democratic and culturally advanced.'

Article 4. The following has been added to the end of the tenth paragraph of the Preamble to the Constitution: 'The system of the multi-party cooperation and political consultation led by the Communist Party of China will exist and develop for a long time to come.'

Article 5. Article 7 of the Constitution reads:

'The state economy is the sector of socialist economy under ownership by the whole people; it is the leading force in the national economy. The state ensures the consolidation and growth of the state economy'.

This has been revised to read: 'The state-owned economy, namely, the socialist economy under ownership by the whole people, is the leading force in the national economy. The state ensures the consolidation and growth of the state-owned economy.'

Article 6. The first paragraph of Article 8 of the Constitution reads:

'Rural people's communes, agricultural producers' cooperatives and other forms of cooperative economy, such as producers', supply and marketing, credit and consumers' cooperatives, belong to the sector of socialist economy under collective ownership by the working people. Working people who are members of rural economic collectives have the right, within the limits prescribed by law, to farm plots of cropland and hilly land allotted for their private use, engage in household sideline production and raise privately owned livestock.'

This has been revised to read, 'In rural areas the responsibility system, the main form of which is household contract that links remuneration to output, and other forms of cooperative economy, such as producers', supply and marketing, credit and consumers' cooperatives, belong to the sector of socialist economy under collective ownership by the working people. Working people who are members of rural economic collectives have the right, within the limits prescribed by law, to farm plots of cropland and hilly land allotted for their private use, engage in household sideline production and raise privately owned livestock.'

Article 7. Article 15 of the Constitution reads:

'The state practices planned economy on the basis of socialist public ownership. It ensures the propor-

rejected, in the "official comments to the proposal with regard to partial revision of the Constitution", which are attached to the "proposal of the CCP Central Committee to the Standing Committee of the NPC with respect to the partial revision of the Constitution". In drafting of the 1993 amendment, the Central Committee received a number of significant recommendations, such as to add

tionate and coordinated growth of the national economy through overall balancing by economic planning and the supplementary role of regulation by the market.'

'Disturbance of the socio-economic order or disruption of the state economic plan by any organisation or individual is prohibited'.

This is revised to read, 'The state practices socialist market economy.'

'The state strengthens economic legislation, improves macro-regulation and control, and prohibits in accordance with law any organisation or individual from disturbing the socio-economic order.'

Article 8. Article 16 of the Constitution reads:

'State enterprises have decision-making power with regard to operation and management within the limits prescribed by law, on condition that they submit to unified leadership by the state and fulfil all their obligations under the state plan. State enterprises practise democratic management through congresses of workers and staff and in other ways in accordance with law.'

This is revised to read, 'State-owned enterprises have decision-making power with regard to their operation within the limits prescribed by law. State-owned enterprises practice democratic management through congresses of workers and staff and in other ways in accordance with law.'

Article 9. Article 17 of the Constitution reads:

'Collective economic organisations have decision-making power in conducting independent economic activities, on condition that they accept the guidance of the state plan and abide by the relevant laws. Collective economic organisations practice democratic management in accordance with law. The entire body of their workers elects or removes their managerial personnel and decides on major issues concerning operation and management', is revised to read, 'Collective economic organisations have decision-making power in conducting independent economic activities, on condition that they abide by the relevant laws. Collective economic organisations practise democratic management and in accordance with law, elect or remove their managerial personnel and decide on major issues concerning operation and management.'

Article 10. The third paragraph of Article 42 of the Constitution reads:

'Work is a matter of honour for every citizen who is able to work. All working people in state enterprises and in urban and rural economic collectives should approach their work as the masters of the country that they are. The state promotes socialist labour emulation, and commends and rewards model and advanced workers. The state encourages citizens to take part in voluntary labour.' This has been revised to read, 'Work is a matter of honour for every citizen who is able to work. All working people in state-owned enterprises and in urban and rural economic collectives should approach their work as the masters of the country that they are. The state promotes socialist labour emulation, and commends and rewards model and advanced workers. The state encourages citizens to take part in voluntary labour.'

Article 11. Article 98 of the Constitution reads:

'The term of office of the people's congresses of provinces, municipalities directly under the central government and cities divided into districts is five years. The term of office of the people's congresses of counties, cities not divided into districts, municipal districts, townships, nationality townships, and towns is three years'.

This has been revised to read, 'The term of office of the people's congresses of provinces, municipalities directly under the central government, counties, cities and municipal districts is five years. The term of office of the people's congresses of townships, nationality townships and towns is three years.'"

the "one country, two system" guiding principle for the Hong Kong handover in the preamble of the Constitution, to institute a regulatory power for the Central Military Commission and to establish under Article 70 a special commission of constitutional supervision to insure that the Constitution is fully respected.[26] The above recommendations were eventually not accepted by the Central Committee. In its official comment, it argued that no amendment was needed on these three specific issues since they could be interpreted as compatible with the current constitution.[27] Remarkably, in doing so, the Central Committee declared it permissible to establish a special commission to supervise the execution of the Constitution, opening up potential space within the current framework to establish an organ for constitutional review.

On 15 March 1999, a new constitutional amendment was implemented, again primarily to reflect and legalise changes introduced by economic reform policies. The private sector was further advanced from "a complement" to "a major component" of the socialist market economy. Public ownership of the means of production would remain dominant, but the acknowledgment of "diverse sectors of the economy" and of the "coexistence of a variety of modes of distribution" testified to the growing legitimacy of market mechanisms in the constitutional order.[28]

However, in subordinating the protection of private property to that of public property, the 1999 amendment fell short of a full recognition of property rights understood as the foundations of the market economy enshrined in liberal Western constitutions. Although the PRC's institutions were for a long time com-

---

26 *Wang, P.Y./Quanguo Renda Chang Weihui Bangongting Mishu Erju,* op. cit., p. 90.

27 Ibid.

28 In particular, Art. 14 of the amendment adds the following paragraph to Art. 6 of the Constitution: "In the primary stage of socialism, the state upholds the basic economic system under which the public ownership is dominant and diverse forms of ownership develop side by side and keeps to the distribution system under which distribution according to work is dominant and diverse modes of distribution coexist." Art. 16 of the amendment stipulates that Art. 11 of the Constitution, which reads: "The individual economy of urban and rural working people, operating within the limits prescribed by law, is a complement to the socialist public economy. The state protects the lawful rights and interests of the individual economy. The state guides, assists and supervises the individual economy by administrative control. The state permits the private sector of the economy to exist and develop within the limits prescribed by law. The private sector of the economy is a complement to the socialist public sector of the economy. The state protects the lawful rights and interests of the private sector of the economy, and exercises guidance, supervision and control over the private sector of the economy", has been revised as follows: "The non-public sectors of the economy such as the individual and private sectors of the economy, operating within the limits prescribed by law, constitute an important component of the socialist market economy. The state protects the lawful rights and interests of the individual and private sectors of the economy, and exercises guidance, supervision and control over the individual and private sectors of the economy."

mitted to the eradication of the private sector, they nevertheless had to tolerate the existence of some individual or non-state ownership at the same time. The Common Principles (*gongtong gangling*) adopted in 1949 provided some guidance for accommodating private economic interests. Similarly, the 1982 Constitution guarantees the "right of citizens to own lawfully earned income, savings, houses and other lawful property". It does not, however, refer to private property as "sacred and inviolable", nor does it provide for its protection as one of the fundamental rights of citizens.[29] As a result, although the market economy is legally recognised as a legitimate instrument of socialist development, it does not rest on fully-fledged property rights. In a context of intensive economic growth and urban development, the implications for enterprises and real estate or land ownership are tremendous. In particular, modernisation in China comes with a very intensive reallocation of land-use within and around cities, frequently imposing the brutal displacement of residents. Naturally, liberal constitutions explicitly or implicitly provide for the possibility of expropriation in the public interest. But the absence of the legal inviolability of private property in the Chinese Constitution and the subordination of private property to public property practically obliterates the possibility of appealing against government abuses if the Constitution is assumed to be a justiciable one.

In such a context, the 2004 amendments attracted considerable attention. At the XVIth Congress held in November 2002, there was further comment on the tension between retaining the public sector as the mainstay of the economy and promoting non-public sectors alongside President *Jiang Zemin*'s report to the plenary session indicated that the two policies should not be "set against each other", but, on the contrary, "unified" in the process of "socialist modernisation".[30] In the same 2002 report, perfecting the legal system to protect "individual private properties" (*siren caichan*) and creating an equally competitive environment for individual and private economic sectors were defined as the state's priorities. Consequently, the 2004 amendments to Articles 11 and 13 proclaimed that "citizens' lawful private property is inviolable", presumably placing the protection of private property on par with that of public property. The state's pledge to "protect the lawful rights and interests of the non-public sectors of the economy" as well as the "rights of citizens to private property" has been hailed as the beginning of the end of the system of public ownership. Whereas the preceding draft of Article 11 called for the state to "guide, supervise and manage" the private sector, the

29 *Blanchard, H.*, op. cit., 386.
30 *Huang, X. F.*: The Path to Clarity: Development of Property Rights in China, in: Columbia Journal of Asian Law, 17 (2004), 202–204.

revised version required it to take a more active role to "encourage and support" the development of the private sector. Finally, the commitment to "make compensation for any expropriation or requisition" of real or private property was also a significant move from mere recognition to a real constitutional protection of private property in China.

In conjunction with the above, the official recognition of private entrepreneurs as constituents of the CCP has attracted the most attention. Aware of the role of entrepreneurs in the development of the Chinese economy and of their growing social leadership, *Jiang Zemin* formally admitted the possibility of entrepreneurs' becoming members of to the CCP in November 2002 by identifying them as "builders of socialism with Chinese characteristics". Their new status was subsequently codified in the 2004 amendment to paragraph 10 of the Preamble, which seeks to include "the builders of the cause of socialism" in the "patriotic united front", a reference to the Chinese People's Political Consultative Congress (CPPCC).[31]

Last but not least, the 2004 amendment had important implications regarding individual rights. Article 23 added one paragraph to Article 14 of the Constitution, which reads: "The state establishes a social security system compatible with the level of economic development." Article 24 added one paragraph to Article 33 of the Constitution, stipulating that "the state respects and preserves human rights". The later followed up Article 13 of the 1999 amendment, modifying Article 5 of the Constitution to provide that "the People's Republic of China governs the country according to law and makes it a socialist country ruled by law".

In substantive terms, the 2004 amendment significantly differed from previous reforms with some real progress in the assertion of rights. In sum, however, it does not come as a surprise that the development of constitutional reform in China has been mainly policy-driven, with revisions subsequently providing the institutional framework for implementing policies initiated by the CCP. We will now turn to the analysis of this reform process in more detail.

---

31 Entrepreneurs' party membership is by no means unconditional. Many current CCP members are either *xiahai*, former government cadres who have "jumped into the sea" of the private sector and therefore possess some degree of political power to begin with, or wealthy managers of large companies who have amassed considerable economic power.

IV. Constitutionalism from Above: Governing by Law

Although various participants intervene in the formal constitutional reform process, the key role rests with the Central Committee of the CCP. According to Article 64 of the 1982 Constitution,[32] only the Standing Committee of the NPC or one-fifth of the members of the NPC can propose a constitutional amendment. However, the wording of Article 64 reflects only one part of the picture. As seen in the previous sections, history shows that it is always the Central Committee of the CCP who initiates the process of constitutional reform and proposes a draft amendment to the Standing Committee of the NPC. Such a constitutional convention[33] places the Central Committee in an exclusive position of agenda setter, both reflecting its pivotal power in Chinese politics and establishing its control of constitutional policy-making.

Constitutional reform in the PRC is also closely related, and indeed subordinated, to changes in the Charter of the CCP.[34] The 1982 Constitution was adopted by the NPC after the XIIth Congress of the CCP had amended its own "constitution" in the same year. Each of the 1988, 1993, 1999 and 2004 constitutional amendments also followed changes in the constitution of the CCP, which took place in sequence in 1987, 1992, 1997 and 2002. The substance of constitutional reform therefore primarily reflects the shifts in ideology of the CCP. For instance, when the resolution of the XIVth CCP's Congress in 1992 declared that China's modernisation would be guided by the theory "to construct socialism with Chinese characteristics" (*jianshe you zhongguo tese de shehui zhuyi*), the 1993 constitutional amendment modified the Preamble accordingly. In 1997, the XVth CCP's Congress added "Deng Xiaoping's theory" as one of the Party's ideological tenets and declared as its objective adherence to a principle of "rule by law" to develop socialism in China. Similarly, the 1999 amendment transposed this ideological change in the Constitution.

The *de facto* monopoly of constitutional initiatives with the Central Committee is not, however, exclusive of any consultation process. Amendment proposals are drafted by a commission appointed by the Politburo of the CCP, a body that seeks advice and comments from four different types of organisations:

---

32 Art. 64, paragraph 1 stipulates that "Amendments to the Constitution are to be proposed by the Standing Committee of the National People's Congress or by more than one-fifth of the deputies to the National People's Congress and adopted by a vote of more than two-thirds of all the deputies to the Congress".

33 *Yin, X.H./Fang, B.G.*: Lun Woguo Xianxing 'Zhengcexing Xiu Xianfa Moshi de Juxianxing [The Limitations of the Current "Policy-oriented" Model of Constitutional Reform], in: Law Info China, 1999 (http://law1.chinalawinfo.com/newlaw2002/SLC/SLC.asp?Db=art&Gid=335566947).

34 Ibid.

- each central ministerial department and commission, including the People's Liberation Army (PLA);
- provincial authorities, including People's Congresses and the CCP's authorities;
- "the eight small democratic parties"[35] and other social organisations; and, finally,
- experts and scholars relevant to the issues involved in the constitutional reform.

On the basis of recommendations collected from these authorities and interests groups, the Commission drafts an initial proposal submitted for review to the Politburo and to the Central Committee.[36] If both approve the draft in principle, it is then submitted to the above governmental and non-governmental organisations for further comments. The commission for constitutional amendment then revises the proposal before re-submitting it to the Central Committee and to the Politburo. The latter in turn reviews the proposal before it enters the legislative process, i.e. when the Politburo submits it to the Standing Committee of the NPC on behalf of the Central Committee.

Normally, the Standing Committee of the NPC strictly follows the wording suggested by the Politburo when the proposal is submitted to the NPC annual meeting in March, the only authority empowered to pass constitutional amendments. However, it is worth noticing that, during the discussion of the proposal for the 1993 constitutional amendment by the Standing Committee of the NPC, some modifications of the CCP's initial version were formulated. The Standing Committee recommended adding one sentence to paragraph 10 of the Preamble, reading "the system of multiparty cooperation and political consultation led by the Communist Party of China will exist and develop for a long time to come".[37] The recommendation was conveyed to the Politburo, which revised its proposal after internal discussion. This was the first time the Politburo reconsidered its own proposal of constitutional reform at the initiative of the Chinese legislature.[38]

---

35 The CCP is indeed not the only lawful political party in China. There are eight other "democratic parties" with legal status in the PRC. These parties supported the CCP during the civil war of 1946–1949.

36 According to Art. 22 of the constitution of the CCP, the Central Committee and the Politburo are the central authority of the CCP. Normally, the Central Committee is convened only during the annual meeting. The Politburo is the standing organ elected by the Central Committee and exercises the power of the Central Committee when the annual meeting of the latter is over.

37 The recommendation eventually became Art. 4 of the constitutional amendment.

38 *Du, Q. Q.*: Woguo 1993 Nian Xiuxian Guocheng zhong Cunzai de Nuogan Chengxu Xiaci [Several Procedural Defects in the Process of 1993 Constitutional Amendment of China], in: Zhongguo Xianfa Shili Yanjiu I [Research on Constitutional Developments in China I], Beijing, 2005, 205.

This move was very remarkable. On the one hand, it can be regarded as a kind of parliamentarisation of Chinese constitutionalism, since it was the first time that the NPC took an active role in initiating constitutional change. On the other hand, the wording of the revision, highly praising both the leadership role of the CCP and the process by which the Politburo still had to approve the modification, was quite eloquent about the strict submission of constitutional developments in China to the initiative and control of the CCP.

V. Constitutionalism from Below: Civil and Legal Activism for the Rule of Law

As we can see from the above, the constitutionalisation of Chinese politics, despite some dramatic changes in ideology reflected in constitutional amendments, has been a gradual and limited process. The picture somewhat changes, however, when constitutionalism is not considered from above, i.e. at the top of the state apparatus, but from below, i.e. the way citizens or legal activists essentially make use of existing procedures.

In the absence of formal provisions for judicial and constitutional review, desperate citizens helped by active lawyers have invoked a legal procedure recently established under Article 90 (2) of China's 2001 Law on Legislation (*Lifa La*). This provision grants Chinese citizens the right to propose that the Standing Committee of the NPC review administrative regulations, the rulings of the Supreme People's Court (SPC) and local laws that they deem legally incompatible with the Constitution.[39]

In a decision of 13 August 2001 (the *Qi Yulin* case), the Chinese Supreme Court, asked to arbitrate a private litigation (usurpation of access to university), considered that the violation of a constitutional right (access to education) could open the way to compensation in the absence of specific legislation. The decision and its justification attracted numerous comments since this was the first time that a court indeed referred to the Constitution in making a decision regarding citizens' rights.[40] Chinese legal commentaries exaggeratedly (and wrongly) referred to the famous *Marbury v. Madison* decision of 1803 by which jurisprudence rather than formal changes of the fundamental law opened the way to judicial

---

39 *Balme, S.*: The Judicialisation of Politics and the Politicisation of the Judiciary in China (1978–2005), in: Global Jurist Frontiers, 5/1, (2005) (available at: http://www.bepress.com/gj/frontiers/vol5/iss1/art1).

40 *Kui, S.*: The Beginning of the Era of the Rule of the Constitution? Reinterpreting China's First Constitutional Case, in: Pacific Rim Law and Policy Journal, 12/1 (2003), 199–231, here 200–215.

review in the US. In the same vein, in 2003 Judge *Li Huijuan* from Henan province refused to implement a local regulation in a civil law case on the ground of its incompatibility with Article 64 of the same Law on Legislation. Initially suspended, the judge finally regained her position after a wide mobilisation of the media, lawyers and legal academics. Again, the affair attracted important controversies about the constitutional status of the law referred to and about the procedure. Finally and more tragically, in 2003 the death of the student *Sun Zhigang* following violence during his detention by the police motivated a group of lawyers to invoke Article 90 of the Law on Legislation to address the Standing Committee of the NPC.[41] They intended to contest the constitutional basis of a form of administrative detention called the "custody and repatriation" regulation under which *Sun Zhigang* had been put under arrest, and they called for the establishment of its constitutional review. Before any decision from the NPC had been taken, the State Council withdrew the corresponding regulations.[42] Finally, the same NPCSC has been put in the position of interpreting the PRC Constitution by political developments in the Hong Kong Special Administrative Region (HKSAR), particularly when amendments to the HKSAR basic law are considered.[43] Ironically enough, the conservative approach of the PRC's authorities to democratisation in Hong Kong and its common law system contributes to a moderate constitutionalisation of politics on the mainland. These different developments are obviously far too limited to be interpreted as a full swing toward constitutional or judicial review. At least they show some juridification of the Constitution, in some instances used by the jurisprudence, and the existence of a vivid debate among legal activists and academics about judicial review either by a specific organ of the NPC or through the creation of an independent court.[44] In that respect they represent some significant developments in the Chinese political and legal culture.

Does this impact on the ordinary life of Chinese citizens through the justiciability of the Constitution? It is hardly disputable that Chinese authorities frequently repress legal activists and make use of arbitrary detention. However, this does not mean that legal recourse is either inexistent or ineffective. Quite the op-

41 *Hand, K.*: Citizens Engage the Constitution: the Sun Zhigang Incident and Constitutional Review Proposals in the People's Republic of China, in: Balme, S./Dowdle, M. (eds.): Constitutionalism and Judicial Power in China, Basingstoke (forthcoming).

42 *Delmas-Marty, M.*: La construction d'un Etat de droit en Chine dans le contexte de la mondialisation, in: Delmas-Marty, M./Will, P. E. (eds.): La Chine et la démocratie, Paris, 2007, 551–575.

43 *Ghai, Y.*: The Legal Foundations of Hong Kong's Autonomy: Building on Sand, in: The Asia Pacific Journal of Public Administration, 29/1 (2007), 3–28.

44 *Balme, S.*, op. cit.

posite, it can be argued that it is today the dominant form of social mobilisation in China and the major channel for constitutional change in the absence of significant political reform. In the course of these struggles, citizens make use of constitutional arguments to contest public policy and to request a legal basis for government action. In doing so, they not only shape public policy, but also claim and actively promote the constitutional foundations of the state. Recent constitutional complaints reviewed by *Keith Hand* that involved tax and compensation issues as well as challenges to the Property-Rights Law illustrate this dynamic.[45]

As indicated above, the NPCSC, not the judiciary, has the power to invalidate regulations that contradict the Constitution and national law.[46] The Legislation Law provided the first concrete legal mechanism through which citizens could advance constitutional claims. Citizens have made active use of this mechanism, submitting more than 50 requests since 2000 for NPCSC review on a wide range of issues.

In July 2006, an annual road fee for car owners attracted public scrutiny after the Chinese media reported that a car owner who failed to pay the fee had been charged 780,000 yuan in back penalties. Soon afterward, lawyers uncovered an apparent conflict between administrative regulations that authorise the fee and two national laws (the Highway Law and the Legislation Law), and they sent a claim to the NPC Standing Committee challenging the legality of the administrative regulations authorising the road fee. After the Ministry of Transportation declared it would continue to collect the fees in 2007, another lawyer submitted a broader proposal to the NPCSC. The Chinese media reported actively on the issue, something that put significant pressure on the Ministry. As public controversy over the road fee mounted, the government responded. In late November 2006, Xinhua News Agency published an interview with NPCSC and State Council legal officials, confirming they had received several citizen's proposals and reviewed them in accordance with legal procedures. They then offered a legal justification for continuing to levy the fee. Although the interview did not constitute a formal legal ruling on the citizen proposals, it was nonetheless the first time that the NPCSC had publicly answered and addressed the legal arguments in a citizen's proposal submitted under the Legislation Law.

Another case in 2006 was related to the death of three students in a traffic accident in Chongqing. Pursuant to a 2003 legal interpretation by the Supreme

---

45 *Hand, K.*, op. cit.
46 Subsequent provisions extended the right to include proposals challenging Supreme People's Court judicial interpretations.

People's Court (SPC), many local courts determine compensation partly on the basis of whether such accident victims hold an urban or rural residence registration. Relying on this standard, the responsible party provided the families of two Chongqing students more than twice the compensation it agreed to provide the family of a third student, who held a rural residence registration. Domestic media reported widely on the case, resulting in public controversy over the unjust compensation disparity and related calls for amending the SPC interpretation.

In the wake of these proposals, both local and national authorities announced legal reforms related to the compensation standard. In 2006, local governments in five provinces and cities adopted reforms to bring compensation for certain migrants into line with that for urban residents. The SPC also began accepting public suggestions about revising its interpretation. In March 2007, NPC delegates introduced motions calling on the Supreme People's Court to equalise the standard. Shortly afterward, SPC Chief Justice *Xiao Yang* announced that the interpretation would be revised after the NPC session. This controversy provides a second recent example of a citizen's proposal that influenced government policy and reinforced constitutional norms.

A third case was the constitutional challenge to the passage of the Property-Rights Law. Originally scheduled for March 2006, the passage of the law was delayed after Peking University law professor *Gong Xiantian* issued an open letter arguing that the bill contravened Article 12 of the Constitution, which declares that state property is inviolable. The appeal generated extensive controversy after its diffusion via the internet. As the NPCSC prepared to deliberate on a revised draft in late 2006, the Chinese government launched an extensive campaign to defend the proposal and its constitutionality. In December of the same year, when the NPCSC approved the Property-Rights Law for consideration by the full NPC, it engaged in an active communication campaign, including a public statement by its chairman, a press conference by senior officials and publication of scholarly defenses of the law's constitutionality by state-run media. Again, although the issue substantially differed in this case, the government had to publicly take action to justify its policy on constitutional grounds.

These events are only small steps toward an active use of the Constitution by citizens and its full effectiveness in guiding policy-making. But their significance in the PRC's context should not be underestimated. Prior to the fall of 2006, the NPCSC had not issued a direct public response to any citizen's proposals filed under Article 90 (2) of the Legislation Law. The fact that China's government publicly reacts to its citizens' legal and constitutional arguments rather than merely ignoring or suppressing them is notable in itself. But these responses also introduce precedents and gradually expand a space for constitutional activism among citizens. Not only do these responses legitimise the idea that legislative acts must comply with national law and the Constitution; they also acknowledge the right of citizens to call legal provisions into question on constitutional grounds and they build public expectations for government responsiveness to future appeals. Anticipating a flood of similar petitions relating to other grievances, the Legal Work Committee of the Standing Committee has established a special office to give preliminary scrutiny to such claims.[47] A series of complaints has reportedly been filed with the Standing Committee against various State Council regulations, particularly by collective groups of Hepatitis B carriers claiming that civil service regulations unlawfully discriminated against them, by female civil servants petitioning to invalidate the requirement that women retire five years earlier than men and by thousands more challenging regulations authorising the demolition of their housing. These complaints have not yet resulted in a constitutional decision by the Standing Committee, but they help to spur administrative reforms and give popular support to Chinese constitutionalism.

VI. Conclusion

Having reviewed constitutional developments in the PRC since the beginning of the reform era, how can we characterise the position of Chinese constitutionalism today? Probably the first element to consider is the long-term perspective and the tumultuous Chinese history we introduced at the beginning of this contribution. The PRC has now accumulated a 25-year period of constitutional government, an unprecedented fact on the Chinese mainland. This can definitely be attributed to the reform policy launched by *Deng Xiaoping* and prolonged by the successive Chinese leaders as the institutional and political foundations of the CCP's policy. It resulted in the establishment of a wholly new political regime, one based on a new constitution for the Chinese state, and in dramatic changes in the political culture that are hallmarked by the role of the constitution in domestic politics. This process can be seen as a second foundation of the PRC by the CCP after the Cultural Revolution, one in which the state once again emanates from the Party. The rooting of constitutional government in Chinese politics is definitely a significant change in the long term.

---

47 *Cohen, J.*: Law in Political Transitions: Lessons from East Asia and the Road Ahead for China, in: New York University Journal of International Law and Politics, 37/3 (2005), 423–439, here 431–436.

Having said that, the major issues are whether the reform policy is in any way conducive to further political change for the PRC and, more precisely, if constitutional reform and constitutional jurisprudence display any signs of political liberalisation. From this point of view, a number of observations can be derived from the above developments. Firstly, while the doctrine of the CCP underwent radical changes regarding economic policy and the status of the market economy in China, amendments on political issues have been far more limited, if not absent. It is true that dramatic advances have been made with the recognition of the rule of law, human rights and property rights in the Constitution, advances that represent significant political changes. But the acknowledgement of rights hardly suffices to serve as a guarantee if the Constitution is not justiciable, and reforms initiated by the Chinese leadership on this issue have been limited to the provisions in the 2001 Law on Legislation we reviewed above.

Secondly, when the process of constitutional amendment is considered, it is remarkable that, up to now, constitutional reform exclusively follows, proclaims and adapts to policy changes initiated by the CCP. Broadly speaking and when key public policies are considered, constitutional change is basically a step in the policy implementation conducted by the CCP and it illustrates the overall submission of the state to the Party. Even when the NPCSC took the unusual step of initiating a change in the amendment suggested by the Central Committee of the CCP, it was to further assert the leadership role of the Party. Beyond that, it can be argued that the Constitution largely exerts a lock-in effect on the CCP supremacy in Chinese politics and therefore fails to truly liberalise the Chinese regime.

Thirdly, it follows that all instances of progress in the rule of law, if they now can find a legal basis in the Constitution, are more likely to be substantial in the areas of judicial reform, legal procedures, law codification, the training of the judiciary and conditions for legal professions than in the Constitution as such.[48] This by no means equates to a sudden advent of the rule of law as an unprecedented state of affairs in China but, quite on the contrary, to a long-term modernisation process by which rights are progressively acknowledged and increasingly respected, if not fully guaranteed. Identifying these developments does not imply that the situation of rights in China is satisfying; rather, it helps to locate the actual sources of substantial changes.

---

48 *Peerenboom, R.*: China's Long March toward Rule of Law, Cambridge, 2002; *id.*: China Modernizes. Threat to the West or Model for the Rest?, Oxford, 2007; *Lin, C.X.*: A Quiet Revolution: An Overview of China's Judicial Reform, in: Asian-Pacific Law and Policy Journal, 4/2 (2003), 255–319.

Finally, if the institutional constitutionalisation of Chinese politics has thus far remained strictly contained by the CCP leadership, it has also opened a limited but significant space for constitutional activism by citizens and legal professionals, indeed probably the most remarkable political trend of recent years in the PRC. These events demonstrate the growing importance of constitutional issues in politics and public opinion, and deserve attention as manifesting a significant evolution of Chinese political culture. Of course, their political implications should not be overestimated. It would be premature to interpret the evolutions described here as the emergence of an institutionalised and independent legal process for constitutional review. China remains far from establishing such a mechanism. Under the current Constitution, judges are not independent of political authorities, and citizens do not have a legal right to compel a review of their constitutional claims. Their capacity to influence the government's decisions is also dependent on their capacity to attract media coverage to generate public-opinion pressure; here again, although the flow of information on the internet is more difficult to control, citizens are confronted with the lack of institutionalised pluralism of Chinese society. Many obstacles remain in the way of China's constitutional development, and constitutional activism as we describe it here is therefore probably more significant in terms of political culture and social mobilisation than in terms of institutional change. It is nevertheless illustrative of a process through which citizens make use of the Constitution to pressure the government and in which the constitutionality of public policy is not left to the exclusive discretion of leadership but also triggers public interactions between citizen and the state.

Whether these developments will indeed nourish further political reforms remains an open question. From a Western and liberal perspective, the rule of law is understood not only as the protection of citizens' rights *by* the state but also *against* potential abuses by the government. It is therefore quite apparent that beyond the recognition of these rights in the Constitution, their effective implementation requires at least some degree of separation of powers, in particular independence of the judiciary, as well as the freedom for citizens to publicly express their grievances and to access legal procedures.[49] It is doubtful from this perspective that the rule of law can be fully established without freedom of expression and association and competitive elections. As was the case in Taiwan and again in South Korea, robust constitutional enforcement is more likely to

---

49 *Killion, M.U.*: China's Amended Constitution: Quest for Liberty and Independent Judicial Review, in: Washington University Global Studies Law Review, 4/1 (2005), 43–80.

follow and consolidate, rather than force, political reform at the top.[50] But China may also follow a different constitutional trajectory referring to "Asian values", and it is obviously trying to do so in adhering to the principle of rule of law while avoiding substantial political reform. In that case, the Chinese concept of rule of law would involve traditional citizen-state interaction, rooted in a Confucian tradition, in which Chinese elites advance moral claims to guide state behaviour rather than the more adversarial process in which constitutional disputes are resolved in liberal constitutional regimes.

The ideological continuity of Chinese leadership with "the people's democratic dictatorship" and democratic centralism do not allow for an accomplished political transition if we understand this to be a full recognition of pluralism including freedom of expression and association, competitive elections and a related inversion of relations between the state and the CCP's respective constitutions. However, this does not preclude some elements of liberalisation *within,* rather than *by,* the regime. The growing references to the Constitution in Chinese politics, initially under the concept of "rule by law", progressively establish some effective elements of "rule of law" by which citizens indeed make use of the Constitution to contest and to limit the government's authority and public policy. Seen from this perspective, the recent constitutional developments in China go far beyond the mere window-dressing that is frequently associated with legal practices in communist regimes.

50 *Cohen, J.,* op. cit.

IV. State Structures and Constitutional Reform

Verfassungsreformen in Bundesstaaten – Fallstricke und Auswege

von Arthur Benz

I. Einleitung

Seit den 1970er Jahren unterliegen moderne Staaten einem fundamentalen Wandel. Dieser wurde ausgelöst durch das Ende der anhaltenden Wachstumsphase nach dem Zweiten Weltkrieg, das den Ausbau wohlfahrtsstaatlicher Leistungen ermöglichte. Verstärkt wurden die Herausforderungen durch die Öffnung der Weltmärkte, welche die Fähigkeiten von Staaten, ihre Wirtschaft und Finanzen autonom zu bestimmen, drastisch einschränkte. Gesellschaftliche Veränderungen wie der Wandel der Altersstruktur und Wanderungsbewegungen erforderten ebenfalls Anpassungen von Politiken und waren mit den bestehenden Strukturen der Leistungserbringung schwerlich zu bewältigen. Infolge dieser Entwicklungen verschoben sich die Gewichte zwischen zentralen und dezentralen Einheiten innerhalb der territorialen Staatsorganisation, weil eine einheitliche Steuerung durch das Zentrum an Effektivität verlor, weil wirtschaftliche Globalisierung zu einem Transfer von Kompetenzen auf supranationale Organisationen führte und gleichzeitig die Regionen stärkte, weil die Pluralisierung der Gesellschaft sich in internationalen Verflechtungen, aber auch in einer regionalen Differenzierung niederschlug, und weil soziale Auswirkungen des gesellschaftlichen Wandels regional differierten. Diese Prozesse förderten gleichzeitig die Internationalisierung von Staatstätigkeit und die Dezentralisierung innerhalb von Nationalstaaten,[1] die zudem mit der Tatsache konfrontiert waren, dass wirtschaftliche und soziale Unterschiede zwischen Regionen zunahmen und nicht mehr aus einem wachsenden Steueraufkommen ausgeglichen werden konnten.

Die meisten westlichen Staaten reagierten auf diese Veränderungen zunächst im Rahmen ihrer bestehenden Verfassungen oder jedenfalls mit begrenzten Änderungen ihrer Verfassung.[2] Mit der Beschleunigung der Globalisierung infolge des historischen Umbruchs nach 1989 leiteten viele Regierungen weiter reichende Verfassungsreformen ein, weil sich die Bedingungen der Staatstätigkeit so sehr

---

1 Ausführlich *Benz, A.*: Der moderne Staat, 2. Aufl., München/Wien, 2008, i.E.

2 *Banting, K.G./Simeon, R.* (Hg.): Redesigning the State: the Politics of Constitutional Change, Toronto, 1985; *Hesse, J.J./Benz, A.*: Die Modernisierung der Staatsorganisation, Baden-Baden, 1990.

verändert hatten, dass Regeln, die Voraussetzung des Regierens sind, nicht mehr geeignet erschienen. Die Reformen betrafen im Kern die territoriale Organisation des politischen Systems und zielten auf eine Neuordnung der Gewaltenteilung und Beziehungen zwischen Gebietskörperschaften und ihrer Institutionen.

Bei aller Aktualität der Ereignisse sollte nicht übersehen werden, dass horizontal und vertikal gewaltenteilige Regierungssysteme einer dauerhaften Dynamik ihrer Strukturen ausgesetzt sind und dementsprechend, je nach der Regelungsdichte ihrer Verfassung mehr oder weniger häufig, ihre Verfassungsordnungen ändern müssen. *„Federalism is by definition an unfinished business because many issues can be neither foreseen nor immediately solved.“* [3] Ursache dafür sind einerseits Spannungen, die in den differenzierten Machtstrukturen angelegt sind, weil Inhaber von Positionen im politischen System immer geneigt sind, ihre Macht auszudehnen. Andererseits wirkt sich die Art der Gewaltenteilung unmittelbar auf die Qualität der möglichen oder realen Politikergebnisse aus, und das gilt insbesondere für die vertikale Dimension der Gewaltenteilung in Bundesstaaten.

Damit stellt sich ein schwerwiegendes Problem. Einerseits sind Verfassungsreformen immer wieder notwendig, andererseits sind sie schwer zu verwirklichen. Letzteres liegt an Regeln der Verfassungsänderung, die qualifizierte Mehrheiten erfordern, darüber hinaus aber auch an den Besonderheiten der Konfliktsituation und der Akteurskonstellation. In Bundesstaaten entscheiden regelmäßig auch Vertreter der dezentralen Gebietskörperschaften in verfassungspolitischen Angelegenheiten mit.[4] Unter diesen Bedingungen ist die Diskrepanz zwischen Notwendigkeit und Machbarkeit von Verfassungsreformen besonders ausgeprägt. Bundesstaaten befinden sich in einer Falle, die *Fritz W. Scharpf* für Strukturen der Politikverflechtung herausgearbeitet hat.[5] Selbst wenn offensichtliche Funktionsprobleme des Regierens eine Verfassungsreform erfordern, ist es eher wahrscheinlich, dass diese scheitert als dass sie gelingt. Darin liegt das fundamentale Verfassungsproblem föderativer Systeme, das im folgenden Abschnitt dieses Artikels näher erläutert wird.

Trotz zahlreicher Einzelstudien zu Verfassungsänderungen vermag die Politikwissenschaft noch keine befriedigende Antworten auf die Frage zu geben, wie Staaten aus dieser Falle herauskommen oder wie sie mit ihr umgehen können.[6]

---

3 *Duchacek, I.:* Comparative Federalism, New York u.a., 1970, 193.
4 Ebd., 230.
5 *Scharpf, F.W.:* The Joint-Decision-Trap. Lessons from German Federalism and European Integration, in: Public Administration, 66/3 (1988), 239–278.
6 Vergleichende Arbeiten gibt es kaum, und die wenigen vorhandenen sind veraltet. Siehe *Banting, K.G./ Simeon, R.,* a.a.O.; *Livingston, W.S.:* Federalism and Constitutional Change, Oxford, 1956.

Die Unterscheidung von Modi der Modernisierung territorialer Staatsorganisationen, die *Hesse* und *Benz* vorgeschlagen haben,[7] weist darauf hin, dass es vermutlich unterschiedliche Wege gibt. Die genannte Untersuchung bezog sich allerdings nicht explizit auf Verfassungsreformen und erfasste nicht deren Besonderheiten. Ich will im dritten Abschnitt Verfassungsreformen im deutschen und im kanadischen Bundesstaat analysieren, um Hinweise zu gewinnen, wie eine Lösung des dargestellten Dilemmas möglich ist. Dabei gehe ich davon aus, dass allein die Tatsache, ob Verfassungsreformen scheitern oder gelingen, wenig darüber aussagt, ob Verfassungsprobleme wirklich gelöst sind. Wir müssen vielmehr das Zusammenspiel von Verfassungsreform und Verfassungsentwicklung in den Blick nehmen, um zu verstehen, wie Staaten mit ihren grundlegenden Strukturproblemen umgehen können. Im abschließenden Abschnitt skizziere ich Thesen zu geeigneten Verfahrensweisen für die Verfassungspolitik im Bundesstaat.

II. Verfassung als Voraussetzung und Problem der föderativen Ordnung

Föderative Systeme benötigen einerseits eine verfassungsrechtliche Stabilisierung der Machtverteilung, andererseits unterliegen sie einem ständigen Veränderungsprozess. Auf diesen Widerspruch machte die Föderalismusforschung immer wieder aufmerksam, wenngleich er selten explizit formuliert wurde.[8] Die Föderalismusforschung konzentrierte sich auf das Problem der Stabilisierung,[9] dagegen wurde selten untersucht, wie die Verfassungsordnung an den Wandel angepasst werden kann. *William S. Livingston,* der sich eingehend mit der Dynamik und der Verfassung föderativer Systeme befasst hat, formulierte das Verfassungsproblem wie folgt:

> „*Every constitution is constantly undergoing changes of various kinds through the impact of new needs upon it. But the means by which these changes take place differ greatly. Necessity for alterations in the institutional structure arises under all systems, but in a federal government the problem is even more acute because the distribution of powers between states and nation, which is not present in unitary systems, gives rise to demands for shifts in the allocation of functions from one government to the other.*"[10]

7   *Hesse, J.J./Benz, A.,* a.a.O.
8   Als Überblick vgl. *Burgess, M.:* Comparative Federalism. Theory and Practice, London/New York, 2006, 156–160.
9   *Filippov, M./Ordeshook, P.C./Shvetsova, O.:* Designing Federalism, Cambridge, 2004; *Riker, W.:* Federalism, Boston/Toronto, 1964.
10   *Livingston, W.S.,* a.a.O., 11 f.

Livingston erkannte dabei, dass der Wandel der Institutionen durch gesellschaftliche Veränderungen verursacht werden kann und föderative Systeme ihre Arbeitsweise kontinuierlich anpassen müssen. Er wies aber auch darauf hin, dass ein
Verfassungswandel durch die politische Praxis oder die Interpretation durch Gerichte oft nicht ausreichen, um auf Veränderungen zu reagieren:

> „*The formal procedure of amendment is of greater importance than the informal processes
> because it constitutes a higher authority to which appeal lies on any question that may
> arise. While changing conventions, new legislative acts, and new interpretations may effect
> serious changes in the constitutional structure, the formal amendment is superior to them
> all: it may override any of the others and none of the others may override it.*"[11]

Notwendigkeiten zur Verfassungsänderungen resultieren aus zwei eng miteinander verbundenen Ursachen, die in der Eigendynamik föderativer Gewaltenteilung
angelegt sind.[12] Zum einen neigen Inhaber von Ämtern auf den verschiedenen
Ebenen und in verschiedenen Institutionen dazu, ihre Macht auszudehnen, und
erzeugen dadurch Instabilität.[13] Zum anderen wirken sich ökonomische und
soziale Entwicklungen auf die Leistungsfähigkeit der einzelnen territorialen Einheiten des Regierungssystems, auf die Ressourcenverteilung zwischen ihnen und
auf die Konfliktstrukturen aus. Beide Ursachen betreffen drei Dimensionen der
Gewaltenteilung, die in föderativen Systemen miteinander verbunden sind: die
vertikale Kompetenz- und Ressourcenverteilung zwischen Ebenen; die horizontale Ressourcenverteilung zwischen den Gliedstaaten; und das Verhältnis zwischen Exekutiven und Legislativen innerhalb der Ebenen des föderativen Systems,
das durch die intergouvernementalen Beziehungen beeinflusst wird.

  Die durch Machtpolitik der Akteure bedingte Instabilität zeigt sich in erster
Linie in der intragouvernementalen Dimension der Gewaltenteilung. Föderative
Demokratien sind anfällig für Machtverschiebungen auf die Exekutive, die für
notwendige Koordination zwischen Ebenen sorgen müssen und die Prozesse der
intergouvernementalen Politik nutzen können, um sich der Kontrolle durch Par-
lamente oder Interessengruppen zu entziehen. Dies ist ein weithin beschriebenes
Phänomen.[14] Nicht übersehen werden darf aber, dass auch Parlamente in der
Lage sind, Handlungsspielräume ihrer Regierungen zu verengen, wenn die De-

---

11 Ebd., 13 f. Ähnlich argumentiert für die USA *Sundquist, J.L.*: Constitutional Reform and Effective
    Government, Washington, DC, 1992, 16–18.
12 *Friedrich, C.J.*: Trends of Federalism in Theory and Practice, New York, 1968; *Vile, M.J.C.*: Federal Theory
    and the New Federalism, in: Jaensch, D. (Hg.): The Politics of New Federalism, Adelaide, 1977; *Watts, R.*:
    The Federal Idea and its Contemporary Relevance, Kingston, 2007, 7.
13 *Filippov, M./Ordeshook, P.C./Shvetsova, O.*, a.a.O.; *Riker, W.*, a.a.O.
14 *Benz, A.*: Föderalismus und Demokratie. Eine Untersuchung zum Zusammenwirken zweier Verfassungs-
    prinzipien (polis-Arbeitspapiere aus der FernUniversität Hagen, Nr. 57), Hagen, 2003; *Smith, J.*: Federalism,
    Vancouver, 2004, 11–37.

mokratiekosten der intergouvernementalen Koordination zu hoch werden, was sich am Beispiel der Reaktion nationaler Parlamente auf die europäische Integration ablesen lässt.[15] In der vertikalen Dimension zeigt sich die Dynamik der Machtverhältnisse in den Bemühungen zentraler wie dezentraler Regierungen, ihre Kompetenzen zu erweitern bzw. zu verteidigen. Die horizontalen Machtverhältnisse zwischen Gliedstaaten sind vor allem dann betroffen, wenn Fragen der Mitwirkung in Entscheidungsprozessen des Bundes oder die Sitzverteilung in Vertretungsorganen zur Diskussion stehen.

Gesellschaftliche Entwicklungen, die sich in neuen Problemlagen oder der Neubewertung von Aufgaben äußern können, wirken sich weniger auf die intragouvernementalen Beziehungen zwischen Parlament und Regierung als vielmehr auf die vertikale und horizontale Kompetenz- und Ressourcenverteilung aus. Die Verwirklichung individueller Rechte, die allen Menschen oder Bürgerinnen und Bürgern zustehen, erfordert zentrale Kompetenzen, weshalb die Erweiterung der Freiheit und Gleichheit im liberalen Wohlfahrtsstaat die Rolle des Zentralstaats gestärkt hat. Aus dem gleichen Grund führte die Liberalisierung im europäischen Markt zu Kompetenzverlagerungen auf die EU. Im dadurch ausgelösten Standortwettbewerb wiederum muss die Infrastruktur verbessert werden, für die meistens regionale Einheiten zuständig sind. Dezentralisierung der Entscheidung und Finanzierung öffentlicher Leistungen reduziert im Allgemeinen die Gleichheit und das Leistungsniveau im Wohlfahrtsstaat. In der Umweltpolitik ermöglicht Zentralisierung die Festlegung von Emissionsstandards, während Dezentralisierung eher an den Ursachen der Emissionen ansetzende Lösungen fördert. Die Kompetenzverteilung zwischen den Ebenen wirkt sich also unterschiedlich auf die Art und Weise aus, wie öffentliche Aufgaben erfüllt werden. Sie ergibt sich daher nicht aus objektiven Eigenschaften von Aufgaben, sondern aus einer Abwägung der Ziele, die erreicht werden sollen. Insofern ist die These der gesellschaftszentrierten Theorie des Föderalismus zu relativieren, wonach die Strukturen der territorialen Staatsorganisation durch gesellschaftliche Prozessen bestimmt werden,[16] und gleiches gilt für die normativen Aussagen der ökonomischen Theorie des Föderalismus.[17] In der vertikalen Dimension hängt die Gewaltenteilung eher von politischen Entscheidungen ab.

---

15 *Auel, K./Benz, A.*: Politics of Adjustment – The Europeanization of National Parliamentary Democracy, in: Journal of Legislative Studies, 11/3–4 (2005), 372–393.

16 *Smiley, D.*: Federal States and Federal Societies, with Special Reference to Canada, in: International Political Science Review, 5/4 (1984), 443–454.

17 *Sauerland, D.*: Föderalismus zwischen Freiheit und Effizienz. Der Beitrag der ökonomischen Theorie zur Gestaltung dezentralisierter politischer Systeme, Berlin, 1997.

Die Theorie des „*society centered federalism*"[18] trifft eher in der horizontalen Dimension zu. Die Ausprägung intergouvernementaler Konflikte zwischen dezentralen Gebietskörperschaften variiert mit der regionalen Entwicklung der Wirtschaft und mit der territorialen Differenzierung der Bevölkerung. Solche Konflikte nehmen je nach den geltenden Normen unterschiedliche Intensitäten an. Wirtschaftliche Disparitäten werden also in Gesellschaften, die eine Gleichwertigkeit der Lebensverhältnisse anstreben, anders behandelt als in liberalen Marktgesellschaften. Und die territoriale Differenzierung der Bevölkerung wird erst dann zum Problem, wenn Unterschiede in kollektive Identitäten umdefiniert werden und Vertreter regional konzentrierter Gruppen besondere Rechte einfordern. Bei aller Persistenz solcher Identitätskonflikte in „multinationalen" Föderationen[19] implizieren auch sie keine festgefügten Strukturen, weil sie von der Abwägung zwischen individuellen und kollektiven Rechten abhängen, wie in der kanadischen Verfassungsdiskussion besonders klar erkennbar wird.[20]

Da die drei Dimensionen der Gewaltenteilung interdependent sind, tangieren sie die genannten Entwicklungen alle gleichzeitig. Je nach Ursachen und Kräften, die Strukturdynamiken auslösen, und je nach politischer Bewertung der Konsequenzen rücken jedoch unterschiedliche Verfassungsregeln in den Mittelpunkt der Reformdiskussion. Wir können analytisch unterscheiden zwischen Demokratieproblemen, die durch eine zunehmende Verflechtung der Ebenen oder durch Zentralisierung zu Lasten der föderativen Gewaltenteilung und dezentralen Demokratie verursacht sind, Effektivitätsproblemen, die entweder in einer Überlastung einzelner Ebenen oder in der Blockade von Koordinations- und Entscheidungsprozessen liegen, oder Integrationsproblemen, die den Zusammenhalt des politischen Systems gefährden. Die Folgen für die Inhalte und den Verlauf von Verfassungsänderungen sind je nach dominierendem Problemtyp unterschiedlich. Unabhängig davon beruhen sie aber in der Regel auf anhaltenden Dynamiken, die Gegenstand der Verfassungspolitik sind und größere Reformen auf die Tagesordnung bringen können.

Dem steht gegenüber, dass Verfassungsreformen gerade in föderativen Systemen besonders schwierig sind und ihr Scheitern grundsätzlich als sehr wahrscheinlich gelten muss. Scheitern können Verfassungsreformen sowohl, weil die erforderlichen Mehrheiten für Entscheidungen nicht zustande kommen, als auch

---

18 *Livingston, W.S.*, a.a.O.; *ders.*: A Note on the Nature of Federalism, in: Wildavsky, A. (Hg.): American Federalism in Perspective, Boston, 1967, 33–40.

19 *Kymlicka, W.*: Federalism, Nationalism and Multiculturalism, in: Karmis, D./Norman, W. (Hg.): Theories of Federalism, New York, 2005, 269–292.

20 *Cairns, A.C.*: Carter versus Federalism. The Dilemma of Constitutional Reform, Montreal u.a., 1992.

weil Verfassungsänderungen durch problematische Kompromisse oder Tauschgeschäfte erreicht werden, womit Probleme nicht gelöst oder negative Folgen pro-
voziert werden. Für die Vermutung, dass Reformen mit hoher Wahrscheinlichkeit
blockiert werden oder misslingen, sprechen folgende Gründe:

- Zwar scheinen erfolgreiche Verfassungsgebungen in vielen föderativen Systemen die hier vertretene These zu widerlegen, generell ist allerdings davon aus-
  zugehen, dass Verfassungsreformen schwieriger sind als Entscheidungen über
  eine neue Verfassung, weil Akteure in einer anderen Situation handeln. Scheitert die Verfassungsgebung, so besteht ein Zustand einer nicht verfassungsrechtlich stabilisierten Ordnung weiter, der im Allgemeinen von allen als un-
  attraktiv abgelehnt wird. Bei der Änderung einer bestehenden Verfassung stellt
  der *Status quo,* der beim Misserfolg bestehen bleibt oder wenig verändert wird,
  in der Regel eine befriedigende und für viele Akteure oft bessere Alternative zu
  einer Entscheidung dar, deren Konsequenzen sie kennen.[21] Vielfach ist der
  Status quo verglichen mit einer Verfassungsänderung für eine Minderheit von
  Akteuren die bessere Alternative, die genügt, um bei qualifizierter Mehrheits-
  entscheidung ein Veto zu erreichen.
- Jede Reform der föderativen Ordnung verändert ein rechtlich geregeltes
  Gleichgewicht der Gewaltenteilung und bedeutet damit eine Umverteilung
  von Macht oder Ressourcen. Nach üblichen Verfahren sind die betroffenen
  Inhaber von Macht und Ressourcen, die von einer Umverteilung betroffen
  sind, an Verfassungsänderungen beteiligt, in den meisten Fällen sogar mit Ent-
  scheidungsrechten. Hinzu kommt, dass die hier angesprochenen Verfassungsregeln die Macht und die Ressourcen von Institutionen betreffen, die durch
  Gruppen von Akteuren in den Entscheidungsverfahren vertreten werden. Konflikte um Umverteilung spielen sich also zwischen kollektiven Akteuren ab, die
  über Vetomacht verfügen. Angesichts der Tatsache, dass Verfassungsänderungen in aller Regel nur mit einer qualifizierten Mehrheit zustande kommen und
  normativ betrachten ein möglichst breiter Konsens gefordert wird, ist offensichtlich, wie schwer unter diesen Bedingungen eine Änderung des *Status quo*
  ist.
- Verhandlungen über eine Änderung von Macht- und Ressourcenverteilungen
  können zu einer Einigung führen, wenn Akteure nicht allein eigene Interessen
  verfolgen, sondern über Normen der Verteilung argumentieren. Dass ein solcher Modus der Verfassungsverhandlung keine idealistische Forderung darstellt, sondern durchaus praktikabel ist, belegen die Untersuchungen *Jon Els-*

---

21 *Banting, K. G./Simeon, R.*: The Politics of Constitutional Change, in: dies. (Hg.), a.a.O., 1–29, hier 25.

*ter*s über Verfassunggebende Versammlungen.[22] *Elster* erläutert eine Reihe von Bedingungen, die Verhandlungen im Modus des *arguing* möglich machen.[23] In Mehrebenensystemen von Bundesstaaten sind diese aber schwer zu realisieren, weil Akteure sich nicht an individuelle Interessen oder fiktive Gemeinwohlinteressen orientieren, sondern an den Interessen der von ihnen repräsentierten Gebietskörperschaften, Parteien oder Institution. Anders als Vertreter in Verfassungsversammlungen unterliegen sie keiner „diffusen" Kontrolle durch die Öffentlichkeit, sondern einer „spezifischen" Kontrolle durch die von ihnen vertretene Interessenkoalition. In einer solchen Konstellation neigen Akteure zu *bargaining*-Verhalten und sind kaum geneigt, im Modus des *arguing* zu verhandeln.

Angesichts dieser Schwierigkeiten wäre es in föderativen Systemen eigentlich angebracht, Reformen der formalen Verfassung zu vermeiden. Allerdings ist dies kaum auf Dauer möglich, weil die Eigendynamik der Verfassungspolitik schwerlich zu kontrollieren ist. Die Normalität der inkrementelle Verfassungsentwicklung genügt vielfach nicht, die Kumulierung von Verfassungsproblemen zu vermeiden. Wenn diese ein bestimmtes Ausmaß überschritten haben, kommt die Verfassungsreform auf die Agenda.

III. Prozesse der Verfassungsreform in Bundesstaaten

Bevor diese Entwicklung und ihre Folgen am Beispiel von zwei Bundesstaaten erläutert werden, sind einige analytische Kategorien zu klären, die zum Verständnis von Verfassungsreformen in föderativen Staaten hilfreich sind.

1. Akteure und Prozesse der Verfassungsreform

Verfassungsreformen seien definiert als politische Prozesse, die auf eine Änderung der formalen Verfassung gerichtet sind. Der Begriff soll zudem eine Untergruppe von Verfassungsänderungen erfassen, die nicht nur einzelne Normen, sondern Bereiche einer Verfassung betreffen. Die Verlagerung einer einzelnen Gesetzgebungskompetenz wird also unter den Oberbegriff Verfassungsänderung subsumiert, während die Änderung der Kompetenzverteilung einschließlich ihrer

---

22 *Elster, J.*: Constitutional Bootstrapping in Philadelphia and Paris, in: Cardozo Law Review, 14/3 (1993), 549–575; *ders.*: Forces and Mechanisms in the Constitution-Making Process, in: Duke Law Journal, 45/2 (1995), 364–396.

23 Ebd.

Prinzipien als Verfassungsreform bezeichnet wird. Verfassungsreformen sind weiterhin zu unterscheiden von der evolutionären Entwicklung von Verfassungen, die durch die politische Praxis, durch die Anpassung des informalen Verfassungsrechts[24] oder durch Entscheidungen der Verfassungsrechtsprechung vorangetrieben wird. Gleichwohl darf Verfassungspolitik nicht mit „normaler", verfasster Politik gleichgesetzt werden. Erstere betrifft die Regeln, die vorausgesetzt werden müssen, um politische Entscheidungen zu ermöglichen. Ferner wird der Begriff der Verfassung hier auf ein gesamtes politisches System bezogen, also auf Regeln, die Institutionen generieren und ihre Beziehungen und Interaktionen betreffen, aber nicht die Arbeitsweise der Institutionen selbst, die in Geschäftsordnungen fixiert sind.

Im Hinblick auf die Akteure der Verfassungspolitik ist zu unterscheiden zwischen jenen, die auf die Agenda Einfluss haben, jenen, die einen Entscheidungsvorschlag aushandeln, und den „Vetospielern", deren Zustimmung für eine Verfassungsänderung erforderlich ist. Zur ersten Gruppe zu zählen sind in der Regel Regierungen der Gebietskörperschaften, aber auch Interessengruppen oder Experten, die über die Medien Diskurse prägen. Ein erhebliches Gewicht als „Agenda-setter" haben meistens auch Verfassungsgerichte, die durch Entscheidungen oft Verfassungsreformen anstoßen.[25]

Verfassungsverhandlungen finden in aller Regel unter Beteiligung von Regierungen der Gebietskörperschaften oder der von ihnen benannten Experten statt. Des Weiteren sind Mitglieder in Gremien zu nennen, die in beratender oder entscheidender Funktion an der Ausarbeitung von Entscheidungsvorschlägen mitwirken. Je nach Verfahrensgestaltung können Vertreter von Interessengruppen oder die Bürgerschaft insgesamt in Verhandlungen involviert sein. Faktisch werden die Verhandlungen aber von Regierungen der zentralen und dezentralen Gebietskörperschaften wenn nicht dominiert, so doch maßgeblich mitgestaltet. Durch ihre Macht, bestehende Verfassungsregeln zu interpretieren und damit den *Status quo* der Verfassung zu verändern, können auch Verfassungsgerichte von außen auf den Verlauf und die Ergebnisse von Verhandlungen einwirken.

Über Vetomacht verfügen alle diejenigen, die nach den Regeln der Verfassungsänderung zu beteiligen sind, die also befugt sind, die „verfassungsändernde Gewalt" auszuüben. In föderativen Systemen gehören dazu die beiden Kammern der

---

24 Zum Begriff *Schultze-Fielitz, H.*: Der informale Verfassungsstaat, Berlin, 1984.
25 *Schneider, H.-P.*: Das Bundesverfassungsgericht als eigenständiger Akteur in Verfassungsreformen. Vortrag auf der Tagung „Verfassungswandel und Verfassungspolitik/Constitutional Change" des Instituts für Europäische Verfassungswissenschaften der FernUniversität in Hagen am 15./16.06.2007 in Hagen (unveröff. Ms.).

Legislative des Bundes mit den zu erreichenden qualifizierten Mehrheiten, zum Teil auch die Parlamente der Gliedstaaten. Sind Verfassungsänderungen durch Referenden zu ratifizieren, liegt diese Kompetenz entweder allein oder gemeinsam mit der Legislative beim Volk, sei es bei der Gesamtheit aller wahlberechtigten Bürgerinnen und Bürger im Bund oder bei den Völkern in den Gliedstaaten.

Verfahren der Verfassungsreform in föderativen Systemen lassen sich danach charakterisieren, ob sie vorwiegend als intergouvernementale, als parlamentarische oder als Prozesse gesellschaftlicher Interessenvermittlung verlaufen. Im ersten Fall sind Regierungen mit ihren Interessen an Kompetenzen und Ressourcen die dominierenden Akteure, im zweiten Fall sind Verfassungsverhandlungen durch parteipolitische Konflikte geprägt, im dritten Modus spielen Gesichtspunkte wie die Qualität des demokratischen Regierens, die Art der Aufgaben und der Aufgabenerfüllung sowie die Rechte von Individuen und Gruppen eine vorrangige Rolle. Nicht immer findet ein Verfassungsreformprozess nach einer einzigen Verfahrensweise statt, sie können je nach Reformphasen wechseln. Wenn der Reformprozess eingeleitet ist, lassen sich typischerweise die Phasen der Diskussion der Verfassungsprobleme, in denen sich Akteure über mögliche Lösungsalternativen austauschen, der Aushandlung von Lösungen, der Formulierung der zu ändernden Verfassungsnormen und der Beschlussfassung unterscheiden.[26] Wechseln die Verfahrensmodi zwischen diesen Phasen, dann ist die Sequenz für die Erklärung der Ergebnisse von maßgeblicher Bedeutung.

Ob Verfassungsreformen erfolgreich sind oder scheitern, ist sowohl abstrakt als auch im konkreten Fall schwierig zu entscheiden. Jedenfalls muss neben dem Ergebnis der eigentlichen Reform auch die Entwicklung der Verfassung in Betracht gezogen werden. Reformen können formal scheitern, aber dennoch Veränderungen im Verständnis von Verfassungsregeln, ihrer Anwendung in der Praxis oder ihrer Auslegung durch Gerichte auslösen. In dieser Vorwirkung der Reformprozesse liegt eine Chance, dass föderative Staaten aus der Falle ihrer Eigendynamik herausfinden können; sie tritt aber, wie zu zeigen ist, nur unter bestimmten Bedingungen ein. Reformen können aber auch verabschiedet werden und dann als erfolgreich scheinen, obgleich sie entweder die politische Praxis kaum verändern oder sogar negative Folgeeffekte auf die Verfassungsentwicklung erzeugen. Ein solches Resultat führt nicht aus den Fallstricken des Verfassungsrechts heraus. Nicht ausgeschlossen werden sollte die Möglichkeit, dass Ver-

26 Vgl. etwa *Benz, A.*: Kein Ausweg aus der Politikverflechtung? – Warum die Bundesstaatskommission scheiterte, aber nicht scheitern musste, in: Politische Vierteljahresschrift, 46/2 (2005), 207–217; *Magnette, P./Nicolaidis, K.*: The European Convention: Bargaining in the Shadow of Rhetoric, in: West European Politics, 27/3 (2004), 381–404; *Russell, P.H.*: The Constitutional Odyssey, 3. Aufl., Toronto, 2004.

fassungsänderungen sowohl formal verabschiedet werden als auch die Änderungen sich inhaltlich als geeignet erweisen, die Probleme zu lösen. Die Beantwortung der Frage, unter welchen besonderen Bedingungen eine solche Reform gelingen kann, erscheint im Hinblick auf die Verfassungsproblematik föderativer Systeme besonders relevant.

Im Folgenden stehen aber die anderen beiden Resultate von Verfassungsreformen im Mittelpunkt, die viel wahrscheinlicher sind als der zuletzt genannte Fall. Die beiden Fallstudien beziehen sich auf in einer bestimmten Hinsicht gescheiterte oder erfolglose Verfassungsreformen. Sie sollen Hinweise geben, ob und wie es gelingt, dass Verfassungsprobleme dennoch gelöst und die Gewaltenbalance in föderativen Systemen stabilisiert werden kann. Nicht beansprucht wird hier, die aufgeworfene Frage nach dem Umgang mit der Verfassungsproblematik im Bundesstaat umfassend zu beantworten. Dazu reichen weder die Informationen aus den hier dargestellten Fällen aus, noch erlauben diese einen systematischen Vergleich. Es handelt sich um Beispiele von Verfassungsreformen in ganz unterschiedlichen föderativen Systemen, in deren verfassungspolitischer Agenda zudem unterschiedliche Problemtypen als vorrangig definiert wurden. Diese können nur erste Hinweise auf den Zusammenhang zwischen Verfassungsreform und Verfassungsentwicklung liefern, der essentiell zu sein scheint, wenn man nach Auswegen aus dem Verfassungsproblem föderativer Systeme sucht.

2. Föderalismusreform in der Bundesrepublik Deutschland

Die mit der Einsetzung der „Kommission von Bundestag und Bundesrat zur Modernisierung der bundesstaatlichen Ordnung" (kurz: Bundesstaatskommission) im November 2003 eingeleitete Föderalismusreform stellte eine Reaktion auf anhaltende Diskussionen über die Regierbarkeit im kooperativen Bundesstaat dar. Seit Mitte der 1990er Jahre verstärkten sich die Klagen über Blockaden bei wichtigen wirtschafts-, sozial- und finanzpolitischen Gesetzen, die der Zustimmung des Bundesrats bedurften. Politikwissenschaftler wiesen schon früher auf die Blockadeanfälligkeit der Politikverflechtung hin, stellten allerdings auch fest, dass Blockaden nur unter bestimmten Bedingungen wahrscheinlich sind und sie zudem in Verhandlungen vermieden werden können. Die Wirtschaftskrise nach der deutschen Einheit machte diese aber schwieriger. In der Folge kritisierten Vertreter der ökonomischen Theorie des Föderalismus den kooperativen Bundesstaat als ineffizient und machten ihn für die wirtschaftlichen Probleme mitverantwortlich. Vor diesem Hintergrund wurden der Grundsatz der gleichwertigen Lebensbedingungen in Frage gestellt, die Gemeinschaftsaufgaben sowie der

Finanzausgleich wegen zu weitgehender Nivellierung und falscher Anreizwirkungen als überflüssig oder reformbedürftig erklärt, ferner eine Entflechtung der Kompetenzen gefordert mit dem Ziel, den Wettbewerb zwischen Gebietskörperschaften zu stärken. Diese Diagnosen und Empfehlungen griffen vor allem die konservativen Regierungen der finanzstarken Länder in Süddeutschland auf,[27] darüber hinaus artikulierten die Landesparlamente ihre immer wieder erhobenen Forderungen nach mehr Gesetzgebungskompetenzen für die Länder, schließlich entwickelte sich eine breite Reformdiskussionen in Politik, Verbänden und Wissenschaft.[28]

Tatsächlich veränderte die deutsche Einheit die Bedingungen der Entscheidungsfindung in Politikbereichen, in denen Gesetze nur mit Zustimmung des Bundesrats verabschiedet werden konnten. Wegen der wirtschaftlichen Situation und der regionalen Ungleichgewichte konnten die alten Muster der Konfliktvermeidung im Föderalismus, die auf der Vermeidung von Umverteilung beruhten, nicht mehr funktionieren. In Bund-Länder-Verhandlungen wurden Parteienkonflikte zunehmend durch intergouvernementale Verteilungskonflikte überlagert und verstärkt. Entscheidungen über Reformen zur Konsolidierung des Sozialstaats wurden schwieriger und kamen nur kleine Schritte voran. Die europäische Integration erhöhte den Reformdruck, weil im erweiterten Mehrebenensystem eine effektivere Bund-Länder-Koordination erforderlich wurde und der Binnenmarkt eine Anpassung der Wirtschafts-, Sozial- und Finanzpolitik erzwang.

In der öffentlichen Diskussion wie auch in der Agenda der Bundesstaatskommission wurden die Verfassungsprobleme, die durch die Reform gelöst werden sollten, als Effektivitätsprobleme definiert. Vertreter der Länder und der Parteien erkannten allerdings, dass der Wettbewerbsföderalismus nach dem Modell der ökonomischen Theorie, als Standortwettbewerb um mobile Steuerzahler, sich als nicht konsensfähig erweisen würde. Angesichts der wirtschaftlichen Ungleichgewichte im Bundesgebiet war es nicht durchsetzbar, Kompetenzen zu dezentralisieren und gleichzeitig den Finanzausgleich zu schwächen. In dieser Situation wurde das Ziel der Entflechtung als Leitlinie definiert. Durch eindeutige Zuordnungen von Kompetenzen auf Bund und Länder und die Reduktion von Mitentscheidungsrechten der jeweils anderen Ebene sollte der Bund an Gestaltungsfähigkeit gewinnen. Dezentralisierung sollte die Landesparlamente aufwerten,

27 *Ziblatt, D.F.*: Recasting German Federalism? The Politics of Fiscal Decentralisation in Post-Unification Germany, in: Politische Vierteljahresschrift, 43/4 (2002), 624–652.

28 *Schatz, H./van Ooyen, R.C./Werthes, S.*: Wettbewerbsföderalismus. Aufstieg und Fall eines politischen Streitbegriffs, Baden-Baden, 2000.

und im Wettbewerb der Länder sollten Politikinnovationen gefördert werden, ein Kampf um mobile Steuerzahler aber vermieden werden. Das föderative Prinzip der Solidarität zwischen Bund und allen Ländern stand nicht in Frage.[29]

Das Prinzip der Entflechtung ließ offen, in welche Richtung sich die Föderalismusreform entwickeln sollte. Die Länder, und unter ihnen insbesondere die finanzstarken, argumentierten, die vielfach geforderte Stärkung des Föderalismus sei nur durch eine Erweiterung ihrer Kompetenzen und ihrer Autonomie zu erreichen. Der Bund war im konkreten Fall aber wenig geneigt, Kompetenzen und Finanzen abzugeben. Für ihn war eine Reduzierung der Zustimmungsrechte des Bundesrats vorrangig, was die Länder aber nur bei entsprechender Reduktion der Eingriffe des Bundes in ihre Zuständigkeiten konzedieren wollten. Damit arbeiteten Bund und Länder zwar auf eine gemeinsame Reform hin, verfolgten jedoch gegensätzliche Interessen an der Umverteilung von Macht.

Das Verfahren, in dem die Konflikte bearbeitet wurden, war formal parlamentarisch organisiert, die Verhandlungen fanden aber im intergouvernementalen Modus statt. Zwar waren die Hälfte der Mitglieder Abgeordnete des Bundestags, die nach dem Parteienproporz bestimmt wurden, faktisch spielten aber parteipolitische Konflikte keine Rolle. Vertreter der Bundesregierung, die beratend an der Kommissionsarbeit mitwirkten, und Abgeordnete des Bundestags trugen keine schwerwiegenden Meinungsverschiedenheiten aus, und ebenso waren Konflikte zwischen den Vertretern der Landesregierungen und den beratenden Vertretern der Landesparlamente nicht bedeutsam. Die entscheidenden Auseinandersetzungen spielten sich zwischen den Ministerpräsidenten bzw. ihren Vertretern auf der einen Seite und den Vertretern des Bundes auf der anderen Seite ab. Gesellschaftliche Gruppen waren nicht direkt beteiligt, sie konnten nur durch schriftliche Stellungnahmen, durch öffentliche Veranstaltungen oder über die Medien auf die Diskussionen einwirken, was in der Arbeit der Bundesstaatskommission aber kaum erkennbar war.

In der ersten Phase der Verhandlungen fand ein offener Diskurs über Ideen der Reform statt, zu dem vor allem Vertreter des Bundestags beitrugen und an dem sich die Sachverständigen, die in die Kommission berufen wurden, intensiv beteiligten. In einer zweiten Phase gingen die Beratungen dann in ein exklusives Aushandeln zwischen Bund und Ländern über. Ausgangspunkt dieser Verhand-

---

29 Die Positionen und Diskussionen sind dokumentiert in *Deutscher Bundestag und Bundesrat, Öffentlichkeitsarbeit* (Hg.): Kommission von Bundestag und Bundesrat zur Modernisierung der bundesstaatlichen Ordnung, Zur Sache 1/2005; *Holtschneider, R./Schön, W.* (Hg.): Die Reform des Bundesstaates: Beiträge zur Arbeit der Kommission zur Modernisierung der bundesstaatlichen Ordnung 2003/2004 und bis zum Abschluss des Gesetzgebungsverfahrens 2006, Baden-Baden, 2007.

lungsphase war ein Positionspapier der Ministerpräsidenten vom März 2004, in dem sie Zuständigkeiten für regionale Lebenssachverhalte forderten, sei es als eigene Kompetenzen oder in Form eines nicht konditionierten Zugriffsrechts auf Bundeskompetenzen. Die Kommission teilte sich danach in zwei Untergruppen auf, die aber wegen ihrer Größe und des Themenzuschnitts keine Konflikte lösen konnten. Ab Sommer 2004 trafen sich dann Projektgruppen zu sieben Teilthemen, in denen Vertreter der Länder und des Bundes über konkrete Fragen und Formulierungsvorschläge berieten. In dieser Struktur gelang es nicht, ein Verhandlungspaket zu schnüren, das aus der Nullsummensituation der Machtverteilung herausgeführt hätte. Dies zu leisten oblag in der letzten Phase den beiden Vorsitzenden und den Obleuten der Gruppierungen. Sie konnten am Ende ein Kompromisspapier vorlegen, das jedoch dem Bund nicht die gewünschten Handlungsspielräume brachte, den finanzstarken Ländern hinsichtlich ihrer Autonomie nicht weit genug ging und von den finanzschwachen Ländern als Weg in den Wettbewerbsföderalismus empfunden wurde.

Die Kommission endete ohne einen Beschluss über einen Vorschlag für eine Verfassungsänderung. Dass sie scheiterte, lag an der Engführung der Diskussion auf den Referenzrahmen der Entflechtung. Dieser lenkte die Verhandlungen auf ein Tauschgeschäft, auf das sich Bund und Länder schon zu Beginn der Beratungen geeinigt hatten. Die Länder wollten auf Zustimmungsrechte des Bundesrats verzichten, wenn sie dafür Gesetzgebungskompetenzen vom Bund erhielten. Das Geschäft erwies sich allerdings in der Umsetzung aus sachlichen Gründen als schwierig, zumal man gleichzeitig als Prämisse der Reform festlegte, den *Status quo* der Finanzverteilung beizubehalten. Bei der Prüfung von einzelnen Materien der Gesetzgebung zeigte sich, dass eine Dezentralisierung in vielen Aufgabenbereichen erhebliche externe Effekte oder Verteilungsprobleme zwischen den Ländern verursachen würde. Dementsprechend konnten Vertreter von Bundesressorts gute Gründe gegen Länderzuständigkeiten vorbringen. Ähnlich argumentierten auch Verbände, die zwar überwiegend für eine Föderalisierung plädierten, aber dann, wenn die Gesetzgebungsmaterie in ihrem Bereich betroffen war, sich einer Übertragung auf die Länder widersetzten.[30] Die Zahl der Zustimmungsgesetze sollte durch eine Änderung von Art. 84 GG reduziert werden, womit der Bund auf verbindliche Regelungen von Behörden und Verfahren des Gesetzesvollzugs in den Ländern verzichten wollte. Die Länder konnten und wollten aber Zustimmungsrechte nicht aufgeben, wenn ein Bundesgesetz für sie

---

30 *Benz, A.*: Verfassungspolitische Alternative zur Entflechtungspolitik – Konzept und Konsequenzen für die Raumordnung, in: Raumforschung und Raumordnung, 63/2 (2005), 123–133.

Kostenfolgen im Vollzug erzeugt. Dies wäre zu vermeiden, wenn dem Bund die Finanzverantwortung übertragen worden wäre, dann aber hätten die ausführenden Länder keine Anreize mehr gehabt, Gesetze effizient und Kosten sparend durchzuführen.

Das eigentliche Problem dieser Paketlösung lag in seinem Ungleichgewicht für die Länder. Der Tausch von Zustimmungsrechten gegen Gesetzgebungskompetenzen lag im Interesse der finanzstarken Länder, während er für die finanzschwachen Länder nur bedingt attraktiv war. Sie sahen sich durch den drohenden Wettbewerb zwischen Regionen bedroht. Die Ministerpräsidenten schlugen daher vor, Kompetenzen der konkurrierenden Gesetzgebung einem nicht konditionierten Zugriffsrecht zu unterwerfen, die Kompetenzdezentralisierung also dem Willen einzelner Länder zu überlassen. Für den Bund hat diese Regel, die für Materien der früheren Rahmengesetzgebung beschlossen wurde, allerdings die Konsequenz, dass er die bundeseinheitliche Geltung eines Bundesgesetzes nicht mehr gewährleisten kann. Wegen Interessenkonflikten zwischen den Ländern erwies sich auch eine Neuordnung von Steuerkompetenzen und des Finanzausgleichs als nicht machbar. Die Länder bemühten sich, in der Föderalismusreform mit einer einheitlichen Position zu agieren. Dies konnten sie jedoch nur um den Preis, dass wesentliche Aspekte der Finanzverfassung ausgeklammert wurden. Die Bundesregierung akzeptierte dies in der Bundesstaatskommission, weshalb selbst pragmatische Vorschläge der Sachverständigen diese Blockierung nicht aufbrechen konnten. Auch andere Handlungsoptionen, die statt auf Entflechtung auf eine flexible Kompetenzzuordnung[31] und veränderte Verfahren der Bund-Länder-Koordination, etwa durch Modifikation der Abstimmungsregel im Bundesrat,[32] zielten, wurden nicht aufgegriffen.

Auch in der wichtigen Frage der Europafähigkeit des Bundesstaats erwies sich die Logik des intergouvernementalen *bargaining* als ungeeignet, Lösungen zu generieren. Eine konsequente Entflechtung hätte bedeutet, einem Mitglied des Bundesrats die Vertretung der Bundesrepublik im Ministerrat der EU zu übertragen, wenn Gesetzgebungskompetenzen der Länder betroffen sind. Genau dieses forderten die Landespolitiker in der Bundesstaatskommission. Der Bund vertrat die konträre Position, wonach er die alleinige Vertretungskompetenz erhalten sollte, um eine effektive Durchsetzung deutscher Interessen in EU-Verhandlungen zu ge-

---

31 *Ders.*: Kein Ausweg aus der Politikverflechtung?, a.a.O.; *Scharpf, F.W.*: Recht und Politik in der Reform des Föderalismus, in: Becker, M./Zimmerling, R. (Hg.): Politik und Recht, Wiesbaden, 2006, 307–332.

32 Zu den Vorschlägen vgl. *Wagschal, U./Grasl, M.*: Die modifizierte Senatslösung. Ein Vorschlag zur Verringerung von Reformblockaden im deutschen Föderalismus, in: Zeitschrift für Parlamentsfragen, 35/4 (2004), 732–752.

währleisten. Letztlich einigten sich Bund und Länder auf einen Kompromiss, der in der Praxis keine Verbesserungen bringt, aber auch kaum Folgen haben wird.

Die Bundesstaatskommission ist an den Konflikten um die Machtverteilung gescheitert, weil die Akteure in den angewandten intergouvernementalen Verhandlungen nicht aus dem Nullsummenspiel herauskamen, das mit dem Ziel der Entflechtung initiiert wurde. Die Frage, welche Konsequenzen die Entflechtung auf die Staatstätigkeit haben kann und die damit verbundene Frage, welchen Föderalismus man verwirklichen will, wurden nicht diskutiert. Für die Vertreter des Bundes und der Länder stellten sie sich nicht, solange sie über Kompetenzen, Ressourcen und Macht verhandelten. Beide Fragen stellten sich schon eher für Verbände, die in ihren Stellungnahmen vielfach widersprüchlich argumentierten, indem sie ein abstraktes Bekenntnis zu mehr Föderalismus ablegten und sich gleichzeitig für ihren Bereich gegen eine Dezentralisierung der Kompetenzen aussprachen.[33] Diese Widersprüche zu klären, waren sie nicht gezwungen, weil sie nicht an den Beratungen der Föderalismusreform teilnehmen konnten.

Dass dennoch eine Reform des Grundgesetzes verabschiedet wurde und im September 2006 in Kraft trat, lag an der Intervention des Bundesverfassungsgerichts. Dieses modifizierte in mehreren Urteilen zwischen 2002 und 2004 seine Interpretation der Voraussetzungen, unter denen der Bund im Bereich der konkurrierenden Gesetzgebungskompetenzen tätig werden konnte. Überließ es das Gericht in der Vergangenheit der Politik, die Voraussetzungen des Art. 72 Abs. 2 GG auszulegen, so erlaubte es Bundesgesetze jetzt nur noch, „wenn sich die Lebensverhältnisse in den Ländern der Bundesrepublik in erheblicher, das bundesstaatliche Sozialgefüge beeinträchtigender Weise auseinander entwickelt haben oder sich eine derartige Entwicklung konkret abzeichnet"[34]. In Reaktion auf die allgemeine Kritik am kooperativen Föderalismus hat es damit die Machtverhältnisse zugunsten der Länder verschoben. Diesen bot sich nun die Chance, durch Anrufung des Verfassungsgerichts den Spielraum ihrer Kompetenzen zu erweitern. Für den Bund war diese Situation nicht haltbar, da die neue Rechtsprechung Unsicherheit über die geltende Kompetenzverteilung erzeugte, die nun von der Meinung des Gerichts abhängig wurde. Er musste daher eine Entscheidung über die Kompetenzordnung herbeiführen. Die Bundesregierung legte deswegen Anfang November 2004 der Bundesstaatskommission einen Katalog von Gesetzesmaterien vor, in denen der Bund sich auf Kernkompetenzen beschränken oder

---

33   *Benz, S.*: Rege Beteiligung konfligierender Interessen. Eine Analyse der Zuschriften an die Kommission zur Modernisierung der bundesstaatlichen Ordnung, in: Zeitschrift für Parlamentsfragen, 36/4 (2005), 741–747.

34   BVerfG, Urteil vom 24.10.2002, 2 BvF 1/01, gleichlautend: Urteil vom 26.01.2005, 2 BvF 1/03.

sich ganz zurückziehen wollte. Da dieser Vorschlag die einheitliche Front der Länder aufzubrechen drohte, war in der kurzen Beratungszeit der Kommission keine Einigung mehr möglich. Der veränderte *Status quo* veranlasste aber Bund und Länder nach der Neuwahl des Bundestags, wieder in die intergouvernementalen Verhandlungen einzutreten, in denen auf der Grundlage der Kommissionsarbeit eine Einigung über Änderungen des Grundgesetzes erzielt werden konnte. Diese kam zustande unter der Bedingung, dass die Verhandlungsposition des Bundes geschwächt war und in den Koalitionsverhandlungen über die Föderalismusreform auf der Länderseite Protagonisten einer Entflechtung dominierten.

Der Referenzrahmen der Verhandlungen, der mit dem Entflechtungsprinzip definiert wurde, ließ jedoch nur noch Kompromisse zu, die die Regierbarkeit im Bundesstaat kaum verbessern. Da man die Kernfrage ausklammerte, welchen Föderalismus man eigentlich verwirklichen will, führten die Verhandlungen zwischen Bund und Ländern, angetrieben durch den vom Bundesverfassungsgericht erzeugten Einigungszwang, zu Ergebnissen, die den Föderalismus in Deutschland kaum effektiver machen. Ein äußerst dürftiger, überwiegend gehaltloser Text der Begründung für die Verfassungsänderungen zeugt davon, dass das Ergebnis auf ein machtpolitisches Aushandeln zurückzuführen ist.[35]

Angesichts der offenkundigen Schwächen der Reform beschlossen Bund und Länder einen weiteren Reformschritt, der als Föderalismusreform II bezeichnet wird. Seit März 2007 arbeitet eine neue Kommission von Bundestag und Bundesrat, die sich mit Finanzfragen befasst. An der Struktur der Entscheidungsvorbereitung und am Modus der intergouvernementalen Verhandlungen hat sich nichts Wesentliches geändert. Dieser Modus wurde eher noch verstärkt, weil nunmehr die Bundesregierung mit stimmberechtigten Mitgliedern in der Kommission vertreten ist und Sachverständige nur zu zwei Anhörungen eingeladen wurden. Die Dominanz des intergouvernementalen Modus zeigt sich schon im Themenspektrum, das neben der Finanzverfassung auch die Verwaltung betrifft und dabei in Details geht, die über das Verfassungsrecht hinausreichen. Ob es dem Erfolg der Kommission dient, solche Fragen zu bearbeiten, muss bezweifelt werden. Skepsis hinsichtlich der Erfolgsaussichten ist auch deswegen angebracht, weil bei Fragen der Finanzverfassung neben den Bund-Länder-Konflikten auch die Meinungsverschiedenheiten unter den Ländern virulent werden. Anders als in der ersten Kommission wurden diese bereits in der konstituierenden Sitzung der zweiten Bundesstaatskommission offen artikuliert. Dies deutet darauf hin, dass

---

[35] Ausführlich zur Bewertung *Benz, A.*: Föderalismusreform in der „Entflechtungsfalle", in: Jahrbuch des Föderalismus, 8 (2007), 180–190.

von Beginn über konkrete Verteilungsinteressen verhandelt wird und nicht über die Regeln der Verteilung. Das Bundesverfassungsgericht bleibt ein wichtiger Akteur im Reformprozess. Es hat mit Entscheidungen zur Staatsverschuldung ein Thema in den Vordergrund gerückt, das grundsätzlich bedeutsam ist und sich als Ansatzpunkt für Paketlösungen anbietet. In zentralen Fragen der Finanzverfassung und des Finanzausgleichs kann die Kommission aber nicht, wie bei der Verteilung der Gesetzgebungskompetenzen, auf Änderungsimpulse des Bundesverfassungsgerichts setzen, da die präzisen Regelungen des Grundgesetzes dem Gericht hier weniger Interpretationsspielraum bieten. Die Chancen, die begrenzten Ergebnisse und Defizite der ersten Reform zu korrigieren, sind daher gering, und es deutet sich an, dass die Verfassung durch weitere Detailregelungen unflexibler wird.[36] Die Folgen zu bewältigen wird dann, wie schon in der Vergangenheit,[37] dem Bundesverfassungsgericht überlassen bleiben.

3. Verfassungsreformen und Verfassungsentwicklung in Kanada

Die Entwicklung des kanadischen Bundesstaats war seit den 60er Jahren des letzten Jahrhunderts durch massive politische Konflikte geprägt. Sie waren in der Geschichte der Staatsbildung angelegt, wurden aber im 20. Jahrhundert durch wirtschaftliche Ungleichgewichte zwischen den Provinzen und das wachsende politische Selbstbewusstsein der französischsprachigen Bevölkerungsmehrheit in Quebec verschärft.[38] Ähnlich wie in Deutschland spielte sich im kanadischen Bundesstaat eine dauerhafte Auseinandersetzung zwischen dem Bund und den Provinzen um die Kompetenzverteilung ab, die mit der Entwicklung des Wohlfahrtsstaats und der ökonomischen Integration Nord- und Mittelamerikas verbunden war. Im Zentrum der Verfassungsproblematik standen aber Integrationsprobleme. Dazu gehörte in erster Linie der Konflikt zwischen der Provinz Quebec, die sich als eigenständige Nation definierte, und dem übrigen Kanada, dessen Bevölkerung und Politiker in der Mehrheit für eine föderative politische Einheit eintraten. Eine zweite, eher durch ökonomische Interessen bedingte Konfliktlinie entstand zwischen den zentralen und dicht besiedelten Provinzen Ontario und

36 Zu dieser Tendenz *Benz, A.*: Über den Umgang mit der Verfassung – Anmerkungen zur Verfassungskultur im deutschen Bundesstaat, in: Gosewinkel, D./Schuppert, G.F. (Hg.): Politische Kultur, WZB-Jahrbuch, Berlin, 2007 (i.V.).

37 *Blair, P./Cullen, P.*: Federalism, Legalism and Political Reality: The Record of the Federal Constitutional Court, in: Jeffery, C. (Hg.): Recasting German Federalism, London, 1999, 119–154; *Kisker, G.*: The West German Federal Court as Guardian of the Federal System, in: Publius: The Journal of Federalism, 19/4 (1989), 35–52.

38 *Stevenson, G.*: The Unfulfilled Union. Canadian Federalism and National Unity, 4. Aufl., Montreal, 2004.

Quebec auf der einen und den übrigen Provinzen auf der anderen Seite; mit dem wirtschaftlichen Strukturwandel wurden diese Interessenkonflikte komplexer, verloren deswegen aber nicht an Bedeutung. Der dritte Konflikt betrifft die Interessen der sog. *„first nations"*, der Ureinwohner des heutigen Kanadas, die erst seit den 1970er Jahren Anerkennung gefunden haben. Diese Trias der Integrationsprobleme hat Verfassungsreformen bislang immer zum Scheitern verurteilt.

Die föderative Ordnung des kanadischen Staats geht auf ein britisches Parlamentsgesetz, den *British North America Act*, zurück, der noch in der Kolonialzeit 1867 erlassen wurde. Das Gesetz wurde, nach Jahrzehnten verfassungspolitischer Debatten, 1982 ohne weitreichende Änderungen in das kanadische Verfassungsgesetz transformiert. Entsprechend der britischen Verfassungstradition, die in Kanada fortwirkt, gehören zur Verfassung auch ungeschriebene Regeln, die sog. *conventions*. Im diesem Rahmen durchlief der Bundesstaat einen Dezentralisierungsprozess, der ohne Reform, mit einzelnen Änderung der Verfassung, überwiegend aber auf der Basis von Parlamentsgesetzen oder intergouvernementalen Vereinbarungen erfolgte.[39] Angesichts der zunehmenden Spannungen im multinationalen Föderalismus versuchte die kanadische Regierung seit Ende der 1960er Jahre, die Verfassung an die veränderten Interessenlagen anzupassen und die Konflikte zu bewältigen. Die Phase der *„mega-constitutional politics"*[40] begann mit der Transformation des *British North America Act* in die kanadische Verfassung (*„Patriation"*), die ein erstes Beispiel für eine gescheiterte Reform darstellt, weil sie wegen des Konflikts unter den Provinzen schließlich nur durch einfaches Parlamentsgesetz und ohne die angestrebten Revisionen gelang. Im Folgenden sollen die späteren Reformversuche, die als *Meech Lake Accord* und als *Charlottetown Accord* bekannten Verfassungsprojekte, ihr Scheitern und ihre Wirkungen im Mittelpunkt stehen.[41]

Hintergrund der beiden verfassungspolitischen Prozesse war die Tatsache, dass das Gesetz, das den *British North America Act* in die kanadische Verfassung transformierte, vom Parlament in Quebec abgelehnt wurde. Nach den seinerzeit gültigen Regeln für eine Verfassungsänderung konnte dies das Inkrafttreten der Verfassung nicht blockieren, die Entscheidung brachte aber die massiven Konflikte zwischen Quebec und dem *„rest of Canada"* zum Ausdruck. Für Premierminister *Brian Mulroney* war dies Anlass, einen weiteren Anlauf zur Lösung der Integrationsprobleme zu starten, die nicht nur den Bestand des Bundesstaats gefährdeten, sondern auch die wirtschafts- und sozialpolitische Handlungsfähig-

---

39 *Cheffins, R.I./Tucker, R.N.*: The Constitutional Process in Canada, 2. Aufl., Toronto u.a., 1976.
40 *Russell, P.H.*, a.a.O, 74 f.
41 Zum Folgenden vgl. ebd.

keit des Bundes zunehmend behinderten. Auf der Agenda standen alle Kern-
probleme der Verfassungspolitik im kanadischen Föderalismus: die Kompetenzverteilung zwischen dem Bund und den Provinzen insbesondere hinsichtlich der
Wirtschafts- und Sozialpolitik sowie der Zuwanderungsregulierung, die Finanz-
hilfen des Bundes, die Ausgestaltung des Senats bzw. die Repräsentation der
Provinzen in der Legislative in Ottawa, die Besetzung des *Supreme Court,* die besondere Stellung von Quebec als eigenständiger Nation („*distinct society clause*"),
die Rechte der *Aborigines* sowie die Regeln der Verfassungsänderung.

Mit der Verabschiedung des *Constitution Act* von 1982 wurden die Regeln der
Verfassungsänderung, die bis dahin nur als Vereinbarung galten, revidiert.[42] Die
Reformen des Senates und des *Supreme Court* erforderten nun die einhellige
Zustimmung des Bundes und aller Provinzen, die übrigen Reformen mussten,
soweit sie die Provinzen betrafen, von sieben Provinzen, die mindestens 50 % der
Bevölkerung Kanadas repräsentieren, ratifiziert werden. Vor dem Hintergrund
dieser hohen Zustimmungshürde erwies sich das gewählte Verfahren der inter-
gouvernementalen Verhandlungen als problematisch.

In Verhandlungen zwischen den Regierungschefs des Bundes und der Provinzen sowie Vertretern der *Aborigines* gelang es schon 1983, eine Verfassungsänderung zu verabschieden, die die Grundbesitzrechte der Ureinwohner anerkannte.
In weiteren Konferenzen kam aber keine Einigung über die Frage der Selbstverwaltungsrechte zustande. Ähnliche Verhandlungen befassten sich mit den
Anliegen Quebecs, die die Kompetenzverteilung, die Finanzierungszuständig-
keiten des Bundes und die besondere Stellung der Provinz einschlossen. In einer
für den kanadischen Exekutivföderalismus typischen Geheimdiplomatie,[43] die
sich in multilateralen Verhandlungen zwischen allen Regierungschefs und in bi-
lateralen Verhandlungen zwischen Regierungen des Bundes und einzelner Provinzen vollzog, konnte schließlich in wesentlichen Fragen eine Einigung erzielt
werden. Das Gesamtpaket brachte, der Natur eines Tauschhandels entsprechend,
für alle Seiten Gewinne und Verluste. Dies reichte aus, um in Regierungsverhand-
lungen zu einer Einigung zu kommen, dem sog. *Meech Lake Accord.* Es reichte
aber nicht aus, um die Zustimmung der Parlamente in allen Provinzen zu erreichen, die erforderlich war, weil mit der Senatsreform und der Reform des
Supreme Court zwei Materien Gegenstand des Pakets waren, die nur mit Zustimmung aller Gebietskörperschaften verabschiedet werden konnten. In der verein-

---

42 *Greene, I.*: Constitutional Amendment in Canada and the United States, in: Newman, S.L. (Hg.): Constitutional Politics in Canada and the United States, Albany, 2004, 249–271, hier 251 f.

43 *Russell, P.H.*, a.a.O., 134; allgemein dazu *Simeon, R.*: Federal-Provincial Diplomacy. The Making of Recent
Policy in Canada, 3. Aufl., Toronto, 2006.

barten Frist gelang dies nicht. Das intergouvernementale Verfahren provozierte Proteste gesellschaftlicher Gruppen, blockierte Kommunikation zwischen Gruppen und Regionen und spaltete die Gesellschaft.[44]

Nach dem Misserfolg der Verfassungsreform in intergouvernementalen Verhandlungen wurde das *Charlottetown*-Abkommen in einem völlig anders gearteten Prozess ausgehandelt, der durch die Parteien, vor allem aber durch gesellschaftliche Interessenvermittlung geprägt war. Zu den auslösenden Ereignissen zählte die Zuspitzung der Konflikte mit den *Aborigines*, die sich 1990 in einem Aufstand der Mohaws äußerte. In dieser Situation initiierte Premierminister *Mulroney* zum einen ein *Citizens' Forum on Canada's Future*, das die Beteiligung von Bürgern an Verfassungsberatungen organisierte. Zum anderen richtete das kanadische Parlament einen Ausschuss ein, der sich mit dem Verfahren der Verfassungsänderung befassen sollte. In einer Regierungserklärung vom Mai 1991 kündigte der Premierminister die Verfassungsreform an. Was folgte waren Beratungsprozesse im gesamten Land, in die die Öffentlichkeit in den verschiedensten Formen einbezogen war. Zum einen waren vielen Verhandlungen der Parlamentsausschüsse im Bund und in den Provinzen nicht nur öffentlich, ihre Arbeit wurde auch über die Medien vermittelt. Obgleich ursprünglich die Forderung nach einer Verfassungsversammlung von der Mehrheit im Parlament abgelehnt wurde, fand schließlich eine Serie von regionalen Verfassungsversammlungen statt, in denen Parteien und Interessengruppen ihre Ideen und Vorschläge einbrachten. Zum zweiten wurden auch außerhalb der Parlamentskomitees auf beiden Ebenen des Bundesstaats Foren und Veranstaltungen organisiert, in denen sich Vertreter von Interessengruppen wie einzelne Bürger beteiligten. Drittens nahmen zahlreiche Experten an den Beratungen aktiv teil, sie leiteten Arbeitsgruppen und verfassten Berichte und Empfehlungen. *Peter H. Russell* verdeutlichte die Intensität der Beratungen wie folgt: „*Canada surely had a look on the entry of the Guiness Book of Records for the sheer volume of constitutional talk.*"[45]

Die gesellschaftliche Interessenvermittlung hatte erkennbare Auswirkungen auf die Inhalte der Verfassungspolitik. Grundlage der Diskussionen waren Materialien der Regierungen. Die Bundesregierung fasste ihre Reformvorschläge in einem umfangreichen Bericht zusammen, und auch die Provinzregierungen bzw. Parlamentsausschüsse veröffentlichten eigene Berichte. Als Folge der Beratungen mit gesellschaftlichen Gruppen und Vertretern der Bürgerschaft wurden signifikante Änderungen zu allen Teilen des ursprünglichen Entwurfs der Bundes-

---

44 *Breton, R.*: Why Meech Failed, Winnipeg, 1992.
45 *Russell, P.H.*, a.a.O., 177.

regierung vorgeschlagen. Demnach sollten etwa die Rechte der englischsprachigen Minderheit gestärkt, die Selbstverwaltungsrechte der *Aborigines* klarer formuliert und ein Verfahren zur Umsetzung dieser Rechte vorgesehen werden. Ferner sollten die Kompetenzen des Bundes zur Regulierung des Handels durch eine Sozialcharta ergänzt werden.

Nach der Phase der gesellschaftlichen Interessenvermittlung wurden die Ergebnisse vom zuständigen Ausschuss des kanadischen Parlaments zusammengefasst und anschließend in intergouvernementalen Verhandlungen weiter beraten. In den ersten beiden Verhandlungsrunden war die Regierung von Quebec nicht beteiligt, die erst beim dritten Treffen mitwirkte, als der *Charlottetown Accord* ausgearbeitet wurde. Dieser enthielt für alle der oben genannten Verfassungsthemen Kompromisse, die teilweise die Probleme nur verlagerten. So sollten Kompetenzkonflikte durch Vereinbarungen zwischen der Bundesregierung und einzelnen Provinzen geregelt werden können, was als „,make a deal' federalism" karikiert wurde. Die Bundesregierung musste, um ihre Kompetenzen in der Wirtschafts- und Sozialpolitik zu sichern, Zugeständnisse hinsichtlich des Finanzausgleichs machen. Die Anerkennung von Quebec als besondere Nation wurde in eine Auflistung von Grundwerten der kanadischen Nation eingefügt. Das Recht der *Aborigines* auf Selbstverwaltung wurde anerkannt, die Umsetzung weiterer Verhandlungen überlassen. Einigkeit wurde über die Reform des *Supreme Court* erzielt. Ebenso bestand Konsens, dass der Senat künftig durch direkte Wahl besetzt werden und an der Gesetzgebung mitwirken soll, seine genauen Kompetenzen blieben jedoch umstritten. Gleichwohl hätten die vereinbarten Reformen wichtige Fortschritte zur Lösung grundlegender Verfassungsprobleme des kanadischen Bundesstaats gebracht, jedenfalls hätten sie eine Basis für eine integrative Entwicklung geschaffen.

Die Verfassungsänderungen[46] wurden in einem Referendum zur Abstimmung gestellt, danach sollten sie von den Legislativen des Bundes und der Provinzen ratifiziert werden. Der Volksentscheid hatte keine bindende Wirkung, jedoch wollten die Parlamente das Ergebnis berücksichtigen. Nachdem dieses eindeutig negativ ausgefallen war, mussten die Regierungen die Reform für gescheitert erklären. Dafür ursächlich war zum einen, dass es der Bundesregierung nicht gelang, rechtzeitig einen ausformulierten Reformvorschlag vorzulegen. Darüber hinaus wirkte sich die Spaltung zwischen Quebec und dem übrigen Kanada nega-

---

46 Consensus Report on the Constitution: Charlottetown, August 28, 1992: final text, Ottawa: Minister of Supply and Services Canada, abgedruckt u.a. in: *McRoberts, K./Monahan, P.J.* (Hg.): The Charlottetown Accord, the Referendum, and the Future of Canada, Toronto u.a., 1993, 279–309; dort finden sich auch Beiträge, die die Ergebnisse analysieren.

tiv aus. In keiner Phase des Reformprozesses kam es zu einer die Grenze dieser Konfliktlinie überschreitenden Kommunikation. Unter diesen Bedingungen wurde der durch die politische Elite formulierte Kompromiss von der Bevölkerung in allen Provinzen mit Misstrauen behandelt. Die Mehrheit in Quebec sah die besonderen Interessen ihrer Nation zu wenig berücksichtigt, die Mehrheit im übrigen Kanada befürchtete, dass die Verfassungsreform die Integration des Bundesstaats gefährden würde.[47] *„In the end, although most Canadians approved of much of the accord, many disregarded with at least one of the elements of it, and so voted against the entire package."*[48]

Das negative Referendum beendete allerdings nicht den Prozess der Verfassungsentwicklung. Zwar waren Bemühungen um eine weitreichende Verfassungsreform definitiv beendet, die Ergebnisse der Verfassungsberatungen lieferten aber die Grundlage für eine inkrementelle Umsetzung einzelner Vorhaben, und der in wichtigen Fragen erreichte gesellschaftliche Konsens verlieh Regierungen und Parlamenten die Legitimität für weitere Schritte.

Zunächst unternahm die Regierung in Quebec einen weiteren Versuch, die Unabhängigkeit zu erreichen, der allerdings im angesetzten Referendum sehr knapp scheiterte. Damit blieb es beim von allen Beteiligten als unbefriedigend empfundenen *Status quo*. In der Folge leiteten der Bund und die Provinzen die Verfassungspolitik in intergouvernementale Verhandlungen über, die zu einer Reihe wichtiger gemeinsamer Entscheidungen führten.[49] 1994 wurde eine intergouvernementale Vereinbarung über den Handelsverkehr in Kanada und 1999 das *Social Union Framework Agreement* beschlossen, das dem Bund das Recht zur Finanzierung sozialpolitischer Programme einräumte, den Provinzen jedoch ein *opting out*-Recht verlieh. Weitere Verfassungsänderungen wurden durch Bundesgesetze implementiert. So wurde 1996 das Verfahren der Verfassungsänderung modifiziert. Ein weiteres Ergebnis war die Bildung des neuen Territoriums Nunavut, das den Inuits die Selbstverwaltung brachte. 2003 wurde der *Council of Federation* etabliert, ein Organ, in dem die Regierungen der Provinzen ihre Politik abstimmen und mit dem eine neue Qualität des kooperativen Föderalismus erreicht wurde. 2004 verkündete Premierminister *Stephen Harper* einen *„open*

---

47 *Monahan, P.J.*: The Sounds of Silence, in: McRoberts, K./Monahan, P.J. (Hg.), a.a.O., 222–248, hier 239.

48 *Greene, I.*, a.a.O., 257.

49 *Broschek, J.*: „Collaborative Federalism" in Kanada: Eine neue Ära in den Beziehungen zwischen Bund und Provinzen, in: Zeitschrift für Parlamentsfragen, 35/3 (2004), 428–447; *Poirier, J.*: Intergovernmental Agreements in Canada: At the Crossroads Between Law and Politics, in: Meekison, P.J./Telford, H./Lazar, H. (Hg.): Reconsidering the Institutions of Canadian Federalism, Kingston, 2002, 425–462; *Cameron, D./ Simeon, R.*: Intergovernmental Relations in Canada: The Emergence of Collaborative Federalism, in: Publius: The Journal of Federalism, 32/2 (2002), 49–71.

federalism", der die Beachtung der eigenständigen verfassungsrechtlichen Verantwortlichkeiten von Bund und Provinzen, aber auch die notwendige Zusammenarbeit in gemeinsamen Aufgabenfeldern betont.[50] Möglich wurde diese verfassungspolitische Praxis neben der Unterstützung durch die Bevölkerung auch durch eine zurückhaltende, in der Sache aber die Entwicklung unterstützende Rechtsprechung des *Supreme Court*.[51] Er förderte durch ausgewogene Entscheidungen die inkrementelle Entwicklung, erzwang aber keine formalen Verfassungsänderungen. Diese bleiben gleichwohl auf der Agenda. Die Senatsreform wird durch ein *Special Committee* des Senats diskutiert, und der kanadischen Premierministers kündigte in seiner Regierungserklärung vom Oktober 2007 einer Stärkung des Föderalismus durch die Senatsreform, eine Begrenzung der *spending power* des Bundes und der Handelsregulierungen durch die Provinzen an.[52]

Die große Verfassungsreform war also zwar gescheitert, aber dies bedeutete kein Ende des verfassungspolitischen Prozesses, sondern dessen Fortsetzung in anderen Verfahren. Die Ablehnung des *Charlottetown Accord* löste eine noch anhaltende Entwicklung aus, in deren Verlauf sich die kanadische Verfassung erheblich wandelte. Man könnte diesen Prozess als Sieg der politischen Eliten über das Veto des Volkes interpretieren. Tatsächlich hat das Volk ihn erzwungen, indem es das Gesamtpaket der Reform ablehnte, wobei allerdings in den einzelnen Provinzen dafür jeweils unterschiedliche Gründen ausschlaggebend waren. Die breite Beteiligung von Interessenvertretern und Bürgern im Verfahren der Verfassungsberatungen zeigte das Interesse weiter Teile der Bevölkerung an einer Überwindung des *Status quo*, und Umfragen direkt nach Abschluss der Vereinbarung belegten die hohe Zustimmung der Bevölkerungsmehrheit mit den meisten Ergebnissen des Verfassungsprozesses, die erst im Laufe der ideologisierten Debatten erodierte.[53] Die Ideologisierung und Emotionalisierung der Debatte traten aber erst im Laufe der Werbekampagnen um Zustimmung oder Ablehnung im Referendum ein, also erst nach der Phase der Verfassungsverhandlungen. Aus diesen gewann die auf das negative Referendum folgende inkrementelle Verfassungspolitik ihre Legitimität, in der sich Pragmatismus durchsetzte, man Divergenzen über Identitätsfragen ausklammerte und Verfassungsprobleme schrittweise abge-

---

50 *Harper, S.*: My Plan for 'Open Federalism', in: National Post vom 27.10.2004; vgl. auch *Banting, K.* u.a.: Open Federalism, Kingston, Ont., 2004.

51 *Baier, G.*: The Law of Federalism: Judicial Review and the Division of Powers, in: Rocher, F./Smith, M. (Hg.): New Trends in Canadian Federalism, Peterborough, Ont. 2003, 111–133.

52 http://www.sft-ddt.gc.ca/eng/media.asp?id=1364 (letzter Zugriff am 31.10.2007).

53 *Monahan, P.J.*, a.a.O., 238.

arbeitet wurden. Die föderative Ordnung konnte dadurch stabilisiert werden.[54] Der kanadische Bundesstaat „*has generally succeeded in striking a balance between unity and diversity. It is an arrangement that has proven to be both flexible and resilient*"[55].

IV. Schlussfolgerungen: für einen demokratischen Pragmatismus in der Verfassungspolitik

Die beiden hier behandelten Prozesse der Verfassungsreform lassen sich hinsichtlich ihrer Ergebnisse kaum vergleichen. Hierfür sind die Strukturen und Probleme der beiden Bundesstaaten zu unterschiedlich. Festzuhalten ist aber zunächst, dass es in Deutschland trotz der auf die vertikale Dimension des Bundesstaats konzentrierten Problemdefinition und eines relativ einfachen Verfahrens der Verfassungsänderung bisher nicht gelungen ist, eine weitreichende Reform der föderativen Ordnung zu verwirklichen, während in Kanada bei wesentlich schwierigeren Konflikten und unsicheren Verfahrensregeln zwar die Reform scheiterte, danach jedoch signifikante Verfassungsänderungen und eine kontinuierliche Verfassungsentwicklung erreicht wurden. Eine Erklärung für die Unterschiede liegt sicher im Problemdruck, der in Kanada Veränderungen erzwang, vor allem nachdem Quebec nicht den Schritt zur Sezession vollzog. Andererseits war der kanadische Bundesstaat viel stärker in der Falle der föderativen Verfassung gefangen, weil wichtige Themen wie die Eigenständigkeit Quebecs, die wirtschaftlichen Disparitäten, die Rechte der *Aborigines* oder institutionelle Reformen relativ unabhängig voneinander zu behandeln waren und sich noch weniger Tauschgeschäfte anboten, als dies angesichts der wirtschaftlichen Ungleichgewichte im deutschen Bundesstaat der Fall ist. Dennoch fand die kanadische Verfassungspolitik den Ausweg aus der Blockade, während die deutsche Verfassungspolitik nach der ersten Reform erst richtig in die Blockadesituation der intergouvernementalen Verhandlungen hineinzugeraten scheint. Dies gibt Anlass, die gewählten Verfahren genauer zu betrachten und zu vergleichen.

---

54 Vgl. *Lazar, H./ McLean, J.*: Non-Constitutional Reform and the Canadian Federation: The Only Game in Town, in: Schultze, R.-O./Sturm. R. (Hg.): The Politics of Constitutional Reform in North America, Opladen, 2000, 149–175, hier 172; *Stevenson, G.*: The Unfulfilled Union, a.a.O., xi–xvi.

55 *Bakvis, H./ Skogstad, G.*: Canadian Federalism: Performance, Effectiveness, and Legitimacy, in: dies. (Hg.): Canadian Federalism: Performance, Effectiveness, and Legitimacy, Don Mills, Ont., 3–39, hier 3. Skeptischer *Broschek, J.*, a.a.O., 447.

(1) Zunächst deuten beide Fallstudien darauf hin, dass es in Bundesstaaten mit einem parlamentarischen Regierungssystem schwierig zu sein scheint, parlamentarische Verfahren der Verfassungsreform zu verwirklichen. Da die Mehrheitsparteien im Bund und in den Gliedstaaten normalerweise von den Regierungschefs geführt werden, und da in der Regeln keine oder nur schwache Strukturen der Parlamentszusammenarbeit bestehen, erfolgt die Konfliktregelung zwischen den Ebenen und Gebietskörperschaften vorrangig in intergouvernementalen Verhandlungen, nicht in parlamentarischen Verfahren. Selbst wenn Parlamentsausschüsse eingerichtet werden, treten weniger die Parteien als vielmehr die Regierungen als verhandelnde Akteure in Erscheinung.

(2) Die Reformprozesse in Deutschland und Kanada belegen, dass intergouvernementale Verfassungsverhandlungen durch ein *bargaining* um Macht und Ressourcen dominiert werden. Je nach Konfliktkonstellation können dabei Kompromisse oder Tauschgeschäfte erreicht werden. Das trifft vor allem für Fragen der vertikalen Kompetenzverteilung zu. Schwierig wird eine Einigung, wenn gleichzeitig horizontale Disparitäten oder Integrationsprobleme zu lösen sind. Der intergouvernementale Modus erlaubt in der Regel nur inkrementelle Veränderungen einer Verfassung, bei denen Leitideen einer Reform gegenüber Detailregelungen in den Hintergrund treten.

(3) Die Beratungen und Verhandlungen, die zum *Charlottetown Accord* in Kanada führten, zeigen (ebenso wie die jüngste Föderalismusreform in der Schweiz), dass komplexe Verfassungsfragen in Verfahren der gesellschaftlichen Interessenvermittlung öffentlich diskutiert werden können und dass dies zu einer Überwindung der *bargaining*-Logik führen kann. Vertreter der Bürgerschaft und gesellschaftlicher Gruppen interessieren sich nicht für Machtfragen, sondern für die Qualität der Aufgabenerfüllung, für Rechte von Gruppen und für Fragen der sozialen Gerechtigkeit. Sie bringen damit eine andere Perspektive in die Verhandlungen ein und handeln nach anderen Orientierungen als die Regierungen, und sie bewirken dadurch nicht selten, dass blockierte Auseinandersetzungen um die Machtverteilung in lösbare Normkonflikte transformiert werden. Sie können auch dazu beitragen, dass sich die Verfassungspolitik auf die wirklichen Verfassungsfragen konzentriert und nicht von Detailinteressen der Regierungen oder ihrer Ministerialbürokratien überfrachtet wird.

(4) Verfahren der Bürgerbeteiligung und der gesellschaftlichen Interessenvermittlung machen allerdings Entscheidungen nicht leichter, und sie verringern nicht das Risiko des Scheiterns. Abgesehen davon, dass sie die Richtung der Verfassungsdiskussion beeinflussen können und diese auf wesentliche Fragen fokussieren, liegt ihre mögliche Funktion in der Erzeugung von Legitimität für eine

geänderte Verfassung, die auch die inkrementelle Entwicklung nach der Reform unterstützen kann. Für diese Vermutung spricht jedenfalls die kanadische Verfassungspolitik, in der nicht das intergouvernemental ausgehandelte *Meech Lake*-Abkommen, sondern, trotz des negativen Referendums, erst das auf gesellschaftliche Interessenvermittlung gestützte Abkommen von *Charlottetown* die blockierte Situation überwinden half und die Verfassungsentwicklung voranbrachte. Und im Fall des Erfolgs ist es wahrscheinlich, dass die auf grundlegende Normen konzentrierte Verfassungsreform die Flexibilität des Bundesstaats für Anpassung erhalten wird.

(5) Der kanadische Fall steht für viele Beispiele, die belegen, dass Verfahren der Ratifikation von Verfassungsreformen erhebliche Risiken in sich bergen, gleichgültig ob sie in Parlamenten oder im Referendum erfolgen. Je höher die Zustimmungsquote festgelegt wird, desto größer sind die Gefahren eines negativen Votums. Und je komplexer das Reformpaket ausfällt, desto mehr haben einzelne Parlamente oder Bevölkerungsgruppen Gründe für eine Ablehnung, weil sie immer nur die sie betreffenden Bestandteile des Pakets beurteilen. Das Beispiel Kanadas deutet aber auch darauf hin, dass nach gescheiterten Reformen Chancen in der Verfassungsentwicklung liegen, allerdings nur unter der Voraussetzung, dass in Verfassungsverhandlungen eine hinreichende Legitimationsbasis für Veränderungen erzeugt worden ist. Dies entspricht der Erkenntnis, dass ein Verfassungskonsens nicht durch einen Akt der Abstimmung erreicht oder zum Ausdruck gebracht werden kann, sondern durch einen dauerhaften öffentlichen Verfassungsdiskurs.[56]

Diese Erfahrungen sprechen dafür, Verfassungsreformen nicht den Regierungen oder politischen Eliten zu überlassen, aber auch die Anforderungen an eine Demokratisierung mit Realitätssinn zu definieren. Für die Verfassungspolitik in Bundesstaaten empfiehlt sich ein demokratischer Pragmatismus. Demnach sollten die Verhandlungen über Entscheidungsvorschläge für gesellschaftliche Interessenvermittlung geöffnet und Verfassungsänderungen nach Regeln beschlossen werden, die eine Konsensfindung im Verhandlungen fördern, aber die Wahrscheinlichkeit von Blockaden durch kleine Minderheiten reduzieren. Zwar sind Verfassungsfragen im Bundesstaat Machtfragen zwischen Gebietskörperschaften, aber sie betreffen auch die Art und Weise, wie öffentliche Aufgaben erfüllt werden und wie politische Prozesse organisiert sind. Damit haben sie weitreichende Folgen für die Bürgerschaft im Allgemeinen und für Interessengruppen im Besonderen. Daher ist es notwendig, Verhandlungen über den Kreis der Regie-

---

[56] Dazu grundlegend *Vorländer, H.*: Verfassung und Konsens, Berlin, 1981.

rungen und Parteipolitiker hinaus zu öffnen. Die Bereitschaft politischer Eliten, sich zu einigen, kann gefördert werden, wenn sie die Zustimmung weiterer Akteure für die Reform benötigen. Der Pragmatismus verlangt aber auch, Vetomacht einzelner Gebietskörperschaften oder Bevölkerungsgruppen möglichst auszuschließen, wenn diese in getrennten Verfahren ihren Willen bilden. Einen Ausweg aus dieser Gefahr könnte die Einrichtung einer gemeinsamen parlamentarischen Versammlung des Bundes und der Gliedstaaten bieten, die für die abschließende Beratung und Beschlussfassung über Verfassungsreformen einberufen wird. Verfassungsreformen sollten jedenfalls so angelegt sein, dass im Fall ihres Scheiterns oder Misslingens der Prozess der Verfassungspolitik nicht blockiert ist und sie mit dem „Überschuss" an Legitimität aus den Verhandlungen in anderen institutionellen Kontexten und Verfahrensweisen fortgeführt werden kann.

Constituting the Cooperative State: Strategies for Collaborative Decentralisation within Unitary States

by Theo A. J. Toonen and Trui Steen

I. The Cooperative State

The concept of cooperative federalism, spilling over into the concept of a cooperative state, is generally connected to the constitutional structure of German federalism.[1] Different administrative functions – most notably policy making and policy execution – are allocated to different layers of government. This creates a basic structure of interdependence across layers. This thus curbs the power of central state government and secures the position of "lower governments". Multilevel governance systems have the advantage of bridging the centralisation-decentralisation divide in a flexible and adaptive manner. This leads to potentially high coordination costs and a fair degree of transaction costs. Adaptive flexibility, stability, self-organising capacity and innovation "from below" are to be set off against time-consuming consensus-forming processes, lagging institutional reform capacity and a potentially high number of veto players in the game of policy making and implementation.

As the concept of the cooperative state is associated with the notion of federalism and the post-World War II development of the German version of federalism, it is easily overlooked that similar principles for designing and constituting intergovernmental systems may apply to non-federal, even unitary systems of governance. The transformation of "cooperative federalism" into the "cooperative state" – encompassing state-federal relations in Germany including central-local relationships within the German *Länder* – implies that there is a broader range of constitutional structures to which this notion applies than formal federal relationships only. It refers to legal (federal) characteristics of intergovernmental relations in a certain country, as well as to the "unitary" structures within states (regions, *Länder*).

This observation creates a starting point for comparative analysis of systems of multi-level governance within countries. The cooperative state may be treated as an analytical concept: a way of looking at the operation of constitutional state

---

1   *Hesse, J. J./Ellwein, T.*: Das Regierungssystem der Bundesrepublik Deutschland, 2 vols., 9th ed., Berlin, 2004.

structures in general and of intergovernmental, central-regional or central-local relations in particular. In this contribution we will take this perspective a step further and provide a comparative view on unitary state systems from a concept of the cooperative state. This concept is our starting point, rather than the hierarchical notions of centralisation and decentralisation – or "the shadow of power" – which more commonly underlies the comparative analysis of unitary state systems on constitutional grounds. While federalism is generally recognised as a multi-interpretable concept, analysts are gradually experiencing that the situation with respect to the concept of unitarism is not very different. As observed earlier: "Indeed, only God knows what the unitary principle is and he has been remarkably reluctant to let mere mortals into the secret."[2] From an empirical viewpoint, the actual relative subsystem autonomy within a unitary state might be as large – or as small – as within a federal structure. The notion of the cooperative state might help in exploring the matter from a comparative perspective.

We will start by addressing the validity of this approach by illustrating and exploring the constitutional nature of the "cooperative state" and the associated concept of collaborative decentralisation in the Netherlands (which from a constitutional perspective is undisputedly a unitary state system). We will do this by referring to late 19th century, early 20th century constitutional theory of the Dutch intergovernmental or multi-level system of governance. The Netherlands is often presented as a mixed state system – an institutional compromise – based on Germanic constitutional principles which – in the mid 19th century – build upon constitutional characteristics of the French (unitary) state system – of the late 18th, early 19th century and the use of British constitutional principles as a foundation and inspiration for further development in the late 19th century. This is most clearly illustrated by an episode in the development of Dutch public and administrative law in the second half of the 19th century. A Dutch constitutional law professor and later Rector Magnificus of Leiden University (*J. T. Buys*) used the writings of and – to many not completely accurate – constitutional interpretation by the German public law scholar *von Gneist* of the British state system to theoretically undergird and defend a constitutional form of decentralisation that had existed within the *Thorbeck*ian constitutional state system from 1848 onwards. It was elaborated in a framework law for Dutch municipal government in 1851. Up until the 1870s, this arrangement was hardly called into effect. With expanding

---

2   *Bulpitt, J.*: Walking back to Happiness? Conservative Party Governments and Elected Local Authorities in the 1980s, in: Crouch, C./Marquand, D. (eds.): The New Centralism, Britain out of Step in Europe?, Oxford, 1989, 56–73; also *Toonen, T.A.J.*: Internationalisering en het openbaar bestuur als institutioneel ensemble: naar een zelfbestuurskunde, Den Haag, 1990.

technological, economic and social developments in Dutch society, the so-called principle of *self-governement* (*Selbstverwaltung, zelfbestuur*) was from then on-wards increasingly called upon to constitute and arrange central-local relation-ships within the context of a rapidly nationalising system of governance.

On the basis of this "constitutional" analysis we will then present a compara-tive overview of institutional developments within some other unitary state sys-tems and analyse the quest for local government autonomy. The concept of the cooperative state will be used as conceptual framework and analytical yardstick for assessing ongoing developments in terms of impact on local government autonomy. This chapter aims to develop a framework depicting the institutional contexts of intergovernmental systems. The framework is applied to outline the basic characteristics of the unitary state systems. We focus on characteristics of local government and intergovernmental relations in England, France, Denmark, Sweden and the Netherlands. The first two are the prototype unitary states to which the Netherlands implicitly or explicitly is often compared. Both British and French traditions have historically affected the design, interpretation and development of the Dutch constitutional system. The Scandinavian countries are included because of the (relatively small) size of the countries – which according to some might matter in state design – as well as the consensual and welfare state nature that these countries have in common with the Netherlands and which might affect the structure and operation of intergovernmental systems. The aim of this contribution is to illustrate that the degree to which an administration is organised at the central or decentralised levels, and the way relations between tiers of government are set up, is of "constitutional importance" to the operation and understanding of multi-level systems of governance.

II. Constituting Collaborative Decentralisation

The Netherlands operates within the evolutionary constitutional framework in-herited from the European revolutionary year 1848. As such, it is now a country with one of the oldest constitutions in Europe.[3] The modern Dutch constitution has thus known many different historical episodes – socially, politically, techno-logically – reflecting and demonstrating its adaptive, flexible and "living" nature. Every now and then the call for a constitutional revision can be heard, often on

---

3   *Toonen, T./Steunenberg, B./Voermans, W.*: Saying No to a European Constitution: Dutch Revolt, Enigma or Pragmatism?, in: Zeitschrift für Staats- und Europawissenschaften (ZSE), 3/4 (2005), 594–620.

the (far too) simple ground that this 19th century constitution is already "so old", (must therefore be) outmoded and (should be assumed) incapable of dealing with the issues of the 21st century. The Dutch constitution is a written constitution, but largely unwritten in the hearts and minds of the Dutch people, mass and elite alike – and therefore hardly known in substance. Closer inspection seldom reveals a real need – apart from modernisation and updating of the language used – for fundamental revision, thus underlining the organic nature of this "living constitution".

The Dutch constitutional system is thereby becoming a critical case for the long-term value and meaning of German, Romanticist 19th century organic state theory. This constitutional approach largely developed as a reaction and alternative to the natural (*Hobbes*) or rational (*Rousseau*) state or social contract theories affecting many acts of institutional state design under the influence of principles of (French) Enlightenment. The design of the current Dutch constitution by *Johan Rudolf Thorbecke* (1798–1872) in the European revolutionary – but for the Dutch nation evolutionary – year 1848 was explicitly informed by reference to German sources, notably the organic state theory of the German historical law school of *K. F. Eichhorn*. *Thorbecke* had become acquainted with this approach during a four-year postgraduate study in Germany (1820–1824). On the basis of his early writings, *Thorbecke* is explicitly seen as a representative of the *Göttinger Schule*.[4] He developed his intellectual capital into an analytical and design perspective of his own, which gave him his distinctly liberal – *liberale* – intellectual position within the broader organic state movement. It later became the intellectual basis for the design of the still operational Dutch constitutional system and the framework (municipal, provincial, water board) laws for the intergovernmental system that he drafted as Minister of the Interior in the first half of the 1850s.[5]

There is no constitutional court in the Netherlands. The right to interpret – and in doing so, substantially change the operational meaning of – the Dutch constitution belongs to parliament. Prudence and gradualism characterise the political and administrative culture surrounding constitutional development. As a consequence, the nature and development of the living constitution is to be found in the administrative substance rather than in the legal constitutional

---

4   *Thorbecke, J. R.*: Über das Wesen und den organischen Character der Geschichte (1824), republished in: Verkade, W. (ed.): Overzicht der staatkundige denkbeelden van Johan Rudolf Thorbecke (1798–1872), Arnhem, 1935.

5   For further elaboration *Toonen, T.*: The Unitary State as a System of Co-Governance: The Case of the Netherlands, in: Public Administration, 68/3 (1990), 281–296.

form and redesign of the institutional framework as such. In this context, the 19th century public law professor *J. T. Buys* (1829–1893) – working in the organic state tradition that *Thorbecke* had helped to establish while still public law professor in Leiden – referred to the wisdom of "the old England", where they understood "that true liberty was not dependent on the constitution but on the administration, not on *words* but on *deeds*"[6].

Buys was living in an era in the second half of the 19th century in which the complexity of Dutch society and the system of governance, particularly at the level of what we would now call the system of intergovernmental relations, was steadily increasing. The Netherlands was a latecomer to the industrial revolution, but from the 1870s onwards quickly caught up. It was developing from a long-term and well-established, merely rural and international trade-oriented society into a socio-economic dynamic one. Industrialisation, urbanisation, transformation of traditional industries and the rise of social issues contributed much to the enlargement of economic scale and social radius and thus to the need to develop an administrative system of multi-level governance. Not so much the autonomy and separation of the (national, regional and local) tiers of government but increasing interaction – be it formal, legalistic or socio-political – and interdependence gradually became characteristic of the system.[7]

Though still limited according to our current understanding, this growing interdependence and nationalisation of local and regional affairs gave rise to strong constitutional debates among lawyers and politicians alike. An important provision in the 1848 constitution drafted and implemented by *Thorbecke,* was the principle that local government could be called upon by the national legislator to carry out national policy in the local context. Throughout the second half of the 19th century, this provision was increasingly used with the expansion of state activity. It also underwent a change in nature: National legislation no longer merely described the administrative activities to be carried out by municipalities in the context of national law. In crucial cases it also required municipalities to regulate a certain domain, activity or policy area, leaving it to municipalities to decide how to carry out provisions. For example, it could legally require municipalities

---

6   *Buys, J. T.*: De strijd tusschen staat en maatschappij, Lecture, Leiden, 05.02.1874, reprinted in: de Beaufort, W.H/Arntzenius, A.R. (eds.): Studiën over staatkunde en staatsrecht van Mr J.T. Buys, Arnhem, 1895, 529.

7   *Toonen, T.*: Change in Continuity: Local Government and Urban Affairs in the Netherlands, in: Hesse, J.J. (ed.): Local Government and Urban Affairs in International Perspective, Baden-Baden, 1990, 291–333.

to regulate local (social) housing instead of formulating a national housing act to be carried out by municipalities.

This construction became subject to criticism as being unwarranted and even as "unconstitutional". "Classical theory" in Dutch public law – thriving in the wake of the development of the modern Dutch state in the 1840s and 1850s – had come to make a strict distinction between (municipal) *autonomie* (autonomy) and (municipal) *zelfbestuur* (self-government or self-administration).[8] This classical theory proposed as a normative principle the strict separation of the three governmental "households" distinguished by *Thorbecke*'s constitution: the national, provincial and municipal households. Each was considered an autonomous domain for (national, regional and local) regulation and legislation. When provincial or municipal authorities were carrying out national legislation, this was considered self-government; under this regime municipal (or provincial) government did not act as local government but as an administrative agent of national government.

An arrangement whereby local governments were not mandated to carry out ("administer") a national regulation but were obliged to regulate ("legislate") a certain area of municipal affairs as part of a national programme, violated this dualism and the principle of the separation of legislative powers ("autonomy") for different governmental households. It was therefore considered a breach of local government autonomy. Many lawyers and local politicians were advocating an either/or approach and a stark if not enumerative differentiation between (the "households" of) national and local governments, thus in effect pleading for a dual executive structure at local government level.

Buys, however, was against a dual and enumerative constitutional strategy. He favoured the cooperative approach and defended the principle of local self-government on grounds of decentralisation and securing the (constitutional) role and position of local government in a dynamic ("living", "organic") state system. In his writings and analyses, *Buys* often referred to the constitutional structures of the British state system as seen through the eyes of the German constitutional lawyer *von Gneist* and his interpretation of the operation of self-government in the British system. Some have therefore seen this as the imitation of a German-English product in the Dutch constitutional order.[9] *Buys* himself, however, saw the principle of self-government as "a real national product, an outgrowth of the autonomy, granted to those bodies, but precisely because of that little honoured

---

8   *Id.*: Denken over Binnenlands Bestuur: Theorieën van de Gedecentraliseerde Eenheidstaat Bestuurs-
    kundig Beschouwd, Arnhem, 1987, 69–88.
9   For example *Brasz, H. A.*: Veranderingen in het Nederlandse Communalisme, Assen, 1960, 60 f.

by those who value a strict line of demarcation" of the different governmental households.[10] He used *von Gneist*'s comparative constitutional analyses – even though they were partly based on a misunderstanding of the British system in its actual operation, as some maintained and *Buys* seemed to recognise – as a source of interpretation to defend an important constitutional principle which in his time, according to *Buys* "was treated as a stepchild, more tolerated than wanted"[11].

Buys hoped – for the sake of freedom and liberty; local government is not an end in itself – that "future generations" would look more favourable on the importance of self-government as a constitutional instrument for safeguarding the role of decentralisation and local government and would want to apply it more extensively. Therefore, the principle of self-government ("self-administration" of national or nationally-induced regulation) next to the principle of autonomy (strictly understood as the right of initiative to legislate at local government level) had to be protected and preserved as a constitutional provision. *Buys* interpreted self-government as a constitutional right of, rather than an obligation for, municipal (and provincial) government. He made clear that the "best" division of labour between layers of government was ultimately a question of frugality, effectiveness and efficiency, and would vary and have to be adapted (organically) to constantly changing social, infrastructural and economic circumstances. He defended the execution of national legislation and regulation by municipal (and provincial) authorities as a right rather than an obligation. If this constitutional provision did not exist, there would be no constitutional limits within the Dutch system to nationalise legislation and rule setting – i.e. nationalising "autonomy" – and have it carried out by a nationalised administration like in the French system. *Buys* located the strategic issue of centralisation within the administrative domain instead of the legislative domain, i.e. in the domain of (government in) action rather than words.[12] Like many other organic state theorists he was against "machinelike" and enumerative constitutional provisions of "checks and balances'" or strictly demarcated "competency blueprints" because of the potential limits this would pose on the system's gradual adaptive capacity.

The constitutional capacity to play a role in the execution of national policy ensured that local governments could continue playing a role in how state affairs were conducted. In addition, instead of sovereign it would make national government agencies dependent on the quality and cooperation of local governments

---

10 *Buys, J. T.*: De Grondwet, Toelichting en Kritiek, tweede deel, Arnhem, 1887, 63.

11 Ibid.

12 *Toonen, T. A. J.*: Denken over Binnenlands Bestuur, op. cit., 83; *id:* Change in Continuity, op. cit.

and would prevent total centralisation. Looking at the British system through the eyes, and following the interpretation of *von Gneist, Buys* concluded that the position of local governments within the overall system was not necessarily served better by "autonomy" – i.e. in the British case legislative powers are restricted to parliament – than by the executive power embedded in the principle of self-government.

The principle of self-government, later translated into *medebewind* – literally: co-governance – has become an important institutional underpinning of the relatively strong and sustained role and position of municipal government in the Dutch state system. It affected later constitutional debates in which *Buys* was declared right and constitutional lawyers and public administration scholars would take his argument one step further. Within the framework of local self-government and the resulting interdependence of national legislation and local execution and administration, *Buys* followed the British dual state model that advocated little administrative interaction and "*tutelle*" in the operational relationships among levels of government. A separation of "policy and execution", therefore, that looks very familiar to contemporary managerial minds. The great Dutch constitutional lawyer *Oud* later challenged *Buys'* ideas and urged to go one step further:

> "Buys was thus on the right track when he established that for the satisfaction of their needs, people turn to the authority they consider most appropriate for the purpose […] But he stopped halfway. He failed to conclude that this same efficiency can also result in *two kinds of government authorities cooperating* in handling an issue."[13]

By that time the first chair in Public Administration, *G.A. Van Poelje,* had already observed that the "modern state", with the perseverance of a "centralistically oriented" constitutional framework, had often adopted a strong decentralisation in the design and organisation of the administration (executive functions) of state affairs, often in collaboration with private initiative and business interest. In the 1920s and 1930s, he spoke of "new forms of decentralisation", which he labelled "decentralisation by cooperation" or "collaborative decentralisation".[14]

---

13 *Oud, P. J.*: Handboek voor het Nederlands Gemeenterecht. Deel 2, Zwolle, 1959, 34, authors' emphasis.
14 *van Poelje, G. A.*: Algemene inleiding tot de bestuurskunde, Alphen a/d Rijn, 1953, 56; *id.*: Wilde groei of organisatie, Alphen a/d Rijn, 1928.

III. Towards a Comparative Framework

The existence of complex, interrelated and interorganisational systems and policy networks are the rule in contemporary "government in action". This observation applies specifically to the complexities of central-local government relations. The organic state perspective on collaborative decentralisation suggests that in a context of change and institutional development, it is particularly the institutional capacity and perseverance to adapt to changing (economic, political, infrastructural, cultural) circumstances – i.e. the capacity for strategic action, resilience, institutional sustainability, survival and innovation of the system – that have to become focal points of attention in comparative analysis.[15]

In the context of a comparative analysis of central-local relationships in unitary systems, two decades ago, *Page* and *Goldsmith*[16] identified three factors which are of crucial importance in assessing the institutional balance among national and local authorities: functions, discretion, and access to relevant decision-making arenas. We assume that these three variables are affected by various institutional factors which in turn influence the adaptive capacity for reform and institutional development. On the basis of our previous constitutional exploration of the concept of collaborative decentralisation, and within the framework of the constitutional design of unitary state structures, we have to discuss two interrelated elements that shape central-local relations: the design of intergovernmental relations and the form of intergovernmental management – i.e. the organisation and management within forms of collaborative decentralisation – applied in a given system or country.[17]

The archetypes of a unitary state are the Jacobin French and the British Westminster varieties, although the distinction between the French "centralised" and the British "decentralised" unitary state came under serious scrutiny in the 1980s.[18]

---

15 *Toonen, T.A.J.*: Administrative Reform Analytics, in: Peters, B.G./Pierre, J. (eds.): Handbook of Public Administration, London, 2003, 467–476; *id.*: Analyzing Institutional Change and Administrative Transformation: a Comparative View, in: Otenyo, E./Lind, N. (eds.): Comparative Public Administration: the Essential Readings, Houghton-Mifflin, 2006, 371–392; *id.*: Substance Came with Little Hype: Public Sector Reform in the Netherlands, in: Hesse, J.J./Hood, C./Peters, B.G. (eds.): Paradoxes in Public Sector Reform, Berlin, 2003, 215–251.

16 *Page, E.C./Goldsmith, M.* (eds.): Central and Local Government Relations: A Comparative Analysis of Western European Unitary States, London, 1987.

17 Cf. *Wright, D.S.*: Understanding Intergovernmental Relations, Pacific Grove, 1988; *Toonen, T.A.J.*: Internationalisering en het openbaar bestuur, op. cit.; *id./van der Meer, F.*: Area and Administration: A Multilevel Analysis of a Multi-layered Phenomenon, in: Burgess, M./Vollaard, H. (eds.): State Territoriality and European Integration, New York, 2006, 71–100.

18 *Bulpitt, J.*, op. cit.

Many consider the decentralised unitary state of the Netherlands as a contradiction in terms – "decentralised centralisation" – revealing characteristics of what can more appropriately be called a "consensus state"[19] but also showing the need to further differentiate the concept of "a unitary state". In many northern European states, local governments play a key role in actually carrying out and "administering" nationally agreed policies. Therefore – formally or *de facto* – decentralised governments have an impact on national government policy formulation that may be compared to that of sub-national systems in some federalised states.

1. Intergovernmental Relations: Horizontalisation and Interwovenness

If anything, our previous exploration of the concept of collaborative decentralisation within the cooperative state requires that we enter the black box of the constitutionally defined unitary state. We have to explore the nature of executive and administrative interrelations that exist and develop within the legal constitutional framework of our unitary states. Relevant intergovernmental relations consist of a configuration of legal, financial, political, administrative and organisational relationships and linkages among the different elements and units distinguished within a state. Most research suggests two important dimensions along which systems of intergovernmental relations might productively be analysed: (1) the horizontal or the vertical nature of relations, and (2) the degree of administrative and political interwovenness of the different levels.

Regarding the first dimension – the horizontal or vertical nature of relations – relationships between different levels of government may be characterised by the horizontal principle according to which units of government at one level carry out legal rules and norms set at another level. This principle applies to systems that are characterised by regional and local self-administration, such as Great Britain, the Scandinavian countries and the Netherlands.

In contrast, the so-called Napoleonic states[20] – with France as the ideal type case – are predominantly characterised by the principle of verticality or administrative deconcentration. The public authority which sets the rule also takes care of the implementation through field agencies in the region. The (former) *préfect-*

---

19 *Hendriks, F./Toonen, T.A.J.* (eds.): Polder Politics: The Reinvention of Consensus Democracy in the Netherlands, Aldershot, 2001.

20 *Page, E.C./Goldsmith, M.*, op. cit.; *Wunder, B.* (ed.): Les influences du modèle Napoléonien sur l'organisation administrative des autres pays/The Influences of the Napoleonic Model of Government on the Administrative Organisation of Other Countries, Brussels, 1995.

oral system of France is the most notable example in this respect, but the category also includes countries such as Italy, Greece or Portugal. In some systems, forms of vertical administration have led to a more uncoordinated "picket fence model"[21] in which national ministries have each set up, more or less independently, their own field agencies and have thus functionalised service delivery. The issue of territorial integration is neglected, causing territorial fragmentation and contributing to a lack of coordination and policy integration. The territorial dimension of the French system has become more political – rather than bureaucratic – in nature during the decentralisation and reform processes of the 1980s and 1990s. The *départements* were granted democratic legitimisation by substituting the *préfet* by a directly elected council as the major way to democratically control executive action at local and supra-local level. Creating more flexibility in the French intergovernmental system was an important reason behind the enhancement and the politicisation of territoriality in public service delivery and control.

The second dimension that needs to be taken into consideration from the perspective of a cooperative state concerns the degree of administrative and political interwovenness of the different government levels of a particular country. Some systems are characterised by statutory regulation and a high degree of separation of the different layers of government. One could speak of steering from a distance. The most notable historical example is the "dual" British system where the principle of *ultra vires*, in combination with an emphasis on local autonomy within these fixed boundaries, has led to a system that "can be called a Dual Polity, a structure of central local relations in which national and local politics, and national and local government, operated, by and large, in two separate compartments"[22].

The "non-executant role" of central government, characteristic of states such as Great Britain, Scandinavian countries and the Netherlands, is traditionally identified as one of the overriding factors in explaining the variety in the share of local government activity in the overall state activities.[23] In these systems, local governments are strongly embedded in the overall state structure, sometimes taking a larger share of government expenditure out of the general budget than the national government. The Anglo-Saxon system of local government and municipal self-administration creates at least a potential dependency of national on lo-

21 *Wright, V.*: Regionalization under the French Fifth Republic: The Triumph of the Functional Approach, in: Sharpe, L. J. (ed.): Decentralist Trends in Western Democracies, London/Beverly Hills, 1979, 148–167.
22 *Bulpitt, J.*, op. cit.; *id.*: Territory and Power in the United Kingdom, Manchester, 1983.
23 *Page, E. C./Goldsmith, M.*, op. cit.; *Rhodes, R. A. W./Wright, V.* (eds.): Tensions in the Territorial Politics of Western Europe, London, 1987.

cal governments for the implementation of public services, while the national "Napoleonic" governments in southern Europe have their own deconcentrated field agencies to carry out their policies.

As we have seen from our historical exercise on Dutch constitutional and administrative law, the degree of interwovenness is usually addressed – and criticised – under the heading of "centralisation". The emphasis is placed on the need for complementarity, coordination, reduction of duplication and overlap or on the desirability of partnership and of disentangling intergovernmental relations for the benefit of the "lower" governments. However, comparative intergovernmental experience and research over the past decade have contributed to a considerable modification of this conventional wisdom. It was precisely the relative lack of direct administrative and political interwovenness of the system in the British setting that allowed the *Thatcher* government to implement its retrenchment policies of the mid-1980s at local government level, without being directly confronted with administrative and political counter forces. These would undoubtedly have been mobilised if the institutional arrangements had allowed bureaucratic and party political access by local interest to the national decision-making centres. It was not until the introduction of the "poll tax" that the national administration became directly involved in "local" issues, and directly experienced the effects which its decisions had at local government level. It marked the beginning of the end of the harsh period – particularly for local government – of *Thatcher*'s rule.

The osmosis of the French system provides a case in contrast. It is more centralist in set-up and nature, but over time has developed into a complex interplay of forces in which more than once central government has not been able to pursue its stated policy preferences against the interests and will of local authorities. The recurrent and systemic inability of one of the supposedly most centralised states to reform the – according to many – archaic French municipal government system is almost legendary.

In sum: A non-executant role of central government and local self-administration are relevant factors in explaining the potential importance of local public economies in intergovernmental systems as a whole and the degree of "cooperation" which the system triggers. In addition, a certain degree of interwovenness of levels of government, connecting national and local agencies even against their will, seems necessary to create the institutional conditions under which local politics and administration may maintain or at times raise their importance for national politics.

2. Intergovernmental Management

The intergovernmental management dimension of multi-level systems of governance refers to the array of problem-solving activities, procedures, techniques and forms of steering, guidance and control mechanisms which operate at the interfaces between government agencies. Different forms of intergovernmental management (IGM) may produce different, and sometimes counterintuitive, results.

The Scandinavian countries and Britain, for example, differ from France and Italy in that they rely heavily on IGM through general norms, statutes, regulations and criteria that must be observed by the authorities involved. In contrast to this management according to statutory regulation, the other countries tend to rely more on administrative regulation through direct and more detailed guidance, involving central government officials in many individual decisions of local authorities. In the northern countries, management by statutory regulation is often practised and advocated in the name of "decentralisation". However, according to *Page*'s and *Goldsmith*'s empirical observation, the intergovernmental management practice underlying administrative regulation implies close links between the centre and specific localities. *Page* and *Goldsmith* conclude that in the investigated southern countries local government has much better opportunities to influence central policy making than in Britain and Scandinavia: "In South Europe, not only is the voice of local government as a whole heard at the centre, but also that of the individual municipality."[24]

Different styles of intergovernmental management and underlying administrative cultures may drastically influence the way in which institutional intergovernmental arrangements operate on a day-to-day basis. In some systems, the supervisory powers of one public authority over another might be used as a mechanism for coordination, consultancy, support, mediation and problem solving among levels of government. In other systems, they might be exploited to try to settle narrow-minded, bureaucratic and political fights and conflicts, or to block or veto developments in adjacent units in the intergovernmental system. The same is true of central-local grant systems. It is often a combination of features at constitutional, relational and managerial levels of intergovernmental systems which determine the nature of the system.

---

24 *Page, E. C./Goldsmith, M.*, op. cit.

3. Comparative Analysis

The configuration of characteristics at the level of both intergovernmental relations and intergovernmental management make up the comparative institutional profile of the unitary state from the cooperative state perspective. Let us briefly survey some developments within various unitary systems and explore them from the perspective of autonomy in a cooperative state structure.

a) England

Local government in England comprises regions – including the Greater London Authority (GLA) –, metropolitan counties, metropolitan districts, unitary authorities, shire (or non-metropolitan) districts, shire councils, town councils and parish councils. The size of the area covered and of the population served may vary considerably between authorities of similar types and with similar functions.

The Westminster tradition is heavily rooted in the common law tradition. There is a written constitution spelling out the position of English local government. Extensive power is conferred on Parliament, i.e. central government. Local authorities work within the powers laid down under various Acts of Parliament. As such, local government has no general competencies but may perform only what is permitted by Parliament which defines the "powers beyond which" (*ultra vires*) it cannot go.[25] However, under this system local government functions may be quite far-reaching, with some being mandatory and others discretionary.

aa) Recent Moves towards Decentralisation after an Era of Centralisation

Since about the 1930s, with the post-World War II welfare state bringing more centralisation in policy making, local government powers and functions have declined. The British entry into the EEC in the 1970s and the necessary loosening of historical ties by the early 1980s had triggered a fundamental reform and re-organisation process among the members of the former Commonwealth. By the 1990s, next to New Zealand and Australia, England had become a main global champion of the New Public Management (NPM) movement. The NPM reforms have modernised but not really changed the institutional characteristics of the "classical" Westminster model.

Centralisation accelerated when Mrs *Thatcher* came to power in 1979. At the time proponents of local government autonomy had a hard time. By all accounts

---

25 *Loughlin, J.*: The United Kingdom: From Hypercentralization to Devolution, in: id. (ed.): Subnational Democracy in the European Union, Oxford, 2001, 37–60.

and in retrospect, when coming into office, Mrs *Thatcher* was confronted with an utterly outmoded system of local government which also in functional terms could not withstand comparison with, for example, Swedish municipalities or French *départements*. In the early stages, the reforms weighed heavily on local government, as the *Thatcher* government had a strong ideological preference for the market – rather than local government – as the main vehicle for decentralisation. The *Thatcher* era has often been labelled as "centralising", but it would be more accurate to stress the "relocative" nature of the reforms in the 1980s. The *Thatcher* government transferred, rather than centralised local government tasks from one (local government) to another institutional domain (the market or public-private arrangements). Central government basically stuck to its "non-executive" – i.e. policy-making – role and under the *Thatcher* regime tried to involve business and for example urban development corporations and other quangos (quasi-autonomous non-governmental organisations) in the production and delivery of services, formerly under the jurisdiction of local government councils. In the later stages of the reform, when privatisation strategies were exhausted or became less popular, executive tasks formerly belonging to the domain of local government were transferred to independent agencies that operated in the region at an "arm's length" of central government. Under *Major's* Next Steps programme, this agencification – i.e. what would be called either "administrative deconcentration" or "functional decentralisation" in continental European systems – became the main institutional expression of the principle of a non-executive national civil service system.

The structure of the "decentralised unitary state" allowed the *Thatcher* government to engage in this far-reaching local government reform process largely in the face of (Labour-dominated) resistance at the local level itself. With the Labour government coming to power in the 1990s, a devolution programme was set up. The functional decentralisation contributed much to the complexity of institutional structures and the need for coordination at the regional – i.e. supra-local – level of governance. This largely triggered the agenda for "rejoining government initiatives" under the later *Blair* regime. Central government established a Central Local Partnership Meeting with the Local Government Association (LGA), which represents the majority of local authorities in England and Wales. As a result, the relations between the centre and the local level have considerably eased.[26] The Department for Communities and Local Governments (DCLG) started a government-wide debate with local government and key stakeholders on the future of

---

26 Ibid.

local government, under the banner of "local:vision". The government's policy to devolve power has been put into practice with the transfer of key powers to the Greater London Authority (GLA). In a recent White Paper (October 2006) the government suggests that counties are becoming stronger and that strong counties represent the best alternative to local power.

Also, from within England there are voices of concern about the so-called West Lothian Question. This concerns the fact that England is lacking a government of its own and is influenced by politicians from the whole of the UK. Suggested solutions have included a fully devolved English parliament, but this has not caught on in British politics. Since Labour came to power, efforts have been made to devolve power to local government, but there have not yet been any radical changes in the administrative system.

bb) Dual Structures and Internal Autonomy

It should be noted that local government in the Westminster tradition is hardly seen as an independent entity; it is to a large extent perceived as a utilitarian arrangement and vehicle for civil society to engage in collective or public affairs at local and regional level. Local government as a form of local self-governance is not the integrated, uniform municipal (executive) government organisation known from the Nordic countries or the European continent. Mayors, for example, are – with the recent exception of the modernised version of the mayor in London – traditionally largely ceremonial figures fulfilling a "honourable" – not a professional – function. The emphasis in the governance of local government (by laymen if not "amateur politicians") is on (functional) policy committees, which are often fragmented and overlapping in nature and even apart from that, not really fit to "manage" large executive organisations.

Within the Westminster model, there are few formal interrelationships for the day-to-day management of individualised central-local relationships. The main vehicle for homogenisation and intergovernmental management – next to the reform and scale enlargement carried out in England in the 1970s as well – is the law. The principal formal interface between local and central government is the Department of Internal Affairs. This "hands-off approach" easily creates an illusion of freedom and lack of central interference in local affairs. However, the vehicles for central government's access to local government agendas are more indirect and are embedded in the overall "constitutional structure" and the (dual) nature of intergovernmental systems. Depending on their political agenda, some governments have been willing to exercise these institutional prerogatives *vis-à-*

vis local government more than others. The eventual outcome of this process is still difficult to predict.

Local government autonomy in the Westminster model is largely administrative and internal in nature. It is a functional, organisational arrangement rather than an institutional value or concept for external societal innovation and problem solving. The scope of this organisational autonomy is externally determined and not vested in the "right of initiative" – legal autonomy – of local government itself. The "debureaucratisation" of local government implied by NPM reforms, fits the utilitarian Westminster tradition of aiming at a minimum of external, individualised and hands-on administrative interrelationships among levels of government.[27] Where they need to exist, they have been redefined as contractual relationships, strictly specifying the object of "discretion" and the conditions of use. The agent is left "free" to do the job as he sees fit and let the manager manage within his mandate.

b) Nordic Countries: Sweden and Denmark

Sweden and Denmark have a model where local government has a strong position, but within a framework that reflects a dominant role of central government and a high ambition in terms of state involvement in society and vice versa. The system as a whole is characterised by a strong participation of civil society at all levels of governance, and the role of the state in public life is generally (still) taken for granted. This has resulted in fairly high "aspiration levels" regarding equity principles within public finance and among local governments.

In Sweden there is much respect for local government and administration in the sense that local administration is said to be very independent from central government in policies and finance. When looking more closely at how Sweden arranges the position of local government, *Loughlin* and *Martin* appear to be right in weakening this statement by saying that "the central-local relations present something of a paradox"[28]. Local and central government cooperate continuously but local government has to operate within limits set by central government and is closely monitored by the county administrator who is appointed by central government. Although the Swedish constitution gives local government a special place and a formal basis, it does not specify the division of responsibilities

27 Cf. *John Halligan*'s contribution to this volume.
28 *Loughlin, J./Martin, S.*: Local Income Tax in Sweden: Reform and Continuity. Paper prepared for the Balance of Funding Review, Centre for Local and Regional Government Research, School of European Studies, Cardiff University, 2004.

between state and local government, which is a matter of principle and a practical issue. This division varies over time following the development of society. The principle of "open households" prevails. Yet, the division of labour is mainly based on special legislation, which, in the more recent past, has also been influenced by EU decisions.

Denmark has a long-standing tradition of a decentralised public sector where most welfare tasks are dealt with by local government. The relationship between central and local government is described as a mixture of control, negotiation and autonomy, but detailed involvement is avoided.[29] A recent reform has weakened the position of the regions (on 1 January 2007, five regions replaced the 13 counties). Municipalities have taken over a number of tasks that were performed by mid-level administrations. The intent is to decrease the level of responsibility for the mid-level administration and to create larger and more sustainable municipalities. These have been put in charge of handling most citizen-related tasks, including most welfare tasks. Local authorities have been given a general competence. The constitution does not provide protection against comprehensive legislative regulation of local authority matters, but in practice local authorities have a considerable degree of autonomy.

aa) Institutionalised Horizontality

The observed "paradox of local autonomy" more or less dissolves when the level of intergovernmental relations is taken into account. The Nordic model represented here is a typical illustration of the balancing act in the trade-off between autonomy and co-decision which a modern local government faces if it aspires a strong position in both society and the intergovernmental system. A strong role of local taxation entails strong state involvement in decisions on how the money is spent, though these interventions are rather institutionalised and seem to work within a statutory framework that gives rights of "access" to both sides of the central-local relationship.

The key concept of the Swedish model of administration is decentralisation of executive power. The strong position of local government in the Nordic model thus derives from the fact that it is crucially involved in the carrying-out – implementation – of important public services. The contrast in our study is the case of France, where the municipal level hardly provides public services and the national state itself maintains a large executive role at local governance level. In

---

29 *Lidström, A.*: Denmark: Between Scandinavian Democracy and Neo-liberalism, in: Loughlin, J. (ed.), op. cit., 343–363.

terms of our framework: The application of the "horizontality principle" gives local government its undisputedly strong position, which, by its very nature, entails a strong relationship with central government policy making.

bb) Equity through Reform

The institutional structure in the Nordic system clearly affects the arrangements for financing local government. Equity is an important value within the rather egalitarian culture associated with the Nordic model. Efforts at equalisation – in a comparative perspective – have to be understood in terms of the correction of a fundamental homogenous if not uniform system, rather than a redistribution of resources within a highly diversified system. In both Denmark and Sweden, the equalisation systems have recently been reformed.

Despite collaborative structures and supervision institutions in the institutional domain of central and local government, the style of intergovernmental management is clearly entrenched by the idea that coordination among levels of government is not a matter of individualised, hands-on administrative control.

If local government as a whole is characterised by a rather uniform and large-scale basic structure, it is easier to leave potentially equity-disturbing tools such as local taxation in the hands of these units. This is particularly the case if the system gives national government "access" to local government decision-making on the nature of these taxes and how they are allocated. In this context, it should be noted that in Denmark's recent local reform process municipalities have gained many tasks, but have also lost responsibilities to the state, primarily as regards the assessment and administration of taxes. Overall, reform of the basic structure of local government is an important tool for "intergovernmental management" in the Nordic countries.

c) France

The French state is traditionally centralised, with sub-national government being strongly influenced by the central level. France is renowned for the fact that – for a long time – it had more local government units than all EU countries together. If that is no longer the case, it is because many new Member States – many of them Napoleonic in character themselves – have entered the alliance and not because France has succeeded in its recurrent attempts to reform a – to many observers – archaic, small-scale local government structure. France is still divided into 22 regions (*régions*) which are subdivided into 96 departments (*départements*). The latter in their turn consist of 329 *arrondissements* subdivided into

3,879 *cantons* which comprise 36,571 municipalities (*communes*). Additionally there are ten "dependent areas". Stricter and looser forms of cooperation between decentral government units exist as well. Indeed, cooperation between the various local government levels is extensive and varied. One of the most important forms of cooperation can be found in the EPCIS (*Etablissements publics de co-operation intercommunale*), which comprises *régions*, *départements* and councils.

There have been considerable reforms in French intergovernmental relations, almost continuously since the early 1980s. The new system that has developed over the past decade seems to be under the strong influence of decentralisation. At the same time, the influence of the central state seems to be as strong as ever. In 2003, the revision of the constitution provided a safeguard for local self-government. This revision must be seen as the next mile-stone in a very gradualist – but stable, long-term and sustained – public-sector reform process that has focused on restructuring the intergovernmental system ever since the early 1980s.

In contrast to the Westminster model of the unitary state, the Jacobin nature of the French unitary state is exemplified by a strong, if not predominant position of the French presidency within the overall governmental system. The French administrative system has strong local governments in parallel with central government branch – or field – offices at local level, which reflect a mix of powers between local and central government. The French state has a reputation as one of the most centralised intergovernmental systems in the world. However, at the same time it may be seen as the classic example that centralisation of tasks and decision-making is not necessarily the same as concentrating effective decision-making power at the apex of an integrated and streamlined governmental machinery.

Decentralisation means transfer of powers, but here it seems to be a transfer of tasks, which is accompanied with the necessary funds. The influence of the central state is illustrated by the role of the prefect (*préfet*), who is the eyes and ears of the central state at local level. However, deconcentration and decentralisation reforms have reinforced the powers of the prefects over field services of central government ministries, more than over local governments.[30]

Devolution and decentralisation policies have been pursued since the 1980s. Functions have been transferred to local governments, but compared to other European countries relatively few tasks have been delegated; the French central state has retained a substantial executive machinery at local level. However, im-

---

30 *Marcou, G.*, e-mail conversation 08.03.2007.

portant transfers of personnel from the field to regional and provincial administrations took place in the 1980s and in the past few years.[31]

The multiplicity and variety of governmental units is complemented by a high degree of interconnectedness of the various levels of governance within the system. The relationships are both top-down and bottom-up. Subsidiarity plays an important role in the French state structure. As a result, territorial units are supposed to take decisions on all matters that are within powers that can best be exercised at their level.

The French system of decentralisation is characterised by a continuous loop of cooperation and co-decision between the various levels of government and frequent interference by the state in local prerogatives.[32] However, it should not be overlooked that many (political) interrelationships work the other way as well, giving local government bottom-up access and influence at the "higher" levels of authority. Very often the – powerful – prefect represents the interests of (the local governments in) his department at the national ministerial level. Both at regional and departmental level, the task of the prefect – the representative of the state – is sometimes more complicated because he finds himself forced to ask for funding for state-run projects.[33] The region is also the layer of government that may be involved in national planning and may accelerate implementation either by being involved in the preparation/approval phase or through *contrats de plan*. Since the 1980s, the *cumul des mandats* – the accumulation of public mandates in one person – has gradually been restricted as part of the intergovernmental reform process but still exists as a phenomenon. Many politicians combine functions at local, regional, national or even European levels. The bicameral parliament comprises the National Assembly, which is elected by direct universal suffrage, and the Senate, which is elected by a body of 150,000 persons through a system of indirect suffrage.[34] Local government is represented in parliament by the members of the Senate. They are elected for a term of nine years by electoral colleges corresponding to the *départements* and composed of deputies and general and municipal councillors. Bills focusing on the organisation of territorial authorities must first be examined by the Senate and then by the National Assembly. As the Senate is the representation of the sub-national authorities, they have considerable influence on this process.

31 Ibid.
32 *Allegri, G.*: Strengthening Regional and Local Democracy in the European Union, Vol. 1: France, CoR-Studies, E-1/2004, Brussels, 2004, 273–354.
33 Embassy of France in the US, 2005.
34 Art. 24 French Constitution.

aa) Deburaucratisation and Professionalisation of Relationships

In the mid-1970s, *Croizier* and *Thoenig*[35] referred to the French system of complex interrelated layers of government as an immobile "honeycomb structure": rigid, and with little flexibility and power to innovate and adapt to new problems and opportunities. It is no exaggeration to say that since its early stages in the 1980s, the decentralisation and devolution process has been a more or less deliberate effort to dismantle the interwovenness of the system. The aim is to create more innovative and problem-solving capacity, most notably at the local and regional levels of governance, which – socially and economically – have become increasingly important with the move towards what has become known as the knowledge-based economy. Original efforts at local government reform in the very early 1980s had failed once again, partly as a result of the political overrepresentation of small municipalities and rural areas at national level. Governments responsible for local government amalgamations very often consisted largely of mayors of small municipalities, and in the early 1980s more than 90 % of the Senate members also held the position of mayor or local, departmental or regional councillor.

Since then, in a slow but steady process of continuous territorial and intergovernmental reform, many plans have been issued and, to a larger or lesser degree, implemented. These plans have been basically oriented at reducing the immobility and complex interdependence of the various layers of the intergovernmental system. They have started out with a steady reduction in the number and types of public mandates that can be accumulated in one person, and, instead of reducing the number of "layers of government'" have made them more visible and transparent by putting them under democratic rather than bureaucratic rule. Gradually, functional powers and responsibilities have been pushed "downward".

bb) Contractualisation

The flexibilisation of relationships has been a key concern, again with small steps to be taken given the complexity of interests involved – not only at national level. As a consequence of the devolution policy, contracts were introduced between the state and local or regional authorities in order to implement various sectoral policies and finance investments.

Relationships among units and levels of government are still heavily politicised and geared to individual units and cases rather than to the local or regional

---

35 *Croizier, M./Thoenig, J.C.*: The Regulation of Complex Organised Systems, in: Administrative Science Quarterly, 21/4 (1976), 547–570.

government as an institution. Still, at the same time the management of relationships among units and levels seems to have become more "contractual" in nature, with formal agreements replacing informal, political arrangements. The cooperation between state and sub-national authorities is laid down in a *contrat de plan*. It is not really possible to say whether this contract is one between equal partners or whether the state is dominant in this regard. On the one hand, local governments can only perform tasks in decentralised fields when they receive funds, which may be a bargaining point for them. On the other hand, the central state may provide funds which local government thinks are inadequate. This again illustrates the continuous loop of cooperation and co-decision between the French levels of government.

Real decentralisation connected with independent powers does not exist in France. This is illustrated by the local financial system which is inextricably bound to the central system. The 2003 revision of the constitution was intended to make things less complicated, but this exercise was not entirely successful. The system is highly complex. The Constitutional Council ensures that the share of own resources in the overall resources of each local authority category does not decrease. But while the state does not finance activities outside its own remit, it requires local authorities to help fund central government projects, especially in the context of the *contrats de plan Etat-régions*.

In sum, administrative centralisation in France has met the countervailing powers of individualised and decentralised functional political interests, networks and relationships. "Organised complexity", rather than centralisation, is probably the key concept in gaining access to what conveniently – but to the regret of some French administrative scholars and political scientists – has been labelled the Napoleonic Model. More generally, organised (social) complexity means: multiplicity, diversity and interdependence.

d) The Netherlands

In addition to what we described earlier, the Netherlands is a less formalised version of a cooperative state. In this version, the unitary legal structure provides national government with considerable leverage over regional and local government, but confers a strong executive role on local governments which contributes to strong interrelationships across various levels of governance. The distinction between autonomy and co-governance as the two classical principles outlining the position of Dutch local government, should not be seen as a tension or conflict, but rather as a trade-off resulting from the interwovenness of the intergovernmental system. This interdependence strengthens rather than weakens the position of local government level *vis-à-vis* national government in that the principle of co-governance makes central government highly dependent on local government for the execution of national policy and provides local government with access to decision-making arenas. Upon a closer look, the conventional idea of the Dutch intergovernmental system as one characterised by a relative high level of centralisation does not provide a full picture. Rather than centralisation, there is a high interdependence between different actors. For lack of a strongly legalised tradition in formal "vertical" cooperation and joint decision-making, this structure evokes a creative use of administrative and bureaucratic instruments to manage intergovernmental relations. Financial tools and arrangements are evidently a major component of the steering repertoire – in both directions. Furthermore, analysis of shifts in central-local relations since the 1980s shows that the balance between national and local authorities is affected by waves of decentralisation of government functions. However, the agenda behind these decentralisation processes was and still is economic rather than aimed at strengthening the position of local government. Overall, the trend seems towards more local autonomy in exchange for financial discipline and "centralisation" of information on local practice and policy performance.

A paradox resulting from the complexity of the Dutch cooperative state is that decentralisation processes are often perceived as (re-)centralisation. Plans aim at the decentralisation of functions, at deregulation and at the introduction of tools for enhancing interactive partnership between government levels. In practice, however, changes in the infrastructure and culture of intergovernmental cooperation are set within the limits of the basic features of the Dutch intergovernmental system – consensus unitarism, interwovenness, and administrative crowdedness. Such changes are hampered in keeping up with the demand to reform intergovernmental relations and management. Despite *Buys*' elusive and persuasive analyses, Dutch local governments still have a hard time accepting that from a constitutional viewpoint, strong central government involvement in local affairs is actually a sign of the sustained strength and importance of local government, rather than of disrespect for local autonomy. The manifestation of certain constitutional issues does not seem to change over a century.

IV. Conclusion

Our explorative comparative analysis shows that it is necessary to understand the larger institutional context and framework of intergovernmental relations in order to perceive possible patterns. There is an intricate balancing system that uses a variety of tools and institutional arrangements to accommodate pulls towards unity, coherence and integration on the one hand and pulls towards selectivity, variety, initiative and innovation on the other.

The analysis also shows that a long-term local government reform process has been and still is going on. It is part of a larger public-sector transformation in the Western world – a process of adaptation to changing global economic conditions and circumstances. Many of the reforms have been budget-driven. The emerging monetary discipline under (European) stability pacts has forced governments to take measures to balance the budget towards local government which perhaps would not have been taken without this external constraint.

However, this process is conducted at different speeds and with different "reform styles" in different countries. Five cases, showing different intergovernmental lay-out within constitutional unitary state structures, have been discussed. England – the model for a Westminster type of unitary state – is strongly centralised, with a tradition of a clear separation of policy making and execution and a preference for generic "hands-off" intergovernmental management. The Nordic countries – though different in political context – share various characteristics and institutional traditions with this category. France represents the Napoleonic – or, if you like, southern European – system, characterised by strong central rule, close – and often highly politicised – administrative interrelationships and a tradition of an individualised, formal (*tutelle*) and fairly "hands-on" intergovernmental management system with direct involvement of higher "authority" in local affairs. Finally, in the Netherlands the unitary legal structure provides national government with considerable leverage over regional and local government, but a strong executive role of local governments contributes to strong interrelationships across various levels of governance.

Under the current conditions of interdependence and scale enlargement, particularly in the European context, it is worthwhile to engage in a renewed debate on local government autonomy. From an institutional perspective, this debate has potentially constitutional ramifications. In designing institutional strategies to secure the role of local government institutions in the emerging Europeanised systems of multi-level governance, a careful comparative understanding of the determinants of local government autonomy and problem-solving capacity is warranted. Different institutional strategies are required to ensure that local and regional government occupy an important position in the emerging European order. A "one size fits all" approach easily divides local governments with different institutional backgrounds in the European arena, even within the unitary state category. Conflict among local governments has over time been the one and overriding force behind centralisation movements.

A contextual and institutional understanding of local government autonomy is required. There are classical indicators such as income from local taxation, managerial autonomy, self-elected officials, reduced supervision structures and the limitation of administrative interrelationships among layers of government. But these do not suffice and tell only part of the story of what it takes to design and constitute a healthy local government system under conditions of Europeanisation in the various meanings of that word.

The theory of the cooperative state suggests that instead of striving for organisational autarky, engaging in various forms of collaborative decentralisation is the way to structurally escape the potentially centralising forces inherent in any process of technological, social and economic scale enlargement. This is hardly a soft approach or throwing in the towel. The previous exploration suggests that local governments mostly gain, rather than loose when they engage in participative strategies towards other levels of government. It is when they become institutionally insulated that they run an increased risk of becoming marginalised and of being bypassed by other social, cultural or political institutions. The overview shows how local governments – each within their national settings, i.e. with respect for their own constitutional traditions – have access to various institutional strategies. It also shows that there is potential for benchmarking, not only of the instrumentalities for local government service delivery in the context of the implementation of European policies and (Lisbon) strategies, but also in terms of the quality of their institutional position and capacity for co-governance in multi-layered systems of government and administration.

Administrative Reforms in Westminster Democracies: the Long-term Results

by John Halligan

I. Introduction

On the occasion of this celebration of an esteemed colleague, it is appropriate to reflect on an era of reform stretching over the last 25 years that coincides with a professional career devoted to comparative government and public sector reform. In ranging across three levels of government, the sub-systems of Europe and international patterns of change, *Joachim Jens Hesse* has been in a unique position to interpret the dynamics and contradictions of comparative reform.[1]

This era has been notable for sustained transformations of public administration internationally. Reform has now continued for a sufficient length of time in Westminster systems to examine the long-term consequences of the changes. Australia, Canada, New Zealand and the United Kingdom are both early and long-term reforming countries by OECD standards and belong to the Anglo-Saxon group that has been identified with new public management.[2] The current decade has been the time for dealing with fallout from this experimentation. The products of two decades or more of activity are clear: The starker manifestations of new public management have less prominence in practice. As well the complexities of managing the modern state have been expanded by the introduction and implementation of new ideas and practices that tend towards more flexible, open, arms-length and diverse government. Yet central steering and direction require capacity, coherence and control. This perennial tension can be expressed in terms of specialisation and coordination, autonomy and control and other combinations, such as increasing agencies in conjunction with greater regulation and auditing.[3]

---

1   See for example: *Hesse, J.J.*: Comparative Public Administration: The State of the Art, in: id./Toonen, T.A.J. (eds.): The European Yearbook of Comparative Government and Public Administration, Vol. 1, Baden-Baden, 1995, 523–549.
2   *Pollitt, C./Bouckaert, G.*: Public Management Reform, 2nd ed., Oxford, 2004.
3   *Verhoest, K./Bouckaert, G./Peters, B.G.*: Janus-faced Reorganization, in: International Review of Administrative Sciences, 73/3 (2007), 325–348; *Richards, D./Smith, M.*: The Tensions of Political Control and Administrative Autonomy, in: Christensen, T./Lægreid, P. (eds.): Autonomy and Regulation, Cheltenham, 2006, 181–202; *Pollitt, C./Talbot, C.* (eds.): Unbundled Government, London, 2004.

The apparent contradictions in reform agendas were recognised at an early stage: Complications are likely to arise from simultaneously drawing on different paradigms in reform.[4] A paradox of discourse in the 1980s was observed by *Hesse* who saw moves to rolling back the state co-existing with interest in "bringing the state back in", thereby underscoring the complexities of interpreting change when confronting diverse challenges. Adapting towards changing environments makes constant demands on the role and organisation of the state.[5]

How such contradictions might be addressed has provided a significant challenge to reformers, often with paradoxical consequences.[6] The results have been interpreted in terms of a new model succeeding another, in particular New Public Management (NPM), or through focusing on the consequences of superimposing a new framework like NPM on existing arrangements, such as the Westminster model.

The article first addresses the long-term impact on Westminster systems of several generations of administrative reform through different reform outcomes, ranging from features of reformed systems that have demonstrated durability and continue to be significant to key reforms that have either been demoted in significance or are subject to debate, and whose longevity may be tenuous. It is also apparent that the preference of Westminster countries is for effective governance through better-integrated and more balanced systems.

II. Westminster Systems and Reform

The four Westminster countries are acknowledged as a coherent group based on a common tradition and historical and continuing close associations and interactions.[7] The "Westminster democracies" form a natural group of industrialised countries that have institutional roots in the British tradition. The group of states is regarded as reasonably homogeneous for analytical and comparative purposes, the assumption being that this comparability results from a shared heritage and continuing associations.

One of the main differentiating elements of this administrative tradition has been the lack of a well-developed concept of the state in the Anglo-Saxon tradi-

---

4   *Aucoin, P.:* Administrative Reform in Public Management: Paradigms, Principles, Paradoxes and Pendulums, in: Governance, 3/2 (1990) 115–137.

5   *Hesse, J. J.:* Constitutional Policy and Change in Europe: The Nature and Extent of the Challenges, in: id./Johnson, N. (eds.): Constitutional Policy and Change in Europe, Oxford, 1995, 3–19, here 8 f.

6   *Hesse, J. J./Hood, C./Peters, B.G.* (eds.): Paradoxes in Public Sector Reform, Berlin, 2003.

7   *Halligan, J.* (ed.): Civil Service Systems in Anglo-American Countries, Cheltenham, 2003.

tion, producing the contrast between the "stateless" tradition of these systems and the "state" tradition of Europe. European observers sensitive to the existence of different state traditions are inclined to choose the Anglo-Saxon as a distinct and meaningful category, whereas others focus on the Westminster system or model, and the fusion of the executive and the legislature under this form of responsible government. Under the Westminster model, the relations between politicians and bureaucrats have traditionally centred on the co-existence of the neutral public service and responsible government.[8]

Despite apparent commonalities from the outside, there is considerable diversity within the group. Substantial variations are apparent in governmental institutions: All have parliamentarianism, but the Australian and Canadian constitutions combine federalism and responsible government on Westminster lines, while New Zealand and the United Kingdom have operated as unitary systems. National factors and prevailing politics have shaped traditions historically and created substantial variation in significant areas. There have also been long debates in these former British colonies about the derivation and ongoing significance of the Westminster model.[9]

In terms of fundamental features of these systems, there have been variations in approaches to and rates of change. This also applies to machinery of government (with different roles and powers for central agencies across the four). They also have different sized public sectors that of Australia being relatively small, the rest falling in the middle range for the OECD. Canada has occupied an intermediate position for some purposes between its North American neighbour and the others.

The tradition's distinctiveness has been reaffirmed during the reform era, since the 1980s. The early identification of NPM – a somewhat imprecise ensemble of reforms – came from British observers who first discerned the trend. In addition to the major reforms in Britain (e.g. privatisation and executive agencies), individual country programmes gained international significance with New Zealand's "public management model" being highly influential. The reform movement therefore served to reinforce the notion of the Anglophone group's identity as distinctive and contrasting with that of other countries. There were strong similarities among reforms of the Westminster countries, with New Zealand and the United Kingdom, and subsequently Australia, being grouped because they adhered more to precepts of New Public Management than other OECD countries, and

---

8   *Aucoin, P.:* The New Public Management, Montreal, 1995.
9   *Patapan, H./Wanna, J./Weller, P.:* Westminster Legacies, Sydney, 2005.

were upheld as the ideal by OECD.[10] Canada was one of the first Westminster countries to explore management reform (in the 1960s), but was slower to incorporate and institutionalise it.

The emergence of this distinctive set of reforms was a product of the features of an administrative tradition that facilitated reform implementation. It also reflected a pattern of interaction that accorded legitimacy and relevance to initiatives within an administrative tradition that provided rapid transmission with systems and acceptance of ideas and practice.[11]

III. Durable Reforms in Public Management

A new management philosophy displaced traditional administration with a package of reforms that focused on results rather than the previous emphasis on inputs and processes. Public management in Westminster systems acquired distinctive features that affected relationships between public servants and politicians on the one hand and between the public and private sectors on the other. Before the reform period the public service was a relatively closed system; the boundaries were fairly tightly drawn and there was a sharp differentiation of the public service from the private sector and the political sphere in addition to a preference for working within accepted bureaucratic principles and practices based on traditional public administration.

Openness and external focus: The traditional public service's identity derived from being relatively closed and clearly demarcated from its environment, particularly the private and political spheres. These boundaries have been systematically eroded since the 1980s. The boundaries that traditionally defined, demarcated and insulated the public service have been substantially eroded to allow greater responsive to the environment. The public service became less self-sufficient and more integrated with other sectors for sharing management practices and personnel. The range of options open to governments was expanded greatly as they went beyond traditional bureaucracy to utilise external contractors and partners. The Westminster countries have been distinguished by the use of management consultants,[12] and the reliance on their specialist capacity.

---

10 *Organisation for Economic Co-operation and Development (OECD):* Governance in Transition: Public Management Reforms in OECD Countries, Paris, 1995.

11 *Halligan, J.:* Anglo-American Systems: Easy Diffusion, in: Raadschelders, J.C.N./Toonen, T.A.J./van der Meer, F.M. (eds.): Comparative Civil Service Systems in the 21st Century, Basingstoke, 2007, 50–64.

12 *Saint-Martin, D.:* Building the New Managerialist State: Consultants and the Politics of Public Sector Reform in Comparative Perspective, Oxford, 2004.

An external focus and learning from the private sector has been integral. Many elements of the reform programmes were based on private sector practices, techniques and modes of operating. Governments have resorted to business people and think tanks, and increasingly management consultants, for advice and regular benchmarking with private sector practice became routine. The influence can be seen in many management processes (e.g. risk and performance), leadership, management improvement, devolution of managerial authority, output assessment and improved financial management and, of course, the focus on competition.

The relatively small nations of Australia, Canada and New Zealand have been externally oriented, with an inclination to scan the experience of larger kindred systems and the broader international environment.[13] The reform programmes have been influenced by the experience of other countries. At various stages of their reform programme, the systems have been willing to draw on each others reforms.

Politicians and public servants: The relationship has traditionally been based on a neutral public service that served the political executive regardless of party. The political executive in turn respected the integrity of the civil service by maintaining its apolitical and professional character. The tension between responsible government and the neutral public service was kept in balance, but an imbalance became apparent and politicians sought to expand their authority in response to the officials' ascendancy. The relationship between public servants and ministers has since been the subject of a redistribution of power in favour of the political executive. This has produced a long-term debate about the consequences of greater political influence on the public service. All systems have experienced much greater use of political (or ministerial) advisers, debate about the handling of appointment processes for department heads, the concentration of power at centre, personalisation of appointments, politicisation of public communications and changing roles for the senior public service.[14]

Even though the quest for responsiveness has eroded traditional boundaries, this has been partly countered by the strengthening of a commitment to public interest and values that affirm the identity of the public service. Traditional prin-

---

13 *Halligan, J.*: Anglo-American Systems, op. cit.

14 *Aucoin, P./Savoie, D.*: The Politics-Administration Dichotomy: Democracy Versus Bureaucracy. Paper presented at the Conference on Canadian Public Administration in Transition, University of Guelph, 21.–22. 09. 2007; *Eichbaum, C./Shaw, R.*: Ministerial Advisers, Politicization and the Retreat from Westminster: the Case of New Zealand, in: Public Administration, 85/3 (2007), 609– 640; *Halligan, J.*: Anglo-American Systems, op cit.

ciples therefore have been fairly resilient, but questions remain about how the relationship works in practice because of pressure exerted by politicians on the concept of a neutral and professional public service. The ambiguities and issues in relations between politicians and public servants are unlikely to be unresolved for some time. The demands of responsible government and the continuing ex-altation of traditional principles provide a dynamic that ensures that the relation-ship will continue to evolve and stretch further this variant of the Westminster model.

Design, delivery and managing change: The range of options available for public agencies in delivering services has been enhanced as they draw on third parties in the private and voluntary sectors and sub-national government. The acceptance of more flexible approaches to delivery systems for public services and the need to move beyond the traditional monolithic departmental structure was an importance change in thinking. This broke the nexus of integrated policy and implementation and lead to greater use of specialised agencies. There have been interesting experiments that have tested the potential of flexible and focused organisation such as alternative service delivery and horizontal management. Canada for example has also become well-known internationally for its early focus on citizens and emerging modes of governance, in particular integrated service delivery, e-governance and other smart practices.[15]

The countries have to varying extents followed international practice for the public and private sectors in workplace relations and with devolution to line de-partments. There have been some movements towards stronger commitments to rebuilding core capacity. The debate continues in about the costs of capacity deficits and the financial tradeoffs and transaction costs of using agents to per-form basic tasks.

The capacity to manage change has been extended with the accumulated ex-perience of reform processes over time. From the initial decade of reform there has been monitoring by central agencies. There has also been the use of collective processes such as the Australian Management Advisory Committee for reviewing issues and setting directions, and improvements in central review of the public service (e.g. the Australian Public Service Commission's annual State of the Ser-vice Report, which surveys employees and agencies on current issues).

---

15 *Zussman, D.*: Alternative Service Delivery, in Dunn, C. (ed.): A Handbook of Canadian Public Admin-istration, Don Mills, 2002, 53–76; *Kernaghan, K.*: Moving Toward the Virtual State: Integrating Services and Service Channels for Citizen-Centred Service Delivery, in: International Review of Administrative Sciences, 17/1 (2004), 119–131; *Campbell, C.* (ed.): Comparative Trends in Public Management: Smart Practices toward Blending Policy and Administration, Ottawa, 2006.

Canada remains the exception among the Anglophone countries in so far as the politicians have generally gone missing from the reform process.[16] They have not taken up the options available under a Westminster system to lead on reform, generally leaving it to the public service leadership.

Leadership development: Westminster systems are inclined to follow a distinctive pattern of senior service, one that has been receptive to management change and leadership concepts, and has become increasingly open (in contrast to systems within state traditions that continue to be relatively closed and less responsive to major change). In the reform era the focus on leadership reflects current management thinking and the need to more effectively deliver change and performance in the public sector. A leadership development approach is important where government is decentralised and comprehensive reform has succeeded incremental change. Where senior service is more managerial and open, leadership is being reviewed and more balance is sought between central guidance and decentralised implementation. Leadership frameworks have been developed and successfully implemented in Westminster systems.[17]

The senior service has been another means for developing leadership in Westminster countries, and may either be termed the senior executive service or go under another name. The efficacy of contracts and performance incentives continues to be debated with mixed reports about how to measure and reward performance. Despite changing values that recognise external influences, there has been a renewed interest in core values that define the publicness of services and the role of leadership in promoting them.

IV. Demotions and Debates as the Pendulum Shifts

Three types of reform are examined, two representing significant shifts in focus and a third, performance management, providing a case of where there is serious debate about its efficacy, at least in certain forms. The fourth area is about the character and condition of hybrid approaches to public management, a highly diverse collection that is being subjected to closer scrutiny.

---

16 *Aucoin, P.*: Beyond the 'New' in Public Management, in: Dunn, C. (ed.), op cit., 36–53.

17 *Halligan, J.*: Leadership and the Senior Service from a Comparative Perspective, in: Peters, B.G./Pierre, J. (eds.): Handbook of Public Administration, London, 2003, 98–108.

1. New Public Management

Movement within the public management reform cycle occurred as the limitations of NPM and neo-liberal reform agenda became understood. The features of New Public Management – disaggregation, devolution, outsourcing, markets and multiple services providers – supported specialisation but encouraged fragmentation, reinforced vertical structures and had impacts on capacity and accountability. Despite the different patterns of change between Westminster countries – e.g. New Zealand's distinctive expression of NPM was imposed rapidly, whereas Australia's full-fledged variant became apparent after over a decade of reform – they found themselves confronting broadly similar issues by the turn of the century. Their neo-liberal reforms provided substantial potential in the 2000s for corrective mechanisms, the rebalancing of operating principles and practice, and for revaluation of the worth of the public service under new leadership that pursued different agendas. In New Zealand, for example, recognition of the need to modify the less successful elements – in areas such as accountability, performance measurement and strategic management – allowed further development and new reform.[18]

Of all four systems, the United Kingdom under *Blair* appeared to remain closer than the others to a variant of NPM. Markets are still most evident in British conceptions with a model that combines top-down performance management; competition and contestability in providing public services; and citizen choice.[19]

2. Disaggregation and Rationalising Public Bodies

The New Public Management phase of reform produced greater arm's length management including the creation of bodies.[20] The pattern was not however consistent in Anglophone countries despite their reputation for being foremost exponents of NPM, with two (New Zealand and the United Kingdom) opting for systemic separation of policy and execution, and two (Australia and Canada) favouring more *ad hoc* approaches. Nevertheless, the general direction was to-

---

18 *Gregory, R.*: Theoretical Faith and Practical Works: De-Autonomizing and Joining-Up in the New Zealand State Sector, in: Christensen, T./Laegreid, P. (eds.), op. cit., 137–161; *Boston, J./Eichbaum, C.*: State Sector Reform and Renewal in New Zealand: Lessons for Governance, in: Caiden, G.E./Su, T.-T. (eds.): The Repositioning of Public Governance, Taiwan National University, Taipei, 2007; *Halligan, J.*: Reintegrating Government in Third Generation Reforms of Australia and New Zealand, in: Public Policy and Administration, 22/2 (2007), 217–238.

19 *Cabinet Office:* UK Government's Approach to Public Service Reform: A Discussion Paper, London, 2006.

20 *Pollitt, C./Talbot, C.* (eds.): Unbundled Government, London, 2004.

wards devolution and experimentation with a range of bodies (executive agencies, statutory corporations and authorities and other variations on non-departmental organisation).

In the 2000s, there have been movements away from arm's length agencies and management as political agendas change. Moreover, there are indicators of this in all four countries. The intensification of central coordination and direction moves towards reintegration of agencies within the core public service, and new mechanisms for controlling and regulating agencies point to system rebalancing.

The roles of and relationships between public and private sectors, and capability and capacity questions have also been revisited. The general direction of change is away from disaggregation, prevalent under NPM, towards re-aggregation. The reversal of the agencification trend internationally, is now most apparent in Britain. From the large-scale disaggregation of the early 1990s policy seems to have almost completely reversed itself, in practice and not in rhetoric. The merger of big agencies has left numerous small agencies that account for a minority of civil servants.[21]

Yet broadly similar movements are underway reflecting a mood to review and tighten oversight through some restructuring and rationalisation of public bodies. An Australian agenda for resurrecting a more comprehensive ministerial department through absorbing bodies and tighter and more direct control over public agencies was given formal recognition through a review of corporate governance. There were two issues: the extent of non-departmental organisations, and their governance. The dangers of "bureaucratic proliferation" were proclaimed with departments of state employing only 22 per cent of public sector employees. The official concern was with different legislative bases, constitutions (boards or not) and opaque governance. In order to drive implementation, it was thought necessary to clarify roles and relationships of ministers, boards and public servants.[22]

Agendas for rationalising non-departmental organisations have also been apparent in other Anglo-Saxon systems.[23] In Canada, government response to the *Gomery* inquiry into the "sponsorship scandal" has been to address control over crown corporations and accountability in general.[24] Similarly, New Zealand has

---

21 *Talbot, C./Johnson, C.*: Seasonal Cycles in Public Management: Disaggregation and Re-aggregation, in: Public Money and Management, 27/1 (2007), 53–60, here 55 f.

22 *Shergold, P.*: Plan and Deliver: Avoiding Bureaucratic Hold-up, Canberra, Australian Graduate School of Management/Harvard Club of Australia, 17. 11. 2004.

23 See *Christensen, T/Laegreid, P.*, op cit.

24 *Aucoin, P.*: Public Governance and Accountability of Canadian Crown Corporations: Reformation or Transformation. Paper presented to Canadian Political Science Association 2007 Annual Conference, University of Saskatchewan, 31. 05. 2007.

moved "to create and grasp more effective levers of control over crown entities" that form part of the broader state services.[25] In response to confusing arrangements for governance, new legislation provided a framework for establishing and operating crown entities, and clarified governance including accountability relationships between entities, board members, ministers and parliament.

3. Performance Management

Performance along with markets has posed one of the big questions in public management during the last 15 years and attracted international debate. Both have recent origins in New Public Management, although their lineage is much longer. Long-term trends now support the ascendancy of performance ideas as a dominant force in public management.

The Westminster systems have been highly committed to performance management over two decades during which they have refined their measurement and performance framework and increased their capacity to monitor performance. The countries have followed different pathways within a performance management framework during these two decades. Their implementation styles have differed in terms of conceptions of the relationship between outputs and outcomes, the responsibilities given to chief executives and the roles of central personnel agencies in handling performance oversight. The exigencies of reform agendas have produced a considerable convergence on public management during the 2000s.

Yet there remain significant differences. Despite common elements, there continue to be differences in approach and with the technical treatment of outcomes and outputs. More importantly, practice continues to fall short of aspirations, and significant questions remain about the quality and use of performance information in the budget process, internal decision-making and external reporting and the variable engagement of agencies. There continue to be other issues about the level of application by public managers in practice, significant challenges to accomplishing sophisticated performance management and limits to a heavy reliance on this approach.[26] The limitations of country approaches include questions in Australia about how well the framework is working; questions in Canada and New Zealand about the level and quality of implementation. There have been a series of issues in the United Kingdom about top-down complexities in unitary

---

25 *Gregory, R.*, op. cit., 153.
26 *Bouckaert, G./Halligan, J.*: Managing Performance, London, 2007 (forthcoming).

system and dysfunctionalities. The use of performance measures against targets in the UK shows performance improvement, but they are modest (and possibly insufficient when other factors such as declining productivity are taken into account).[27]

A new generation of studies is now addressing the pervasive influence of the burgeoning performance movement on governments. Positions on performance management have been polarised between its advocates and dissenters who argue that the fundamental premises are wrong and produce dysfunctional behaviour. There is now a growing middle ground of analysts who see the limitations of performance management but believe there is something worthy of careful investigation through examining assumptions and means of narrowing the gap between rhetoric and practice. Performance management is arguably at a turning point with this questioning by external observers as well as insiders struggling with its limitations in practice.[28] Performance management systems have been modified to improve operability, but unless they serve better internal and external needs, particularly those of politicians, their integrity will be undermined.

4. Hybrids at the Interface

Public administration at the interface has been subject to substantial change, which has been interpreted in terms of hybridisation. The distinctiveness of the public and private sector has been described as "a useful fiction for governments", for there are many historical precedents of melding between private and public sectors across several fields.[29] In the reform era, the range and extensiveness of hybrids have expanded greatly. The question is what direction is hybridisations now taking for the tendencies are contradictory, both favouring more hybrid arrangements and pointing to moves against certain forms?

The modes of hybridisation cover models, relationships, boundaries and organisational forms. A broad conception for one of the countries is of the "hybrid state", which is "one that has not returned to the statism of the [Keynesian welfare state], but neither has it maintained the neo-liberal, limited state aspirations of

---

27 *Flynn, N.*: Public Sector Management, London, 2007.
28 *Bouckaert, G./Halligan, J.*, op. cit.; *Massey, A./Pyper, R.*: Public Management and Modernisation in Britain, Basingstoke, 2005; *Radin, B.A.*: Challenging the Performance Movement, Washington, DC, 2006; *Flynn, N.*, op. cit.
29 *Wright, V.*: Blurring the Public-Private Divide, in: Peters, B.G./Savoie, D.J. (eds.): Governance in the Twenty-first Century, Montreal/Kingston, 2000, 155–177.

the New Right"[30]. In direct terms the common cases involve personnel, management, delivery and various forms of technical advice. Another cut on the mixes is to focus on boundaries as hybrids.[31] There are of course significant organisational implications with the proliferation of organisational hybrids around the margins of the state.[32] A significant source of these developments has of course been New Public Management, which itself was "hybrid, complex and inconsistent, both in its main ideas and in its more specific reform instruments". Countries are reported as combining "different theoretical and practical elements of NPM in their reforms, meaning that the degree of hybridisation varied"[33].

A reaction against some hybrid forms has occurred across the Westminster countries. There has been a move to clarify the governance of public agencies with hybrid boards that do not accord with a particular corporate (and therefore private sector) governance prescription in Australia and New Zealand. In a number of significant areas there have been highly public experiments that have produced mixed results, such as public private partnerships for financing infrastructure in Britain and Australia.[34]

The question is not of course whether hybrid approaches will remain significant for they will continue to be a source of experimentation and even growth in areas such as collaboration with the third sector. Rather the pattern of engagement can be expected to be uneven and dependent on experience with specific arrangements in different sectors and countries.

IV. Reconstituting the State: Integration and Westminster Systems

A distinguishing feature of reform in Westminster systems reform is that it has been comprehensive, involving different generations, multiple stages and programmes over time. Where public service systems are under consideration, several arenas of reform and a number of organisations of different types are involved. There are further challenges with complex and lengthy reform processes. Com-

---

30 *Richards, D./Smith, M. J.:* The 'Hybrid State', in: Ludlam, S./Smith, M. J. (eds.): Governing as New Labour, Basingstoke, 2004, 106–125.

31 *Pierre, J.:* Externalities and Relationships: Rethinking the Boundaries of the Public Service, in: Peters, B. G./Savoie, D. J. (eds.), op. cit., 332–357.

32 *Wettenhall, R.:* Three-Way Categorisations, Hybrids and Intersectoral Mixes in the Governance Equation, in: Asian Journal of Public Administration, 25/1 (2003), 57–86.

33 *Christensen, T./Laegreid, P.:* New Public Management – Undermining Political Control?, in: id. (eds.): New Public Management, Aldershot, 2001, 93–121, here 94.

34 *Flynn, N.,* op. cit.

prehensive reform involves greater complexities and is more likely to lead to garbage can processes.[35]

The state has also become more complex. This complexity is arguably greater in the more devolved of the two federations, Canada, which also is responsive to its Anglophone and Francophone identity, and the United Kingdom with EU membership as well as internal devolution to executive agencies and to sub-nations.[36]

Fundamental to comprehensive reforms in Westminster countries have been the different approaches. These may be implemented and applied in stages over time or in tandem. One may invoke another as seemingly complementary strategies, thus the injunction to centralise in order to decentralise, long familiar in organisational analysis,[37] may apply also within the broader public service system (an early case being the combination of devolution of management and the centralisation of policy). Experience indicates that it is just than likely that reforms may be contradictory. Some interpretations have recognised the complexities by distinguishing tiers of NPM or contending models based on traditional control and autonomy tensions, and it is clear that coordination and integration have co-existed with disaggregation. British observers have sought to unpack the most complex case – a large unitary system of government – by distinguishing levels and co-existing models.[38] The United Kingdom has displayed several tendencies concurrently as it wrestled with different demands to deregulate and regulate, devolve and control. Ultimately, "the reason that governments have pursued contradictory actions is that there are real contradictions that cannot be reconciled"[39].

It is clear that new conceptions of governance address a different mix of features than those that have been prevalent during the last 20 years. The reaction against New Public Management features has produced similar trends in Westminster countries,[40] and there are now a number of country-derived interpretations. Where once reinventing government was seen as the pathway, the mid-

---

35 *Brunsson, N./Olsen, J. P.*: The Reforming Organization, Bergen, 1993, 26.

36 *Holliday, I.*: Executives and Administrations, in: Dunleavy, P./Gamble, A./Holliday, I./Peele, G. (eds.): Developments in British Politics 6, Basingstoke, 2000, 88–107.

37 *Metcalfe, L./Richards, S.*: Improving Public Sector Management, London, 1987; *Perrow, C.*: The Bureaucratic Paradox: The Efficient Organization Centralizes in Order to Decentralize, in: Organizational Dynamics, 5/4 (1977), 3–14.

38 *Richards, D./Smith, M.*: The Tensions of Political Control and Administrative Autonomy: from NPM to a Reconstituted Westminster Model, in: Christensen, T./Lægreid, P. (eds.), op. cit., 181–200; *Dunleavy, P./ Margetts, H./Bastow, S./Tinkler, J.*: New Public Management is Dead – Long Live Digital-Era Governance, in: Journal of Public Administration and Theory, 16/3 (2006), 467–494.

39 *Flynn, N.*, op. cit., 283.

40 *Christensen, T./Laegreid, P.* (eds.): Autonomy, op. cit.

2000s indicators in several contexts point to reintegrating governance as one means of depicting the trends. It is apparent that such a model is an amalgam of new elements and design features derived from previous models. This mix can be represented as moving away from a previous model (hence the "beyond NPM" perspective) or moving towards some form of amalgam based on features derived from different models. There has been a reconfirmation of the organisational components of the traditional machinery of government such as cabinet, ministerial department and central agency. There have also been indications of the revival of features associated with traditional bureaucracy – such as risk aversion in fields with an external and international focus – suggesting the emergence of neo-Weberianism.

However, there are a number of significantly different features from the earlier hierarchical model of integration. The public service operates under a political executive with more instruments for securing and sustaining control and direction. There is a brace of instruments for working the system strategically and at several levels, as mentioned earlier. Empowered departments may have greater responsibilities than traditional arrangements, and performance is conceived differently and receives priority. Management processes are well institutionalised. The options of choosing some form of market solution and the private sector as provider are integral elements of flexible management.

The resulting synthesis of elements suggests integrated governance has become the prevailing approach, at least in Australia and New Zealand. An integrated governance conception derives from the focus on different modes of coordinating and control designed to confer greater coherence and capacity on the public sector. While New Zealand's commitment to integration appears to be somewhat less developed, the era of "contract governance" has gone and the mode of governance favoured by *Boston* and *Eichbaum* is a variation on "joined-up governance"[41].

The main themes resonate across Westminster countries: horizontal collaboration through whole of or joined-up government; the reassertion of the centre giving central agencies greater capacity for leadership and direction; re-aggregation and rationalising public sector bodies; new instruments for securing and facilitating delivery and implementation. Under this conception, elements of New Public Management persist. This is especially the case with performance manage-

41 *Boston, J./Eichbaum, C.*: State Sector Reform and Renewal in New Zealand, in: Caiden, G. E./Su, T.-T. (eds.): The Repositioning of Public Governance, Taipei, 2007; *Halligan, J.*: Reintegrating Government in Third Generation Reforms of Australia and New Zealand, in: Public Policy and Administration, 22/2 (2007), 217–238.

ment, which continues to provide a cornerstone of the public management framework of Westminster countries as indicated by the growth in and continuing high commitment to performance despite the overall fate of the NPM model.

Integrated governance has two purposes: renewing the public sector to improve capacity, and resetting and refocusing the core public service to increase performance. The term reflects the strong impulse to integrate, recognition of its attendant features that cover whole of government and coordination, roles of central agencies, and line departments, autonomy and governance of public bodies, delivery and implementation and the performance focus. The roles of and relationships between public and private sectors and capability and capacity questions have also been revisited.

At the same time, under the British system the Westminster model is still regarded as conditioning how civil servants and ministers operate. Public service reform has invariably been "contained within the existing constitutional framework, and this has limited the scope for overhauling the institutional arrangements that condition the bureaucracy. For example, the political cost to the *Thatcher* Government of reforming the constitution was too great". Similarly, the *Blair* Labour government was "constrained by continued deference to the ideas associated with the parliamentary state"[42].

The working through of the tensions between political control (or variants of the Westminster model) and administrative autonomy (variants of New Public Management) in Britain has demonstrated the dynamic interplay between contra-directional reforms.[43] One schema sees a tendency "for many governments in the Anglo-Saxon world to move from the Westminster Model 1 to a New Public Management Model 2". The more recent development of what is termed Westminster Model 2, "is an attempt to re-impose WM1 mechanisms of control onto NPM2 systems of delivery and, in doing so, reconstitute many of the key features of the original Westminster model"[44]. These features cover in particular political authority in the centre and re-imposition of central control using direct political control as well as regulation and targets.

---

42 *Richards, D.*: The Civil Service in Britain: A Case Study in Path Dependency, in: Halligan, J. (ed.): Civil Service Systems in Anglo-American Countries, Cheltenham, 2003, 27–69, here 28.

43 *Richards, D./Smith, M.*: Tensions of Political Control, op. cit.

44 Ibid., 298.

V. Concluding Remarks

This article has addressed the long-term significance of extensive public sector reform. The long-term impact has been to produce a reformation in organisation and relationships and public services that are more streamlined to respond to political, economic and social environments. At the same time there has been a shift towards a more balanced and effective public management that can avail itself of a range of options but is less subject to ideological or fad driven movements. The familiar verities of public administration continue to have relevance to reformers. In the end the reform era provided salutary reminders of how much environment matters and that ultimately political executives' need for effective governing systems – whether for delivering services or international security – will drive change.

Independent Civil Service Systems: a Contested Value?

by Tony J. G. Verheijen

I. Introduction[1]

The importance of a professional and impartial civil service has been a virtually uncontested notion ever since *Woodrow Wilson*'s seminal work on the topic at the end of the 19th century.[2] Even in cases where practice was far removed from the ideal, the need to move closer towards the norm of impartiality, merit and professionalism has tended to be the starting point for academic analysis and, indeed, political discussions. *Joachim Jens Hesse* has in his work always emphasized the importance of these values and the need for states, especially the transition states in Central and Eastern Europe, to develop civil service systems that reflect these values.[3] An additional point highlighted by *Joachim Jens Hesse* in his frequent publications on the issue is the need to clearly enshrine the principle of an independent civil service in legislation, preferably anchoring it in the constitution or constitutional legislation.[4] However, the question of how to handle cases and contexts in which the creation of civil service systems that reflect these principles proves to be elusive, even if legally or constitutionally prescribed, remains unanswered. This also applies to a largely unexplored area of further research that is nevertheless becoming increasingly relevant: The values underlying the classical model are being challenged even in states where this was not expected, notably the new member states of the EU.

The classical model of the civil service survived as the key benchmark for the development of civil service systems throughout much of the 20th century and arguably it still survives in that sense today. The advent of New Public Management (NPM) in the late 1980s was initially seen as a potential challenge to the

---

1 The views expressed are those of the author and do not represent the official position of the World Bank.

2 *Wilson, W.*: The Study of Administration (1887), in: Shafritz, J./Hyde, A. (eds.): Classics of Public Administration. 4th Edition, New York, 1997, 14–26.

3 *Hesse, J. J.* (ed.): Administrative Transformation in Central and Eastern Europe, Oxford, 1993; *idem*: Rebuilding the State. Public Sector Reform in Central and Eastern Europe, in: Lane, J.-E. (ed.): Public Sector Reform, London, 1997, 114–146.

4 The case of Brazil, where the principles of an independent and merit-based institution were elaborated in detail in the Constitution and thus made obligatory for Brazil's constituent states, is one of the more recent key examples of such practice.

hegemony of the model. However, most analyses today find that NPM has not significantly altered the underlying values of civil service systems. NPM-based reforms did contest the notion of administrative autonomy, calling for more direct engagement of elected politicians in the management of the public sector and, specifically, the public service.[5] Whereas this has led to a higher degree of direct political influence on civil service management in some states, the debate on the nature of the civil service remained in essence unchanged; the notion of a permanent and professional civil service as an important institutional value in liberal democracies was not fundamentally challenged.[6]

In this article the continued global applicability of the model will be examined. A large number of states, in very diverse developmental and regional contexts, remain stubbornly outside the confines of this value system. Analyses of such cases remain rare. Whereas in the past this concerned mainly systems in developing countries and states with authoritarian regimes, more recently the relevance of the classical model of civil service has also been questioned by leaders in the new EU member states and in other post-communist countries. This would appear to indicate that, regardless of the fact that academic and political beliefs on the importance of politically impartial, merit-based and professional civil service systems have been relatively consistent for more than a century, there might be more fundamental questions regarding the relevance of the model that require further analysis.

This article will review two rather different cases in which the classical model has failed to make a breakthrough. First, the continued stalemate on civil service development on most of the African continent will be discussed as a case of the long-standing and consistent failure of the classical model to make an impact. Second, the more recent reversal of trends towards establishing civil service systems based on classical principles in a number of new EU member states is reviewed. The analyses of these two cases would help provide insight into why the classical model, although still alive and well in OECD states, has not made as many universal inroads as analysts might have expected. It will also help establish whether this is a temporary phenomenon or one that gives rise to the need to think in terms of alternative models for the organisation and management of civil service systems.

---

5   *Metcalfe, L./Richards, S.*: Improving Public Management, London, 1987; *Hood, C.*: A Public Management for All Seasons?, in: Public Administration, 69/1 (1991), 3–19.
6   See, for instance, *Hood, C./Lodge, M.*: The Politics of Public Service Bargains, Oxford, 2006.

II. The Classical Model in OECD States: Increasing Variations and Some Cases of Erosion

The classical model defines the civil service as an institution with a *status sui generis* with employment conditions and a form of organisation that is distinct from the private sector. The status of civil servants in this model is protected not only (or not even primarily) by law and, in most instances, the constitution, but also by conventions and norms that limit the scope for changes affecting the core aspects of the organisation and the management of the civil service: the non-interference of politicians in appointments, dismissals and career management beyond defined boundaries, the strict adherence to merit principles in career management and an emphasis on professional competencies in selection and career development.

Although this model remains the norm in most OECD states, the variations on the model have certainly increased. States in Southern and much of Central Europe,[7] but also in established democracies in South and East Asia (such as Japan, South Korea and India), still operate relatively unchanged variants on the classical civil service model, although management and accountability systems have often been reformed to reflect demands for open and service-oriented government.

Many of the Anglo-American states, and in particular Australia, New Zealand and the UK, have introduced radical reforms, bringing their civil service systems close the private sector models, without, however, compromising on merit and professionalism. Notions of the political impartiality of the civil service are also considered to be largely unaffected, protected by conventions and traditions.[8]

Reforms in some of the Nordic states, in particular Sweden, and also in the Netherlands, have led to a reduced level of differentiation between employment conditions in the public and the private sector. In these two particular cases, this has led to a creeping politicisation of the very top positions in civil service systems,[9] though this is not considered to have changed the core values underlying the civil service system.

---

7 The new EU member states form an exception in this context; they are discussed in section V. (see below).

8 *Halligan, J.* (ed.): Civil Service Systems in Anglo-American Countries, Cheltenham, 2004.

9 *Van der Meer, F./Dijkstra, G.*: The Development and Current Features of the Civil Service of the Netherlands, in: Bekke, H. A. G. M./van der Meer, F. (eds.): Civil Service Systems in Western Europe, Cheltenham, 2000, 168–172; *Pierre, J.*: Parallel Paths, Public Policy, Administrative Reform and Politico-Administrative Relations in Sweden, in: Peters, B.G./Pierre, J. (eds.): Politicians, Bureaucrats and Administrative Reform, London, 2001, 132–141.

On the other hand, the gradual erosion of the civil service as a permanent and impartial institution in the USA is well documented.[10] Starting in the 1980s, the number of political appointees in the US system has gradually increased, and now numbers in the thousands at the federal level. Even though this erosion is largely a feature of the federal administration, some US states, notably in the South, show similar features of patronage and politically-based recruitment and career management systems. Although this situation has been accompanied by reforms of management systems in these administrations, analysts consider it to be mainly a feature of the changing political culture under which the value of an independent and impartial civil service is increasingly being contested.

Similarly, European states such as Greece and, to some extent, Italy, with longstanding issues of the politicisation of the civil service, are also seen as exceptions. However, reforms introduced in these states generally aim at restoring or forming a civil service system that meets the norm, rather than creating an alternative form of civil service management.

Overall, therefore, NPM and post-NPM reforms do not appear to have significantly changed the value systems that underpin the organisation and management of civil service systems in those countries, mostly OECD member states, which have adhered to these values for over a century. The USA might be the exception that confirms the rule, though this applies largely to the federal administration and still does not affect large parts of even the federal system. This is indeed noteworthy, considering the deep and fundamental reform in internal management, organisation and accountability systems over the last three decades which have affected these systems virtually without exception.

In general, therefore, the classical values that have been at the core of the academic and professional debate on civil service systems appear to have continued relevance regardless of the sweeping changes that have taken place in the management and the organisation of civil service systems.

III. The Classical Model: an OECD+ Model?

Based on analyses of OECD states, it would appear that the classical model of civil service is alive and rather well regardless of almost two decades of managerial reform. Today, it is usually asserted that managerial reforms have certainly altered

---

10 Cf., for instance, *Peters, B. G.*: Administrative Traditions and the Anglo-American Democracies, in: Halligan, J. (ed.), op. cit., 10–26.

but not significantly changed the model. It is important to note, however, that most analyses of civil service system that confirm this trend focus on OECD states and a still relatively small group of developed economies that tend to follow their lead. Similar variations on the developmental patterns discussed above can be found among these states.

To mention a few of the more prominent variations, the often discussed Singapore model emulates elements of the Anglo-American managerial reforms in combination with career guarantees and safeguards against politicisation. Another frequently cited case is Brazil, which has moved forward on a reform agenda that aims to strengthen merit and professionalism in the civil service throughout the state.[11] The Brazilian case is somewhat unique since it enshrines merit and career principles directly in the Constitution, thus making them mandatory for all states under the federation. Some of the more advanced Brazilian states have subsequently moved forward by introducing performance-management elements while simultaneously strengthening career and merit principles.

Recent reformers such as Russia and Kazakhstan have also opted to mix classical principles (career system, merit, etc.) and modern management tools by introducing performance-management principles at government, organisational and individual civil servant levels. Even though in the Russian case in particular the implementation and application of merit principles have proven difficult,[12] this has not as yet led to a reversal of political course. Moreover, the fact that these reforms are enshrined in organic legislation makes such a reversal more difficult.

However, regardless of the resilience of the classical model and moves towards its expansion, a large and diverse set of states remain stubbornly outside the model, including several large states in South Asia (notably Bangladesh and, to a lesser degree, Pakistan), most of the Near and Middle East, most African states (with the exception of Botswana, Namibia, South Africa and possibly Tanzania) and a significant number of states in East Asia, Latin America and Central America.

Interestingly, a number of post-communist states, including several of the new EU member states, have recently started challenging the relevance of the classical model and have argued that it is ill-suited to rapidly growing states with dynamic labour markets.[13] This has added a new dimension to the debate on the relevance of the classical model.

---

11 See the discussion on Brazil in *World Bank:* Institutional Reform in Russia. From Design to Implementation in a Multi-Level Governance Context, Washington, DC, 2006.

12 Cf. *World Bank,* op. cit.

13 *Verheijen, T.*: Administrative Capacity in the New Member States: the Limits of Innovation? World Bank Working Papers 115, Washington, DC, 2007.

IV. Remaining Outside the Model: the Case of Africa

Of the groups of states mentioned above, the almost complete failure of trans-posing the classical civil service to the African continent case is one of the most startling cases. Whereas most other continents and regions present a mixture of states that have created variants on the classical model and others that have retained patronage-based and often marginalised civil service systems, in Africa only very few states have successfully introduced functioning civil service systems, and these are limited mainly to Anglophone Africa.

Apart from South Africa, which has successfully managed a transformation of its institutions, including the civil service, and Tanzania, which remains potentially the most interesting case of institutional reform in a relatively large country with limited mineral wealth, success stories are limited to small and relatively resource-rich states bordering on South Africa, notably Botswana and Namibia.

Botswana in particular has used its mineral wealth to rebuild and invest in a strong and professional civil service system which is known for its high ethical standards. Compression ratios in civil service pay are high (1:20), up to double that of most OECD states, making it attractive for qualified staff to seek a longer-term career in the civil service. Performance principles are strongly engrained in the system. Discussions on Botswana focus mainly on whether the country will be able to sustain its institutional development efforts and advance further towards establishing a performance-based public management system.

Similarly, the case of Tanzania remains interesting. As in the other three states mentioned above, Tanzanian reforms aim to establish a merit-based, permanent and professional civil service while introducing performance principles. However, since the country lacks the resources of its southern neighbours, the introduction of merit-based pay incentives is largely donor-funded. The Tanzanian approach was based on donor-funded advance payments through a Selected Accelerated Salary Enhancement (SASE) system, which brings civil servants in a selected set of positions up to a pay level that, under normal circumstances, they would have achieved only in five to seven years time.[14] The positions which could be integrated into the mechanism were pre-defined and based on development priorities. Although the model was slow to take off (SASE was launched in 2000, and until 2004 only five agencies were integrated into the system, leading to an

---

14 *Kigaru, K./Mukandala, R./Morin, D.*: Reforming Pay Policy: Techniques, Sequencing and Politics, in: Levy, B./Kpundeh, S. (eds.): Building State Capacity in Africa, Washington, DC, 2004, 109–148.

eventual watering down of the model)[15] and did not fully manage to deliver on its promises, it is an important example of an attempt to break with the vicious circle that has plagued most African systems, this being a combination of political strife and a lack of resources, which leads to a downward spiral in institutional development. Rather than attempting to obtain a universal top-up of wages, which is at best a temporary solution to the problems of African public service systems, Tanzania was a pioneer in trying to introduce reforms that combined incentives with a package of institutional reforms aimed at creating a merit-based and professional civil service.

However, the four cases mentioned above remain the main exceptions to the rule that classical model-based civil service systems, in whatever variety, have failed to take hold in Africa. This is most notably the case in Francophone Africa, where there remains little to report on the development of modern civil service systems.

Francophone states[16] continue to operate all-encompassing integrated public service systems, including both the core civil service and public service providers such as teachers, medical personnel and others. Although some of the rules inherited from the former French (or Belgian) rulers still formally exist, public service systems bear little resemblance to the model they were expected to emulate. Merit-based recruitment systems have been effectively abandoned, pay systems have developed into a myriad of bonuses and supplements (in some cases constituting 90 %–95 % of actual wages),[17] cabinets have replaced the civil service in its policy design role (with cabinet officials often earning 10–15 times the wage of a permanent secretary) and career perspectives have been effectively eliminated by the bonus and supplement-based wage system and the abandonment of step-advancement inside grades. These are features of systems that can be found in a range of variations from Senegal to Burundi and from Chad to the Republic of Congo.

The integrated nature of public and civil service systems have made reforms virtually impossible to introduce because often militant trade unions tend to fight any significant change in existing systems that would uncouple the ties be-

---

15 *Valentine, T.*: Budget Analysis to Facilitate Pay Reform. Final Report. Tanzania Public Service Management Office, 2004, 9 f.

16 For the present purpose the Democratic Republic of Congo (DRC) is also included although it is not part of the French colonial system.

17 This is partly due to attempts to circumvent restrictions on wage bill levels, often agreed in the context of IMF programmes. However, in some cases, such as in the DRC, this has led to civil and public servants being unable to retire since retirement benefits are calculated over base wages only.

tween different sections of the public service, thus creating a vicious circle of veto points.

In Anglophone systems, however, except for the cases mentioned above, there are fewer veto points because civil and public service systems are not integrated. Nevertheless, similar patterns of distorted wage systems, ineffective recruitment and career management systems and resulting low moral and ethical standards persist, including in states such as Zambia, Kenya and Malawi.

One question that the daunting situation in African civil service systems poses is why systems that are essentially based on the same principles as the French and British civil service have degenerated to an extent rarely seen elsewhere in the world, even in states with a similar colonial inheritance and, supposedly, similar resentment against externally imposed institutional models.

Three sets of explanations are generally given for this. First, the low degree of legitimacy of transferred systems among post-independence leaders, who considered civil service systems as an alien and implanted notion. Whereas leaders could not necessarily do without the civil service if they were to rule effectively (or, in other cases, to extract resources), they sought to marginalise the institution of the civil service. Systems subsequently developed as an extension of political power and were intended to effectively support the exercise of control and resource extraction and to provide employment.[18] This particular phenomenon is by no means limited to Africa. Latin America and Central America have seen a fair share of similar patterns of development, though most states in that region appear to have overcome this form of resentment and to have moved towards civil service modernisation, though by no means universally successfully.

Second, the "medicine" prescribed by international financial institutions in the 1980s and the first half of the 1990s, an emphasis on reducing public sector employment and the public sector wage bill as a way to enhance public investment spending, further aggravated the situation since the remaining talented staff left the administration by choice. The medicine did not work because states rapidly found ways to work around the imposed restrictions on wage bill and employment levels. Arguably this approach worsened the condition of some of the "patients": Public sector employment was not significantly reduced, but mandatory wage reductions and hiring freezes did further damage to what remained of the system.[19] In addition, it made pay systems even more opaque than they had

18 See, for instance, *Hyden, G.*: Opportunities and Constraints to Reform in Africa. Paper Presented at the Workshop "Administrative Traditions: Inheritances and Transplants in Comparative Perspective", Hong Kong City University, 23–24 June 2007.

19 *World Bank:* Civil Service Reform. A Review of World Bank Assistance, Washington, DC, 1999.

already been by adding more supplements and allowances to increase wage levels without touching base wages. Again this is not unique to the African case; as the same "medicine" was administered in other parts of the world, though nowhere was the record as negative as in Africa.

Finally, underlying tribal loyalties continue to permeate African societies, something that does not fit well with the idea of a state service that should remain above such interests. This is possibly the most unique factor to Africa in terms of explaining why the classical civil service model has never taken root in the overwhelming majority of African states.

At the same time, regardless of a pattern of institutional development that goes back almost five decades in most states, little thought has been given to the development of alternative approaches to build institutional systems that could take root in the specific socio-cultural context of most African states. Examples of good practice that are cited in the region are those of the four countries discussed above and, for the case of Francophone Africa, the still timid efforts of states like Burkina Faso and Senegal to re-establish a civil and public service system based on the classical principles of competitive access, career development based on merit and protection from political interference.

Thought has been given to designing approaches to reform that could reverse long-standing trends in the erosion of public sector values. For instance, an increasing number of analysts have argued that generating demand-side pressure for improved public service quality might lead to a re-consideration of government policies, while others have suggested that cultivating leaders with a commitment to democratic values could be a way forward. The latter approach in particular has received increasing support in recent years and has been bolstered by the (relative) success of cases such as Botswana and Tanzania.

However, little academic thought has been given to whether there might be alternative solutions to the African dilemma and, if so, what these could be. Demand-side and leadership approaches are certainly a worthwhile effort towards re-opening the debate on institutional and, in particular, civil service development. However, questions remain as to whether these can bring about the significant shifts in perceptions and political culture that are required to reverse a set pattern of erosion of the state and, in particular, the civil service. More important to the discussion in this article, there still does not seem to be an alternative paradigm to the classical model, even if over five decades the model has made few inroads in this part of the world.

V. Central and Eastern Europe: a Challenge to the Classical Model?

Civil service reform in Central and Eastern Europe has not lived up to what was widely expected to be a process of convergence with the principles of the classical model: the creation of permanent and merit-based civil service systems aligned with the European mainstream. This expectation was raised by *Joachim Jens Hesse* in the early 1990s[20] and by most other analysts, regardless of the lack of progress on public administration and civil service reforms in the first years after the start of the transition. The expectation was that, on the road towards integration into the European Union, demoralised civil service systems would inevitably and willingly adapt to the "European Administrative Space", a concept coined by *Jacques Fournier* in 1996.[21] The principle of mutual trust, one of the keystones of the operation of the EU, would make it difficult, if not impossible, for states with anything but a permanent and reliable administration to be good member states.[22] The impetus of the start of accession negotiations in 1997 added further credence to this assumption.

Reform and development patterns in the following five years strengthened this assumption as EU candidate states moved forward in establishing civil service systems in line with EU accession criteria.[23] Reviews of the public administration systems in the years immediately prior to the accession of the "eight", both in the context of academic publications[24] and the annual assessments conducted by OECD/SIGMA for the European Commission, showed a tendency for these states to move towards systems within the range of the baselines established by the EU to measures progress towards European standards. However, assessments also showed that a number of them were well removed from meeting European standards on core aspects of civil service, policy management and budget management practices. Much more progress had been made on core technical competences directly related to EU policy implementation (and the associated EU funds), such as procurement and internal and external audit.

---

20 *Hesse, J. J.*: Administrative Transformation, op. cit.
21 *Fournier, J.*: Governance and European Integration – Reliable Public Administration in OECD, Preparing Public Administrations for the European Administrative Space, SIGMA Papers 23, Paris, 1998.
22 *Hesse, J. J.*: Rebuilding the State, op. cit.
23 The EU accession criteria on administrative capacity were developed by the OECD/SIGMA programme and consist of six sets of baseline criteria on key aspects of administrative capacity, including the status and quality of the civil service.
24 *Dimitrova, A.*: Enlargement, Institution-Building and the EU's Administrative Capacity Requirement, in: West European Politics, 25/4 (2002), 171–190.

Especially in the area of civil service, progress in these cases did not go beyond the adoption of legislation. Even at the point of EU accession, doubts were expressed on the true commitment of the political elite to the creation of civil service systems reflecting European values and traditions such as merit, permanency, political impartiality/clear separation of career and political aspects of the civil service and professionalism.

An assessment conducted by the World Bank in 2006 [25] looked into (a) the extent to which the new member states were able to perform effectively in the EU during the first three years of membership and (b) the extent to which their civil service and policy-management systems had moved closer to the standards set under the baseline and CAF assessments. Even though the assessment did not address all aspects of these issues for all new member states (and did not include Bulgaria and Romania, which both joined in 2007), the conclusions were striking. As the focus of this contribution is on civil service systems, the discussion will be limited to the findings on this particular issue.

1. Baselines on Civil Service

In their original design, baseline assessments used a seven-point rating system, ranging from "baseline achieved" (1) to "baseline not achieved and unlikely to be achieved under current arrangements" (7). Despite the fact that the rating scale was used only during the first two years of the application of the baseline system, it is nevertheless a useful tool to visualise the level of approximation of systems to European minimum standards. For convenience of presentation, the scale has been inversed in this article. Thus "7" represents "baseline achieved" in the four charts below, which depict four essential elements of the baseline assessment system as reviewed in the World Bank Assessment. A "4" rating implies that reforms are on a positive trajectory (baseline not achieved but progress being made), while 1–3 ratings imply a significant deviation from minimum standards and a lack of initiatives that could address this situation.

2. Review of the Current Context: Legislation, Incentives, Politicisation and Management Systems

On the issue of civil service legislation, all the eight new member states would have at least rated at "4" at the time of accession since legislation had been drawn up in all states except the Czech Republic (which was about to adopt a law).

25 *Verheijen, T.*, op. cit.

Although there were reservations about the applicability of some of the laws (notably in Slovakia), it was expected that this would be addressed through amendments. Several states had drafted legal systems that constituted an adequate basis for the development of a civil service system based on classical values.

At the time of the review in 2006, however, civil service legislation had been revoked in Poland and Slovakia, with no legal framework for the civil service effectively in place and no clear perspective for the development of a new one. Legislation in the Czech Republic had never been implemented and seems unlikely to ever be implemented. The Hungarian and Estonian systems are considered inadequate and in need of significant reform. The Hungarian framework has gone through several sequences of amendments, all of which limit coherence. Only Latvia and Lithuania have drawn up legislation that can be considered an adequate basis for a professional, impartial and merit-based civil service. Thus, of the eight new member states, only two now have a legal framework that would move them towards the establishment of a civil service based on classical principles, while Slovenia might also move in this direction. Five others have either abandoned civil service legislation altogether or have a legal framework that does not allow for effective civil service management.

Chart 1: Civil Service Legislation

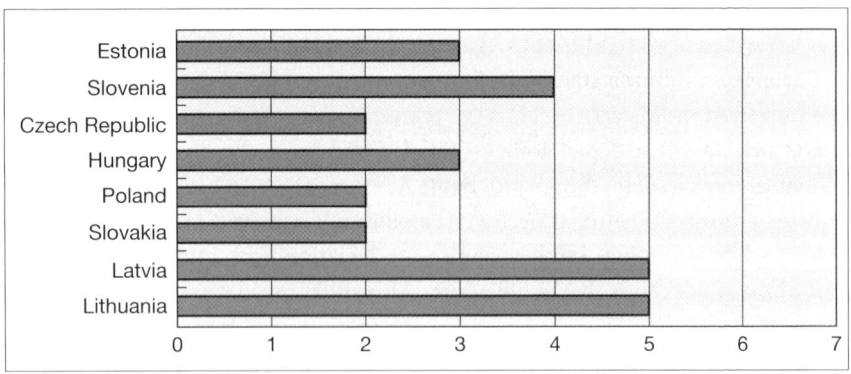

Source: Verheijen, T., op. cit.

Integrated human resource management systems are a second crucial element of classical civil service systems because they guarantee the consistent application of merit principles and professional standards and safeguard against the risk of politicisation. On this particular element, none of the eight new member states would obtain an adequate rating: Civil service agencies were abolished in Poland and Slovakia and effectively marginalised in Latvia. Rudimentary structures remain too weak to have a real impact in Estonia and Slovenia, while in the Czech Republic and Hungary horizontal management systems were never properly established.

Chart 2: Human Resource Management Systems

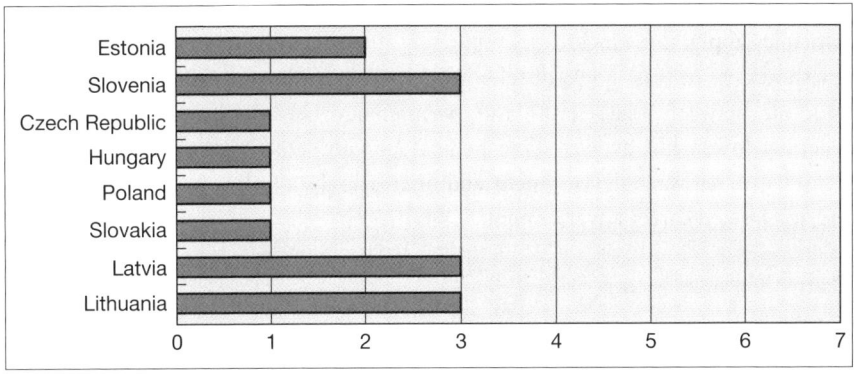

Source: Verheijen, T., op. cit.

Chart 3: Politicisation

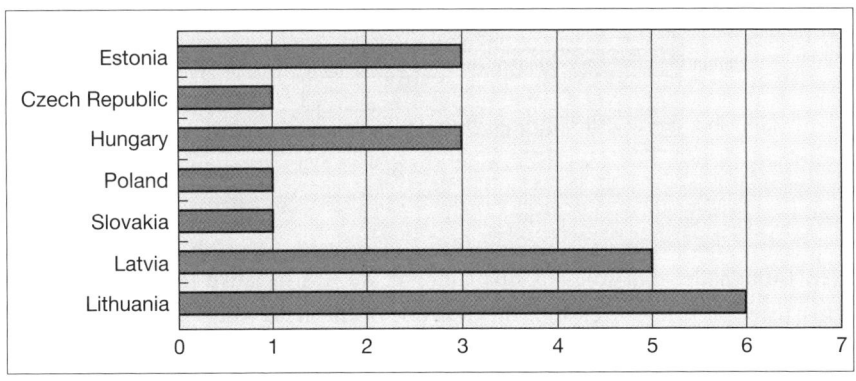

Source: Verheijen, T., op. cit.

A politically impartial administration with safeguards against undue political interference in appointments, dismissals and career management is a key feature of the classical model. Whereas there are various ways of providing a degree of managed political involvement in top-level appointments, all of these aim at creating a clear boundary between the political and career-administrative worlds while ensuring adherence to the principle of a permanent, professional civil service.[26] Of seven states reviewed on this particular issue, only Latvia and Lithuania have adequate systems for managing politico-administrative relations; in all other cases (with the possible exception of Hungary), the dynamics of the last three years have been negative. Once again, there has been a reversal in dynamics, away from convergence and increasingly towards a spoils system.

Incentive systems are a fourth key element for discussion since relatively clear principles apply; these include transparency (the generally held principle that base pay should be at least 80 % of take-home pay, according to OECD standards), a trade-off between wage levels and permanency (i.e. public sector wages are generally lower, but at a credible percentage compared to those in the private sector), gradual wage development and, increasingly, a link between performance and accelerated career advancement.

Chart 4: Incentive Systems

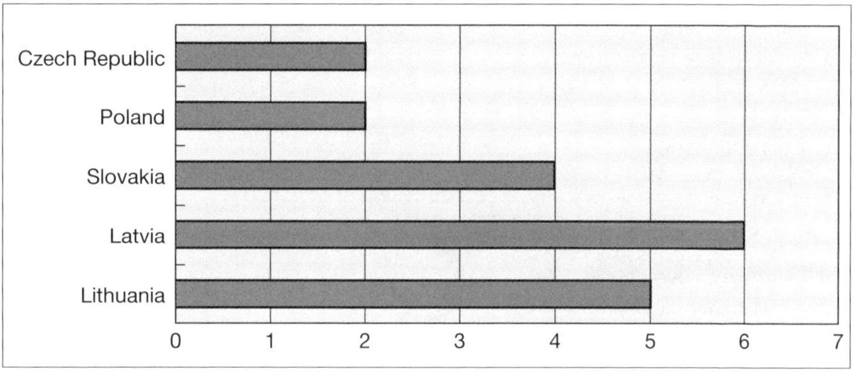

Source: Verheijen, T., op. cit.

Even though the dynamics of this element are less negative than those of the other three points (at accession this was one of the areas where the least progress had been made), the inability of Central and East European states to establish reward systems that allow them to attract and retain a sufficient number of talented staff has been a further obstacle to the development of permanent career civil service systems. The main problems that remain are opaque reward structures, low compression ratios (and thus limited career incentives) and large disparities between private and public sector wages.

26 *Peters, B. G./Pierre, J.:* Civil Servants and Politicians: the Changing Balance, in: id. (eds.), op. cit., 1–11.

The reversal in patterns of administrative (and specifically civil service) development after EU accession has come as a surprise to many observers (who had expected more convergent dynamics upon socialisation in the EU) and is seen as having negatively affected the performance of new EU member states,[27] and the general performance indicators (such as fiscal management, business environment, anti-corruption efforts, etc.). In addition, and more important in the context of this article, the reversal of reforms appears in most instances to have been a conscious move by politicians away from the development of a more classical civil service model. The arguments given against the latter development are threefold:

- the poor suitability of classical civil service models to the rapid growth context of the new member states, which renders aspects of permanency and gradual career paths unattractive for potential candidates;
- politicians' prerogative to be free to appoint and dismiss staff in the civil service;
- low levels of trust between politicians and civil servants as a result of an established pattern of political appointments and dismissals over a prolonged period of time.

The first argument, though based on reality, is somewhat dubious in that several other states in the region, Latvia and Lithuania among the new member states and countries such as Serbia and Macedonia among the (potential) EU candidates, have in fact been successful in creating a more permanent professional civil service system. These systems are based on traditional notions with elements of performance management successfully blended in.[28]

The second and third arguments are potentially more worrying since they point towards a more permanent reluctance among politicians in key states, especially Poland and the Czech Republic but also Slovakia and Hungary, to invest in the development of a system of public administration and civil service that would be professional and permanent and that would correspond to classical values. Unlike the case of African states, this reluctance is not driven by fiscal constraints or by historical aversion to classical civil service systems but rather by labour market considerations and a political obsession with controlling the administration.

It is clear that if work on civil service reform in Central and Eastern Europe is to advance, two conditions need to be fulfilled. First, the design of systems that reflect the new labour market realities in the region, based on performance prin-

---

27 For a more in-depth analysis of the performance issues see *Verheijen, T.,* op. cit., 3–6.
28 *Verheijen, T./Dobrolyubova, Y.*: Performance Management in the Baltic States and Russia: Success Against the Odds?, in: International Review of Administrative Science, 73/2 (2007), 205–215.

ciples, properly designed and linked to incentive systems and fair and transparent application of rules. Second, the development of both a common understanding among politicians that a well functioning civil service is a public good rather than an extension party politics and a set of principles that politicians promise to abide by when addressing civil service staffing issues. Without a commitment by politicians to accept the notion of the civil service as a public good, little progress can be made on this issue.

The question of whether the classical model is the right one "for all seasons" also arises in this particular case, and the absence of alternative paradigms makes it highly difficult to find solutions to what are obviously deep-seated problems of institutional development. Pairing flexibility in the internal labour market of the civil service with a more rigorous application of performance principles and pay flexibility would appear to be potential solutions, but this would not address the preoccupation of politicians with their right to exercise political control over appointments, career management and dismissal procedures, which is at odds with the accepted principles of civil service management and the idea of central, impartial control (by a civil service agency or unit) over the application of such standards.

VI. Can We Go Beyond the Classical Model?

The classical model of civil service, based on principles that emerged in the late 19th century, remains the dominant paradigm on civil service development. The notion of an independent and permanent civil service, protected from undue political interference by law and, most often, by constitutional provisions and managed on the basis of transparent and universally applicable rules enforced by an independent body remains alive and well in most OECD states. Despite the fact that the increased use of performance standards and the diversification of accountability mechanisms have altered the model, it has not been fundamentally changed.

However, the weakness of the paradigm is that it has not travelled very well beyond the realm of OECD+ states. Two diverse cases where the classical model did not (at least so far) make inroads were presented, raising a number of factors that can impact the levels of acceptability and applicability of the model.

The factors highlighted in the African cases (fiscal constraints, reluctance to accept a colonially imposed model, tribal loyalties) are very different from the – more surprising – backlash against the classical model among a significant number of new EU member states (poor compatibility with labour market realities, lack of opportunities for awarding spoils, lack of trust in the civil service). However, both cases do raise the need to pursue some alternative solutions to civil service development if the classical model does not thrive. The negative impact of a demoralised and poor-quality civil and public service on African development is well established, and recent assessments of the performance of Central and Eastern European states on business climate, corruption levels and macro-fiscal issues show a gap between those that have established functioning civil service and public administration systems and those that have not.

The (partially failed) attempt of the EU to convert the new member states to adopt the classical model shows that external insistence on moving towards variants of that model might not bring the desired results. Diverting some of the intellectual energy of the academic public administration community to thinking outside the box and finding practical solutions to the institutional dilemmas of states that remain outside the "OECD+" model therefore need to be made a more important part of the global public administration development agenda.

V. The Future of Constitutionalism in Multi-level Environments

Perspektiven des europäischen Verfassungsrechts – Verfassungsdämmerung?

von Gerhard Robbers

I.

Vor einem Jahr wäre die These klar und einfach gewesen. Sie hätte gelautet: Die Europäische Union hat längst eine Verfassung. Die europäische Verfassung besteht in den Gründungsverträgen und in anderem Primärrecht, durchaus auch in Grundaussagen der Rechtsprechung des Europäischen Gerichtshofs. Der Entwurf der Verfassung für Europa, gescheitert oder nicht gescheitert, erschien als weiterer Schritt in der Fortentwicklung dieses Verfassungsrechts. Heute ist die Situation anders.

Drei Schritte weiter, und Europa steht in einer anderen Welt. Zunächst gab es die aufgeregte Lähmung nach der Ablehnung des Verfassungsentwurfs in Frankreich und den Niederlanden. Der erste Schritt war der Europäische Rat vom 21./22. Juni 2007 mit den Schlussfolgerungen des Vorsitzes, der „Merkel-Gipfel".[1] Der zweite Schritt war die Regierungskonferenz vom 23. Juli 2007 unter portugiesischem Vorsitz. Dieser Schritt hat den „Entwurf eines Vertrags zur Änderung des Vertrags über die Europäische Union und des Vertrags zur Gründung der Europäischen Gemeinschaft"[2] hervorgebracht. Der dritte Schritt, der informelle Europäische Rat vom 18./19. Oktober 2007, hat diesen Entwurf mit einigen Änderungen angenommen,[3] so dass er nun zur Ratifizierung in den Mitgliedstaaten ansteht.

Drei Schritte, drei Sprünge. Wir sind mitten in einem Dreisprung. Der Europäische Rat im Juni hat entschieden, den ursprünglichen Verfassungsentwurf aufzugeben, viele seiner Inhalte aber in die bestehenden Verträge einzuarbeiten. Der Gipfel hat die Einzelbestimmungen des Verfassungsentwurfs den verschiedenen bestehenden Verträgen zugeordnet. Die Regierungskonferenz vom Juli hat daraus

---

1 *Europäischer Rat (Brüssel, 21./22.06.2007):* Schlussfolgerungen des Vorsitzes, 11177/1/07 REV I vom 20.07.2007.

2 *Konferenz der Vertreter der Regierungen der Mitgliedstaaten:* Entwurf eines Vertrags zur Änderung des Vertrags über die Europäische Union und des Vertrags zur Gründung der Europäischen Gemeinschaft, CIG 1/07 vom 23.07.2007.

3 Vgl. *Konferenz der Vertreter der Regierungen der Mitgliedstaaten:* Entwurf eines Vertrags zur Änderung des Vertrags über die Europäische Union und des Vertrags zur Gründung der Europäischen Gemeinschaft, CIG 1/1/07–4/1/07 REV 1 vom 05.10.2007.

konkrete Entwürfe gemacht. Sie sind im Wesentlichen vom Europäischen Rat am 18. Oktober 2007 angenommen worden.

Alles steht jedoch unter dem Vorbehalt erneuter Ratifizierung in den Mitgliedstaaten. Der gesamte Ratifizierungsprozess muss vollständig neu aufgenommen werden. Bevor dieser Prozess nicht erfolgreich abgeschlossen ist, lassen sich Perspektiven des Europäischen Verfassungsrechts auf dieser Ebene in allen Himmelsrichtungen denken. Alles bleibt Spekulation. Alles bleibt von politischen Unwägbarkeiten abhängig.

Aber unterstellt, es bleibt in der Substanz bei dem, was im Oktober 2007 beschlossen worden ist. Unterstellt auch, der Ratifizierungsprozess verläuft erfolgreich. Dann wird es drei Verträge, drei Grundverträge, geben. Sie werden alle den gleichen Rang haben. Der erste Vertrag ist der Vertrag über die Europäische Union. Der andere Vertrag ist der Vertrag zur Gründung zur Europäischen Gemeinschaft, er wird dann heißen: Vertrag über die Arbeitsweise der Europäischen Union. Der dritte Vertrag ist die Europäische Grundrechtecharta.

II.

Die Aufspaltung in drei Verträge bewirkt tiefgreifende Verschiebungen der Systematik. Der Wortlaut vieler Normen aus dem Verfassungsentwurf mag unberührt bleiben. Die Folgen für die systematische Interpretation sind erheblich.

Zunächst betreffen die Verschiebungen Einzelfragen. Das betrifft etwa die Europäische Zentralbank. Ihre Unabhängigkeit muss gewahrt bleiben. Nach Art. 88 des Grundgesetzes dürfen die Aufgaben und Befugnisse der Deutschen Bundesbank als Währungs- und Notenbank auf die Europäische Zentralbank nur übertragen werden, wenn die Europäische Zentralbank unabhängig ist und im vorrangigen Ziel der Sicherung der Preisstabilität verpflichtet ist. Im neuen Entwurf wird die Europäische Zentralbank als ein Organ neben den anderen Organen der Europäischen Union aufgezählt, aber gleichrangig, gleichgeartet wie das Europäische Parlament, der Rat oder der Europäische Gerichtshof. Eine besondere Stellung der Europäischen Zentralbank ist insofern nicht vorgesehen. Das birgt immerhin die Möglichkeit, dass die Europäische Zentralbank eingebunden wird in die Verpflichtung zur Organtreue gegenüber den anderen Organen. Das könnte die Pflicht zur Rücksichtnahme auf politische Prioritäten anderer Organe mit sich bringen. Das könnte die Unabhängigkeit der Europäischen Zentralbank beeinträchtigen.

Aber eine grundsätzlichere Perspektive ist sichtbar. Diese Perspektive ist „Verfassungsdämmerung". Eine Perspektive des Europäischen Verfassungsrechts ist das Ende von Verfassung überhaupt, jedenfalls das Ende einer grundlegenden herkömmlichen Funktion von Verfassung. Der Streit um den Entwurf der Verfassung für Europa war im Kern ein Streit darum, ob die Europäische Union eine Verfassung hat und eine Verfassung haben soll. Nur ein Staat könne eine Verfassung haben, sagten manche. Die Europäische Union sei kein Staat und dürfe kein Staat werden und dürfe deshalb auch keine Verfassung haben. Diese Stimmen haben sich politisch durchgesetzt. Einstweilen jedenfalls. Die Europäische Union soll keine Verfassung haben. Der gescheiterte Verfassungsvertrag hatte ausdrücklich von der Verfassung für Europa gesprochen. Die neuen Verträge streichen den Begriff Verfassung aus dem Vokabular. Alles ist gestrichen, was für manche Staatlichkeit, wenigstens Verfassung suggeriert: die Hymne etwa.

Damit ist mehr getroffen als eine bloß begriffliche Entscheidung. Vor der Debatte um den Verfassungsvertrag konnte ohne weiteres gesagt werden, die Europäische Union habe eine Verfassung, weil Verfassung nicht am Begriff hängt, sondern an der Substanz, an der Qualität der Normen. Verfassungsrecht, *leges fundamentales* der Europäischen Union, fand sich danach in allen Verträgen. Der Europäische Gerichtshof sprach ausdrücklich vom Verfassungsrecht der Europäischen Union, von sich selbst als ihr Verfassungsgericht.

Das Argument vom materiellen Verfassungsrecht sticht jetzt nicht mehr. Die Europäische Union soll nun geradezu ausdrücklich keine Verfassung haben. Es hieße, die Debatte und die Entscheidung um den Verfassungsvertrag ignorieren, wollte man jetzt weiterhin von einer Verfassung der Europäischen Union sprechen. Aber vielleicht führt kein Weg daran vorbei, diese Debatte letzthin zu ignorieren. Denn es besteht die Gefahr der Verfassungslosigkeit insgesamt. Mehr noch: Verfassungsrecht hört auf.

III.

Zur Begründung dieser Perspektive ist zunächst ein Blick in das nationale, das mitgliedstaatliche Verfassungsrecht erforderlich, hier auf Deutschland konzentriert. In seiner Europäisierung erlebt das Verfassungsrecht Deutschlands und der anderen Mitgliedstaaten einen ähnlichen Prozess wie das Verwaltungsrecht, das Zivilrecht, das Strafrecht. Kein Rechtsgebiet kann sich diesem Umwandlungsprozess entziehen, und er ist oft beschrieben worden. Die Europäisierung des Verfassungsrechts erfasst den Normtext; sie verändert Wirkungsbereich und Binnenstruktur der Verfassung; die Europäisierung prägt die Verfassungsinterpretation.

Der Normtext: Von den 16 verfassungsändernden Gesetzen der letzten 15 Jahre stehen mindestens acht in unmittelbarem Bezug zu europarechtlichen Anforderungen. Sie reagieren auf europäische Entwicklung, zum Teil setzen sie Europarecht schlicht um. Aber auch die Entwicklung zur Privatisierung vormaliger Staatsaufgaben ist europäisch geschuldet – vielleicht ist sie jedenfalls mittelbar europarechtlich veranlasst. Deshalb kommen die beiden Änderungen zur Privatisierung von Post und Telekommunikation[4] sowie der Luftverkehrsverwaltung[5] hinzu. Das sind insgesamt 63 % der verfassungsändernden Gesetze seit 1991. Immerhin zwölf Artikel des Grundgesetzes enthalten inzwischen ausdrücklich die Begriffe Europa, europäisch oder entsprechende Formen.

Die europarechtlich begründeten ausdrücklichen Verfassungsänderungen sind inzwischen oft bloße technische Umsetzung europarechtlicher Anforderungen. Dazu gehört die kommunale Wahlberechtigung von Unionsbürgern, sie ist notwendige Folge europäischer Rechtsakte. Ausdrücklich inkorporiert Art. 28 Abs. 1 Satz 3 GG das Recht der Europäischen Gemeinschaft in das deutsche Verfassungsrecht. Die kommunale Wahlberechtigung von Unionsbürgern erfolgt von Verfassungs wegen nach Maßgabe des Rechts der Europäischen Gemeinschaft. Die Verfassung enthält also eine dynamische Verweisung auf Gemeinschaftsrecht. Zugleich zeigt sich der Vollzugscharakter deutschen Verfassungsrechts: Die Verfassungsänderung setzt Art. 17 II, 19 I EG schlicht um.

Ähnliches gilt für Art. 16a GG – das Asylrecht, für Art. 16 GG – die Auslieferung Deutscher, für Art. 87e GG – die Privatisierung der Eisenbahnen. Art. 16a GG[6] begründet den Vorrang völkerrechtlicher Verträge von Mitgliedstaaten der Europäischen Gemeinschaft untereinander – und mit dritten Staaten – bei der Asylrechtsgewährleistung. Das Asylgrundrecht ist vergemeinschaftet. Völkerrecht – und insbesondere Gemeinschaftsrecht – geht von Verfassungs wegen der Grundrechtsgewährleistung vor.

Art. 16 GG[7] macht die Auslieferung Deutscher an einen Mitgliedstaat der Europäischen Union möglich als Reaktion auf den Impuls der Tagung des Europäischen Rates in Tampere von 1999. Damit hat das Grundgesetz zugleich Art. 7 Abs. 1 des Übereinkommens vom 27. September 1996 über die Auslieferung zwischen Mitgliedstaaten der Europäischen Union Rechnung getragen.[8]

---

4   BGBl. 1994 I, 2245.
5   BGBl. 1992 I, 1254.
6   Vgl. auch *Bonk, H.J./Pagenkopf, M.*: Kommentar zu Art. 16a, in: Sachs, M. (Hg.): Grundgesetz. Kommentar, 4. Aufl., München, 2003, hier Rn. 106.
7   BGBl. 2000 I, 1633.
8   BT-Drs. 14/2668, 5.

Die Neuordnung des Eisenbahnwesens von 1993[9] mit ihrer Umwandlung der Bundeseisenbahnen in handelsrechtliche Gesellschaften nach Art. 87e GG bezieht sich direkt auf die Richtlinie 91/440/EWG, die die Unabhängigkeit der Geschäftsführung von Eisenbahnen fordert.[10] Diese Entwicklung ist Teil eines europaweiten Prozesses der allgemeinen Wandlung von Staatsaufgaben.

Die Änderung des Art. 12a Abs. 4 Satz 2 GG,[11] wonach Frauen auf keinen Fall zum Dienst mit der Waffe verpflichtet werden dürfen – früher hieß es: auf keinen Fall Dienst mit der Waffe leisten dürfen –, ist unmittelbare Folge der Rechtsprechung des Europäischen Gerichtshofs.[12]

Das verfassungsimmanente System der Gleichheitssätze verschiebt sich. Was gleich und was ungleich zu behandeln ist, hängt nicht mehr nur primär von der mitgliedstaatlichen Verfassung ab. Die Idee der Gleichheit bestimmt sich vielmehr vorrangig aus europäischen Quellen. Und überhaupt betrifft die europarechtliche Prägung der Grundrechtsentwicklung primär Gleichbehandlung und Nichtdiskriminierung.

Wirkungsbereich und Binnenstruktur der Verfassung: Die vielfältige Übertragung von Hoheitsrechten verengt – selbstverständlich – den Wirkungskreis der nationalen Verfassungen. Die komplexe Struktur der Informations-, Mitwirkungs- und Mitentscheidungsrechte im Verhältnis der Verfassungsorgane zueinander nach Art. 23 GG ist so entscheidend, dass sich der verfassungsändernde Gesetzgeber im Zuge der Föderalismusreform genötigt gesehen hat, wiederum Vereinfachungen vorzunehmen. Der europarechtliche Willensbildungsprozess zwingt also verfassungsintern zu Verschlankung und Rationalisierung der Entscheidungsprozesse. Leitender Gesichtspunkt der Verfassungsentwicklung wird die Brückenfunktion zur Europäischen Union.

Dies gilt auch innerhalb von Verfassungsorganen. Reaktionsschnelligkeit auf europäische Vorgänge ist Grund der Einführung von Europaausschuss und Europakammer, insoweit der Bundestagsausschuss für die Europäische Union die Rechte des Bundestages nach Art. 23 GG gegenüber der Bundesregierung wahrnehmen kann (Art. 45 GG) und die Beschlüsse der Europakammer als Beschlüsse des Bundesrates gelten (Art. 52 Abs. 3a GG). Die europäische Einigung hat dabei im Übrigen den Rechtscharakter des Bundesrates selbst geprägt und verändert. Dass durch den Bundesrat die Länder in Angelegenheiten der Europäischen

---

9 BGBl. 1993 I, 2089.
10 BR-Drs. 130/93.
11 BGBl. 2000 I, 1755.
12 BT-Drs. 14/4380; EuGH, 11.1.2000 – Rs. C-285/98.

Union mitwirken (Art. 50 GG), lässt dem Bundesrat gesamtparlamentarische Funktionen zuwachsen.

Auch Verfassungsinterpretation ändert sich europäisch. Verfassungsintegration ist dem Interpretationstopos der Integrationsoffenheit verpflichtet. Die Völker- und Europarechtsfreundlichkeit des Grundgesetzes[13] bindet auch die Interpreten der Verfassung. Wer Deutscher im Sinne unionsrelevanter Grundrechte ist, wird zunehmend von der Unionsbürgerschaft her gesehen, um Diskriminierungen zu vermeiden – beim Berufsgrundrecht des Art. 12 GG zum Beispiel. Nun wird man nicht gut gegen den offenbaren Wortlaut der Deutschengrundrechte und des Art. 116 GG alle Unionsbürger schlicht als Deutsche umdefinieren können. Aber schon die prozessrechtliche Stellung von Unionsbürgern lässt sich über den Weg des Art. 2 Abs. 1 GG dem der Deutschen angleichen, und die materiellrechtliche Gleichstellung erfolgt dann über die verfassungsmäßige Ordnung im Sinne des Art. 2 Abs. 1 GG. Damit nivelliert die Europäisierung des Verfassungsrechts die Schrankensystematik des Grundgesetzes. Unionsbürger dürfen in den relevanten Bereichen nicht stärkeren Beschränkungen unterworfen werden als Deutsche.

Zunehmend wird angenommen, dass die verfassungsmäßige Ordnung als Schranke der allgemeinen Handlungsfreiheit und des Persönlichkeitsrechts auch das Gemeinschaftsrecht umfasst.[14] Damit erweitert sich der Horizont der verfassungsmäßigen Ordnung um weite Rechtsgebiete, die zwar unter Beteiligung, kaum aber unter konkreter Letztverantwortung mitgliedstaatlicher Verfassungsorgane gestaltet werden.

Europäische Rechtsauslegung misst europäischen Grundrechten und Grundfreiheiten in weitem Umfang Drittwirkung zu – z. B. die Ansätze neuer Freizügigkeit. In der Tendenz wird dadurch die deutsche Unterscheidung zwischen mittelbarer Drittwirkung und unmittelbarer Drittwirkung überdeckt, marginalisiert, vielleicht obsolet. Europarechtliche Drittwirkung ist eine neue, weitere Art unmittelbarer Drittwirkung, auch soweit Richtlinienrecht der Umsetzung bedarf. Diese Entwicklung wird gestützt von der unionsrechtlichen Wertedogmatik, die Betonung europäischer Werte als Grundlage der Rechtsgemeinschaft. Werte gelten allgemein. Werte sind nicht auf das Verhältnis Staat – Bürger beschränkt. Werte hängen in ihrem Wirkungsanspruch nicht von freier Entscheidung eines Parlaments ab. Werte gelten, und sie gelten allgemein. In der Tendenz wird die unmittelbare Drittwirkung der Grundrechte gestärkt.

---

13 BVerfGE 113, 273 ff., hier 295.
14 *Dreier, H.*: Kommentar zu Art. 2, in: ders. (Hg.): Grundgesetz-Kommentar, Bd. 1, 2. Aufl., Tübingen, 2004, hier Rn. 58.

Insgesamt zeigen die Beispiele: Verfassung wird – auch – zum Vollzugsinstrument von Richtlinienrecht und gemeinschaftsrechtlicher Rechtsprechung. Europarecht verschiebt die staatliche Binnenstruktur. Europarecht prägt die Verfassungsinterpretation. Verfassung erscheint nicht als Basis und Fundament. Verfassung zeigt ihren Charakter als Entwicklungsordnung und Richtungsgeber. Verfassung beschreibt, Verfassung bestimmt die Entwicklung eines Gemeinwesens.

Das Verhältnis von europäischer und mitgliedstaatlicher Verfassung wird heute verbreitet als ein Mehrebenensystem beschrieben.[15] Europäische und mitgliedstaatliche Verfassungen sind dabei nach dem Subsidiaritätsprinzip aufeinander bezogen. Das Mehrebenenmodell besitzt wichtiges Erklärungspotential. Es weist auf die Relativierung des nationalen Verfassungsgesetzes.[16] Letztlich aber ist das Mehrebenenmodell inadäquat. Zumindest gilt dies für die Begriffsbildung. Sie wird der politischen Wirklichkeit, die das Recht strukturieren muss, allenfalls in Teilen gerecht. Das Mehrebenenmodell folgt der herkömmlichen Hierarchisierung der Rechtsordnung. Es geht dabei von einer Hierarchie politischer Macht, des Rechts und der Legitimität aus. Diese Hierarchievorstellungen sollte man in der Tat nicht vorschnell verabschieden. Sie sichern die demokratische Legitimation politisch-rechtlicher Macht. Aber das Mehrebenenmodell impliziert eine Rangordnung, eine Über- und Unterordnung, eine Überordnung des europäischen Rechts über das nationale, mitgliedstaatliche Recht. Es findet seine Fortsetzung in der herkömmlich akzeptierten bundesstaatlichen Überordnung des Bundesrechts vor dem Landesrecht, wie sie Art. 31 GG normiert. Damit eignet dem Mehrebenenmodell im Blick auf die Europäische Union rechtspolitische Funktion. Es suggeriert bundesstaatliche Attribute, eine dem mitgliedstaatlichen Recht übergeordnete Ebene des Europäischen Rechts.

Dem widerspricht der Grundsatz der begrenzten Einzelermächtigung, der die Kompetenzen der europäischen Institutionen bei aller Breite auf umgrenzte Bereiche reduziert. Dem widerspricht der Grundsatz des bloßen Anwendungsvorranges des Unionsrechts, der den Vorrang eng begrenzt. Dem widerspricht aber auch die tatsächliche politische Existenz.

Souveränität löst sich auf nicht in Ebenen, Souveränität löst sich auf in Bereiche. Umfassende Souveränität im Sinne einer Allkompetenz und einer Zuhöchstkompetenz gibt es nicht mehr. Die Nationalstaaten in der Europäischen Union haben in weitem Umfang Souveränitätsrechte an die europäischen Institutionen abgegeben. Dem muss auch ein angemessener Verfassungsbegriff Rechnung tra-

---

15 Statt vieler *Pernice, I.*, in: Veröffentlichungen der Vereinigung der Deutschen Staatsrechtslehrer 60 (2000), 173 ff. m.w.N.

16 *Huber, P.M.*, in: Veröffentlichungen der Vereinigung der Deutschen Staatsrechtslehrer 60 (2000), 226.

gen. Ein solches Verfassungsverständnis muss auch die außerstaatliche Wirklichkeit erfassen. Transnationale Wirtschaftsunternehmen haben sich zu Machtzentren entwickelt, die praeterstaatliche Existenz genießen. Ähnliches gilt für transnationale Werteinstitutionen wie *Greenpeace* oder *Amnesty International*.

Diese Wirklichkeit wird mit einem Mehrebenenmodell nicht angemessen erfasst. Diese Wirklichkeit existiert nicht in Ebenen. Es haben sich Schwerkraftzentren gebildet, die aufeinander Einfluss nehmen. Diese Schwerkraftzentren mögen in mancherlei Hinsicht einander vorgeordnet und nachgeordnet sein. Das ist etwa beim Anwendungsvorrang des Gemeinschaftsrechts – aber eben nur punktuell – der Fall. In anderen Bereichen ist das Über- und Unterordnungsverhältnis umgekehrt – die Mitgliedstaaten sind weiterhin Herren der Verträge. In wieder anderen Bereichen herrscht Gleichordnung, etwa im institutionellen Geflecht der innergemeinschaftlichen Rechtsetzung. Und in wiederum anderen Bereichen haben die Träger von Hoheitsgewalt nichts miteinander zu tun, etwa in Bereichen, in denen sich keine Kompetenzüberschneidungen oder Kompetenzüberlagerungen ergeben. Damit löst sich auch der Stufenbau der Rechtsordnung auf.

Verfassung wird dadurch Bereichsverfassung. Verfassung verliert den Anspruch, den Gesamtzusammenhang staatlich verfasster Gemeinschaft zu organisieren. Die Deutung der Kompetenzzuordnung von Bundesverfassungsgericht und Europäischem Gerichtshof (bei der Grundrechtsgewährleistung) als Kooperationsverhältnis bestärkt die Entwicklung des Grundgesetzes zur Teilverfassung.

IV.

Die mitgliedstaatlichen Verfassungen sind längst Bereichsverfassungen geworden. Sie sind nicht mehr Grundlage, sie sind nicht mehr Fassung für öffentliche Herrschaft überhaupt. Zu viel an Hoheitsrechten ist dafür auf die europäische Ebene übertragen worden. Europäisches Recht überlagert, verschiebt, verdrängt mitgliedstaatliches Verfassungsrecht. Gemeinschaftsrecht geht mitgliedstaatlichem Verfassungsrecht vor.

Das aber birgt die Gefahr, dass Verfassungsrecht vergeht – vollständig vergeht. Wenn die Europäische Union keine Verfassung hat, wenn die mitgliedstaatlichen Verfassungen nur Bereiche abdecken, so sind weite Bereiche des Rechts verfassungslos. Die Europäische Union hat dann keine Verfassung. Die Mitgliedstaaten haben dann keine Verfassung. Mitgliedstaaten haben nur noch Bereichsverfassung – und die Europäische Union darf keine Gesamtverfassung haben.

Aber wo Gefahr ist wächst das Rettende auch. Europäisierung des Verfassungsrechts ist auch Europäisierung des Verfassungsbegriffs. Für das Verfassungsrecht bedeutet die Europäisierung aber letztlich eine Verdeutlichung seines modernen Wesens. Der Befund ist im Grundsatz für alle Mitgliedstaaten der Europäischen Union ähnlich. Für das Grundgesetz ist er aber besonders klar, und im Vergleich erscheint die Europäisierung des Grundgesetzes besonders weit fortgeschritten. Bereichsverfassungen haben Brückenfunktion, weil sie andere Bereiche und deren Verfassungen voraussetzen und sich zu ihnen verhalten, auf sie verweisen. Bereichsverfassungen schlagen Brücken nach Europa, zu anderen Mitgliedstaaten. Verfassung ist nicht mehr Staatsgrundlegung. Verfassung ist nunmehr Entwicklungsordnung. Dieser Verfassungsbegriff folgt aus der Entwicklung der Europäischen Union. Aber er kann nur Bestand haben, wenn die Verfassungsverneinung aus der Debatte um den Verfassungsvertrag ignoriert wird. Die europäische Verfassungsverneinung führt mit ihrem Beharren auf einem überkommenen aber überholten Verfassungsbegriff nicht zurück zur Nationalstaatlichkeit. Diese Verfassungsverneinung führt zur Aufgabe von Verfassungsrecht überhaupt. Aber wenn wir denn eine Verfassungsdämmerung erlebten. Auf jede Abenddämmerung folgt eine Morgendämmerung.

The New Regional Organisation:
Incentives, Rules and Constitutional Implications

by Jan-Erik Lane

I. Introduction

Regional organisation above the level of the nation-states is very popular with early 21st-century governments. The pace of regional organisation will probably pick up speed after the failure of the so-called Doha Round with the World Trade Organisation (WTO) and its global approach: multilateralism. One can now speak of a set of regional blocks of states that engage in certain activities that were previously run by the nation-state. Most of these blocks have promised more in the years to come, but it is a typical feature of these new regional organisations that their ambitions outpace what they can deliver.

Depending on the nature of the treaties signed between the governments of states, there are different modes of regional organisation. They range from a mere discussion forum to a compact monetary union. They may start out as a simple cooperative mechanism and end up being a co-ordination mechanism that impinges upon the constitutions of member states. Thus, one may raise the question: When does regional organisation call for constitutional regulation?

II. Regional Organisation and Incentives

Regional organisation is intimately linked with the incentives of the governments. It is these interests that lead the governments of states into various modes of regional organisation. The economic interests behind regional blocks cannot be doubted, given the global emphasis upon trade and trade liberalisation. It is when governments take further steps beyond the Free Trade or Preferential Trade Agreements that they have to clarify what interests they aim at pursuing in terms of a specific organisation. Regional organisation entails costs for the participants, who also need to take into account the risks involved. When regional organisation replaces state organisation, the participant governments need to be well aware of the benefits and the costs.

The bilateral regulation of reciprocities between states may appear to involve extremely heavy transaction costs. But multilateral regulation may not always be possible because of conflicts among a major set of countries in the world. Thus, regional organisation offers a promising mode of handling the interdependencies among countries that the ongoing process of globalisation generates. But once regional organisation has been achieved, it may have constitutional implications and it certainly involves costs. Public organisation deals with competences, rights and duties. When regional organisations multiply, the pertinent question is what competences do they handle. My argument is that the more compact the regional group of states becomes, the more it calls for some form of constitutional regulation.

An attempt has been made to theorise regions as a new emergent level of the macro-organisation of societies, a level displaying "regioness" as well as "actorness".[1] The difficulty involved is that such an approach to regionalism could defy the principle of *methodological individualism* for the social sciences. The actors participating in the new regionalism are, *inter alia,* governments representing the states of the world. They support regional arrangements when the benefits outweigh the costs. Regions are not actors in themselves but emerging aggregates of human beings. Thus, regioness greatly varies, depending upon how compact regional integration or regional organisation tends to be. Similarly, actorness also varies considerably because only few regional organisations possess supranational bodies. Economic blocs as regional organisations include free trade areas and customs unions with preferential trade agreements somewhere in-between. A trade bloc is established through a trade pact (or pacts) covering different issues of economic integration. However, "regioness" and "actorness" surface only when a common market is established.

Regionalism is often modelled as an impersonal process of change, forcing the nation-states to give up sovereignty and establish new forms of public organisation. Thus, one speaks of "imperatives", "functional necessity" and major "social transformation" as if regionalisation is on par with urbanisation or industrialisation. I believe this is incorrect. Regional organisation is fundamentally a principal-agent phenomenon. Governments as the principals agree to set up, instruct, pay and monitor agents to handle certain tasks for them. They do this mainly because the total gain to the states or countries they represent is larger than the total costs. As long as the transaction benefits (TB) exceed the transaction costs (TC), they will continue to push for deeper and deeper regional integration, but once TB < TC, the process of regional organisation will come to a halt.

---

1   *Hettne, B.*: Regionalism and World Order, in: Farrell, M./Hettne, B./van Langenhove, L. (eds.): Global Politics of Regionalism, London, 2005, 269–286.

Regional organisation promises benefits but it also incurs costs. Thus, the participating governments will consider the ratio: benefits/costs. If this ratio is larger than 1, they may decide to proceed. Benefits and costs involve both short-run and long-run considerations. Economic benefits and costs will be given much attention, but so-called "intangible" benefits and costs may also be involved. Two key principles may be identified:

(1) *Pareto improvement:* The regional group as a whole must bring forth a better ratio of benefits/costs for its members as a collective than no regional organisation at all. Thus, changes in the *status quo* which do not increase benefits/costs for the group as a whole should not be made (group rationality).

(2) *Nash rule:* Every member of a new regional organisation will demand that, sooner or later, the new organisation improve its benefits/costs ratio. This can be done through compensation from the other members. But a member that looses out cannot stay in the new group, even if the first principle is fulfilled (individual rationality).

Regional organisation is often inherently instable because member states are not always convinced that its total benefits will make them a winner. Consequently, regional organisation tends to proceed with much uncertainty, as individual member states reconsider their obligation to the group while fearing that the promises of future benefits may not be forthcoming for their sake. It is not enough that regional organisation involves a *Pareto* improvement in relation to the *status quo* because each member state needs to be convinced that it will benefit sooner or later.

III. Regional Organisation versus Regional Integration:
the Economic Approaches

Regional organisation ranges from a trading block to a common market with a monetary union attached to it. It exists to the extent that ambitions expressed by governments at regional meetings are really put into practice. It is often not easy to tell exactly how far the ambition to create a compact regional organisation has actually been realised. This difficulty is caused not merely by poverty, overstated ambitions and lack of transparency; the achievements of the Gulf Cooperation Council (GCC) are also difficult for an outsider to judge.[2]

---

2   Cf. *Fasano, U.*: Monetary Union among Member Countries of the Gulf Cooperation Council, Washington, DC, 2003.

There is no self-evident manner in which the planet is to be divided into a set of regions. Countries may be part of several regions and regions may overlap considerably. Region is a geographical concept. It may exhibit homogeneity in culture or economics. Economic processes of regional integration have attracted much interest in the rapidly swelling literature on regionalism. A number of regionally-based blocs have emerged recently to promote trade between member states through trade liberalisation measures.

One may wish to make a distinction between regional integration and regional organisation. The first form of regionalism would consist of real economic outcomes that make countries within the same region more interdependent: trade, investments, and migration. The second form of regionalism would consist of public organisation such as agreements between governments, the setting up of common institutions and the making of federal arrangements. Although these two forms of regionalism may go together in reality, they are conceptually different phenomena.

Regional economic integration refers to the growing and deepening size of the market, making two or more countries interpenetrate in terms of goods and services, jobs and capital. It is to a large extent a spontaneous process of social change – resulting in a spontaneous order. Regional organisation results from deliberate action, aiming at the realisation of plans and ambitions by governments. The latter may promote the former, but the success of regional organisation is a probability phenomenon.

From an institutional point of view, there is a clear variation in the modes of regional organisation. It is worth an explanation, but it is not enough to rely only upon economic theory. The key economic approaches to regionalism do not really address the key issues in, respectively, the institutionalisation and constitutionalisation of regionalism.

The present-day variation in regionalism goes beyond the simple *Balassa* framework for the analysis of the *dynamics of regional organisation*: from the free trade area over the monetary union to political federation.[3] The theory of monetary unions or the *Mundell* model of *optimal currency areas*[4] are not clear about what its implications are for a region of states. If an optimal currency area requires labour mobility, this will lead to the common market. *De facto* currency areas seem to arise more from the collapse of the local currency than from explicit macroeconomic considerations about how an area will react to so-called

3   *Balassa, B. A.*: The Theory of Economic Integration, Westport, CT, 1982.
4   See *Calvo, G. A./Obstfeld, M./Dornbusch, R.* (eds.): Money, Capital Mobility, and Trade. Essays in Honor of Robert A. Mundell, Boston, 2004.

shocks, i.e. unanticipated economic adjustments that cause high unemployment. When regional organisation is deliberately designed to provide regional public goods, then the relevant theory about regional facilities is to be found in the so-called *club theory.*[5] Regionalism today tends to proceed according to the logic of the *Bergsten* model of *open regionalism* instead of the old framework of closed regionalism[6] favoured especially by the Economic Commission for Latin America and the Caribbean (ECLAC) and the European Community (EC), raising the *Viner-Meade* objection that trade diversion could be larger than trade creation.[7]

From the perspective of political science, the crucial question is: When do states cross the borderline where regional organisation is not merely just another free trade treaty but where it takes on constitutional implications?

IV. Regional Institutions and State Regalia: the Constitutional Approach

A state operates with certain typical characteristics. Regional organisation becomes an alternative to state organisation when one or several of these characteristics are moved from the level of the state to that of the regional organisation. The more this is done, the stronger the demand for a constitutional regulation of regional organisation. Let me call these state characteristics *regalia.* Some of the characteristics belonging to the set of regalia are:

- passports and embassies
- taxes
- army
- police
- money
- higher education
- environmental management, and
- social security and unemployment.

The state operates a number of bureaux or agencies in order to provide these regalia. Since their provision requires institutions, there will normally be a constitution that instructs about how institutions can be created and changed. The state wishes to identify its citizens, provide for law and order, pay for public

---

5   *Cornes, R./Sandler, T.*: Theory of Externalities, Public Goods, and Club Goods, Cambridge, 1996.
6   *Bergsten, C. F.*: Open Regionalism, in: The World Economy, 20/7 (1997), 865–888.
7   Cf. *Viner, J.*: The Customs Union Issue, New York, 1950; *Meade, J. E.*: The Theory of Customs Union, Amsterdam, 1955.

services with at least partial taxation, constitute the monetary authority, run higher education and research in the best interests of the country, survey its land and natural resources as well as help the needy.

Regional organisation may be low-keyed, not touching upon these regalia. Sometimes regional organisation is solely a discussion forum between governments. Or it involves merely a trade agreement. Sometimes regional organisation involves more, much more at times. When a regional organisation takes on one or several of the regalia, then constitutional regulation will become relevant. Let me now develop this theory in relation to real-life examples of regional organisations.

V. Basic Modes of Regional Organisation

Several outlines or designs of modes of regional organisation can be found in the many regional blocks of states. But it is far from certain that there is a corresponding institutional reality. Although decisions about plans of regional organisation may have been made, the implementation of such designs tends to be slow and open to many reversals. Yet, it would be fruitful to survey the new political units in regional blocks of states in order to pin down what they are actually doing. In Africa for instance, there are a large number of regional organisations, but not all of them are actually operational since some of these free trade areas or common markets in Africa remain promises or projects only. It is impossible to achieve much in terms of regionally coordinating states when the governments involved are not in control of their own territories.

A regional organisation is *not* the same as a free trade agreement, although it may include that. One motive for setting up a regional organisation is clearly economics, but a regional organisation should include more than a mere contract to liberalise trade among a set of states. Typical of a regional organisation is that it takes over certain government tasks from the nation-state. The crucial question is to pin down what these competences tend to be. There are many bilateral trade agreements, and some of them do not imply that state competences are somehow to be handed over to a regional organisation somehow. A regional organisation at least includes a discussion forum, where the governments of sovereign states meet on a regular basis to deliberate common problems. Often regional organisations devote much time to spectacular conferences only to show a *façade* of unity where there is division and conflict. Yet, a regional block of states must devise and run a minimum of common institutions in order to qualify as an organisation.

Setting up a continuous schedule for a round of talks between sovereign states does require some planning and information-gathering that commit governments to collaborate and coordinate their efforts.

If the creation of a regional forum for continuous information-sharing and debate on issues is the starting-point of regionalisation, then one may distinguish between alternative modes of regional organisation, depending on how the set of competences is identified:

(1) Politics: A Regional Forum
(2) Policies: Regional Facilities
(3) Economics I: Trading Blocks or Customs Union
(4) Economics II: Currency Areas
(5) Economics III: Common Markets, and
(6) Federation: Common Defence.

I would argue that descending the list above results in an increasingly complex coordination mechanism, requiring some form of constitutional recognition at the end of the day. Regional co-operation may be discussion and information-sharing, the running of a common facility, or various forms of economic collaboration. A common market is the most demanding form of regional economic organisation because of all that it requires in terms of public regulation as well as dispute settlement. A federation would entail the regional organisation becoming a new state and replacing the existing ones, but no regional organisation has gone so far.

1. The Regional Forum

Governments are increasingly attracted by the idea of a forum, i.e. a regular meeting place for rounds of talks about common problems. This amounts to a minimum level of organisation, involving a small secretariat with the resources necessary to hold meeting once or twice a year and engage in information-gathering. The secretariat may only possess some intelligence resources, such as collecting data, preparing reports and disseminating information, but its planning may have a large impact upon future events.

The Forum may look innocuous, but it could serve basic political interests such as clarifying defence and foreign policy issues among states where relations are tense. One example comes readily to mind: the South Asian Association for Regional Co-operation (SAARC), covering Bangladesh, Bhutan, India, the Maldives, Nepal, Pakistan and Sri Lanka. Although created in 1985, it did not delineate a free trade area until 2006 (SAFTA). How could such a regional organisation really work, given the Kashmir problem between Pakistan and India or the internal turmoil within Nepal and Sri Lanka? War-torn Afghanistan has been accepted as a member, and unruly Iran has also expressed interest in joining. Could that really work? It depends on what the real objectives in regional organisation are. Promoting peace and avoiding war is no small ambition, especially if some of the governments involved have nuclear weapons.

By debating issues of conflict between states, governments may promote peace. Although a long round of regular meetings may not resolve the fundamental conflicts, at least military confrontation is avoided. The longer this period of instable peace lasts, the more one may hope that the worst outcome can be avoided. Such purposes of debating thorny issues between states may consist not only of the question of war and peace but also of migration, border controls, transnational crime and the spread of diseases. Many of the regional organisations today are merely Forums, meaning that governments meet and sign letters or treaties of intentions in various fields.

The Forum model is also attractive when the goals of regional cooperation are mainly cultural ones. Governments may wish to identify a common culture or historical legacy for a number of states, despite all economic differences between them. Culture would deliver the cement of cohesion for a regional block, especially if economics creates divergence among the countries involved. Here, the regional efforts in the Muslim civilisation come to mind: the Arab League and the Organisation of Islamic Conference, focusing upon Islam and its cultural roots in the Arab civilisation.

Another example of regional organisation as a Forum is the Association of Southeast Asian Nations (ASEAN),[8] although it also manifests an ambition to create stronger forms of regional integration. The ASEAN regularly conducts dialogue meetings with other countries and an organisation, collectively known as the *ASEAN dialogue partners,* during the ASEAN Regional Forum (ARF). The ARF, which met for the first time in 1994, is an informal multilateral dialogue of 26 members concerned with security issues in the Asia-Pacific region. An ideal-type example of a Forum is the Asia-Pacific Economic Cooperation (APEC), covering the entire Pacific Ocean area with the exception of the small island states there. The APEC is only a forum for facilitating economic growth, cooperation, trade and investment in the Asia-Pacific region. It operates on the basis of non-binding commitments, open dialogue and equal respect for the views of all participants. Unlike other multilateral trade bodies, APEC requires no treaty obli-

8 *Beeson, M.*: Regionalism and Globalization in East Asia. Politics, Security and Economic Development, Basingstoke, 2006.

gations of its participants. APEC has 21 members, which account for approximately 40 % of the world's population, approximately 56 % of world GDP and about 48 % of world trade. APEC, established in 1989, has worked to reduce trade barriers across the Asia-Pacific region. Its goal is to have realised the "Bogor Goals" of free and open trade and investment in the Asia-Pacific region by 2010 for industrialised economies and by 2020 for developing economies.[9] Yet, what APEC has actually created is a combination of open and shallow regionalism.

The Forum may simply serve as a tension-reduction mechanism between states, pushing issues further into the future without resolving much. Or a Forum may provide the framework for regional planning, having a huge impact upon the member states' governments. It may be highly successful in setting the agenda for several governments, enhancing common plans about, for instance, global warming and environmental degradation. The Forum may also be a façade that creates an illusion of regional cooperation and understanding. Take the example of the Commonwealth of Independent States (CIS), which replaced the Soviet Union. What has come out of this Forum is the plan of the Eurasian Economic Community (EURASEC): In 1995 Russia and Belarus created a customs union, which Kazakhstan and Kyrgyzstan later joined. Belarus, Kazakhstan, Kyrgyzstan, Russia and Tajikistan signed the treaty creating the EURASEC in 2001. One objective is to develop a full-scale customs union and common economic space and another objective is to harmonise customs tariffs. It is difficult to tell whether the CIS or its offspring have booked any real results.

The Forum is politics, often *high* politics. But regional organisation may also be low politics or the implementation of a set of common facilities serving educational, health or communication policies.

2. Regional Facilities

The pooling of country resources to set up regional organisations within a public law framework is hardly anything new. It was done in the past outside of the regional integration ideology that is now so strong in all parts of the world with the possible exception of Japan and China. Such regional facilities offer a springboard for further integration, underlining the fact that economies of scale play a major role in organisation. The set of regional facilities is a broad one, including a common airline, common university education, a common space exploration

---

9   *Ravenhill, J.*: APEC and the Construction of Pacific Rim Regionalism, Cambridge, 2002.

policy, a common air navigation policy, common cultural institutions as well as common sports and leisure activities.

Both rich and poor regional organisations operate one or another regional facility. From a club-theory point of view, the tiny states of the world would have most to gain from offering regionally based services. Take the case of the Caribbean Community and Common Market (CARICOM), for instance.[10] CARICOM was established by Barbados, Jamaica, Guyana and Trinidad and Tobago in 1973, replacing the 1965–1972 Caribbean Free Trade Association (CARIFTA), organised to provide a link between the English-speaking countries of the Caribbean upon the dissolution of the West Indies Federation. A revised treaty to establish the Caribbean Community including the CARICOM Single Market and Economy (CSME) was signed 2001. The CARICOM now has 15 small states as members. It operates a large number of common facilities, such as the Caribbean Disaster Emergency Response Agency, the Caribbean Food Corporation (CFC), the Caribbean Environment Health Institute (CEHI), the Caribbean Agriculture Research and Development Institute, the Caribbean Development Bank (CDB), the University of Guyana (UG) and the University of the West Indies.

CARICOM also uses economies of scale in diplomatic mission, one ambassador serving all 15 small states in Brussels and Geneva, for instance. The partners in a regional group may of course use private organisation too, setting up joint-stock companies in the economy. However, economic organisation is oriented mainly towards facilitating trade and may go so far as the setting up of a community, i.e. a single market.

3. Economics I: Free Trade Associations and Customs Unions

Economic factors are important incentives when setting up a regional organisation. Trade looms large in regionalisation since fundamental trade theory promises considerable benefits if trade is liberalised. Countries that attempt to capture the benefits from trade liberalisation constitute themselves as trading blocs, whether this be as a free trade association (FTA) or a customs union or something in-between. A number of countries have set up secretariats in order to implement free trade agreements: FTAs or preferential trade areas (PTAs). Such a secretariat defines and interpret rules with regard to the FTA or a preferential trade agreement. Managing a free trade area involves so-called *facilitation meas-*

10 *Bulmer-Thomas, V.*: Regional Integration in Latin America and the Caribbean. The Political Economy of Open Regionalism, London, 2001.

ures, but FTAs or PTAs do not need to have any special common institutions such as a judiciary, police and court. All countries have some bilateral trade agreements, but they would require some special institutions for their enforcement only when a group of states consists of more than five or ten member states.

The difference between an FTA and a customs union is blurred when countries operate a preferential trade agreement. A PTA gives preferential access to certain products from certain countries by reducing, although not completely abolishing tariffs. An FTA is a designated group of countries that have agreed to eliminate tariffs, quotas and preferences on most goods traded between them. To avoid evasion through re-exportation the countries use so-called rules of origin, in which there is a requirement for the minimum extent of local material inputs and local transformations adding value to the goods. Such rules may actually be used as a trade policy restricting imports. The principal difficulty with customs unions is the *Jacob-Viner* balance between trade *creation* versus trade *destruction*, which may turn negative.[11] There are so many FTAs or PTAs that they cannot be enumerated here. They require only a minimum level of organisation, such as the Lome-Cotonou Agreements between the EU and the African, Caribbean and Pacific states.

A customs union is a free trade area with a set of Common External Tariffs. The participant countries set up a common external trade policy, but in some cases they use different import quotas. In addition to fostering economic efficiency, the purposes of establishing a customs union include closer political and cultural ties between the member countries. A customs union is established through trade pacts: the Southern African Customs Union, the East African Community, the Gulf Cooperation Council, MERCOSUR, the Central American Customs Union, the Economic and Monetary Community of Central Africa (CEMAC), the West African Economic and Monetary Union (UEMOA) and the Andean Community (CAN).

A customs union needs to have some administrative capacity; the common framework of tariffs and quotas must have surveillance. However, there is hardly any need for common political institutions because these trade tasks can be handled through delegation to some agency at arm's length from the different governments.

Regional trading blocks may include some organisations that exist on paper only. One may distinguish between several regional organisations depending upon how strong they integrate the various national economies. Regional organi-

---

11 *Viner, J.*, op. cit.

sations often have ambitions but their implementation tends to be projected into the future. One may, for example, question the existence of the following examples of trade blocks:

- The African Economic Community (AEC): Although supported by several African regional organisations like the Economic Community of West African States (ECOWAS), the Common Market for Eastern and Southern Africa (COMESA), the Economic Community of Central African States (ECCAS), the Intergovernmental Authority on Development (IGAD), the Southern African Development Community (SADC) and the Arab Maghreb Union (UMA), there has been little progress in implementing the AEC in their respective regions.

- COMESA: In 1978, it was decided to create a sub-regional economic community with a PTA, beginning with a sub-regional preferential trade area which would be gradually upgraded over a ten-year period to a common market until the community had been established. The PTA treaty envisaged its transformation into a common market: the Common Market for Eastern and Southern Africa, COMESA, in an agreement signed 1993.

- *Comunidad Sudamericana de Naciones* (CSN): a continent-wide free trade zone that will unite two existing trade organisations – Mercosur and the Andean Community – will eliminate tariffs for non-sensitive products by 2014 and sensitive products by 2019.

Although these are trade pacts endorsed by regional organisations, in reality they are only plans and ambitions. Regionalism in sub-Saharan Africa appears to be problematic when it comes to the actual enforcement of agreements.[12]

4. Economics II: Monetary Unions

Monetary unions can be found in many regions: the Economic and Monetary Union of the Caribbean Community (CARICOM), the Economic and Monetary Union of the Economic Community of West African States (ECOWAS), the Economic and Monetary Union of the East African Community (EAC) (due in 2009), the Economic and Monetary Union of the Gulf Cooperation Council (GCC) (due in 2010), the Economic and Monetary Union of the Southern African Development Community (SADC) (due in 2016), the Economic and Monetary Union of the South American Community of Nations (CSN) (due in 2019) and

---

12 *Fawole, W. A./Ukeje, C.* (eds.): The Crisis of the State and Regionalism in West Africa: Identity, Citizenship and Conflict, Dakar, 2006.

the Economic and Monetary Union of the African Economic Community (AEC) (due in 2028).

De facto monetary unions arise whenever two or more countries use one and the same currency. There have been several currency unions between countries not having a common market, e.g. the CFA franc BEAC, the CFA franc BCEAO and the CFP franc. Actually, a monetary union does not need a common central bank or a common facility issuing legal tender. It is enough that one country merely adopts the currency of another country. Sometimes countries use two currencies, the national official one and a shadow foreign currency. For instance, the United States dollar is used in Palau, Micronesia, the Marshall Islands, Panama, Ecuador, El Salvador, East Timor, the British Virgin Islands and the Turks and Caicos Islands. The Australian dollar is used by Kiribati, Nauru, and Tuvalu, while the New Zealand dollar is used by Niue, the Cook Islands, Tokelau, and the Pitcairn Islands.

Yet, it is true that when countries formally set up a monetary union, they then construct some money-issuing authority. For example the Organisation of Eastern Caribbean States (OECS) supports a central bank since most member states adhere to the Eastern Caribbean Central Bank (ECCB) monetary authority. This regional central bank surveys the financial and banking integrity of the OECS economic bloc of states in order to maintain the financial status of the Eastern Caribbean dollar (EC$). The British Virgin Islands do not use the Eastern Caribbean dollar as their *de facto* native currency, but the East Caribbean dollar is used by Anguilla, Antigua and Barbuda, Dominica, Grenada, Montserrat, Saint Kitts and Nevis, Saint Lucia, and Saint Vincent and the Grenadines. The South African rand is legal tender in South Africa, Swaziland, Lesotho, and Namibia through the Common Monetary Area.

5. Economics III: the Common Market

A common market is a quantitative leap compared with the FTA and a customs union. Here, common institutions must be set up in order to handle the administration of the rules of the regional group. A common market can be erected only if it handles all questions relating to product acceptance and product comparability. This will require court action in settling disputes. A currency area will need a central bank that is responsible for the supply of common currency and that sets the interest rates in the area, but the organisational requirements of a common market go much further.

The common market requires far-reaching economic regulation in order to define how goods, services, capital and labour can move across borders. A typical sign of a common market is the regional passport that abolishes border controls. If the market is big, then economic regulation needs considerable regulatory resources besides a judicial organisation that can settle ensuing disputes. There may be such a sizeable need for administrative capacity to handle a common market that this replaces the nation-state. Regulatory tasks will have to be transferred to a regional organisation of some sort.

A single market poses a great organisational challenge. The rules of economic activity will have to be defined for a number of states having different regulatory traditions. Various strategies may be employed: harmonisation (different rules will be made similar), mutual recognition (each state reciprocally accepts the rules of another state) and new legislation (a body of new regulation is created). It is well known that harmonisation takes time, as it is transaction costs heavy. Mutual recognition is quicker, but it may not cover all aspects of the new common market. Finally, legislation requires new institutions such as a legislative body as well as a judicial body.

One of the typical problems encountered in setting up a common market is the creation of a common passport. It is easy to promise but harder to arrive at in reality. The free movement of persons implies a common passport, but migration is a sensitive state issue. It is when regional organisation takes on such a scale that the nation-state is mirrored in new bodies – legislative, executive and judicial – that regionalism becomes a substitute for the nation-state. It is the creation of a common market that calls for a structure of new political bodies and new agencies.

VI. Constitutionalisation of Regional Organisation

The more complicated and compact the regional organisation becomes, the more relevant is constitutional regulation. Thus far, only the EU has attempted a full-scale constitutional codification of regional treaties among member states' governments. However, several regional blocks have set up institutions whose operations have constitutional relevance.

How much new regional organisation is required depends upon the size of the single market. But even small common markets, like CARICOM and OECS, have had to set up new public bodies in order to deal with the implications of a common market.[13] Thus, in the Caribbean we find:

---

13 *Hall, K. O.*: Re-Inventing CARICOM. The Road to a New Integration, Kingston, 2003; *Hall, K./Benn, D.*: Caribbean Imperatives. Regional Governance and Integrated Development, Kingston, 2005.

- The executive consists of a rotating prime ministerial chairmanship of CARICOM (head of CARICOM), the CARICOM secretary general (chief executive) and the CARICOM Headquarters secretariat (chief administrative organ). There is also a quasi-cabinet of individual Heads of Government who are given specific responsibilities or portfolios for overall regional development and integration.
- The Council consists of ministers responsible for community affairs and any other minister designated by the member states in their absolute discretion. It is one of the principal organs (the other being the Conference of the Heads of Government) and is supported by four other organs and three bodies: The Council for Finance and Planning (COFAP), the Council for Trade and Economic Development (COTED), the Council for Foreign and Community Relations (COFCOR) as well as the Council for Human and Social Development (COHSOD).
- The Legal Affairs Committee provides legal advice to the organs and bodies of the community. The Budget Committee examines the draft budget and work programme of the secretariat and submits recommendations to the Community Council; the Committee of Central Bank Governors provides recommendations to the COFAP on monetary and financial matters.
- The Caribbean Court of Justice (CCJ) acts as the original jurisdiction for the settlement of disputes on the functioning of the Caribbean Single Market and Economy (CSME) and it serves as an appellate court of last resort for member states which have severed their country's ties with the Privy Council in London, United Kingdom. The CCJ is based in Port of Spain, Trinidad and Tobago.

In addition, there are new structures that comprise the Caribbean Community (CARICOM), such as the CARICOM Heads of Government consisting of the various heads of government from each member state. Moreover, there is a standing committee of ministers because ministerial responsibilities cover specific areas; for example, the standing committee of ministers responsible for health will comprise of ministers of health from each member state. The secretariat of the Caribbean Community is located in Georgetown, Guyana. Running these operations results in costs that must somehow be covered.

For the much smaller OECS, we also find new regional political or administrative bodies: (1) The secretariat consists of four main divisions responsible for external relations, functional co-operation, corporate services and economic affairs. These four divisions oversee the work of a number of specialised institutions, work units or projects located in six countries (Antigua and Barbuda, the Commonwealth of Dominica, St. Lucia, Belgium, Canada, and the United States of

America). (2) The Eastern Caribbean Supreme Court (ECSC) today handles the judicial matters in the Organisation of Eastern Caribbean States. When a trial surpasses the stage of the High Court in an OECS member state, it can then be passed on to the ECSC at the level of the Supreme Court. Cases appealed from the ECSC Supreme Court will then be referred to the jurisdiction of the Caribbean Court of Justice (CCJ).

VII. RTAs, Institutionalisation and Constitutionalisation

The explosion in the number of regional trade agreements (RTAs) during the last decade raises not only economic questions about the compatibility of increasing regionalism with the multilateralism of WTO. Open regionalism may actually conform more to the classical ideal of global free trade and factor movements than old regionalism, focusing on *Prebisch*ian import substitution as well as shallow integration. From the point of view of politics and administration, the new regionalism replaces shallow integration with deep integration. Thus, some RTAs lead to more than trade or customs unions.

Deep regional integration emerges with the establishment of the common market and the monetary union. The qualitative leap occurs here, as shown by the enormous difficulties that regional organisations such as the CARICOM, the OECS, the Central American Common Market (CACM) and the GCC have experienced. Until now, only the European Union (EU) has mastered the organisational challenges that a common market and a monetary union pose. It is no surprise that the EU attempted to create a constitution since it has progressed further in *deep integration* than has any of the other regional organisations.

Constitutionalisation in relation to regional integration becomes an option when governments create a common market and a monetary union. The process of rule-making, rule application and rule adjudication needs to be formalised and entrenched in a predictable manner in relation to so-called *Ordnungspolitik* and the implications of supranationality must be addressed and solved somehow.

Yet, constitutionalisation is far from an automatic process that is released once regional integration goes beyond a certain point. Country legacies matter; adherence to a civil law tradition makes a country more prone to engage in an attempt at constitutionalisation than does adherence to a common law family. Three issues are of particular concern where institutionalisation may not be enough, viz:
• the recognition of a supreme court for adjudicating disputes about the rules for the common market;

- the establishment of a central bank for the monetary union; and
- the clarification of competences between the regional bodies and the national ones.

These pressing issues in processes of regionalisation can be handled by mere institutionalisation, focusing upon some vague principles like the sovereignty of the European Court of Justice (ECJ), the independence of the European Central Bank (ECB) and the flexibility of subsidiarity. Yet, in a long-run perspective, constitutional codification becomes increasingly relevant in order to establish what these notions entail.

I would suggest that the threshold between institutionalisation and constitutionalisation is found in-between the common market and the political federation, i. e. in setting up an economic union. It requires the elaboration of fiscal, monetary and environmental policies with great impact upon taxation and employment. It presupposes a list of intergovernmental bodies and perhaps some supranational ones as well. And the relationships between these bodies and civil society call for a clarification of patterns of influence and even democracy.

As long as the union bodies are weak and ill-defined, institutionalisation may be sufficient. However, as the regional organisation grows to maturity with *deep* integration, one may conjecture that the demand for constitutionalisation will increase. As a matter of fact, affluence is a nice predictor of the level of transparency of institutions, the EU scoring high while the Andean Community, the CACM and the CARICOM score low.

VIII. Conclusion

The new phenomenon of regional organisation harbours an interesting variety in public organisation. There are now many regional organisations, at least on paper. One may expect that some of them will achieve a more firm structure in the decade to come. Countries may be members of several regional organisations, especially when it is only a matter of trading blocks. Regional organisation replaces the state to some extent only when a common market is set up. Monetary unions require a central tender-issuing authority when it is not a case of simply using another country's money. Constitutionalisation becomes a relevant option when member states move to set up an economic union with deep integration.

The next decade will show which regional organisations are durable and whether some of them really achieve a community, i. e. a common market with the four freedoms: goods, services, capital and labour. When a common market is set up, then new institutions will be created, some of which may call upon consti-tutional recognition such as a tribunal monitoring the harmonisation of the common set of rules for the economy and the various markets. The more com-pact the regional group of states tends to be, the more relevant the call for consti-tutionalisation becomes. Thus, the competences of intergovernmental or supra-national bodies need to be defined in a transparent manner and the role of civil society in influencing policy-making must be identified.

Constitutional Principles and Internationalisation

by Michiel Scheltema

I. Introduction[1]

The most basic legal instrument of almost all national legal orders around the globe is the constitution.[2] In democracies, constitutional principles provide for a democratic and accountable government by stipulating checks and balances between the competencies of the various state authorities, and by protecting the fundamental rights of citizens against potentially capricious government. In many countries, constitutional courts are set up to guarantee that the constitutional order is observed by all government bodies and to give special attention to the protection of the citizens against infringements by the government. If a constitutional court is absent, other (high) courts fulfil this task.

These principles have been developed as part of the constitutional order of *nation*-states with a view to guaranteeing good government at the national level. Thus, they are tailored to suit circumstances for which they have been developed: nation-states that operate as clearly separate political entities, their respective national legal orders being "closed" and self-contained and the main powers vested exclusively in national institutions. In the present era of globalisation and internationalisation, however, this situation is changing rapidly.

Many rules that used to be laid down in national legislation are now laid down in treaties or in instruments of international organisations. Sometimes those rules are executed by international executive bodies. They are bound only by the rules of their organisations, which do not always include the kind of constitutional

1   This contribution is mainly based on a lecture given in the Spring 2007 Faculty Speakers Series of the Benjamin N. Cardozo School of Law in New York, organised by Prof. *Michel Rosenfeld*. Parts of the text were also used for the development of the research programme "Constitutional Principles and Internationalization" of the Hague Institute for the Internationalisation of Law (HiiL). The author thanks *Sam Muller, David Raic* and the members of HiiL's Programmatic Steering Board for their stimulating remarks, and especially *Morly Frishman* for his great contributions to the final version of the text. For further information on the HiiL's research programme see www.hiil.org.
2   The Constitution acts as the foundation of a state's government. Its content varies according to the intent with which it was made. While descriptive constitutions "merely describe the existing system of government, proclaim societal goals, promise programs and policies", "constitutionalist" constitutions contain proscriptions and prescriptions which bind all branches of government. See *Dorsen, N./ Rosenfeld, M./Sajó, A./Baer, S.*: Comparative Constitutionalism, Thomson West, Minnesota, 2003, 11. In the few states where there is no constitution as such, one may still identify constitutional principles of the normative system, which have a role similar to that of formal constitutions.

principles we are used to at the national level. In most cases, international rules are executed by national authorities. Even if the execution of international decisions is the task of national authorities, these are bound by international norms that can take precedence over national principles. This means that it is not self-evident that national constitutional rules can be observed. Furthermore, the emerging phenomenon of *informal* international rule making, i.e. norm-creation outside the area of treaty-making and treaty-based decision-making, may constitute another problem because it may take place without due regard to constitutional principles and may be beyond the reach of the protection that national constitutions traditionally provide.

Realistically, we have to acknowledge that nowadays international institutions have become so important, and international rule making (both formal and informal) so dominant in various fields of the law, that we cannot do without them. Consequently, the question arises to what extent this development undermines the national constitutional guarantees for good governance. Is it clear that the national courts cannot control international rules or international decisions the way they control national rules and decisions? Can the international level provide compensating guarantees? Or should the national level still play a role in this domain?

It will be argued that national constitutional law remains very important, but that it has to "open up" in order to remain pertinent and play a crucial role in the internationalised world of today. It has to be re-conceptualised to a certain extent and develop constitutional principles that are no longer purely national, but have a transnational character.

II. Does the International Legal Order Sufficiently Provide Compensating Constitutional Guarantees?

It may be tempting to take the view that if there would indeed be an identifiable decrease of national constitutional control, this might be compensated for by international constitutional guarantees. International law could provide the same kind of guarantees as the constitution does at the national level. So, the first question to be addressed is: To what extent does the international legal order provide compensating guarantees? *It may be all too easy to assume that international law alone can sufficiently provide such guarantees.*

It is true that, since World War II, international law has had a great influence on the development of an important area of constitutional principles: human rights. Following the UN General Assembly's Universal Declaration of Human Rights in 1948, in 1966 both the International Covenant on Civil and Political Rights and the International Covenant on Economic, Social and Cultural Rights were adopted, to name the most important instruments.[3] There is an interesting interplay between domestic and international law in this field. The international provisions are quite clearly based on national concepts of fundamental rights and the textual expressions of those rights already existed in the constitutional traditions of several states. The international instruments are based on the principle that human rights have to be observed at national level. Even though these instruments have become part of international law to enhance their effect, the legal regimes or mechanisms they have created for the purpose of enforcing compliance are rather limited. Consequently, human rights are still the rights that protect individuals against intrusion by *national* authorities, and the domestic legal systems and the domestic courts have to provide legal remedies.

There have been additional regional initiatives for the protection of human rights. International (regional) courts entrusted with the task of ensuring compliance with the respective (regional) human rights treaties have been established by the European Convention on Human Rights (creating the European Court of Human Rights) and (to a lesser extent) by the American Convention on Human Rights (with the later creation of the Inter-American Court of Human Rights). Nonetheless, the main responsibility of protecting human rights remains with national authorities (including domestic courts) and only if they fail to protect these rights the regional court may intervene, guaranteeing the protection of fundamental rights by providing legal remedy against a state which does not respect them.

At any rate, the important point for us here is that all these instruments focus on the national level. Consequently – and here lies the problem – human rights may not receive an equivalent level of protection when it comes to decisions taken at international level, for example, by certain international organisations and authorities that are not directly bound by these instruments. The problem can also occur, as shall be demonstrated below, when states find themselves in a position where they are bound to comply with – or implement – decisions taken at the international level. Such compliance might threaten the civil liberties of their citizens and thus run counter to a long-standing national tradition of constitutional principles protecting human rights.

---

3   Both entered into force in 1976, and by now their ratification is almost universal.

In general, and outside the field of human rights, there are several factors which mitigate the view that international law already contains compensating constitutional guarantees or that it will provide these in the near future. The first factor is that, historically, the tradition of constitutionality has not been very strong in international law. Important constitutional principles, such as accountability, transparency, democracy and the protection of the rights of individuals were not the core issues when international law was developed. This can be explained by looking at the development of international law until the middle of the 20th century. The rules of international law of this period concerned the relations between states and particularly the delimitation of the sovereignty of states as well as the use of those areas which fell outside this sovereignty (such as the high seas). The interests of individuals as such and the regulation of their behaviour were considered to be outside the scope of international law. When individuals within the jurisdiction of states derived benefits under international law, such benefits were enjoyed not by virtue of a right which individuals themselves had under international law, but by reason of a right appertaining to the state which exercised jurisdiction over the individual. Despite the use of the terms inter*national* law and law of *nations,* international law was first and foremost *interstate* law. But this has all changed.

As referred to in the introduction, current international law regulates a large number of issues which were formerly dealt with in the national context only, including the legal position and interests of individuals. Individuals have not only become direct objects of international law, but also its subjects. In some situations this has strengthened their legal position, that is, their protection against capricious government, as under the European Convention on Human Rights. But in many situations international rules or decisions are made that directly affect the legal position of individuals without the provision of international constitutional guarantees.

Observance of human rights and fundamental freedoms for all is supposed to be among the guiding principles in the minds of those who draft treaties.[4] There is no real mechanism to guarantee this, however. Treaties are often prepared outside the scope of direct national parliamentary control. The texts are negotiated by government officials (in many cases behind closed doors), and eventually national parliaments may well be confronted with long-negotiated texts which they can hardly reject. Moreover, many treaties do not provide for a judicial settlement procedure in which individuals have *ius standi.*

---

4   Compare the Preamble of the 1969 Vienna Convention on the Law of Treaties.

The problem can be said to be more pertinent in the context of rules or decisions made by international organisations. The decision-making process in international organisations is not as transparent as it is in democratic states, and there is no parliamentary control of decision-making (even in the European Union – probably the most advanced form of international co-operation – the European Parliament has still considerably less controlling powers than national parliaments have). Moreover, except for rare situations, neither individuals nor states can dispute the legality of decisions of international organisations before an international court.[5]

III. The Problem of Multi-level Government

Yet another factor comes up, showing that the problem is even more complex. It is open to doubt whether international law can provide adequate constitutional principles at all. Although many issues that were regulated on the national level have now gone to the international level, it cannot simply be concluded that the international level can provide the same kind of constitutional principles that exist on the national level. The situation is much more complicated. Most rules that are made on an international level and most decisions that are taken on that level have to be executed by national authorities within national legal systems. International law has become much more dependent on national law than is often thought.

As long as international law was restricted to the relationship between nations, international law could be seen as a separate legal system. But when international law deals with subjects that come from the national level, international law cannot act without the help of the domestic legal systems. International agreements on financial and economic transactions and relations, on the combat of crime, on the protection of the environment, or on the safety of aeroplanes, ships or goods have to be executed within the domestic legal systems. Modern international law can therefore not function without effective national legal systems.

The example of the European Union may illustrate this. More than any other international organisation, the EU has developed institutions resembling those of a nation-state. The Union has a Parliament, a Court and a Commission with (some) executive powers. Nevertheless, the EU has made it clear that it cannot

---

5   Neither can these decisions be dealt with by national courts (except for cases of explicit waiver), because principles of immunity from national jurisdiction apply.

accept new Member States unless those states observe the rule of law and have a democratic system of government. Even in the EU, the Union's own legal order is so dependent on the legal orders of the Member States that it had to formulate strict requirements in this respect (the so called "Copenhagen Criteria").

Since institutions of the international legal order in general have far less power to bring their rules into effect than the EU has, their activities are far more dependent on the national legal orders than those of the EU. Consequently, when international decision-making is at stake, it is not enough to establish constitutional principles only at the international level. Those principles should also pertain to the national level where international instruments are to be executed. In other words: in a system of multi-level government the constitutional guarantees should cover the whole system, i.e. all levels of the system.

It seems necessary to conclude that – if only for practical reasons – international law is not (yet) very strong in developing constitutional principles. Together with the theoretical reasons, this shows that constitutional principles originating from the national level remain very important, also for international decision-making. National constitutional law thus continues to be essential for the observance of constitutional principles in an internationalising world.

The complicated interaction between international and national law is clearly demonstrated in situations where states are in fact bound – as a matter of international law – to implement certain decisions and take measures which may potentially infringe individual rights protected by the national constitution as well as by international human rights law. The way EU Member States were required to take action against individuals in their territories as part of the fight against terrorism serves to illustrate this point.

Since modern-day terrorism is to a large extent a transnational phenomenon, the fight against terrorism requires international co-operation. Following the attacks of 9/11 the UN Security Council adopted certain resolutions – binding upon all Member States – with a view to making it difficult for organisations and individuals that were suspected to be involved in international terrorism to carry out their plans. This was done by way of imposing personal financial sanctions, such as the freezing of assets. As part of this process, so-called "terrorist lists" were created; the assets of persons on these lists are to be frozen by national authorities of the countries where the assets are located.[6] In some cases the lists have been

---

6   For the current purpose, it is not possible to offer a detailed analysis of the legal mechanisms which function as the normative basis for such processes, or of recent case-law pertaining to such cases (of the European Court of Justice, the European Court of First Instance, and the European Court of Human Rights). For an up-to-date analysis of these issues see *Hoffmann, J.*: Information: The Essence of Justice.

compiled by the Security Council (in point of fact by the Sanction Committee created for that purpose) while in others this task has been left to the national authorities. In the case of EU Member States, the Union "intervenes" in the process by adopting a Common Position and corresponding regulations, in order to implement the resolutions of the UN Security Council in a unified manner across the EU. The problem with these terrorist lists is that certain fundamental rights of the suspected terrorists – who might, of course, not be terrorists at all – are infringed in a way which lacks transparency and accountability and which does not make it clear how – if at all – persons can be "de-listed", if there are no real proofs as to their involvement in terrorism. It is not at all clear whether the courts of the European Community are in a position to review these sanction mechanisms and to offer a real remedy, when the circumstances seem to justify this.[7]

Generally speaking, international law has only recently started to address this kind of questions.[8] This is an important development because, as explained above, an increase in international constitutional guarantees could compensate for the decrease of those guarantees at the national level. National constitutional law could be an important source of inspiration, and constitutional lawyers should take part in the developments on the international level. However, at this point it must be concluded that current international law does not sufficiently provide these guarantees. This in turn leads to the conclusion that the internationalisation of law still poses a serious challenge from a constitutional point of view.

IV. Constitutional Guarantees on the National Level and Informal International Rule Making

The importance of constitutional principles at the national level can be further underlined by another phenomenon: the emerging field of international rule making outside the area of treaty-making and treaty-based decision-making, i.e.

Public Interest, the Law and the Facts in Terrorism Blacklisting (tentative title, forthcoming) and the references cited there. It should also be mentioned that the most recent (relevant) cases known to the author are *Sison v Council* of 11.07.2007 (T-47/03) and *Stichting Al Aqsa v Council* of 11.07.2007 (T-327-03).

7   Further see *Lavranos, N.*: UN Sanctions and Judicial Review, in: Nordic Journal of International Law, 76/1 (2007), 1–17.

8   See *Ruiz Fabri, H.*: The Constitutionalization of International Law. Benjamin N. Cardozo School of Law, Spring 2007; available at: http://www.cardozo.yu.edu/uploadedFiles/FLOERSHEIMER/ATT00040. pdf (last accessed 15.09.2007).

informal transnational rule making. This includes cases in which national authorities come together to discuss their policies without the objective of converting political agreements in legally binding instruments or decisions. They often try to come to an agreement on a policy that they all will adhere to in their home countries, for instance, the rules made by central banks for the purpose of controlling commercial banks in the so-called Basel agreements.[9] There are also many activities of this kind in the fields of food safety, drugs, aeroplanes, ships, etc.

Public authorities are active in the field of informal rule making, but the same is true for private actors. Self-regulation by transnational private actors is a growing phenomenon that is seen in various fields. Private actors make rules on corporate governance, business relations, industrial standards and certifications as well as on professional activities. Furthermore, private actors make efforts to regulate environmental matters and sometimes even demonstrate a commitment to human rights. In some cases public and private actors work together, for instance in situations in which a certain task or responsibility is carried out by public authorities in some countries and by private actors in others.

Admittedly, these forms of international co-operation have become so essential that one cannot do without them. The safety rules for an aeroplane cannot be different in each country. Nor can the norms for supervising banks or international transactions vary from country to country. The influence of all this informal normativity is enormous and it affects citizens in various ways. This creates a need for constitutional guarantees, pertaining both to the protection of fundamental individual rights, and the questions of the authority and legitimacy of such rule creation, including the existence of appropriate checks and balances.

Even if constitutional guarantees would already exist at the international level, their formal power with respect to informal rule-making would be called into question. Consequently, the legal norms regulating these developments have to come from the national legal systems. There are just no other sources of law for them. National law is involved anyhow, since informal international co-operation needs national instruments to be executed. Thus international settlements such as the Basel agreements have to be translated into national policy rules or into national regulations. In other cases the instruments have a private law character, and are governed by contract law at the national level. All disputes relating to

---

9   Cf. *Barr, M. S./Miller, G. P.*: Global Administrative Law: The View from Basel, in: European Journal of International Law, 17/1 (2006), 15–46.

informal international co-operation have to be solved under national law. In this field the protection of citizens is therefore in the hands of national legal systems, and constitutional principles can be applied by national courts only.

V. National Constitutional Law Remains Very Important, but it has to Open up to the International World

My conclusion is that national law remains very important in an internationalising world. A well-functioning national legal system is a prerequisite for the development of modern international law. Besides, until international constitutional principles will have matured, principles originating from national jurisdictions will be necessary to provide the most essential constitutional guarantees in decision-making at the international level. Moreover, it seems that the national level is where the growing area of informal and private international law-making can be effectively controlled, as far as constitutional guarantees are concerned.

At the same time, however, the character of national law has to change. It cannot fulfil its functions in an international world if it remains an isolated legal order. It has to open up to the transnational community. National legal systems have to be interconnected and have to co-operate with each other to function as a foundation for international law-making. They have to become a part of a transnational legal order. This also means that they cannot exclusively serve the interests of the national community, but have to take the interests of the outside world into account as well.

All this has consequences for the way constitutional principles are formulated. A process of rethinking those principles is needed.[10] In this context, a number of questions arise, such as:

(1) What changes are needed within the national legal system when it transforms from an isolated legal system to an integrated part of a transnational legal order?

(2) What constitutional principles should be developed for national review of international and transnational law-making and adjudication?

(3) What is the potential contribution of international law to the development of constitutional principles?

---

10 Rethinking constitutional principles was the subject of the Spring 2007 Faculty Speakers Series of the Benjamin N. Cardozo School of Law, organised by *Michel Rosenfeld*.

1. What Changes are needed in the way Constitutional Principles are framed at National Level?

The constitution of every country is written for the national community. The authorities act in the national interest, parliament represents the population, and the constitutional principles protect the citizens. But internationalisation changes the system. As a part of a larger, transnational legal order the national constitutional system cannot be oriented on the national interests alone: It has to take the interest of other countries and their citizens into account as well.

The European Union provides a telling example of this development. National governments and other state authorities in Europe execute some of their tasks on behalf of the EU. This may be illustrated by the role of the courts. Although these are national courts, they have to apply European law, even if it contradicts national law. This is not the only example. In the Netherlands there was an interesting discussion on the task of the National Audit Office. It had taken the initiative to control the expenditure of funds the Dutch authorities had received from Brussels (Social Fund). Brussels had set rather strict conditions, and the inquiry by the Audit Office concluded that the conditions were not met. The publication of the Audit Office's report resulted in a request from Europe to pay the money back. The inquiry was clearly in the interest of the EU, but not in the interest of the Netherlands and therefore the question came up whether this kind of inquiry is a task of the National Audit Office. The Dutch Parliament concluded that it was. The tasks of many other national executive authorities have been similarly broadened. For example, supervision of the quality of food and goods is done in the interest of the health of all the inhabitants of the EU, since the foods and goods that are admitted to the market in one country may circulate freely in the other Member States. These examples demonstrate that the activities of national authorities of EU Member States are nowadays serving the interests of a broader community than the national citizenry.

It is important to note that the European Union is not unique in this respect. In fact, international co-operation must in most cases be implemented by national authorities within the national legal order. This is true for the decisions of international organisations like the UN, for many treaties that ask for measures on the national level, and for informal forms of co-operation.

Traditionally, however, domestic constitutional systems do not really take into account this international role of national law and national authorities. Consequently, in the present day constitutional system of control over the executive, the government remains for the most part accountable to the national parliament. And the national parliament represents national interests only. The other interests that are affected have no position in the process. In the light of what was described above, it seems inevitable to conclude that something in this normative system has to change and that this process has in fact already started. Democracy in an isolated country needs other institutions than democracy in a country that is an integrated part of the international community. The way in which constitutional principles are translated into national institutions has to be reconsidered in the light of internationalisation. But how is it possible to adapt our national instruments and processes, which bring constitutional principles into effect, to the new circumstances?

The research programme of the *Hague Institute for the Internationalisation of Law* (HiiL) raises this question and corresponding matters.[11] These relate to the long-standing idea of the *trias politica*, with the fair balance of power between the legislative, the executive and the judiciary branches of government. This balance is changing rapidly. As a result of the growing international and European rule making, the influence of the national legislature is weakening, while the executive (and the courts) are becoming more influential. What consequences does this have? Other questions relate to new forms of accountability and transparency that might supplement or replace existing ones. As mentioned before, national authorities often affect the interests of people outside their nations, e.g. when they execute international agreements, and in a democracy all those affected by governmental actions should have a position in the accountability process. How should the outside people get a position in this process? Instruments for account-ability to the general public and a greater emphasis on transparency might help to solve this problem.

2. What Constitutional Principles should be developed for National Review of International and Transnational Law-making and Adjudication?

a) Formal Law-making

As stated above, international law is no longer confined to the relations among states, but is also regulating subjects that used to belong to domestic law. Decisions of the EU, but also of the UN sometimes expressly deal with individual persons or organisations. A clear example of difficulties that may arise was mentioned above, concerning the work of the UN Sanctions Committee to fight terrorist organisations. The more international law is concerned with matters

---

11   The programme can be found at www.hiil.org.

formerly belonging to domestic law, the more it should be subject to the same standards of legitimacy. But the constitutional principles that govern domestic law-making and that protect the rights of individuals, do not yet apply at the international level.

This could be a reason to suggest that national courts should review decisions based on international law. National courts can come in at the moment international decisions are executed by national authorities, especially if the rights of individuals are concerned. However, the supremacy of international law over national law might forbid constitutional review by domestic courts.[12] Notwithstanding the rule of supremacy, cases of this kind are brought before national courts and in some instances they did give precedence to constitutional principles over international decisions. For instance, in a famous decision the German Constitutional Court denied to give effect to a judgment of the European Court of Human Rights, because it restricted the fundamental rights under the (German) Constitution.[13]

Given the apparent lack of constitutional principles at the international level, such an approach may seem to be justified. But it has a clear disadvantage: If domestic courts would move in, and would see it as their task to review international law according to the standards of *their own* constitutions, that might cause an important danger to international law. The precise meaning of particular constitutional principles, including the scope of protection they provide, may vary from one state to another and therefore the standards for review are different. If international law would come in the hands of so many different domestic courts, it might lose much of its power and normative authoritativeness.

That is why, if national courts are to have a task – and we believe that they must – they have to do something other than just applying their domestic constitutional standards. Rather, they should try to develop common sets of constitutional standards or principles to be used in a more or less similar manner by all domestic courts.

b) Informal Rule-making

The problem of national review of international law-making and adjudication is even more important in the area of informal and private international co-operation. Here the problem is twofold: firstly, constitutional guarantees which can be developed as part of international law may not be applicable to such informal

---

12 It depends also on the domestic law what the relationship is between international law and national law. So, the situation differs from country to country.

13 BVerfGE 111, 307 ff.

rule-making; secondly, since such rule-making avoids the conclusion of treaties, national parliaments are generally excluded from this process. For this reason, it seems that the only way to control this type of activities is through domestic courts.

But again, it is difficult to see how national law could control activities that are of a transnational character. If the policy rules that were agreed upon in international co-operation were challenged in different countries, and the courts of those countries would use their national standards to assess those claims, the outcome might become chaos.

In other words, there is a dilemma. On the one hand, the only way to control the lawfulness of informal international agreements is through national institutions, especially national courts. On the other, a review based on national law is arguably inadequate because an international act would be reviewed on the basis of a great number of different standards. Here again the need for common standards across the borders becomes clear.

c) The Need for Transnational Constitutional Principles

Formal and informal agreements, rule making and decisions at the international level lack the kind of constitutional control that is essential in a constitutional state. It cannot be expected that the international system will provide this kind of control in the near future. The European Union has made most progress in that direction, but it still has a long way to go. The examples above show that the position of national authorities who execute European decisions in the interest of the EU at large deserves more attention. International constitutional provisions are almost absent in international co-operation in other organisations and in the extensive field of informal public and private co-operation.

Consequently, constitutional principles have to be developed for the application at national level, and have to be applied by national courts. At the same time, those principles cannot be seen as purely national: International rules and decisions cannot be controlled by national institutions, like courts, purely on the basis of national standards. These differ from each other considerably, and if several national courts apply their own standards to the same international rule or decision, they would come to contradictory judgments. The status of instruments of international co-operation could become uncertain, because they can never meet all these different standards. It could also mean that international instruments would not be reviewed by national courts because this form of control might make international co-operation impossible.

The only solution seems to be to develop common constitutional principles that are applied at the national level, but have a transnational character. They should not reflect the law of the national court that reviews an international instrument, but the principles that are common to constitutional states. In deciding cases, courts should pay attention to the law in other states, especially those taking part in the process of international co-operation. This also includes judgments of courts in such foreign countries. This is to some extent what the German Constitutional Court did in the case mentioned earlier. It referred to common European principles, which seems to indicate that the simple application of German law would have been inadequate in that case. It is also interesting to note that a provision in the Constitution of South Africa explicitly provides that when interpreting the South African Bill of Rights, a court, tribunal or forum must consider international law and may consider foreign law, including (constitutional) decisions of other domestic courts.[14] Several participants in a recent panel on the internationalisation of constitutional law also emphasised that it is important that national courts adopt a comparative view of constitutional principles.[15] Not only the representatives of states with a relatively young constitutional tradition such as South Africa and South Korea took this view, but also the representative of the United Kingdom's House of Lords.

In general, internationalisation asks for the development of constitutional principles, neither as part of international law nor as part of purely domestic law. Although applied at the national level, these principles should have a transnational character.[16] However, two questions still need to be discussed.

In the first place: What arguments could a national (constitutional) court have to use other standards than the national constitutional principles? National law is the basis of these courts. The answer is that national law is made for domestic situations. Not for decisions that are taken in the context of international co-operation. Although constitutional principles should also apply in such cases, we must be aware of the fact that we simply cannot use those principles in the same way as in domestic situations. We have to take the international setting into account, where some principles do not work. In an international context, democ-

---

14 Section 39 of the South African Constitution, adopted 1996 as amended 1997.

15 This took place as part of the VIIth World Congress of the International Association of Constitutional Law in Athens, Greece, on 15.06.2007.

16 The kind of interaction needed for this is described by *de Búrca, G./Gerstenberg, O.*: The Denationalization of Constitutional Law, in: Harvard International Law Journal, 47/1 (2006), 243–262, who offer an interesting view on this development. They give special attention to the European experience, which includes the interaction between the European and the national institutions.

racy cannot be realised in the same way as at the national level. Public participation in the rule-making process is much more difficult than within a national setting. For this reason, constitutional principles are needed that are formulated in such a way that they take the international setting of the cases into account.

The second question is: How can those principles be developed? Obviously, they cannot be developed on a national basis. To be effective, they need to be international and they should be applied by all domestic courts in the same way. It has been proposed to develop global standards of administrative law.[17] This means seeking solutions at the international level, whereas this paper suggests seeking solutions at the (trans)national level. While a common understanding of those principles is indeed essential, it cannot be expected that those principles will be set in a binding instrument of international law in the near future. Only the domestic courts will therefore be able to apply the principles, and their input in the process of development of the standards is essential.

3. The Role of International Law in the Development of Constitutional Principles

International law has had a great influence on the development of human rights protection, as evidenced by the adoption of several key instruments (international and regional). The protection of human rights, however, is still more focused on the activities at the national than at the international level. Furthermore, the protection of human rights is only a part – though an important one – of the field that is covered by constitutional principles. Principles concerning the separation of powers, government accountability or democracy have received scant attention in international law-making. It should therefore be encouraged to continue the development of constitutional principles as part of the international legal order. This would be complementary to the development of transnational constitutional principles. Given the present world of multi-level government, in which the international level and national level have to co-operate, there is a great need for both.

Consequently, constitutional principles have to pertain to both levels. Principles that only govern the international layer would cover only part of the

---

17 See *Kingsbury, B./Krisch, N./Stewart, R. B.*: The Emergence of Global Administrative Law. New York University School of Law, 2005 (As international organisations take over tasks which used to be nationally regulated, the lack of global administrative law enables "national regulators participating in this extranational governance […] to shelter their actions from effective review at the domestic level").

problem. The development of transnational principles requires a common effort of a great variety of national jurisdictions. At the international level, there is no unity: Every international organisation and every form of supranational government has its own rules. No forum exists that can lay down rules for all these forms of government, and no international court has a general jurisdiction. In fact, the competent courts are the national courts, apart from the rare cases in which a supranational court is set up, such as in the EU.

Two developments are interesting in this situation. Firstly, there is the idea of formulating constitutional principles for international governance. Formulating global standards of administrative law can be seen as a step in that direction. These standards will be based on the standards that are used at the national level, but will also consider the differences between international organisations and international decision-making on the one hand, and the national context on the other. When standards of this kind become generally accepted, they might also become part of the rules of many international organisations.

An international jurisdiction that maintains those standards cannot be expected to emerge in the near future. For that reason, only national courts are in a position to base their judgements on those standards. International agreement would help them enormously to fulfil their task of developing common standards for review of international decisions.

Secondly, the national part of multi-level government comes within the realm of international or transnational law. A decent system of domestic law can be regarded as a prerequisite for international decision-making, because the execution of international rules and decisions has to take place within that system. Consequently, the international community has an interest in the quality of domestic legal orders in every country that is participating in international activities.

In fact, international organisations increasingly impose conditions on the quality of national legal systems. The highest level of requirements has been established by the European Union in the Copenhagen criteria. This means that a country can only become a member of the EU if its legal system is based on an extensive set of constitutional principles, including the rule of law, democracy and the protection of human rights.

The same development can be seen at a lower level, when international organisations like the UN, the World Bank and the IMF require adherence to a number of constitutional principles as a condition for international co-operation or participation in a programme. The term "rule of law" is mostly used to express this requirement, but this term can be said to express the idea of constitutional principles rather vaguely. It is perhaps too vague to be of real practical help when trying to determine what is meant exactly.[18]

Thinking in terms of constitutional principles is essential to make progress. In doing so, one should realise that constitutional principles at the international or transnational level are different from principles at the national level. The former have to take into account that historical contexts vary from country to country, so they have to leave room for adaptation. Consequently, they should not go further in formulating obligations than is really necessary from the perspective of the international community. One of these obligations which leaves room for the national level could be that the national constitutional principles do not discriminate against the rights and interests of foreigners.

V. Concluding Remarks

Constitutional principles have been developed as a part of national legal orders. They were formulated in the situation of an isolated and sovereign national legal order, in which only the interests of the national community were taken into account. Internationalisation has changed this situation radically. Constitutional principles are essential for the development of an international and transnational legal order. But they have to be reformulated to adjust them to the new situation.

The development of constitutional principles at the international level is not the only answer to the new situation, although it is of great value. The national courts will also play an important role by judging the adherence to constitutional principles in international and transnational co-operation. The courts cannot do this when they rigidly adhere to the principles of their domestic legal system, however. Those principles should be adapted to the international setting, and should develop into common principles for the national courts across the borders.

---

18 This is one of the topics discussed in the HiiL Research Programme, and it is also the focus of the HiiL Annual Conference, taking place in The Hague in October 2007.

Conclusion

Constitutional Analysis and Institutional Redesign in an Era of Internationalisation: Ten Reflections

by Theo A. J. Toonen and Florian Grotz

I. Re-introducing Constitutions

As the end of an age of managerialism seems to be approaching, it is refreshing to reflect once again on the fundamentals of governance in the public sector. The contributions in this volume represent two ways of understanding and conducting constitutional analysis. Both merit more attention given the operational and even the managerial challenges facing modern government in an age of internationalisation. On the one hand, we have the *analysis of constitutions,* which can be narrowly defined as the "basic" or "higher" legal framework that forms the source and fundament of public legislation and political action. It can also be used more broadly in the public choice meaning of the "rules of the game". On the other hand, we have *constitutional analysis* as an analytical approach to the study of government structures, policy and management. These are then explored from the viewpoint of underlying institutional patterns and actor configurations that are aimed at securing the balance, adaptation, resilience and future development of the economic, social, political or administrative systems under consideration.

It goes without saying that the constitutions of nation-states in both understandings face many challenges under the current conditions of internationalisation. The analyses presented here make clear that national constitutional systems are there to stay for the foreseeable future, despite all kinds of external challenges. At the same time, the increased cooperation among national legal and judicial systems is needed and implies a cross-border and comparative approach by constitutional lawyers and legal specialists in the international arena. The development of regional systems of governance, functionalised in nature and with various degrees of "depth" at a supra-national level (*Lane*), may serve as a practical meeting place. From a methodological point of view, case-law analysis and benchmarking of national cases in a cross-national perspective, rather than institutional comparison in the light of general international rules of law, seems to be the best way to make progress.

II. Constitutional Analysis as an Approach

Many contributions to this book invite scholars and practitioners alike to engage in a less specialised and disciplinary orientation in the study of institutional development and public sector transformation and to complement legal analyses of constitutions with operational and interdisciplinary approaches. This amounts to a plea of using an analytical perspective that focuses on questions of constitutional evolution and redesign as the basis of understanding the operation and development of legal, political and administrative systems (*Benz*). Contrary to the analysis of constitutions, constitutional analysis in this sense approaches issues such as economic transformation (*Csaba*), administrative reform (*Halligan*), civil service values (*Verheijen*) or democratisation in centrally guided systems (*Jung/Kim*) from a viewpoint of sustainability, adaptive capacity and social support. Managerial and policy questions may be addressed based on these "constitutional" values, concerns and angles to add perspective to ongoing processes of public sector reform. The analysis of formal constitutions and constitutional policies from a broader perspective represents an interesting emerging field, as it is shown by the Chinese case (*Balme/Lihua*). This study presents decision-making on constitutional reform as a relatively independent transformation force and "logic" in itself. Another example of the merits of a constitutional analysis is the contribution on the US system (*Rockman/Waltenburg*), begging the question which strategies are available that would facilitate the balanced, sustained and resilient operation of a formal constitution.

III. Constitutions as Beautiful Accidents

Although crafting constitutions is a specialist and high-quality enterprise, various contributions suggest that constitutional design – in any of the meanings distinguished above – should not be analysed by using an all too rational, deliberative and constructive type of approach or argument. The fact that constitutions have been strongly and meticulously studied and scrutinised in the national context, often as part of a long-term endogenous cultural development, easily creates the impression of a well thought of, almost rational and teleological design by "great architects", conscious acts by (We) the People or Conventions of Wise Men.

Most essays in this volume address the issue of constitutional design and (re-) development from an evolutionary perspective. Various contributions explicitly identify the analytical approach of the German historical law school and organic state theory as an important source of power and inspiration for constitutional developments in Germany and elsewhere (*Langewiesche; Nishikawa; Toonen/ Steen*). It is also remarkable, however, that several authors refer to a less than "rational" relationship between design and outcome. This volume reflects a broad variety of relevant cases, from a drafter of the Weimar Constitution whose early writings were inspired by a thorough understanding of the historical background of a "nation without state" (*Langewiesche*), to the discovery of a highly influential German historian in the Japanese environment who argued from a distinctly Europe-centred and at the time already outmoded perspective (*Nishikawa*). Yet another instance is the reinterpretation of existing constitutional provisions in the Dutch case on the basis of – perhaps partly misunderstood – comparative observations of British self-government by a German scholar (*Toonen/Steen*). And the contributions also include the Chinese example of largely "pro forma" constitutional exercises, which have the potential for or may result in starting a "constitutional life" of its own (*Balme/Lihua*).

Many existing constitutions seem to be the product of cross-border intervention and impregnation of various kinds and have been invented in the process. Why should we therefore adhere to the ideal of the consciously designed and rational framework as the basic assumption from which many constitutional analyses, particularly by laymen and practitioners, often depart? The variety of experiences highlighted in this book seems to suggest that it is worthwhile to engage in the comparative study of the birth of constitutions in more detail. In doing so, special attention should be paid to the behaviour and values that shape this process as well as the conditions for surviving the first rounds of creating and gaining legitimacy among stakeholders and vested interests.

IV. Transnationalisation and the Constitutional State

The contributions to this volume present an array of factors that make it necessary to think "out of the box" while studying and analysing constitutions that typically have been developed in the context of or parallel to the development of the nation-state. There are many reasons for "denationalising" our constitutional understanding. National constitutions currently find themselves within a complex of forces, ranging from the "hollowing out" of the state (*Lane*) and redesigning the role of courts and judges (*Scheltema*) – historically considered by some as "the least dangerous branch of government" (*Rockman/Waltenburg*) – to efforts of and a potential for supra-national constitution-building in the various merging regional blocks and trade unions, particularly within the European Union (*Robbers*). These regional organisations gradually seem to manifest themselves as the institutional carriers of the economic underpinnings of the developing global market economy.

However, globalisation is not only an economic process. The world-wide increased attention to human rights has contributed significantly to the transformation of international law from "law among states" to "law among individuals". This raises questions and a legal, or even constitutional logic which obviously becomes a force in itself, not in "limiting government" but in addressing the issues of accountability, transparency, democracy and the protection of individuals in a transnational context. Many constitutional principles and values at the international level are being advocated and promoted by institutions and intergovernmental types of cooperative arrangements that do not meet standards of constitutional quality generally thought to apply to respective institutions in the national context. This has the potential to raise a dynamic which might become as strong as the economic logic underlying current developments in the internationalisation of states and societies. It is an open question whether these forces are to any extent less robust – both in terms of benevolence and prosperity as in terms of cynicism and brute force – than the economic logic that is more generally seen as a cross-national mega-trend.

The contributions in this volume also show that the development of international terrorism represents the clearest challenge to existing constitutional arrangements. One of the core functions of the nation-state as having the monopoly of violence and force "in the binding allocation of values" – i.e. politics – is at stake. Both in the German (*Badura*) and US cases (*Rockman/Waltenburg*), it is the question of international safety that triggers constitutional debates and constitutional change. The distinction between matters of internal and external security has started to lose its meaning. This has consequences for a constitution primarily designed and developed for regulating "internal" affairs and constraining external behaviour. Obviously, international economic matters come out in third place as a force of change. However, many contributions suggest that constitutional issues linked to economic transformation seem to be more opportunistic than is often thought, and do not always lead to lasting constitutional reforms (*Verheijen*). This is strengthened by the image that traditional – even communist – constitutions may come a long way in accompanying economic transformations (*Csaba; Jung/Kim; Balme/Lihua*).

V. Beyond Exceptionalism

Internationalisation creates the need for opening up and the need for comparative analysis and understanding. Constitutional law has often been understood as the intricate knowledge and study of the legal fundaments of a single country, although it operates on the basis of more general values and principles. Books on comparative constitutional law were limited in number, specialised and used formal descriptive terms, although they were often powerful as a source of thought and inspiration. But they were usually considered to be not very "practical" or applicable to other contexts. Many countries and analysts have basically operated from the idea of the exceptionalism of their constitutional systems.[1] Rooted in a long and distinct history, with sometimes very specific legacies – both in terms of institutional arrangements and of historical traumas, formative conjectures or peak events – constitutions have been approached as idiosyncratic in practical terms: each nation its own system. Therefore, comparative institutional analysis is often limited by the unique and "own" characteristics of each nation-state.

In this volume, we encounter many authors that have to tackle and work with the idea of German (*Langewiesche*), Japanese (*Nishikawa*), French (*Caracassonne*) or American "exceptionalism" in terms of historical development and constitutional framework. Only a smaller country as the Netherlands (*Toonen/Steen*) is analysed here in terms of a compromise of different national constitutional traditions, which in such uniqueness also creates problems for a comparative understanding, as it paradoxically feeds the notion of idiosyncratic exceptionalism as the starting point for constitutional analysis.

Several contributions underline the notion of path dependence in constitutional development. Interestingly enough – and also paradoxically – a constitutional analysis conducted within the French context is able to put, for example, the uniqueness of *Sarkozy*'s reform policies in the perspective of a cyclist development that shows the seeming "exceptionalism" of the current president as a recurrent pattern (*Carcassonne*). Also in the US case, the role of the *Bush* administration in changing the constitutional balance to the advancement of the position of the executive within the system of checks and balances (*Rockman/Waltenburg*), can only be viewed as an extreme, but not unique case of usurpation of constitutional power. *Abraham Lincoln*, for example, acted quite forcefully and used the discretion which the US constitution grants to the executive to the fullest – as a

---

1   The most prominent case in point is the US. See *Lipset, S.M.*: American Exceptionalism: A Double-Edged Sword, New York/London, 1997.

zealous "human right activist" *avant la lettre* – but the results have proved him right from a historical perspective. At any rate, *Lincoln*'s political purposes have been clearly evaluated differently than the current case of the *Bush* administration.

Constitutional analysis is partly also the writing and rewriting of history: It is the future that stays the same, but also the history that constantly changes, particularly in an era of internationalisation. Historical traditions and constitutional structures do shape patterns and styles of reform and transformation and seem to contribute to the vigour with which, for example, countries with a British constitutional tradition pursue some kind of administrative innovation and change. This is basically done within certain constraints, opportunities and dilemmas set by the Westminster system (*Halligan*). In combination, these observations indicate that it might be fruitful to focus on constitutional analysis, not only in terms of norms, rules, structures and frameworks, but also in terms of patterns of idiosyncrasy which different countries might have in common.

VI. Transnational Constitutions: Functions or Frameworks?

The traditional questions, however, remain relevant. How do we substantiate constitutions in a context of globalisation? Constitutions are both a framework and a programme. The essays in this volume confirm this analytical starting point, adopted by *Hesse* and *Ellwein* throughout their work.[2] Constitutions could be, but hardly ever are, the embodiment of the "framework state". The contributions on Germany and Canada (*Benz*), Japan (*Nishikawa*), Central and Eastern Europe (*Csaba*) and even the People's Republic of China (*Balme/Lihua*) suggest that a focus on the framework state alone – constitutions as meta-structures for decision-making about decision-making – somewhat reflect the luxury position of "arrived" nations, states or regions. The historical examples presented in this volume all seem to indicate the sensibility of a less highbrow and more mundane "bread and butter" attitude to the question of constitution building. For instance, *Ludwig Riess* brought the provision of safety-first measures, infrastructure and the regulation of the use of military force to the attention as part and parcel of a constitutionalisation process (*Nishikawa*). The contemporary examples of China, the Central and Eastern European countries or Korea given in this volume might suggest that the establishing of frameworks and conflict

---

2   Cf. *Hesse, J. J./Ellwein, T.*: Das Regierungssystem der Bundesrepublik Deutschland. 2 vol., 9th ed., Berlin, 2004.

regulatory systems is a vital, but subordinate, part of the broader process of building prosperity and economic growth, or at least needs to be embedded in such a more encompassing perspective. From an empirical point of view, regional organisation seems to become an alternative to state organisation when one or several core characteristics of state sovereignty – *regalia* in terms of *Lane* – are moved from the national to the supra-national level. A subsequent institutional logic of building transnational constitutional networks, as outlined by *Scheltema*, could then differentiate the "framework part" from the "regalia part" of constitution building.

The US constitution might indeed be the closest to the ideal of a "postmodernist's dream" (*Rockman/Waltenburg*), but it should not be forgotten that the framework of a competitively shared power system was designed to curb internal conflict and violence and to further the use of options for economic growth and development. The notion of, for example, external safety could be relatively neglected, creating an open space for a presidency with a vested interest in (international) crisis. Comparatively speaking, it would be interesting to see whether this is also true for constitutions with a different purpose. For example, constitutions may limit the legislative powers of a national assembly because of regionalist tendencies or curb executive powers because of a history of abuse and dominance. This might leave room for the judiciary to develop itself from the countries' least dangerous into the most activist branch in securing safety and human rights. The question is where and under what conditions this activism can turn the judicial branch into a dangerous one. This is a highly relevant question in view of the formation of legal frameworks at the supra-national level, most clearly visible within the EU where the European Court of Justice has substantially been setting the tone and the standard in cross-national constitutional development (*Robbers*). If courts and not (We) the People have to become the carriers of – international – constitutional development, the question of whether and how to limit these powers constitutionally might become an acute one. Constitutional policy in the democratic nation-state to a large extent had to do with limiting the powers of the state on behalf of its citizens, because the state could be considered the institution to be controlled. Who or what will "check and balance" the judiciary if it enters an open playing field and if it were to get a "vested interest" in crises and conflict?

VII. The Tacit Constitution

The notion of "implied powers" within a constitution merits further development in a comparative perspective. It may become part of the analysis of a political power game, as the current US case illustrates. But combined with the notion of "tacit knowledge", we are encouraged to embark upon a quest to unveil the implicit dimensions of constitutional provisions. What values are implied by which constitutional arrangements? Constitutional lawyers often take the "implied value" of constitutional configurations simply for granted and merely focus on the system and structure of rules in itself. Internationalisation will become a force for unfreezing – "de-institutionalising" – the structural embodiment of these values. But what, precisely, are they? And do they mean the same to different people in different regions of the world?

When we are looking at formal constitutional arrangements, we are tacitly assuming that a certain degree of quality or "value" is implied. This insight is important for the investigation and evaluation of ongoing reform and transformation processes by which deprived regions and peoples try to get their share of wealth and prosperity. The separation of structure and value in a process of internationalisation offers a unique opportunity to study the "assumptive world" of certain constitutional arrangements. Several contributions to this volume seem to suggest a "loose coupling" between constitutional arrangements and the quality of life under that constitution, although many constitutional analysts would claim precisely the opposite. It goes without saying that not everything can be "guaranteed" by a constitution. However, it is unclear which values need to be respected in a constitutional model to make it viable. It is also unclear to which extent, for example, "professionalisation" of political and administrative behaviour would be able to serve as a substitute for legal regulation.[3]

Is a balance of power, or better: a system of shared powers only a good in itself within a more or less shared system of values, or is it a good in itself under all circumstances? Many constitutions are directly or indirectly based on the proposition that authority – if not government in itself – is both necessary and dangerous. Some seemingly promising institutional developments and social experiments across the world are "centrally guided", whereas the assumption of the need for "rolling back the state" without any consideration for implied values, or the lack thereof, has created many corrupt situations. In several countries,

---

3 Cf. also *Hesse, J. J./Grotz, F.*: Europa professionalisieren. Kompetenzordnung und institutionelle Reform im Rahmen der Europäischen Union, Berlin, 2005.

parliament – not a constitution limiting governmental decision-making – is more important as the institutional seat and guarantee of a democratisation process, as the Korean case shows (*Jung/Kim*). In a nutshell, the de-institutionalisation implied by the internationalisation process opens possibilities to discover and reveal the values behind existing constitutional models.

VIII. The Administrative System as a Constitutional Power

There was a time that administrative systems, in more than one way, belonged to the tacit constitution of well-functioning democracies. An important question emerging from the contributions to this volume is the relationship between the constitution and the – quality of – public administration. If the judiciary is considered by many as the "least dangerous branch", it follows that the executive – that is to say: the administrative system – is the "usual suspect" when looking for the most forceful if not dangerous branch of government. We seem to have come a long way from observing that administrative systems are the units that distinguish the dignified from the efficient part of a constitution. Administrative systems seem to have arrived in the "suspect" part of the tacit constitution.

In theory, civil service systems are supposed to bring impartiality, professionalism, competitive access, accountability, merit and protection from daily politics to the system (*Verheijen*). These are still important values for assessing the question of "how to run a constitution". The current bureaucratic model for securing this in many countries seems to have lost much of its attraction. It remains to be seen which alternative paradigms will arrive. Referring back to neo-*Weber*ian systems is begging the question rather than providing an answer. It is striking, however, that the current stage of internationalisation shows much resemblance to the rapid scale enlargement, dynamics and growing complexities associated with socioeconomic development in the 19th century in Europe, which inspired *Weber* to look for the reasons behind this development. With the advantage of hindsight, he eventually identified the quality of organisation and governance in the form of "rational bureaucracy" as the key administrative factor to understand the success behind the broader constitutional development.

The main question is what the current institutional features for securing authority, trust and confidence in the working parts of the constitution are, and where in society they may be found under conditions of de-institutionalisation and internationalisation. Many countries are in need of a civil service that is professional, impartial, evidence based, trustworthy and reliable. The institutional features by which the values of a well-functioning civil service in a cross-national context may be institutionalised still have to be identified. It is most likely, however, that we have to look for them in the general way the systems are constituted, rather than in their internal organisational or managerial components. The characteristics of the rational bureaucracy model that *Weber* identified as a cornerstone of the modern state were detected by focusing on the broader constitutional and socioeconomic development in the late 19th century. This is still a worthwhile approach as part of a cross-national public administration research agenda.

IX. Layers and Levels

The observation that the development of an international constitutional order is based on the quality of national constitutional systems presents another interesting paradox. Even where international legal development exemplifies acknowledged constitutional qualities, as in the field of human rights, implementation and compliance critically depend on the operation of national courts and legal systems (*Scheltema*). It is, however, important to note the parallels between the process of scale enlargement in the second half of the 19th century and the current process of internationalisation, both reported in this book. One and a half centuries ago, the nationalisation of local and regional affairs was at stake, much in the same way as the internationalisation of national affairs is presently regarded as key feature of public sector development.

Of course we have come a long way, and securing national autonomy in an internationalising world might not be quite the same as securing local autonomy within a nationalising system. However, it is striking to observe the resemblance in constitutional discussions and changes. The current development contributes to a focus on multi-level governance, much in the same way as the nationalisation of public affairs did in many countries during the 19th century. The construction of local governments carrying out national legislation shows – from a constitutional perspective – many similarities with the structure in which an international constitutional order has to be implemented and secured by national courts and national administrative systems. This similarity seems to beg for a comparative analysis, not only cross-nation or cross-culture, but also across time.

Furthermore, the arguments against the EU construction of setting supranational guidelines and directives that have to be carried out by national administrations, closely resemble the discourse on the pros and cons of local self-govern-ment in a context of nationalising public affairs in the 19th century. Both regarding the lack of enforcement and compliance power at the "central" level as well as the erosion of autonomy at the local level, there are strong analogies that ought to be explored in more detail. Comparative constitutional analysis "across time" might provide more insight in the long-term development of multi-level systems of government. These are often considered novel and innovative, while we are actu-ally dealing with a very classical "cooperative arrangement" for organising rela-tions among various layers of government. Multi-level systems exist in both uni-tary and federal states, as the contributions to this volume indicate (*Benz; Toonen/ Steen*). But what is more: Existing comparative research on intergovernmental systems within federal constitutions points to the importance of citizens and social interests not in blocking, but in furthering and "freeing" the continuous adaptation of (federal) governance structures to changing circumstances (*Benz*). A comparison across time may help to understand what it takes to engage citizens and social interests in multi-level development and to join and complement judicial branches to keep a check on "the most dangerous part" of any constitu-tion, still most likely to be the executive.

X. Crossing Borders

The need for interdisciplinary and applied research in an internationalised con-text could hardly be illustrated better than by the various contributions to this volume, brought together in honour of *Joachim Jens Hesse*. An interdisciplinary approach, respecting the lasting importance of legal analysis in the context of constitutional development, is required in which legal perspectives are combined with the insights from political science, history and the administrative sciences, in order to investigate the implied powers of certain constitutional arrangements. Many of the questions raised and addressed in the preceding chapters need the development of an intercultural perspective and a solid confrontation of *Staats-wissenschaften* and *Staatspraxis*.

Constitutional policy is both an art and a craft, carried out by a huge variety of actors in a process that is functional as well as symbolic. Constitutional de-velopment is not merely a matter of instrumentalities. If we think of constitutions as expressions, rather than instrumentalities, we need to be able to investigate a multitude of identities at various levels of meaning or identification. Constitu-tions as sets of norms and expressions may also gradually contribute to an empirical development securing rights and protecting against abuse, which is embedded in and part of ongoing political and administrative processes. If we accept this notion, we need to understand that constitution building is not done by lawyers only, but also – and especially – by practitioners. Therefore, it takes a strong "cross-border alliance" among academically-oriented practitioners and policy-oriented academics to contribute to this understanding and to create a process of learning from experience, rather than learning by doing.

Authors

Professor em. Dr. *Peter Badura*
Lehrstuhl für Öffentliches Recht, Rechts- und Staatsphilosophie
Ludwig-Maximilians-Universität
Professor-Huber-Platz 2
80539 München

Professor Dr. *Richard Balme*
Sciences Po, Global Public Policy Program in China
School of Government
Peking University
Beijing 100871
rbalme@pku.edu.cn

Professor Dr. *Arthur Benz*
Institut für Politikwissenschaft
FernUniversität Hagen
Universitätsstr. 41
58084 Hagen
Arthur.Benz@FernUni-Hagen.de

Professor Dr. *Guy Carcassonne*
Université de Paris X (Nanterre)
200, av de la République
F-92001 Nanterre Cedex
guy.carcassonne@wanadoo.fr

Professor Dr. *László Csaba*
International Relations and European Studies Department
Central European University
Nador u. 9
HU-1051 Budapest
Csabal@ceu.hu

PD Dr. *Florian Grotz*
Lehrstuhl für Vergleichende Politikwissenschaft und Systemlehre
Julius-Maximilians-Universität
Wittelsbacherplatz 1
97070 Würzburg
florian.grotz@uni-wuerzburg.de

Professor Dr. *John Halligan*
School of Business and Government
University of Canberra
ACT 2601 Canberra
Australia
John.Halligan@canberra.edu.au

Professor Dr. *Yong-duck Jung*
Graduate School of Public Administration
Seoul National University
Seoul, 151–742
Republic of Korea
ydjung@snu.ac.kr

Cheongsin Kim
Graduate School of Public Administration
Seoul National University
Seoul, 151–742
Republic of Korea
cheongsk@usc.edu

Professor Dr. *Jan-Erik Lane*
Département de science politique
Université de Genève
40, boulevard du Pont d'Arve
CH-1211 Genève 4
Jan-Erik.Lane@politic.unige.ch

Professor Dr. *Dieter Langewiesche*
Historisches Seminar
Eberhart-Karls-Universität
Wilhelmstr. 36
72074 Tübingen
dieter.langewiesche@uni-tuebingen.de

Yang Lihua
Legal counsel, Yongjin Group Company
6 M, Hong Qiao Business Center, No. 2272 Hong Qiao Road
Shanghai 200336
Yanglh@yongjin.com.cn

Professor Dr. *Yoichi Nishikawa*
Graduate School of Law and Politics
University of Tokyo
7-3-1 Hongo Bunkyo-ku
Tokyo 113-0033
Japan
brasym4@dolphin.ocn.ne.jp

Professor Dr. *Gerhard Robbers*
Institut für europäisches Verfassungsrecht
Universität Trier
Universitätsring 15
54286 Trier
robbers@uni-trier.de

Professor Dr. *Bert A. Rockman*
Department of Political Science
Purdue University
100 N. University Street
W. Lafayette, IN 47907-2098, USA
barockma@purdue.edu

Professor em. Dr. *Michiel Scheltema*
Chair of the Programmatic Steering Board
Hague Institute for the Internationalisation of Law (HiiL)
PO Box 93033
2509 AA The Hague, The Netherlands
M.Scheltema@law.uu.nl

Dr. *Trui Steen*
Department of Public Administration
Leiden University
Wassenaarseweg 52, P.O. Box 9555
23000 RB Leiden, The Netherlands
tsteen@fsw.leidenuniv.nl

Professor Dr. *Theo A. J. Toonen*
Faculty of Social and Behavioural Sciences
Leiden University
Wassenaarseweg 52, P.O. Box 9555
23000 RB Leiden, The Netherlands
toonen@fsw.leidenuniv.nl

Dr. *Tony Verheijen*
Institutional Reform and Capacity Building Unit
Africa Region
The World Bank
1818 H Street NW
Washington, DC 20433
USA
averheijen@worldbank.org

Professor Dr. *Eric N. Waltenburg*
Department of Political Science
Purdue University
100 N. University Street
W. Lafayette, IN 47907-2098, USA
ewaltenb@purdue.edu